AMITĀBHA-BUDDHA-ŚRĪḤ

GEMS OF BUDDHISM

KALIDASA ACADEMY OF SANSKRIT MUSIC & FINE ARTS SERIES No. 2

AMITĀBHA-BUDDHA-ŚRĪḤ
GEMS OF BUDDHISM

Principal Investigator & Editor
PROF. SUSHMA KULSHRESHTHA
D.Phil.; D.Litt.; F.R.A.S.(London)
Visiting University Professor
Department of Sanskrit
Ranchi University, Ranchi

EASTERN BOOK LINKERS

DELHI : : (INDIA)

Published by
EASTERN BOOK LINKERS
5825, New Chandrawal, Jawahar Nagar
Delhi-110007
Phone : 2520287

Kalidasa Academy of Sanskrit
Music & Fine Arts Series No. 2

Publication Secretary
Ms. Anju Bala

First Edition : 1996

I.S.B.N. : 81-86339-39-6

Price EBL Rs. 1000-

Printed in India
AMAR PRINTING PRESS, DELHI-110009
Phone : 7252362

कालिदास संस्कृत सङ्गीत कला एकेडमी ग्रन्थमाला संख्या-2

अमिताभ-बुद्धश्रीः

GEMS OF BUDDHISM

प्रधान अनुसन्धात्री एवं सम्पादिका

प्रो० सुषमा कुलश्रेष्ठ

डी० फिल०; डी० लिट०; एफ० आर० ए० एस० (लन्दन)

निदेशिका

कालिदास संस्कृत सङ्गीत कला एकेडमी

दिल्ली

ईस्टर्न बुक लिंकर्स

दिल्ली :: (भारत)

प्रकाशक :
ईस्टर्न बुक लिंकर्स
5825, न्यू चन्द्रावल, जवाहर नगर
दिल्ली-110007
दूरभाष : 2520287

दूरभाष : 7120287

कालिदास संस्कृत सङ्गीत कला
एकेडमी ग्रन्थमाला सं०-२

प्रकाशनसचिव
कु० अञ्जुबाला

प्रथम संस्करण : 1996

I.S.B.N.: 81-86339-39-6

मूल्य Rs. 1000-

मुद्रक :
अमर प्रिंटिंग प्रैस, दिल्ली-110009
दूरभाष : 7252362

DEDICATED TO THE LOVING &
EVERLASTING MEMORY OF MY
DEAR DHAWAL & DEAR MONIKA
ON THEIR TWENTYFIRST
BIRTH-ANNIVERSARY
(11th JUNE, 1996)

EDITORIAL

शीलश्रुतत्यागदयादमानां तेजः क्षमाधीधृतिसंनतीनाम्।
अनुन्नतिह्रीमतिकान्तिकीर्तिदाक्षिण्यमेधाबलशुक्लतानाम्॥
नमामि बुद्धं सुगुणोदयानामलङ्कृतानामिव यौवनेन।
विशुद्धतौदार्यमनोहराणां चन्द्रं कलानामिव संश्रयं तम्॥

Today, on the auspicious occasion of the 2540th birth anniversary celebrations of Lord Buddha, it is our proud privilege to offer our adorations to Him in the form of *'Amitābha-Buddha-Śrīḥ*-Gems of Buddhism.'

It was the auspicious evening of 17th July, 1995, when *Saṁskṛta-Saṅgīta-Jagadīśvarī* (Jewels in Sanskrit & Musicology), a Felicitation volume in honour of Prof. J.S. Kulshreshtha was ceremoniously released by Prof. A.P.Mishra, Ex.Vice Chancellor, Allahabad University at Federation House, New Delhi. Prof P.N.Kawthekar was the chief guest of this function which was presided over by Prof. R.K. Sharma. When the function was over at about 10.00 p.m., we all came out and assembled in an adjacent hall for dinner. While dining, everyone was busy in discussion on one or the other topic. In the course of discussion, our esteemed *Guru*, Prof. Sumati Mutatkar, herself an ardent lover of Buddhism came forward with a novel and excellent idea of bringing out a volume entitled *'Amitābha-Buddha-Śrīḥ*-Gems of Buddhism' comprising learned papers by eminent scholars on Buddhism and Buddhist studies befitting our adoration and devotion to Lord Buddha. The idea was welcomed and applauded by everyone present at the moment. Hence, Prof. Mutatkar truely deserves our hearty gratitude for being the chief planner of this volume. The planning for preparation of *Amitābha-Buddha-Śrīḥ* was started the same day with the firm resolve that this volume 'Gems of Buddhism' would see the light of the day on the coming *Buddha-Purṇimā*, the 3rd May, 1996.

We are happy to present this volume *Amitābha-Buddha-Śrīḥ* comprising thirty articles and research papers that have been included to serve as a *floral adoration of vāk* to the grandeur and magnanimity of the illustrious Tathāgata Amitābha Gautama Buddha. This volume 'Gems of Buddhism' is divided into six sections :

(i) *Śrīsaṁvarodayatantrarājaḥ* (Unpublished Text)

(ii) Buddhism & Society

(iii) Buddhist Philosophy

(iv) Buddhist Literature & History

(v) Music In Buddhist Literature

(vi) Jātaka-Studies

This volume *Amitābha-Buddha-Śrīḥ* is a garland of thirty flowers in the form of thirty learned papers from renowned scholars of India and abroad (few maiden papers too from our researchers), covering diverse aspects of Buddhism, Buddhist Studies and Indology. A brief appreciation of the papers is presented herewith. The volume opens with an introductory note by Sri Naresh Man Bajracharya on the unpublished text entitled *Śrīsaṁvarodayatantrarājaḥ* of unknown authorship and then follows the edited text (chapters I-IV) of this work which is being published here for the first time. This work *Śrīsaṁvarodayatantrarāja* has been extracted from a voluminous work *Śrīherukābhidhānamahātantrarāja* comprising fiftyone chapters and 3,00,000 stanzas. *Śrīsaṁvarodayatantra* belongs to the school of *Mantranaya (Mantrayāna)* which is a branch of *Mahāyāna*. The chief deity of *Śrīherukābhidhānamahātantrarāja* is *Śrīheruka* who is also known as Cakasaṁvara.

The Cakasaṁvara is still very widely popular in Nepal and Tibet. The text published here is based on five manuscripts of *Śrīsaṁvarodayatantrarāja* found in Nepal. We are looking forward to publishing the complete edited text of *Śrīsaṁvarodayatantrarāja*.

Prof. Phra Soonthorndhammathada deals at length with the concept of compassion in Buddhist view in general and earlier

Buddhism in particular in his paper 'Compassion: Buddhism vis-a-vis Purāṇas.' He suggests the possibility of comparing the Buddhist view with purāṇic legends. Prof. S.G. Kantawala has highlighted the development of Buddhism with regard to its ethical and social values in his paper 'Buddhism and socio-cultural values'. He is of the view that significant role was played by modern Buddhism in bringing social and political changes.

In his analysis of Buddhism in the context of socio-cultural values, Dr. S.G. Kantawala has drawn attention to the fact that the societies practising Buddhism have moved away significantly from its basic tenets in some respects, one of the most glaring examples of this pointed out by him being the tenet of *Ahiṁsā* which presupposes non-killing of beings, not being followed in matter of food by large Buddhist societies the world over, in feeling no compunction in being non-vegetarian necessitating animal slaughter. Further, the Buddha was against idol worship. Interestingly, his were the largest number of idols made and worshipped, so much so that in Persian, *But* which is a partially changed form of the word *Buddha* became a synonym of idol.

The Buddha had raised his voice against the birth-based superiority of the Brahmins as per the authority of the *Soṇadaṇḍa Sutta* and the *Dhammapada* cited by Dr. Kantawala. But he was probably not the first to do so. There already was a distinct undercurrent of opposition to this. Apart from the oft-quoted *Gīta* verse *cāturvarṇyaṁ mayā sṛṣṭaṁ guṇakarmavibhāgaśaḥ*, there is a reference in the *Mahābhārata*, not so well-known, which is much more direct in not accepting birth as the basis of caste. In answer to the query of a python (who was none other than Nahuṣa come to assume that form out of the curse of the sage Agastya), Yudhiṣṭhira says that a Brahmin is one who is endowed with (qualities like) truth, charity, mercy, forgiveness, righteousness and kindness. If the Sūdra were to have the same, he would not be a Sūdra; if the Brahmin does not have them, he is not a Brahmin, call him a Śūdra (*Vanaparvan*, 180,21-26). (Quoted from the Foreword to 'Studies In Indology & Musicology' {Dr. Prabhakar Narain Kawthekar Felicitation Volume} recorded by Prof. Satyavrat Shastri.)

Prof. Kewal Krishan Mittal has explained the Buddhist approach of individual and social identity on the basis of ethical values which are flexible in practice. The variations in food habits are local and individual. The Buddhist approach guides us to take things calmly and quietly in various social contexts.

In his paper 'B.R. Ambedkar's Religious Legacy', Prof. Sanghasen Singh throws light on the reasons and circumstances which led Baba Saheb to get converted to Buddhism from his parent religion. In Prof. Sanghasen Singh's view, the advent of Bhimrao Ambedkar on the Indian scene has made enormous difference in the social, political and religious aspects.

Ms. Abha Kulshreshtha has discussed judiciously some legal problems and their remedies as found in the Buddhist literature. She has also compared the remedies prescribed in Buddhist texts with the modern ones laid down in the Indian Penal Code. Dr. Subhra Barua Pavagadhi emphasizes that on the earth, humanity and world peace can be established through Buddhism.

Dr. Krishnakant Trivedi in his paper 'The social behaviour of man as reflected in the Pāli Nikāya' discusses at length the high virtues of a human being that bring forth unity, co-ordination and universal brotherhood in society. The life on earth becomes easier, more comfortable and enjoyable if people imbibe in them, good qualities and act according to the norms laid down in the Pāli Nikāya. A person acquires greatness and fame, when he averts sufferings of the mankind—is the view of Buddhist thinkers.Dr. Urmila Srivastava propounds in her paper that the Lord Buddha was not against the Vedas or the performance of sacrifices as prescribed in the Vedas. He was dead against the animal slaughter in the sacrifices.

Prof. Sanghasen Singh has discussed at length the problem of existence and non-existence in Buddhism in his paper. During the period of the Buddha, the most debated problem was whether the soul and the world are eternal or are subject to decay or annihilation. During the course of discussion, Prof. Sanghasen throws light on the four Noble Truths, the twelve links which cover the past, the present and the future life of a human being, the Eightfold Noble Path and the *Nibbāna*. '*Nibbāna* is profound like an ocean, lofty like a mountain-peak and sweet like honey'—thus explains Nāgasena to his disciple, the Greek King, Menander (Milinda).

Prof. K.K. Mittal traces the root causes underlying the concept of tolerance in various schools of philosophy in general and particularly in Buddhism. Dr. T.R.Sharma has analysed the relation between dependent origination and *Śūnyatā* from the point of view of *Sāṁvṛtikasatya* and the *Pāramārthikasatya*. Summing up various concepts and meanings of both the doctrines, Dr. Sharma opines that the law of dependent origination is a mataphysical ladder to reach the high pedestal of *Śūnyatā* at the transcendental level.

Prof. Chandrakant Shukla has tried to establish links between the doctrines propounded in Upaniṣads and in Earlier Buddhism. He has cited a number of examples to substantiate his view. Dr. Veena Gaur highlights the contribution of Lord Buddha to mankind. Discussing various possibilities of the principal sentiment in the *Nāgānanda* of Śrīharṣa, Prof. N.P. Unni applied traditional and modern ingredients to come to the assumption that *Vīra* is the principal sentiment in the *Nāgānanda*.

Prof. K.T.S. Sarao has made a praiseworthy attempt to highlight categorically the contribution made by Campā Mahānagara in nursing Buddhism in its nascent phase. Campā had the honour of being a place where on the banks of the Gaggarāpokkharṇī, *Suttas* like the *Soṇadaṇḍa, Dasuttara, Kandaraka* and the *Kāraṇḍava* were preached. Campā is adorned with the honour of producing high personalities like Soṇa Kolivisa Thera, Soṇadaṇḍa, Jambūgāmika Thera, Nandaka Thera, Bharata Thera, Pessa, Vajjiyamāhita and others.

In the light of the *Saundarananda* of Aśvaghoṣa, Dr. S.M.P.N. Singh Shahi presents a picturesque view of Nanda's journey from passion to Enlightenment. Through repeated endeavours only, of Lord Buddha, Nanda could pave the tough path of his goal and attain Salvation-Enlightenment-the Supreme Truth. Dr. Priyasen Singh, in his paper has tried to trace the causes of the decline of Buddhism in India. Ms. Sanghamitra Bauddha has given a beautiful account of the contributions made by Bhikṣuṇī (Princess) Saṅghamitrā, the worthy daughter of King Aśoka in the propagation of Buddhism in India and Sri Lanka. She was the first lady preacher of Buddhism outside India.

She founded *Bhikṣuṇī-saṁgha* in Sri Lanka. The significance of Bodhi tree in Buddhism has also been highlighted.

Prof. Lokesh Chandra in his paper, shares his personal experience of the bliss of music which he enjoyed in Japan. He has given detailed account of the musical rederings in Sanskrit prevalent in China, Korea and Japan. Besides referring to 3000 musical compositions, he has referred to a number of instruments and dance forms popular in China and Japan.

Dr. Sushma Kulshreshtha has subjected the *Buddhacarita* of Aśvaghoṣa to a searching scrutiny from the point of view of music. She has found references in the work to all the three types of the discipline, vocal, instrumental and dance. These references she has pieced together to form a connected picture of music in the work under study. It had been the practice in ancient India that the poets before taking to poetry would acquire a thorough and faultness knowledge of various disciplines : *Śrutaṁ ca bahu nirmalam,* which knowledge they brought to bear on their poetic compositions. Aśvaghoṣa is the second author that Dr. Kulshreshtha has taken up for study from the point of view of musical content, the earlier one being Kālidāsa. It is to be hoped that she will follow it up by taking up other authors in course of time thus preparing the ground for, the grand work : 'Music in Sanskrit Literature-Theory and Practice' (Quoted from the Foreword to *'Prabhākara-Nārāyaṇa-Śrīḥ'*-'Studies In Indology & Musicology' composed by Prof. Satyavrat Shastri).

Prof. Sushma Kulshreshtha in her paper 'Music and Dance in Buddhist Literature' has tried to collect references pertaining to the threefold music, *viz,* vocal, instrumental and dance, scattered here and there in Buddhist literature and bring to light the prominence of the art of music in those days. Music found in Buddhist literature has been beautifully presented in India's ancient sculpture and paintings through which a thorough study of music and dance of those days can be accomplished. This paper was first published in the proceedings of seventh World Sanskrit Conference (Leiden, the Netherlands, August 23ṛḍ to 29ṭḥ, 1987) entitled 'Indologica Taurinensia', official organ of the International Association for Sanskrit Studies, Volume XV-XVII, Torino, Italy in July, 1991.

Dr. Kamlakant Mishra has made an attempt to collect different shades of meaning of the epithet 'Bodhisattva' and has critically examined them in his paper. He has presented an appraisal of the magnanimous deeds of Bodhisattva painted in the stories of the *Jātakamāla* of Āryaśūra. This paper has been thankfully extracted from Dr. K.K. Mishra's work *Āryaśūra-kṛta Jātakamālā-Eka Adhyayana* published in 1977.

There are two contradictory views as regards the image of woman found in the Jātakas. Some stories denegrate women, paint them as licentious and caution the Bhikkhus to keep wide awake, whereas some other stories eulogize women as *therīs,* whose life-sketches in the form of *Therīgāthā* form an integral part of the Buddhist canon.

This contradiction of views has been critically examined by Dr. Harcharan Singh Sobti in his paper 'Image of Women as reflected in the Jātakas' citing all relevant examples from Jātakas. He is of the opinion that the Jātakas present a balanced view with regard to the image of women. Dr. Krishnakant Trivedi has made an attempt to present a complete picture of the status of women from various angles as found in the Buddhist Jātaka. He has given numerous references and illustrations to substantiate his view.

Ms. Anju Bala has presented a critical appraisal of the ten *Pāramitās* in her paper. She has defined and illustrated all the *Pāramitās* as found in the *Jātakamālā* of Āryaśūra. In her subsequent paper, she has given poetic appreciation of *Jātakamālā* in the light of the application of figures of speech. She has successfully searched the illustrations of various figures of speech, *viz.; Anuprāsa, Upamā, Mālopamā, Yamaka, Rūpaka, Utprekṣā, Arthāntaranyāsa, Parisaṁkhyā, Paryāya, Ullekha, Viṣama, Svabhāvokti, Viśeṣokti, Vibhāvanā, Vyatireka* and *Yathāsaṁkhya* and beautifully described and discussed their application in the *Jātakamālā* giving their definitions from noted woks on rhetorics.

In her last paper entitled 'Heroic Sāttvika Guṇas in *Jātakamālā*' Ms. Anju Bala has delineated for the first time, the eight *sāttvika guṇas* of the *Nāyaka* as found in the *Jātakamālā*. Bharatamuni in his *Nāṭyaśāstra,* propounded for the first time that a hero should possess eight *sāttvika guṇas* namely *Śobhā, Vilāsa, Mādhurya, Gāmbhīrya, Sthairya*

(Dhairya), Lalita, Audārya and Teja. Scores of Ācāryas, right from Bharatamuni to the rhetoricians of the twentieth century, have emphasized the importance of these heroic qualities. Ms. Anju Bala has traced all these eight *Sāttvika guṇas* in the *Jātakamālā* of Āryasūra and presented in her paper a critical study giving definition of each *guṇa* from five treatises and then discussing its application in the examples available in the *Jātakamālā.*

After these thirty interesting and learned papers are included two appendices. In Appendix I, Prof. Sushma Kulshreshtha and Ms. Anju Bala have compiled titles of 213 research papers related to Buddhism and Buddhist Studies, which were presented at seven International Conferences held abroad during 1979-94 along with the names of their authors. In Appendix II is given the list of our contributors.

We have only pointed out here some of the special features of this volume and leave the rest to the connoisseur and discerning reader of Buddhism, Buddhist Studies and Indology.

We wish to record our sincere thanks and gratitude to all the scholars who spontaneously responded to our invitation enabling us to succeed in the venture of this volume through their learned papers sent well in time. We wish to place on record our gratitude and indebtedness to all our friends, colleagues and disciples who spontaneously offered their valuable services and made themselves available to us in the preparation and printing of this volume. We are thankful to all the members of the Publication Committee-Ms. Abha Kulshreshtha, Ms. Anju Bala and Mrs. Meena Chandra who successfully performed their meticulous job. We extend our affectionate blessings to our dear disciples Ms. Abha, Ms. Anju & Mrs. Meena. May God bless them!

We express our sincere thanks to Shri Sham Lal Malhotra (Proprietor, Eastern Book Linkers) and his son Shri Ravi Malhotra who undertook the publication of this work and brought it out with attractive presentation in record time. For beautiful computer-composing, our special thanks are due to Shri Hira Lal (Proprietor, Amar Printing Press) and Shri Inder Raj (computer-designer and pagemaker).

It gives me great pleasure and solace to dedicate this work 'Gems of Buddhism' to the loving and everlasting memory of my dear Dhawal (Dhawal Chandra-Dhawal Kishore) (Born 11.6.1975-left for his heavenly abode on 28.8.1990) and dear Monika (Mohini-Mauni) (Born 11.6.1975–left for her heavenly abode on 7.2.1991) on their twentyfirst birth anniversary (11.6.1996). They, though born as pets (dogs), were great source of inspiration to me in my research. Due to them alone, I could write a book entitled *'Music of Animals & Birds in Kālidāsa'* which had the honour of being ceremoniously released by the then Vice President of India, Hon'ble Dr. Shankar Dayal Sharma on 18ṭḥ January, 1990 at a special function held at Uparashtrapatiniwas. Although, they are no more now, still they continue to inspire me to do something or the other. Gautama Buddha (Bodhisattva) in his previous births was born in many forms, *viz.*, divine being, human being, bird or animal. In one of his previous births, he was born as dog too. Hence my dedication of *Amitābha-Buddha-Śrīḥ* to dear Dhawal and dear Monika.

Inspired by the fond and everlasting memory of my dear Dhawal and Monika, I have been tracing the references pertaining to music and dance of birds and animals in Vālmīki's *Rāmāyaṇa* and wish to present a critical appraisal in near future.

In the end, through this volume *'Amitābha-Buddha-Śrīḥ*-Gems of Buddhism', on the auspicious occasion of His 2540ṭḥ birth anniversary celebrations, we offer our sincerest adorations to the Exalted One, the Lord Buddha. May the Apostle of world peace, Amitābha Gautama Buddha inspire and live for ever in the memory of all those who love Buddhism and Buddhist literature ! May Lord Buddha bestow on us His choicest blessings!

MANIKA-DHAWAL
KC/12 B, Ashok Vihar
Delhi
Buddha-Pūrṇimā
3ṛḍ May, 1996

SUSHMA KULSHRESHTHA
DIRECTOR
Kalidasa Academy of
Sanskrit Music & Fine Arts
Delhi

CONTENTS

SECTION I

ŚRĪSAṀVARODAYATANTRARĀJAḤ

(Unpublished Text)

ŚRĪSAṀVARODAYATANTRA

(A Brief Introduction)

Naresh Man Bajracharya

The *Śrīsaṁvarodayatantra* consists of thirtythree chapters. The first chapter commences with a series of questions put by Bodhisattva Vajrapāṇi to Lord Buddha. The remaining chapters are the answers, given by the Lord Buddha in the assembly of Bhikṣus, Avalokiteśvara and Yogīśvaras. The colophon of the last chapter of *Saṁvarodayatantra*, identifies that the *Saṁvarodayatantra* has been extracted from the *Śrīherukābhidhānamahātantrarāja* which consists of 3,00,000 stanzas. And the tewntyfifth stanza of the same chapter advocates about *Śrīherukābhidhānatantra*.[1] It makes clear that the *Saṁvarodayatantra* is not an independent text but a part of *Śrīherukābhidhānamahātantrarāja*. Indeed, the *Śrīherukābhidhānamahātantrarāja* which consists of fittyone chapters, deals with the Śriheruka, the chief deity of the *Śrīsaṁvarodayatantra*.

The *Śrīsaṁvarodayatantra* clearly indicates the division of *tantra* into two categories namely *Yogatantra* and *Yoginītantra*. The unknown author made attempt to explore the view that the two categories of the *tantras* had descended from Lord Buddha himself.[2]

The *Saṁvarodayatantra* belonged to the school of *Mantranaya* (*Mantrayāna*) which is a branch of *Mahāyāna*.[3]

The *Samayi* seems to be the highest degree in *Mantranaya*. A student of *Mantranaya*, after obtaining a series of initiations is called *Samayi*.[4]

The *Saṁvarodayatantra* deals with three *cakras* namely *kāya*, *vāk* and *citta*. Each *cakra* consists of eight nerves (total twentyfour). Apart from these nerves, the *Lalanā*, *Rasanā* and *Avadhūti* are mentioned as the three chief nerves. It is a matter of great interest that the *tantra* deals with the twentyfour outer-sites (*Bāhyapīṭha*) such as

Pullinamalaya, Jālandhara, Ondiyāna etc., which could be more informative in order to know the practice and boundary of *Mantranaya* in ancient India.[5]

The deities, such as *Saṁvaras, Dākinīs* etc. in the *Maṇḍala* and the account of nerves are two of very common characteristics among the many in Buddhist *tantras*. The *Saṁvarodayatantra* states that all the *Dākinīs* of *Maṇḍala* are the nerves' system, *Skandhas* and *Āyatanas*. And it further enlightens readers that the concept of Śrīheruka, the central figure of the tantra is originated from the union of the nerves, *Skandhas* and *Āyatanas*. This statement points out that the Heruka is noting more than the personality of beings. The concept of Śrīheruka leads us to the primary Buddhist thought.[6]

As mentioned above, the chief deity of the *Saṁvarodayatantra* is Śrīheruka who is also known as Cakrasaṁvara. The Cakrasaṁvara is still very widely popular in Nepal and Tibet.

The school of Cakrasaṁvara was carried out by Vāgīśvarakīrti[7] a Nepalese scholar in Nepal. He was popularly known as Pham-thin-pa by Tibetan people.

Vāgīśvarakīrti had three brothers. The elder was Dharmamati. Dus-Khor-pa and Than-Chun-pa were younger and youngest respectively. All the four brothers were direct disciples as well as contemporary of Naropā (978-1026 A.D.) Among the four brothers, first of all, Dharmamati became disciple of Naropā. He spent twelve years with him in ancient India. Then Vāgīśvarakīrti went to invite his brother Dharmamati. But instead of coming back to homeland, Dharmamati told him to stay there with Naropā.

Vāgīśvarakīrti attended on Naropā for nine years and was initiated in many doctrines including Cakrasaṁvara and Hevajra. He obtained the lower and intermediate *Siddhi* with the help of Cakrasaṁvara. He became the gatekeeper Paṇḍita at the Southern gate of Vikramaśilā University. Gradully, younger brother Dus-Khar-pa came and attended on Naropā for five years. He was also initiated in Cakrasaṁvara and others. Finally, the youngest brother Than-chun-pa came to invite Dus-Khor-pa. But he also became a disciple of Naropā from whom he learnt a few *Tantras*.

Vāgīśvarakīrti came back to Nepal after learning from Naropā. While he was in Nepal, he made many Tibetan disciples. He gave initiation of Cakrasaṁvara to Lo-tra-ba klog-skya-ses-rab-rtsegs. In course of time, he proceeded to Tibet. There he initiated Mal-gyo-lo-tsa-ba blo-gros-grasgs in Cakrasaṁvara. According to another version, Vagīśvarakīrti had also given initiation of Cakrasaṁvara to Ngag-dVang-Grags-Pa. Thus a lineage of Cakrasaṁvara school was established in Tibet.

Later on, Vāgīśvarakīrti returned to Nepal. It is stated that the Tibetan scholar Mal-gyo-lo-tsa-ba bLo-gros-grags later on, himself came to Nepal and again learnt the Cakrasaṁvara from Vāgīśvarakīrti, from Bodhibhadra, and from Mahākaruna. This time also Vāgīśvarakīrti gave the initiation of Hevajra and others according to the system of Naropā to a Tibetan scholar named Se-tsha-bsod-names-rgyal-mtshan who came from Tibet. Mar-pa-do-pa, a Tibetan scholar had also visited Nepal and learnt the exposition of the Naropā's system from Vāgīśvarakīrti, from his brother Vāgīśvara and from Kanakaśrī, a Nepalese scholar. The youngest brother of Vāgīśvarakīrti was Than-chun-pa who had practised the meditation of Vāgīśvara. Because of this reason he is sometimes known as Vāgīśvara.

Ratnarakṣita (app. 1160-1230 A.D.) was the Nepalese scholar who had also carried out the Cakrasaṁvara school in Nepal after Vāgīśvarakīrti. He had also initiated Tibetan scholars into the school of Cakrasaṁvara.[8]

Ratnarakṣita was conferred with the title 'Mahāpaṇḍita'. He was great scholar in Tibetan history. He had initiated many Tibetan disciples in Nepal. He was a well known scholar in Sanskrit, Logic, as well as in Buddhist *Tantras*.

Ratnarakṣita taught Sanskrit grammer and Logic to Phur-pa-skyabs, a Tibetan disciple who passed away in 1237 A.D. He gave the initiation of Cakrasaṁvara to anothr Tibetan Scholar named Ko-brag-pa bSod-nams-rgyal-mtshan who was born in 1182 and died in 1261 A.D. Similarly, Khams-pa-slon-grags met Ratnarakṣita at Svayambhū mount, Kathmandu. He and other Tibetan people were also initiated by Ratnarakṣita. During the initiation rites, Chag-chos-rje-dpal played the role of translator.

Besides teaching, Mahāpaṇḍita Ratnarakṣita had also composed a commentary entitled *Śrīsaṁvarodayatantrasya Padminī nāma Pañjikā*. The colophons of the commentary identifed that Mahāpaṇḍita Ratnarakṣita was a Bhikṣu.

The Lineage of Cakrasaṁvara Tantra in Tibet

Vajradhara
↓
Vajrapāṇi
↓
Suraha
↓
Nāgārjuna
↓
Śrī Savari
↓
Luipā
↓
Slob-dpon-rje-drill-bu-pa
↓
Kacchapā
↓
Jalandharada
↓
Kṛṣṇācāryapāda
↓
Guhya
↓
Vijayapāda
↓
Taio-pā
↓
Na-ro-pā
↓
Vāgīśvarakīrti
↓
Naga-dVang-Grags-pa
↓
Ngag-gi-dVang-phyug
↓
gLag-skya-ses-rab-brtegs.
↓
hGro-mGon-hPhags-pa-kun-dGah-sNing-po (1233 A.D.) etc.

Here, the editor has collected total five photocopies of manuscripts of the *Śrīsaṁvarodaya-tantra* namely M1, M2, M3, M4, M5 from Nepal.

The M1 denotes the manuscript which is underpossession of a Vajrācārya at Kathmandu. The manuscript was written in Devanāgari script with Newari translation. It does not give any date and name of the copy-writer. It seems to be copied later. The text, chapter one to four which has been edited here was extracted from M1.

The M2 refers the manuscript which was copied by Amṛtānanda Vajrācārya for the sake of his disciples in 1854 A.D.

The M3, M4, and M5 identify the manuscripts which are under possession of different Varacharyas at Kathmandu. These manuscripts do not mention the date and names of the copy-writers.

The editor is eagerly awaiting the opportunity to publish the remaining chapters.

REFERENCES & NOTES

1. *Iti Śrīherukābhidhānamahātantrarāje trilakṣodhṛta sahajodayakalpe Śrīsaṁvarodayatantrarāje sarvayoginīrahasya paṭhitasiddhi trayastriṁśatitamapaṭalaḥ samāptaḥ. Herukābhidhanatantrasya pāṭhasvādhyāya lekhanāt Siddhirṛdhiñca saubhāgyaṁ bodhisattvatvamāpnuyāt/25/*
2. *Yoginīyogatantrasya rahasya buddhagocaram/* Chapter-22
3. *ehi vatsa mahāyānamantracaryanayani vidhi/ deśayiṣyāmi te samyagbhajanastvani mahanaye//*Chapter-18
4. *ācāryābhiṣekasaṁpūrṇaṁ dvitīyaṁ guhyamuttani/ a prajñā jñānatritayam tu caturtha tatpunastathā/ etābhiṣekasampannaḥ samayī so vidhīyate/* Chapter-18
5. Chapter 7
6. *Dākinyo nāḍikāssarvaḥ skandhāyatanamandatani/ śarvanyeka rasāpattace sphūrjitāni Herukākṛti./* Chapter-29
7. Bajracharya, N.M., *A Survey of Buddhism in Nepal,* (Dissertation), Delhi University., pp. 57-62.
8. *Ibid.*

Delhi

ŚRĪSAṀVARODAYATANTRARĀJAḤ

CHAPTERS I-IV

Edited by

Naresh Man Bajracharya

॥ श्रीसम्वरोदयतन्त्रराजः ॥

सम्पादकः—नरेश मान बज्राचार्यः

प्रथमः पटलः

ओँ नमः श्रीहेरुकाय ।[1]

एवं मया श्रुतमेकस्मिन्समये भगवान् सर्वतथागत कायवाक्चित्तवज्रयोगिनीभगेषु विजहार । आर्यानन्द-प्रभृतिभिर्वीतरागप्रमुखैराय्यावलोकितेश्वरादौ[2] अशीतिकोटीयोगीश्वर[3] मध्ये वज्रपाणिं व्यवलोक्य स्मितमकार्षीत्[4] । वज्रपाणिरुत्थःयासनादेकांशमुत्तरासंग[5] कृत्वा दक्षिणजानुमण्डलं पृथिव्यां[6] प्रतिष्ठाप्य कृतकरपुटो भूत्वा भगवन्तमध्येषयामास ।

श्रोतुमिच्छामि भगवन्नु[7] त्पत्ति[8] योगलक्षणम् ।
समुत्पन्नं[9] कथं देव सर्वाकारैकसम्वरम् ॥1 ॥
कथं वाय्वग्निआपस्य[10] पृथिव्याकाशमेवच[11] ।
पञ्चाकार कथं देव षड्विषयाः कथं[12] प्रभो ॥ 2 ॥

---

1. M2. ओँ नमः श्रीहेरुकवज्राय । M 3. राधै नमः श्रीसम्वराय । M5. ओँ नमः श्रीहेरुकाय ।
2. M2. ० राद्यै
3. M5. ० योगेश्वर
4. M2. ० अकरोत्
5. M2, M3, M4, M5. ० रुत्थायासनात्समुत्तरासंग
6. M2, M4, M5. पृथिव्यां
7. M3. हे भगवन्
8. M3. उत्पत्ते
9. M2, M3 उत्पन्नं
10. M2. ० त्रि नीराणां; M2, M4, M5. ० आपश्च
11. M2. ० आकाशयोरपि
12. M2, M3, M4, M5. ततः

त्रिकायकमधिष्ठानं[13] बाह्या चाभ्यन्तर[14] स्थितिः ।
कथं ते देवतारूपं कथयस्व[15] देवती प्रभो ॥ 3 ॥
चन्द्रसूर्य[16] कथं देव पथ[17] पञ्च कथं भवेत् ।[18]
कथं ते[19] शारीरस्वभावं तु नाडीरूपं कथं[20] ततः[21] ॥4 ॥
के ते[22] नाडी प्रमाणस्य शारीरपिण्डत[23] त्कथं ।
समयसंकेत छोमस्य कथयस्व[24] मम[25] प्रभो ॥ 5 ॥
के ते[26] पीठादिसंकेत[27] बाह्याध्यात्म[28] कमेव च ।
कथं भूम्यादिलाभस्य[29] कथं निमित्तदर्शनम् ॥ 6 ॥
कथं ते द्वादशं कर्म मन्त्रजाप[30] कथं भवेत् ।
अक्षमाला कथं युक्तिः के ते[31] जापस्य लक्षणम् ॥ 7 ॥

---

13. M2, M3, M4, M5. कथंत्रिकायाधिष्ठानं
14. M3. अभ्यन्तरे
15. M2. कथं च, M3. कथयश्च
16. M2. चन्द्रः सूर्यः
17. M3. पर्व्व
18. M5. भवे
19. M2. omits ते
20. M3. वाथ
21. M5. भवेत्
22. M2. किन्तद्
23. M2. ०पिण्डकं
24. M3. कथयसमसय
25. M3. omits मम
26. M2. किं तद्
27. M3. पीठसंकेत
28. M2. ०ध्यात्मिक ।
29. M2. लाभस्यात्, M4. लाभञ्च
30. M3. ०जापः
31. M2. किं तद्

के ते[32] मण्डलमावर्त्त[33] देवताकारयोगतः ।
सिद्ध[34] मन्त्र कथं देव कौमारीतर्पणं कथम् ।।8 ।।
के ते[35] दिवसेन कर्तव्यं[36] अलिबलि[37] कथं प्रभो ।
पञ्चामृतादि[38] कथं देव पञ्चाङ्कुश कथं[39] भवेत् ।।9 ।।
कथयस्व[40] मण्डला[41]लेख्यं सूत्रपात[42] कथं भवेत् ।
कथं[43] भूमिसंशोध्य[44] रक्षाचक्रं[45] कथं भवेत् ।।10 ।।
आचार्य[46] केन कर्तव्यं[47] कथं शिष्यस्य संग्रहं ।[48]
के ते सेक[49] प्रमाणञ्च[50] चतुर्थञ्च कथं भवेत् ।।11 ।।

---

32. M2. किं तद्
33. M2. आवर्त्य
34. M2, M3, M5. सिद्धि
35. M2. किं तद्
36. M3. कर्तव्या
37. M2. अलिबलिः
38. M2, M4, M5. पञ्चामृत
39. M2. कथं पञ्चाकुश
40. M2. कथं च,M3. कथयश्च
41. M2. मण्डलं
42. M2. सूत्रपातं,M3. सूत्रपातः
43. M2. कथं तु, M2. कथं ते
44. M2. ०संशुद्धिः,M3. ०संशोधौ,M4, M5. ०प्रसंशो(स्व)ध्य
45. M4, N5. रक्षा चक्र
46. M2, M3. आचार्यः
47. M2, कर्तव्यः,Ms. कर्तव्य
48. M3, M4. संग्रहः
49. M2, M4, अभिषेक,M5. भिषेक
50. M2. प्रमाणं किं

कथं[51] कालस्य नियमं मृत्युवञ्चन[52] मेव च।
के ते[53] चतुर्युगांकस्य[54] चतुर्द्वीप[55] कथं भवेत् ॥ 12 ॥
युगे युगे[56] कथं सिद्धिश्चर्याचारी[57] कथं भवेत्।
के[58] ते योगिनीतन्त्रस्य योगतन्त्र कथं भवेत् ॥13 ॥
कथं सूत्रान्तप्रमाणं[59] के ते पारमितास्तथा।
प्रतिष्ठा[60] होमयोगस्य सिद्धिमन्त्र[61] कथं भवेत् ॥14 ॥
रसायनं च[62] कथं देव मद्यपानं[63] कथं भवेत्।
मन्त्रोदय[64] कथं देव मन्त्रोद्धार[65] कथं भवेत् ॥ 15 ॥
निग्रहञ्च कथं देव अनुग्रहं च कथं प्रभो।[66]
तत्वानां[67] च कथं भगवन् शून्यता[68]करुणा कथं ॥ 16 ॥

---

51. M3. कथं ते
52. M2, M5. ०वचन
53. M2. किं तद्
54. M3. चतुर्युगोन्तस्य
55. M3. ०द्वीपः
56. M3. युगोयगे M5. जुगयजुग्य
57. M3. ०चर्याचादी
58. M2. किं and omits ते
59. M2. ०प्रामाण्यं, M4. प्रामाणं
60. M4. प्रतिस्था
61. M2. मन्त्रं
62. M2, M4, M5. omit च
63. M2. मद्यपानं
64. M2. मन्त्रोदयं
65. M2. मन्त्रोद्धारं
66. M5. omits प्रभो and reads भवेत्
67. M2. तत्वानि
68. M2, M5. शून्यतां

कथं शून्य[69] स्वभावत्वं कथं तथता स्वरूपकं ।[70]
देवरूप कथंनाम योगिनीलक्षण बलिः[71] ॥ 17 ॥[72]
सर्वधर्मपरिज्ञानं[73] भावना कथय[74] प्रभो ॥

॥ इति श्री[75] सम्वरोदयतन्त्रस्य[76] अध्येषणा पटलः प्रथमः ॥[77]

---

69. M3. शून्यतां
70. M2. स्वभावकं
71. M5. omits बलि and reads कथं
72. M3. omits the two quarters.
73. M3. परिज्ञायन
74. M2, M4. कथ्यते, M5. कठते
75. M3. omits श्री
76. M5. ० तन्त्रराज
77. M4. reads only इति अध्येषणा

द्वितीयः पटलः

भगवानाह ! साधु साधु वज्रपाणि[1]र्हस्योत्पत्ति[2] मुदानयामास[3] ।
अथातः संप्रवक्ष्यामि उत्पत्तिक्रम भावनां ।
चतस्रो योनयो[4] भूता[5] नानाकर्मस्वभावतः[6] ॥1 ॥
अण्डजा[7] जरायुजाश्च[8] संस्वेदजोपपादुकाः ।[9]
हंसक्रौञ्च[10] मयूरा[11] श्च शुकसारादि[12] अण्डजाः ॥ 2 ॥
हस्त्यश्वगोमहिषा[13] श्च खर[14] मानुष[15] जरायुजाः ।
कृमिकीट[16] पतङ्गा[17] श्च मशकादि[18] स्तु स्वेदजाः ॥ 3 ॥
देवनरक[19] सत्वानामन्तराभवमेव च ।

---

1. M2, M3. वज्रपाणे
2. M2. उत्पत्ति लक्षणं
3. M3. उदानयामासः, M2. omits उदानयामास
4. M2. भूतयो
5. M2, M5. भूत्वा
6. M5. omits भूता.
7. M2, M3, M5. अण्डजाश्च
8. M2, M3, M5. जरायुश्च
9. M2, M5. औपपादुका
10. M2. क्रेञ्च
11. M3. मयूरश्च ।
12. M2. शुकश्येनादयो ,M2. शुकसारिकादि
13. M3. महिष
14. M2. खरा
15. M2, मनुषा, M2. नरा
16. M2, M3. क्रिमि
17. M3. पतर्गालि,M5. पतंगी
18. M2. मत्स्यादय,M5. मत्सकादि,M5. मन्सकादि
19. M2, M5. नारका

एते[20] औपपादुका:[21] सत्त्वाः प्राथम[22]कल्पिकादयः ॥ 4 ॥
पूर्वविदेहापरगोडानी[23] उत्तरकुरुमेत्र च ।[24]
महाभोगेन संवर्ता[25] धन्वा[26] जडा[27] विवेकिनः ॥ 5 ॥
त्रय[28] द्वीप[29] मनुष्याणां निर्विकल्प[30] विचारिणाम् ।
जम्बुद्वीपेषुजातस्य[31] कर्मभूमि[32] प्रशस्यते[33] ॥ 6 ॥
सुकृतं दुष्कृतं कर्ममध्यमाधममुत्तमाः[34] ।
पूर्वजन्मविपाकोत्र दृश्यते सर्वजन्तुषु ॥ 7 ॥
मदमात्सर्य्यदुष्टानां शठकपटाभिमानिनः[35] ।
रागद्वेषादिमोहानां जराव्याधिं तु पीडिताः[36] ॥ 8 ॥
जम्बुद्वीपे[37] वरश्रेष्ठ मध्य[38] देशोपपद्यते

20. M2. वउपजजमक एते,M4, M5. एता
21. M4. ओपपादुका
22. M2, M3, M5. प्रथम
23. M2. अपरगोदान्यू,M5. पूर्वविदेहोजम्बूद्वीपऽपरगोडायनी,M4. अपरगोदायनी
24. M2. उत्तरकुरुस्तथा
25. M2, M3, M5. सवंर्य,M4. संवर्यः
26. M2. धन्या,M5. धम्बा ।
27. M2.omits जडा and reads यत्रा
28. M2. त्रयो
29. M2. द्वीपा,M3. द्वीपः
30. M3. निविकल्पा,M5. नाविकल्प
31. M2. जातानाम्
32. M2, M3. भूमिः
33. M2. प्रशस्यते, M3. प्रशम्यते, M4. प्रशंस्यते, M5. प्रशंस्यते
34. M2. अधमोत्तममध्यमं, M3. अधमोत्तमयध्यमाः, M5. मध्येमाधर्म्मनुत्तमा
35. M2. ० अभिमानिनाम्
36. M2. ० व्याधियुषां तथा
37. M4. ० द्वीप
38. M2. मध्यम नोपपद्यते

मृदुमध्यतीक्ष्णेन्द्रिया[39] जन्म पूर्वकुशलमपेक्षितं[40] ॥ 9 ॥
मनुष्यजाता[41] प्रथमस्य सत्फलम्[42] ।
स्वगृहान्निष्क्रान्त[43] द्वितीयस्य सत्फलम्[44] ॥ 10 ॥
कुशले प्रव्रज्यासाधनं तृतीयम्[45] ।
एकाग्रमानसं[46] लाभश्चतुर्थन्तु उदाहृतः[47] ॥ 11 ॥
मायोपम[48] समाधिञ्च न प्रजानन्ति मानुषाः ।
अनादिकालिक[49] क्लेश[50] वासनाप्रबली[51] कृताः[52] ॥ 12 ॥
तेन पुराकृतं कर्मच्युतिउत्पत्ति[53] संभवेत्[54] ।
सामग्रीन्न लभ्यते[55] तावत् सप्ताहमन्तराभवे तिष्ठति ।[56] ॥ 13 ॥
अन्तराभवसत्त्वस्य देशान्तरगामिवत् ।
कथंचित्कर्मसूत्रेण षड्गतिञ्च प्रजायते ॥ 14 ॥

---

39. M2. मध्येत्रीज्ञेन्द्रिया, M3. तीक्ष्येन्द्रिया, M4. तीक्षेन्द्रियो, M5. मध्येस्तीक्ष्णेन्द्रिया
40. M2. ०प्रेक्षितं, M3. ०येक्षितं M5. ०पक्षितं,M4. ०यक्षितं
41. M2. ०जातं
42. M2, M4, M5. महत्फलं
43. M3. गृहं निष्क्रान्ता, M5. नीष्क्रान्त
44. M2. लाभ
45. M3, M4, साधनस्तृतीयम्
46. M2. मायुषः
47. M2, M3, M4, M5 उदाहृतम्
48. M2. मायोपमं
49. M3. कालिका, M4. कालिकं
50. M2,M3. क्लेशा
51. M3. प्रवसी
52. M2,M3. कृता, M5. कृत
54. M2. कर्मजानंत्युत्पत्ति, M3. च्यूतोत्पत्ति, M4. जातोत्पत्ति,M5. च्युत्युत्पत्ति
55. M2. सभवं
56. M2. लभेत्,M3, M5. लभते

मात्रापित्रादि[57] संयोगादै[58] क्षयेद्भव जन्मनि[59] ।
अतिनिर्भरमानन्द[60] सुखमार्गे[61] प्रवेश्यते[62] ॥ 15 ॥
अश्वारोहवज्ज्ञानं वायुवाहनरढवत्[63] ।
शीघ्रतरेण[64] आगत्य[65] मूहूर्तं[66] क्षणमात्रकं ॥16 ॥
द्वासप्ततिसहश्रञ्च नाडी संचोद्यतत्क्षणो[67] ।
परमानन्दसंप्राप्तमालिकालिद्रवीकृतं ॥ 17 ॥
शुक्र[68] शोणितयोर्मध्ये बिन्दुरूपेण तिष्ठति ।
प्रथमं कललाकारमर्वुदञ्च द्वितीयकं ॥ 18 ॥
तृतीयं पेशिजातश्चतुर्थघनमेव च ।
वायुना प्रेय्येमाणस्य मत्स्या[69] कारं च यद्भवेत्[70] ॥ 19 ॥
पञ्चमासगतं बीजं पञ्चस्फोटं[71] प्रजायते ।
हस्तपादमुखश्चैव षण्मासेन तु जायते[72] ॥ 20 ॥
केशरोमननखचिन्हं सप्तमासेन जायते ।
इन्द्रियाणि च रूपाणिव्यंजनाष्टकमासतः ॥ 21 ॥

---

57. M2. ०पित्रादि, M3, M4, M5. ०पितादि
58. M3, ०दै, M5. ०द्वै
59. M3,M4,M5. जन्मिनः
60. M2, M3, M4. निर्भरसानन्द
61. M3. म्मुखमार्गे
62. M5. प्रवेशयेत्
63. M5. वायुवाहनमरुट्टवत्
64. M2. शीघ्रतरां, M3. शीघ्रतरणं, M4. शीघ्रतलं, M5. शीघ्रन्तरेत्
65. M2, M4. समागम्य
66. M2,M3. मुहूर्तं
67. M2. क्षणो, M5. जनैः, M4. फणे
68. M4, M5. शुक्ल
69. M3, M5. मान्सा
70. M2,M3,M4,M5. omits यद् and reads वत्
71. M2. पञ्चस्कन्ध
72. M2,M3,M4. omit the two quarters.

संपूर्ण नवमासेन चेतना दशमासतः ।
कललादक्षोभ्यरूपेण[73] अर्बुदं रत्नसम्भवं[74] ॥22 ॥
पेशी[75] अमितनाथस्य घनो अमोघसिद्धयः[76] ।
प्रशाखा[77] वैरोचनस्यापि पञ्चाकारन्तु दर्शयेत् ॥ 23 ॥
अक्षोभ्य[78] मूत्र[79] रक्तस्यामिताभशुक्र[80] रूपिणः ।
पिण्डमात्रन्तु रत्नस्य स[81]न्मिश्रं वैरोचनं[82] स्थितः ॥ 24 ॥
द्वेनाद्योयोनिमध्ये[83] तु वामदक्षिणयोस्तथा ।
वामे[84] शुक्रं[85] विजानीयाद् दक्षिणे[86] रक्तमेव च ॥ 25 ॥
तयोर्मीलनमेकत्वं[87] धर्मधातुस्वभावतः ।
कर्मबीज[88] वशात्प्राप्त[89] वायवो[90] परिवर्त्य च ॥ 26 ॥

---

73. M2. कललमक्षोभ्यरूपेण, M3. कललाक्षोभ्यरूपेण
74. M3, अर्बुदरत्नसम्भवः
75. M4, M5. पेशितो
76. M2. अमोघसमृद्धिकः
77. M2. omits प्रशाखा and reads केशा
78. M2. अक्षोभ्यो
79. M4, M5. मुर्ति
80. M4, M5. शुक्ल ।
81. M2. omits सन्
82. M2. वैरोचनः
83. M5. ०मध्य
84. M3, M4, M5. वाम
85. M4, M5. शुक्ल
86. M3. दक्षिण
87. M2. ०एकत्वे
88. M2. कर्मजीव
89. M2 प्राप्तं
90. M3. वायुभिः

धर्मोदयानि द्वाराणा[91] मभिमुखं भवति निश्चितम्।
दक्षिणकुक्षिमाश्रित्य उत्कुटुक[92] स्थितमाभिमुख[93] ॥ 27 ॥
वामकुक्षिसमाश्रित्य प्रज्ञाउदरमुखी भवेत्।
बीजाधान[94] क्रमे काले मुहूर्तं लक्षयेत्सुधीः ॥ 28 ॥
दक्षिणे वहति[95] यो वायुः पुरुषो भवति सर्वदा[96]।
वामे[97] वहति[98] मारुत्[99] स्त्रीणो[100] भवति निश्चितं ॥ 29 ॥
उभयोर्मध्यगतं बीजं नपुंसकं सदा[101] भवेत्।
अब्धातु[102] पैतृको ज्ञेयो[103] तेजोधातुश्च मातृका[104] ॥ 30 ॥
त्वक्[105] मांसश्च रक्तश्च मातृजा[106] इति कथ्यते।
स्नायुमज्ज[107] श्च शुक्रं च पितृजा इति कथ्यते ॥ 31 ॥
एवं षट्कौशिकं[108] पिण्डं[109] वज्रसत्ववचो यथा।

---

91. M2. धर्मोदयाख्य द्वाराणां,M3. धर्मोदयोयोनिहारणां,M4, M5. धर्मोदयायोनिद्वारानां
92. M3. उत्कुटक
93. M2, M4, M5. ०सन्मुखं
94. M4,M5. बीजाधान्य
95. M2. वहते
96. M2, सर्वथा
97. M3. वाम
98. M2. वहतो
99. M2. मरुतः
100. M2. स्त्रियो,M3,M4,M5. स्त्रीणां
101. M4. तदा
102. M2,M4,omits अब्धातु and reads अथातः, M3. आपधातु
103. M2. ज्ञेयः,M3, M4, M5, ज्ञेया
104. M2. मातृकः, M3,M4,M5. मातृकाः
105. M2. त्वक्च
106. M2. मातृज्ञा
107. M2,M4 ०मज्जा
108. M3. omits षट्
109. M3. पिण्ड

रूप[110] वेदनासंज्ञासंस्कार[111] विज्ञानमेव च ॥ 32 ॥
पञ्चबुद्धस्वभावं तु स्कन्धोत्पत्ति विनिर्मिताः[112]
जन्मोत्पत्तिक्रमं ज्ञात्वा[113] सम्यक्संबुद्ध[114] माप्नुयात्।
एतत्स्कन्ध[115] परिज्ञानं[116] कथितं तत्त्ववादिना ॥ 33 ॥

॥ इति उत्पत्तिनिर्देशपटलो द्वितीयः ॥ 2 ॥

---

110. M2. रूपञ्च
111. M3. संस्कार संज्ञा
112. M2. सूनिश्चिताः, M3,M4, M5. विनिश्चिताः
113. M3, M5. ज्ञानं, M4. ज्ञातुं
114. M2. सम्यक् बुद्धावं
115. M5. omits स्कन्ध
116. M5. ज्ञात

तृतीयः पटलः

अथातः[1] संप्रक्ष्यामि[2] उत्पन्नक्रमभावना[3] ।
येन विज्ञान[4]मात्रेण आशुसिद्धिमवाप्नुयात् ॥ 1 ॥
कायमण्डलमाश्रित्य धर्मसंभोगविग्रहम्[5] ।
देहमण्डलमित्युक्तं संबोधिक्रमसाधनम् ॥ 2 ॥
उत्पत्तिमृदुमध्यायोगिध्याया[6]न्मण्डलभावनाम्[7] ।
अधिमात्र[8]झटिताकारं[9] मण्डलं[10] चित्रमात्रतः[11] ॥ 3 ॥
झटिता[12] कारयोगेन उत्पन्नक्रमभावना ।
त्रैधातुकमयं कूटं[13] प्राणिनो माण्डलेयकाः[14] ॥ 4 ॥
तन्मध्ये झटिताकारं[15] योगी[16] स्यात्मण्डलाधिपः ।
ओँ आः हूँ इतिमन्त्रेण कायवाक्चित्तमण्डलम्[17] ॥ 5 ॥

---

1. M3. अथात्र
2. M2,M3,M4,M5. संप्रवक्ष्यामि
3. M2. ०भावनाम्
4. M2,M4,M5. विज्ञात
5. M2,M3, M4. ०विग्रहे । M5. ०विग्रहाः
6. M2. ० मध्याद्योक्रमात्,M3. ० मृदुमध्यादिध्यायात्, M4. ० मृत्युमध्यात्माध्यायात्
M5. मृदुमध्यात्माध्यायात्
7. M3,M4, M5. ०भावना
8. M2. ० मात्रे, M5. ०मात्रो ।
9. M2. झटित्याकारं
10. M2. मण्डले
11. M2. चित्तभावना, M3. चित्तमात्रताः, M5. चित्रमात्रक M4. चित्रमात्रता
12. M2. झटित्या
13. M2. मयकूट,M4. त्रैधातुकमयंकृतं
14. M2. प्राणिनामण्डलेयता, M3. ०यताः
15. M2. झटित्याकारं
16. M2. M3. स योगी,M4. योगीन्तु
17. M4.reads differently as the following : त्रिकायं शोधन कुर्यु कायवाक्चित्तमण्डलम्

स्वर्गमर्त्यचपाताल[18] मेकमूर्त्ति भवेत् क्षणात्[19] ।
झटिता[20]कारयोगेन झटिता[21] मन्त्रमुच्चरेत्[22] ॥ 6 ॥
सर्ववीरसमायोग[23] डाकिनीजालसत्सुखम्[24] ।
चत्वारो धातवः[25] स्कन्धाः[26] षट्विषयात्मकस्तथा ॥ 7 ॥
देव्याहेरुक[27] ज्ञानन्तु तस्य भेदं न कल्पयेत् ।
तथता मुद्रितं[28] चक्रं खमिव शून्यता तथा ॥ 8 ॥
नैरात्मा तथता विश्वं उपाय[29] करुणावलः[30] ।
युगनद्धमनाभोगं[31] मण्डलं सारमुत्तमम् ॥ 9 ॥
चिन्ताविकल्पयोगेपि तद[32] चिन्त्यमकल्पकम् ।
सर्वाकारवरं सर्वं निराकारं सुखेन्द्रियम्[33] ॥ 10 ॥
भावाभावात्मकं चैव भावं[34] कृत्वा नित्योदितम् ।[35]

---

18. M2. स्वर्भुर्मण्डलपातालेषू
19. M3. तत्क्षणात्
20. M2. झटित्या
21. M2. झटित्या
22. M2. ०मुच्चरेन्
23. M3. ०योगं, M4, M5. ०योगा
24. M2. डाकिनीजालमुत्तमम्, M4, M5. जालसमुखम्
25. M4 धातवे
26. M3. स्कन्धो, M5. स्कन्ध
27. M3. ०हेरुकं
28. M3. ०मुदिता
29. M2. उपायः
30. M3. ०वलं, M4. ०वर, M5. ०वल
31. M3. omits मनाभोगं
32. M2, M3, M4, तदा, M5. सदा
33. M3. निराकार०
34. M4. भावां
35. M2. निवेदितं

नानारोप[36]मनोभोगं[37] नित्योदितं[38] महासुखम्[39] ॥ 11 ॥
तत्तत्प्राप्त[40] समुत्पन्नमनुत्पन्नस्वभावतः ।
अजडत्वात्स्वसंवेद्यमजानकमपश्यकम्[41] ॥ 12 ॥
नी[42] रुपत्वादकूटस्थं नित्यं तदविकारतः[43]
न चाभावोप्यनुच्छेदात्सांवृतो[44] त्यादसंभवात् ॥ 13 ॥
सहजं[45] सर्वधर्माणां निजानन्दस्वरूपतः ।
स्वाधिष्ठानं[46] स्वयं भूत्वा [47]दनाहतमनाशतः[48] ॥ 14 ॥
अनुत्पादरसावेधाद्भावनापितथाविधा ।
प्रज्ञैवहिभवेध्यान[49] शून्यताप्रतिवेदिका[50] ॥ 5 ॥
सर्वधर्मपरिज्ञानं[51] भावनानैव भावना ।
महासुखाभिसंबोधि[52] महामुद्रापरा[53] तथा ॥ 16 ॥

---

36. M3. नानारुप
37. M2. नानारोपनानाभाग
38. M2,M3,M5 नित्योदित
39. M2, M3. महत्सुखम्
40. M2, M3. तत्तत्प्राप्य
41. M2,M4.० महास्यकं
42. M3, M4, M5. निरूप०
43. M2. विकारकम्
44. M2,M3,M4,M5.० संवृतो
45. M3, M5. सहज
46. M2. स्वाधिष्ठान,M3. स्वाधिष्ठाधिष्ठान
47. M3. भूया
48. M2. ० नागतम्
49. M4. प्रज्ञावहतीभवेत्मानं,M4. प्रज्ञैवयदिभवेत्मानं
50. M2,M3,M4,M5.० वेधिकाः
51. M5. ० परित्याग
52. M2. महासुखानिसर्वाणि,M3, ० संबोधे,M5. ० सर्वाणि ।
53 M3. omits परा

धर्मतत्त्वा[54]वताराय तेभ्यो भेदं प्रदर्शितम्।
सद्गुरोरुपदेशेन स्फुटो भवति नान्यथा॥ 17 ॥
संवरं सर्वबुद्धानामेवंकारे[55] प्रतिष्ठितम्।
कायवाक्चित्तसं[56] कर्म सर्वाकारैकसम्वरम्॥ 18 ॥
सम्वरं सुखवरं बोधिमवाच्यमनि[57] दर्शनम्।
रहस्यं सर्वबुद्धानां[58] मीलनं सम्वरं वरम्॥ 19 ॥
स्वाधिष्ठानुक्रमो ह्येषः स्फुटाः[59] सद्गुरुकौशलात्।

॥ इति उत्पत्ति[60] निर्देशपटलस्तृतीयः॥ 3 ॥

54. M2. धर्मधात्व, M3. धर्मतस्या
55. M2, M4. ०एवंकारं
56. M2, कायवाक्चेतसां,M3. चेतसं
57. M4. बोधिमाचार्य्यमणि
58. M3, M5 रहस्यसर्वबुद्धानां
59. M2, स्फटः,M5. स्फुटो
60. M2,M3.उत्पन्नक्रम,M4, M5. उत्पत्तिक्रम

चतुर्थः पटलः

अथातः संप्रवक्ष्यामि[1] चतुर्भूत स्वभावतः।
यत्तद्वस्तु सर्वाणि तद्भूत[2] स्वभावतः ॥ 1 ॥
पृथिवी तत्र वस्तुनि अग्निना सर्व[3] पाच्यते[4]
आपेणच[5] द्रवीकृत्य वायुना सह प्रेरितम् ॥ 2 ॥
आकाश[6] शून्यदेशस्थं[7] तेन सर्वत्र जायते।
यत्रैक[8] स्तत्र चत्वारि तत्सर्वमुपतिष्ठते ॥ 3 ॥
तृणगुल्मलतावृक्ष[9] जडोविज्ञानमात्रकम्।
षड्गतिकाश्च ये सत्वा विज्ञान[10] सह वर्तते ॥ 4 ॥
तेन सर्वत्र पिण्ड[11] स्याज्जानीयद्भवधीधना:[12]
मरणादिषु सत्वानां वायु[13] सर्वत्र चाल्यते ॥ 5 ॥
तत्क्षणेऽग्निना त्यजति आपं शुष्क[14] स्तदा[15] भवेत्।
सर्वत्र सन्धि[16] सन्धितु गतानिश्चेष्टता[17] भवेत् ॥ 6 ॥

---

1. M3,M5. संप्रवक्षामि
2. M2, M4. तत्तत्भूत
3. M2,M3,M4,M5. सर्वत्र
4. M4. पच्चते
5. M2. अद्भिश्चैव
6. M2. आकाशं
7. M3,M4. ०देशस्य,M5. ०देहस्य
8. M3. यत्रैकं,M4. यत्रैको
9. M2, M3. वृक्षा
10. M2. विज्ञानं
11. M2. पिण्ड
12. M2. जानीभोभवधीधना:,M3. जानीयवधकः धीधना:, M4. जानीयोभवभीषन, M5. जानीया भवधीधनः
13. M2. वायुः
14. M2,M4. शुष्कं
15. M2,M3,M4,M5. सदा
16. M2. संधिः
17. M2. ०वैष्टता

पृथिवीमात्रकाठिन्य[18] स्थितादेहादिमात्रकम् ।
जायन्ते[19] च म्रियन्ते च चत्वारि भूत[20] सर्वगाः[21] ॥ 7 ॥
देवासुरमनुष्याणां विनाभूतै[22] न जायते ।
देवतालोकपालादीन्सर्वत्रसहसंस्थिताः ॥ 8 ॥
समस्त देव[23] सिद्धान्त[24] मन्यते भाविते सदा ।[25]
सर्वत्र सर्वगं[26] सर्व[27] यत्र तिष्ठन्तु[28] भूमिसम्[29] ॥ 9 ॥
चतुर्भूतपरं श्रेष्ठं सर्वशास्त्रेषु संमताः ।
प्राणवायु[30] समादृश्य[31] अग्निजीवतु[32] लक्षणम् ॥ 10 ॥
अमृतस्वभाव आपस्य पृथिवीक्षेत्रमात्रता ।
तत्र तिष्ठेत्सदा देव[33] विज्ञानं परमेश्वरम्[34] ॥ 11 ॥
स्माद्वर्तते ज्ञानं[35] आकारं[36] पंचदेवताः ।

---

18. M3. काषिन्य,M4. कोष्टिन्य, M5. काष्ठिन्य
19. M5. जायते
20. M2. चतुर्भूत
21. M2. शगताः,M3. सर्वगः,M4. सर्वतः
22. M2, M5,० भूत सर्वगः,M4. ० सर्वतः
23. M2, वेदा M3,M4. वेद
24. M2, M3, M4. सिद्धान्ते,M5. सिध्यन्ते
25. M2. सति
26. M2, सर्वगः,M2, M4,M5. सर्वग
27. M2. सर्वो
28. M2, तिष्ठति M3, M5. तिष्ठन्ति
29. M2,M3,M4,M5. भूमिजं
30. M2. ० वायुं
31. M5. समोदृस्य
32. M2. ० जीवित,M3, M4. ० जीवत,M5. ० जीवन्तु
33. M2. देवो,M3, M4, M5. देवं
34. M2. परमेश्वरः
35. M3. ज्ञानदेवं,M3,M4,M5. देवं
36. M3. आकार

रूपवेदनासंज्ञासंस्कार[37] विज्ञानमेव च ॥ 12 ॥
आदर्शसमता[38] प्रत्यवेक्षणाकृत्यानुष्ठानमेव च।
[39]सुविशुद्धधर्मधातुश्च एता[40] ज्ञानप्रतिष्ठिताः[41] ॥ 13 ॥
वैरोचनं रत्नसंभवमिताभामोघा[42] क्षोभ्य एव च।
पंचाकारैकरसंबोधि[43] विषयाश्च[44] षट्[45] स्मताः[46] ॥ 14 ॥
रूपशब्द तथा गन्धरसस्पर्शधर्ममेव च।
एता[47] विशुद्धिमाख्याता धातुरष्टादशा[48] स्मृता[49] ॥ 15 ॥
एतेषां स्कन्धरूपत्वाद्भावयेत्परमाक्षरः[50]
बुद्धत्वफलहेतुस्याच्च[51] क्षुरादिषुभावयेत् ॥ 16 ॥
चक्षुरिन्द्रियविज्ञानं चित्तवज्रविकुर्वितम्[52] ।
त्रयः स्वभाव[53] विशुद्ध्यार्थ[54] प्रभास्वरपद[55] भवेत् ॥ 17 ॥

---

37. M2. ॰संस्कारं
38. M5. आदर्शभ्यता
39. M2. M3, शु॰
40. M2. एतत्
41. M3. ॰प्रतिष्ठिताः
42. M2,M3. मोघो
43. M2. ॰सबोधिं
44. M2,M3. omit च
45. M2. षडपि,M3. षद,M4. षड
46. M2,M3,M4,M5. स्मृता
47. M2. एतद्
48. M2, M3.॰देश
49. M3. मताः
50. M2. ॰क्षरं
51. M4, M5. ॰फलमेवस्यात्
52. M5. ॰विकुर्वित
53. M2. त्रिस्वभाव,M3,M5. त्रयस्वभाव
54. M3. विशुद्धयार्थं
55. M5.॰परं

विज्ञान[56] श्रोत्रशब्दस्य अनुपलम्भ[57] स्वभावतः[58] ।
घ्राणगन्धन्तु विज्ञानं विशुद्धिस्तथता स्मृता[59] ॥18॥
रस[60] जिह्वाविशुद्धित्वाद्धि[61] ज्ञानं परमार्थतः[62] ।
कायस्पर्शविज्ञानं[63] मायोत्पन्नस्वभावतः ॥ 19 ॥
मनो धर्ममनोविज्ञानं[64] हृदयेति[65] विशुद्धितः[66] ।
षट्प्रवृतिविज्ञानं[67] आलयं तु तथागतः[68] ॥ 20 ॥
श्रीहेरुकसमाधिस्थं[69] प्रभास्वरपदमाप्नुयात् ।
विषय[70] विशुद्धि[71] योगेन निर्विकल्पवपदं भवेत् ॥ 21 ॥
विषयविशुद्धिबोद्धव्याः[72] सर्वाकारवर[73] स्थितिः[74] ।
बुद्ध[75] धर्मस्तथासंघ एकोपि कल्पनात्रयम् ॥ 22 ॥

---

56. M2,M3. विज्ञानं
57. M2. अरुपलंभ
58. M5. स्वभावत
59. M3,M4. स्मृताः
60. M2, रसं,M3. रसः
61. M3. ०विशोधित्वाद्
62. M3. परमार्थत,M5. परमार्थयः
63. M2. कायविज्ञानसंस्पर्शविज्ञानं,M3. कायकस्पर्शविज्ञानं,M4. कायस्पर्शकविज्ञानं
64. M2. मनोधर्मस्यविज्ञाने,M3. मनोधर्म्ममनोविज्ञाने,M4, M5. ०विज्ञानं
65. M3. तथतेति
66. M2,M5. विशुद्धिता, M3. विशुद्धताः,M4. विशुद्धिताः
67. M2,M5. ०विज्ञाने, M3. वद्यमुक्ति विज्ञाने,M4. ०विज्ञान
68. M2,M3. तथागताः, M5. तथागता
69. M3. ०स्य,M4. श्री संवरसमाधिस्थं
70. M2. विषयो
71. M3, M4. विषयि
72. M2,M4. ०बोधव्यो
73. M2,M4,M5. वले
74. M2, स्थिता,M5. स्थिती
75. M2. बुद्धो,M3. बुद्धा

त्रिशरणं[76] त्रितत्त्वस्तु[77] त्रिकाया[78] स्त्रिविमोक्षतः[79] ।
त्रिमुखः त्र्यक्षरः[80] त्रिदेवः[81] स्यात्त्रैधातुकः[82] स्वरूपतः[83] ॥ 23 ॥
त्रिमण्डलः त्रियोगंतु[84] त्रीणिमार्गन्तुदेशिताः[85] ।
त्रिसमयः त्रिकल्याणः[86] कायवाक्चित्तमेव च ॥ 24 ॥
प्रज्ञायाश्च उपायाश्च योग[87] तस्य तृतीयकम् ।
त्रिगुह्यं च यथा दृष्टं[88] धर्मोदय[89] स्वभावतः ॥ 25 ॥
त्रितया[90] नुपम्भयोगेन त्रयाणां मन्त्ररूपतः ।
त्रय[91] नाडीस्वरूपाश्च बाह्याभ्यन्तर वस्तुतः[92] ॥ 26 ॥
बाह्यलौकिकोधर्मं[93] मभ्यन्तर[94] देवतादिकम्[95] ।
बाह्याभ्यन्तर विशुद्धित्वा[96] द्योगी बुद्धत्वमावहेत् ॥ 27 ॥

76. M2. त्रिशरण्यं,M3. त्रिशरणः
77. M2. त्रितत्वं,M3. त्रितस्वस्थ
78. M2,M3,M4,M5. त्रिकायः
79. M3. त्रिविमोक्षणो,M5. त्रिविमोक्षत
80. M5. त्रेक्षर,M4. त्रिदेवस्या
81. M2. त्रिमुखस्त्रयक्षरस्त्रिदेवः
82. M3. त्रैधातुकः,M4. त्रिधातुकः
83. M5. स्वरुपत
84. M2. त्रीणिभार्गानिदेशिताः
85. M2. त्रीणिमार्गनिदेशिताः
86. M2. त्रिविमोक्षस्त्रिकल्पंच,and omits त्रिसमयःत्रिकल्याणः,M3, M4,M5.त्रंयकल्यान
87. M2. प्रज्ञायाश्चैवपायस्य योगं,M3. प्रज्ञाया चउपायश्चयोगं,M5. प्रज्ञायश्चउपायश्चयोगं
88. M2,M3,M5. दृष्टं
89. M2. धर्मोदया
90. M3. त्रिम्त्रया,M4. त्रितयो
91. M2. त्रयो
92. M2,M3. वस्तुच,M4,M5. वस्तुनः
93. M2. बाह्याश्चलौकिकाधर्मा,M3. बाह्यंलौकिकधर्मं , M4. बाह्यालौकिकधर्मा,M5. बाह्यालौकिकधर्म
94. M2. आन्तरा,M4. अभ्यन्तरे
95. M3. देवतादिकाः
96. M5. सुधात्वा

धर्मधातुस्वभावन्तु देवतालम्बन[97] प्रति।
सर्वाकारस्वरूपत्वाद्देवती[98] परिकल्पितम् ॥ 28 ॥
आदिदेवत[99] रूपंतु वज्रसत्व[100] व्यवस्थितः[101] ।
पीठक्षेत्रेषु[102] संकेत[103] योगिनीयोग[104] मेलकम्[105] ॥ 29 ॥
तथाद्वयसभायोग[106] स्फारयित्वातु दवेतां[107] ।
असंख्य[108] देवतास्फरणं[109] संख्यामण्डलकल्पयेत्[110] ॥ 30 ॥
अचिन्त्यदेवतायोग[111] मचिन्त्यं बुद्धनाटकम्[112] ।
श्रीहेरुकसमायोग[113] डाकिनीजालरूपतः[114] ॥ 31 ॥
तयोरभिन्नरूपत्वं[115] भावना कथिता[116] मया।

---

97. M4. आलम्बन
98. M2,M5. ०देवता
99. M2. ०दैवत,M3.०देवतः
100. M2.वज्रसत्वे
101. M2.व्यवस्थितं,M3, M4. व्यवस्थितिः, M5. वेवस्थितः
102. M2. ०क्षेत्रन्तु,M3. ०क्षेत्रेतु,M4. ०क्षत्र,M5. क्षत्रंतु
103. M2. संकेते,M3. संकेतः
104. M4.योगिनीगन
105. M4. मरकं
106. M2,M3,M4. योगं,M5. योगा
107. M2. देवता,M3,M4,M5.देवताः
108. M2,M3. असंख्यं
109. M2.०स्फारण
110. M2. ०कल्पना
111. M2. अचिन्तादेवयोगं,M5. अचिन्तेदेवतायोगं
112. M3. बुद्धनाद्यकं,M4. बुद्धनायकं
113. M5. ०योगा
114. M5. ०रूपत
115. M5. रूपत्वा
116. M3. कथित

सर्वं[117] अद्धयतां प्राप्य ग्राह्याग्राहकवर्जितम्[118] ॥ 32 ॥
स्थूलं शब्दमिति प्रोक्तं[119] सूक्ष्मं[120] चिन्तामयं भवेत्।
चिन्तयारहितं[121] तत्वं तत्पदं[122] परिकीर्त्तितम् ॥ 33 ॥

॥ इति चतुर्भूतपञ्चाकारषट्विषया[123] देवता[124] विशुद्धिपटलश्चतुर्थः ॥ 4 ॥

Kathmandu, Nepal

---

117. M2. सर्वे
118. M2, M5. ०वर्जिता
119. M2,M3,M4,M5. स्थूलशब्दमिमिप्रोक्तं
120. M2. शुक्ष्मे
121. M3. चिन्तर्य्यलहितं, M5. चिन्तियामिहितं, M4. चिंतयासिहितं
122. M5. तत्पदंपदं
123. M3. ०कारषजिष्य
124. M2. देता

SECTION II

Buddhism & Society

COMPASSION : BUDDHISM VIS-A-VIS PURĀṆAS

Phra Soonthorndhammathada

Religion is a matter of experience, it cannot be entirely theoretical. Although every religion has a ceremonial aspect, yet religion in its true sense is actually a direct awareness of the world of values. The rites and ceremonies are often nothing but indirect methods to prove the importance of these basic values. The culture of a country is reflected in its religion and that of India is no exception. Each civilisation has its own pivot, i.e. ancient Greece was devoted to art and ancient Rome was committed to politics. If we compare these civilisations with that of India, we find that the civilisations having their feet on secularism have faded into oblivion while Indian civilization stood undaunted weathering many a fierce storm of changed political and religious atmosphere, because her foundations are the eternal values of philosophy and moral code, and not the sifting sands of pseudo-secularism. There came a succession of spiritual leaders who are the true bearers of culture which is a synthesis of sweet compassion and truth. Sweetness is what expresses itself as universal love and truth is what is called spiritual enlightenment. Their call is not meant for any particular sect or school but for the whole of humanity. Their message is not for a particular time or place, but for the entire world and eternity.

Buddha and Buddhism are the perfection of love compassion. In fact the nine virtues of Lord Buddha are *"itipi so bhagavā archam sammāsaṃbuddho vijjacaraṇasampanno sugato lokavidu anuttaro purisadammasārathi satthā devamanussānam buddho bhagavati"* i.e. Indeed the exalted one is thus : the accomplished destroyer of defilements, a Buddha perfected by himself, complete in clear knowledge and compassionate conduct, supremely good in presence and in destiny, the knower of the worlds, incomparable master of men to be tamed, the teacher of celestials and men, the awakener, and the Lord by skilful means apportioning Dhamma.

There is another method of summing up the virtues of Buddha. This is to classify them in three categories, that is to say, the virtues of wisdom, of purity and of compassion. The nine epithets above may be included under these great virtues as follows :

Wisdom and purity - accomplished destroyer of defilements

Wisdom - a Buddha perfected by himself (*sammāsambuddha*), the knower of the worlds (*lokavidu*)

Wisdom and compassion - complete in clear knowledge and compassionate conduct (*vijjacaraṇasampanno*), the awakened and awakener (*Buddho*) the lord by skilful means apportioning Dhamma

Compassion - supremely good in presence and in destiny (*Sugato*), incomparable master of men to be tamed (*anuttaro purisadammasārathi*), the teacher of celestials and men (*satthā devamanussānam*)

Buddha believes that the perfection of loving-compassion and thought is the key to enter into the world of emancipation. He once says to Sumedha to fulfil the perfection of loving - compassion. He ordains "O wise Sumedha! be of the same frame of mind towards those who are well and ill disposed towards you. As water extends its coolness equally alike to both the wicked and the virtuous, you too remain with the same frame of mind, with thoughts of love towards all creatures and become a Buddha. Reflecting thus, he firmly resolved on the perfection of loving-compassion. The following anecdote reveals the essential points in the perfection of the loving-compassion.

At one time, the exalted one was staying at Sāvatthi, in Prince Jetas Grove in the park of Ananthapiṇḍika. Then the exalted one spoke thus to the *Bhikkhus*–"When the heart's deliverance of loving-compassion is made use of, developed, made much of, used as one's vehicle, used as one's foundation, established, consolidated and properly managed, then eleven advantages can be expected. These are : one goes to sleep happily, one wakes up happily, one sees no evil dreams, one is dear to men, one is dear to non-men, the Gods protect one, neither fire, nor poison, nor the weapons can harm one, one's mind is easily concentrated, the colour of one's face is radiant, one dies unconfused, and one attains the *Brahma*-world even if one penetrates to nothing higher.

When the heart's deliverance of loving-compassion is made use of, developed, made much of, used as one's vehicle, used as one's foundation, established, consolidated and properly managed, these eleven advantages can be expected.

Praising the development of loving-compassion which holds these eleven advantages, a *bhikkhu* ought to show compassion to all creatures whether by means of specific practice or generally he should be a friend to the friendly, even a friend to the unfriendly, and a friend to the indifferent. Thus to all without distinction whether by some special practice or general principles, he should develop loving-compassion, he should develop compassion with other's sorrow, gladness with other's happiness and equanimity and thus work should be done by means of the four divine abidings. By doing so he will reach the world of *Brahma* even though he does not gain path and fruit. Wise men, by cultivating loving-compassion for seven years, have dwelt in *Brahma's* world for seven *aeons* of involution and evolution.

In a former *aeon,* the Bodhisatta was born in a Brāhmaṇa's family. When he grew up, he forsook sensuality and embraced the holy life and attained the four divine abidings. His name was Araka and he became a teacher and lived in the Himalayan region with a large body of followers. Admonishing his band of sages, he said, one who has gone forth must develop loving kindness, compassion (with other's sorrow) gladness with other's happiness and he should develop equanimity : for this thought of loving-compassion, he repeated these verses.

The heart that boundless pity feels for all things that have birth in heaven above, in realms below, and on this middle earth, filled full of pity infinite, of infinite charity. In such a heart nought, narrow or confined can ever be.

Thus did the Bodhisatta discourse to his pupils on the practice of loving-compassion and his blessings. And without a moment's interruption to his concentration (at the death of his body), he was born into *Brahma's* world and for seven *aeons* of involution he did not return to the world.

Buddha's possession or clear knowledge shows the greatness of wisdom, and his possession of conduct the greatness of compassion. It was through wisdom that he reached the kingdom of *Dhamma* and he fully understood others' suffering and that he bore it. It was through compassion that he undertook to counteract it. It was through understanding that he was brought face to face with *Nibbāna* and through compassion he attained it. It was through wisdom that he himself crossed over and through compassion that he brought others across. It was through wisdom that perfected that enlightened one's task.

It was through compassion that he faced the round of rebirths as a Bodhisatta, through wisdom that he took on delight in it. By means of compassion he practised non-cruelty to others and he protected others to protect himself. That he did not torment others was largely due to his compassion. So of the four types of persons beginning with the one who practises his own welfare, he perfected the fourth and the best type. Likewise, it was through compassion that he became the world's helper, he had humanity (as a Bodhisatta), helped all beings as a father. In fact, Buddha's compassion was devoid of sentimental affection or sorrow. The following event may be pointed out in this connection.

A certain *bhikkhu* was once sick with dysentery and he lay fouled in this own urine and excrement. As Buddha was going round the lodgings with his disciple Ānanda as his attendant, he came to that *bhikkhu's* dwelling. When he saw him lying where he was, he went up to him and said: "What is your sickness, *bhikkhu*?" "It is dysentery, Blessed One." "But *Bhikkhu*, have you no attendant?" No Blessed One." "Why other *bhikkhus* do not look after you, *Bhikkhu*". "I am of no use to the *bhikkhus*, Lord; that is why, they do not look after me." Then Buddha said to Ānanda "Go and fetch some water. Let us wash this *bhikkhu*." Ānanda brought some water. They poured out the water and washed the *bhikkhu*, raised him up and put him on the bed.

With this as the occasion and this as the reason Buddha summoned the *bhikkhus* and asked them: "*Bhikkhus*, is there a *bhikkhu* sick in a certain dwelling?" "There is Blessed One." "What is the *bhikkhu's* illness?" "He has dysentery, Lord". "Had he anyone to look after one who is sick? If he has a preceptor, his preceptor should as long as he lives look after him until his recovery. His teacher, if he has one, should do likewise. Or his pupil or one who has the same preceptor or one who has the same teacher. If he has none of the three, the community should look after him. Not to do so is an offence of wrong doing, for compassion must be voluntary and eternal.

When a sick man has five qualities, he is hard to look after. He does what is unsuitable, he does not know the measure of what is suitable, he does not take medicine, he does not disclose his illness to one who seeks his welfare, or tell him that it is better when it is so, or worse when it is so, he is of a type unable to endure arisen bodily feelings that are painful, harsh, racking, piercing, disagreeble, unwelcome and menacing to live. When a sick man has the five opposite qualities, he is easy to look after.

The following *Dhamma* talk is also very important to show the importance and role of compassion in Buddhism.

A certain youth who lived at Sāvatthi heard that teacher preach the *Dhamma,* yielded his heart to the *Sarora,* went forth to homelessness, and after full admission to the *Sangha* became known as the Thera Tissa. As time passed on, an eruption broke out on his body. At first appeared postules no bigger than mustard seeds but as the disease progressed, they assumed successively the size of kidney-beans, chick-peas, jujube stones, embryo myrobalans and then *bilva* fruit. Finally they burst open and his whole body became covered with open sores. In this way, he came to be called Thera Putigatta (rotten-bodies) Tissa. After some time, his bones began to disintegrate and no one was willing to take care of him. His under and upper robes which were stained with dried blood, looked like fibrous *pancaks*. His fellow residents, unable to care for him, cast him out, and he lay down on the ground without a protector.

Now the Buddha never fail to survey the world twice a day. At dawn, they survey the world looking from the fragrant cell taking cognizance of all that is without. Now at this time, the Thera Putigatta Tissa appeared within the net of Buddha's knowledge. Buddha took compassion on him and knew that *Bhikkhu* Tissa was ripe for Arhantship, thought to himself"That *bhikkhu* has been abandoned by his associates; at the present time he has no other refuge than me".

Accordingly he went to the hall where fire was kept. He washed the boiler, placed it on the brazier, waited in the fire room for the water to boil, and when he knew it was hot, went and took hold of the end of the bed where *bhikkhu* was lying. He caused a measure to be brought and sprinkled hot water, lay it in the sunshine to dry. Then he went, and taking his stand near Tissa, moistened his body with hot water and rubbed and bathed him and thereafter changed his robes. With his heart full of compassion for Tissa took his stand at his pillow and said to him "*Bhikkhu,* consciousness will depart from you, your body will become useless." At the conclusion of his teaching, Thera Putigatta Tissa attained Arahantship and passed to final *Nibbāna*. Buddha himself performed the funeral rites over the body and taking the relics, caused a shrine to be erected. Thus it has been declared that dedication of his life for the sake of mankind (and other beings) reveals the perfection of giving and loving-compassion (*mettāpāramī*). In fact the three worlds–of Brahma, the *Aśwas* and men–are consumed by the sufferings of disease and old age, they are devoured by the fire of death and deprived of all guidance. The life of a human being is like a flesh of lightening in the sky. Or as a torrent rushed down a mountain so life flows on with irresistible rapidity. Beings in the abodes of men and gods are on the way to three evils (birth, old age and death) by the fact of their existence and because of craving and unknowing. Every creature, the fairest, the most beloved, disappears for ever like a leaf or fruit fallen into a stream, it is whirled away and lost for ever to our eyes. So practice of loving-compassion in the heart must be developed to overcome these sufferings.

The transient pleasures, the robbers of our happiness and our wealth and which float empty like illusions through the world, infatuate men's minds even when they are only hoped for,still more when they take up their abode in the heart. The victims of pleasures do not attain happiness even in the heaven of the gods, still less in the world of mortals. He who craves is never satisfied with pleasures. The *Purāṇas* also mention that when it had rained a golden shower from the heavens, and when he had conquered the continents and the four oceans and even had obtained half of Indra's throne, king Māndhātā was still unsatisfied with objects of the world. When they heard of the miseries of those who are intent or devoted to worldly pursuits, such as agricultures and the rest and the self content of those who are careless of pleasure, it well befits self-controlled to fling it away. The very conditions which mark pleaure also bring in turn pain. Heavy garments and fragrant aloe-wood are pleasant in the cold but an annoyance in the heat; and the moon-beams and sandal woods are pleasant in the heat but painful in the cold, since the well-known pairs of opposites, such as gain and loss and the rest are connected inseparably with everything in this world; therefore, no man is invariably happy on the earth, nor invariably wretched. Buddha taking into consideration the category of men for which there are no necessarily entailed results, and being aware of those evil and false views which had arisen among the Brāhmins and laymen of Magadha aware of the entreaty of Great Brahmā, aware of his own vow made *aeons* and incalculable age conceived a great compassion for the people. Buddha ultimately addressed great Brahmā with a verse :

Opened wide are the doors of deathlessness
Compassion, love and compassionate love.
Those who hear let them show forth their faith
For Dhamma is sublime with love and compassion.

Dhamma of love and compassion leads to passionlessness not to passion. They lead to bondlessness, not to bondage. They lead to non-accumulation, not to accumulation. They lead to wanting little, not to wanting much. They lead to contentment, not to discontentment. They lead to solitude, not to sociability. They lead to making an effort not to laziness. They lead to ease in maintenance, not to difficulty in maintenance.

Through the stories of Devadatta, the prince and Nalagiri the elephant, the power and excellence of compassion and kindness have been fully exhibited. The philosophical conception of compassionate love has been analysed. Venerable Yasoja at the beginning of the rains addressed the *bhikkhus* in the following way, "Your reverences, we have been dismissed by the Lord Buddha for our own good and profit, out of compassion for us, because he felt compassion for us. Come now, your reverences, let us dwell in such a way that Lord Buddha may be well-pleased with our way of dwelling. And finally it is Lord Buddha himself who thus addressed his followers, "O *Bhikkhus,* the secure, safe path leading to joy has been opened by me, the treacherous path blocked off, the decay disturbed, the lure let loose. *Bhikkhus*, whatever may be done out of compassion by a teacher seeking the welfare of his disciples, that has been done by me out of compassion for you. So be compassionate and full of love. The *Purāṇas* also are the embodiment of love, sympathy and compassion. The *Purāṇas* are generally considered posterior to Vedic literature although some of the legends are really very old. They betray their intimate relationship with common people. Like a living organism, it has undergone changes from time to time with the changes in the social and religious life of the people and has thus been able to preserve considerable material for the study of the life of common people.

The religion of the Hindus is not at all stoic. It has the broadness to acknowledge and accept demands of the changing time. A living society must have been the power of continuity and the power of change to prove its life force. The current of religion always changed its course according to the trend of different ages and made neccessary adjustments. Thus the *Purāṇas* clearly show popularity of differnt deities favoured in different ages.

The *Purāṇas* are taken as substitutes for the Vedic literature. They show the easiest way to attaining peace and perfection in life through myths and stories. It is wonderful to note the way in which *Purāṇas* make a synthesis among the different doctrines, between Vedic and non-Vedic views of life and conduct. Purāṇic literature presents all religious faiths most respectfully and somehow make them look unified, a unity in diversity.

The harmony which the *Purāṇas* brought about in the doctrines of knowledge, notion and devotion and the Vedic and non-Vedic views of life and conduct exerted its influence in all strata of Hindu society, with the result that the life of the average Hindu of the present day, presents a texture into which various ideas and practices of different times and regions have been interwoven with an unparalleled symmetry. Even an illiterate Hindu, living far away from the seats of learning, is not totally ignorant of the principles and philosophical truths taught in the *Purāṇas*. As a result, he has a very broad view of life and a deep sense of tolerance and adjustment which can rarely be expected elsewhere from a person like him. This is so only because of the fact that the *Purāṇas* have played a very important part in the life of the Hindus for more than two thousand years. They have brought home to the common man the wisdom of the saints of the highest order without creating any discord. The author or authors of these works took every individual into consideration and made such prescriptions as would benefit him in his social and religious life. The sense of values developed by these works and the moral codes set in these works smack of practical wisdom. It accepts certain lapses of human nature and offers to show ways to set over them. This acceptance of the human beings as a whole is the basic proof of human aspect of these sacred books.

According to the *Purāṇa* writers, compassion is a unique word. It includes in its periphery, a variety of noble feelings like love, devotion, generosity, affection, forgiveness, sympathy etc. These feelings should be the basis of life. The instinct of give and take, forgive and forget makes the life worth living for a person and his associates. This message is delivered over and over again like a refrain in these popular works through numerous legends and anecdotes. To err is human, but the effort to rectify the mistakes elevates one to a super-human level.

Hinduism has a wide compass. It is like an ocean where different streams of sectarian thoughts and beliefs merge. The Vedic religion, although principally ceremonial, has an underlying philosophical basis which allowed all basic truths in their proper perspective. These truths blossomed in genuine emotions. Compassion was their common name. This word has a rainbow like character which contains a variety of love sentiments like love, devotion, rights, duties, sympathy, affection. The attitude of a particular god towards the devotee, penances, repentance---everything has bearing on compassion.

The *Purāṇas* preach the same Hinduism as the Vedic scriptures but in a different manner. They mainly preach through stories. Many stories may apparently be simple anecdotes without any such religious colouring but minute or close observation will prove that these legends also have some lessons in compassionate thoughts.

It is true that the spirit of the *Purāṇas* is religious. For this, virtue plays a prominent role in the legends. This virtue can be interpreted in many ways, in the duties of a son, of a wife, of a disciple. Devotion is another emotion which is found in many aspects. We cannot actually categorise these emotions but they all come under the broad term compassion.

There are large number of stories, legends and myths in the *Purāṇas* that depict one or the other facet of compassion. And it is sufficient to show and establish beyond all doubt that Hinduism in the age of the *Purāṇas* was, like Buddhism, a compassionate religion. This is the inherent mobility that made Hinduism immortal. It is also to be borne in mind that a religion cannot develop this mobility all of a sudden. It is true that Hinduism from the day of its conception has gone through many stages over thousand of years and has retained many characteristic features of outside influences within itself, but the trend was there all along. The spirit of the early vedic religion, however primitive it might look, has generosity and broadness of thought as the basic principles and with the right background, later Hinduism blossomed into a truly compassionate religion.

Bangkok, Thailand

BUDDHISM AND SOCIO-CULTURAL VALUES

S.G.Kantawala

India is a land of diverse faiths and religions and Buddhism is one of the religions practised in modern India. This is the land wherein it originated, from where it spread and wherein it declined.[1] The recent statistical data show that the number of Buddhists has shot up in the last few decades. In this paper it is proposed to discuss some of the Buddhistic socio-cultural aspects and values in their relevance to contemporary India.

India is a classical land of caste-system, wherein Brahmins stood on the highest rung of the social ladder enjoying high respect and favourable position in the *varṇa*-structure of the society. With the passage of time, the birth came to be the determinant of the caste-status and Buddha was not in favour of caste-system.[2] He was harsh in the valuation of Brahmins[3] and was opposed to them because they sacrificed innocent cows and other animals.[4] According to the *Soṇadaṇḍa-sutta*, Buddha spoke against the birth-based superiority of Brahmins.[5] The *Dhammapada* declares that a Brahmin is not a Brahmin by wearing the matted hair. He is not a Brahmin because of birth or *gotra*. He must practise *dharma* and must possess purity. The virtuous man is a Brahmin. The external paraphernalia do not make one a Brahmin. One, who remains untainted by passion and pleasure and who is given to truth-speaking and practising *ahiṁsā* is a Brahmin. An *arhat* is a Brahmin.[6] The *Tevijjasutta*[7] states that Kṣatriyas are higher and Brahmins are inferior.

This shows that according to Buddhism, the value of a man is to be judged on the basis of character and not on the basis of birth. This tends to suggest a change in the social status-value of Brahmin. This gains insignificance in the light of the fast-disappearing and loosening barriers and shackles of the caste-system and its changing values in modern times. Values are largely moulded by environment.[8]

With the change in socio-cultural environment, values in India are undergoing a change.

With the passage of time, the caste-rules etc. hardened and the Śūdras inclusive of "untouchables" came to suffer from many a disability. In modern times, Mahatma Gandhi and Dr. Bhimrao Ramji Ambedkar started a movement for the removal of untouchability and uplift of the depressed class. In 1956, Babasaheb Ambedkar announced his formal conversion to Buddhism. He recommended this course of action to the entire community of scheduled castes. Before his conversion to Buddhism in 1956 A.D. he exhorted in May 1936 the Mahar Community of Maharashtra that "they would have to leave the Hindu fold in order to secure true freedom".[9] He, further, pointed out that they had nothing to lose except chains, and everything to gain by changing their religion,[10] because to him "Buddhism was the preferred alternative religion"[11] for their uplift. After his death, this policy is pursued by his successors and the converts are known as "neo-Buddhists" and there is a "fairly benign Indian attitude towards Buddhism..."[12]

It may be observed that in ancient India, Buddhism arose out of protest and revolt against certain ritual practices of the Brahmanical religion whereas this recent new Buddhistic movement (neo-Buddhism) owes its origin to protest and revolt against the oppressions etc. by the so-called "higher"caste Hindus in the caste-ridden society. This tends to suggest how a change in religion has a resultant impact on the caste-status and caste-structure.

The *Theravada* school of Buddhism emphasised the non-political nature of Buddha's teachings. It is a non-political and anti-political regligion of a social class according to Max Weber. The early Buddhists tried to evade implications of their religious movements in political and social matters as far as possible, but in contrast to this, the Buddhism in modern times has played a significant role in social and political changes. In modern times, the Buddhism in its actual manifestation, *i.e.*, "as a part of an integrated religious system including popular religious beliefs", gets involved in some countries in political and social developments and the implications of this involvement are felt in some Buddhist countries. In this connection, one may refer here to the history of modern Buddhism in Ceylon

(Sri Lanka). It is well known that in 1945 A.D. and in the succeeding years the Buddhism got connected in Sri Lanka with the problem of "*śāsana*-reform" in the light of the modern conceptions of state and society.[13]

Buddha emphasised moral qualities like wisdom, asceticism, self-control, desirelessness etc., and he threw his order open to all. In ancient India, there was a time in the history of the Vedic religion, when "animal sacrifices were quite reputable and of high other-worldly value."[14] Because of the consequent excess of this practice of animal sacrifice, *ahiṁsā* came to the fore in the later Upaniṣadic times and this doctrine of *ahiṁsā* was then strongly recommended by the then emerging religions, *viz.*, *Bhāgavata*-religion, *Bauddha* religion and *Jain* religion.[15] In the Buddhist religion, *ahiṁsā* implies causing no pain to all beings at all times by thought, word and deed according to the *Sāmāñña-phala-sutta*. In this context, it is significant to note that Buddhists in Sri Lanka, China, Japan, Thailand and many other countries have no objections to non-vegetarian food. This reflects a change in the social attitude and value of the doctrine of *ahiṁsā* in a counter-direction.[16]

Moreover, the doctrine of *ahiṁsā* gains significance, when "violence and peacelessness continue to erupt all over in all the systems"[17] and when proposals for disarmament are being moved by different countries for a peaceful and non-violent world-community. This brings out the great bearing of the doctrine of *ahiṁsā* in modern times. Gautama Buddha did not think much of worship or prayers. What mattered to him was the freedom of man from sorrow and suffering and the attainment of *nirvāṇa*. With the passage of time, the iconic worship of Buddha entered the Buddhist religion; in the *Mahāyāna*, Buddha is worshipped as a god; one comes across several temples of Buddha in different countries. This relfects a change in the entire value-system of worship in the Buddhism. *En passant* it may be mentioned here that from the seventh century A.D., Buddha came to be recognised as an incarnation of Viṣṇu in the *daśāvatāra*-list. This brings out the catholic and absorbent nature of the Purāṇic Hinduism.[18]

The worship-aspect of Buddha has a natural consequence of the introduction of the *bhakti*-element, which is traceable to the Ṛgvedic hymns in honour of Indra and Varuṇa.[19] This reflects upon the religio-cultural impact. Some of the virtues recommended in the early Buddhism seem to be negated in its later phase, *e.g.*, self-control, renunciation of wealth, etc. The inscriptional evidence of Kuda and Bhilsa shows that Buddhist monks and nuns were rich and they were great donors.[20]

The high moral ideals preached by Buddha were found annoying and burdensome to some members admitted to the order and this feeling is echoed in the address of the barber on Buddha's *nirvāṇa* in *Mahāparinibbānasutta.*[21] This is significant. There are cases which reflect the loseness in the moral standards. In the *Śāriputraprakaraṇa* of Aśvaghoṣa there is a character of a young Buddhist monk named Somadatta. He is very voluptuous and roguish and he pretends allright to be a monk of the Buddhist order; but in contravention to the rules and regulations governing the conduct and life of monks, he keeps in privacy his relations with a courtesan Magadhavatī by name. Here the dramatist affords a peep into the realistic working of the monks' institution in relation to the theoretical code of conduct and life of Buddhist monks.

It may be noted here that the *Andhaka* school referred to in the *Kathāvattu*[22] permits copulation (*maithuna*) for a special object. The Tantric practices of the *Vajrayāna* school are too well-known to be mentioned here.[23] This shows that the earlier values had undergone a radical change in the social and religious life and practices of the Buddhistic followers, monks and nuns.

To sum up, the above-going discussion tends to show how in modern times the Buddhism works as one of the major factors for a social and political change. It also shows that some very valuable socio-cultural values have lost their significance in later times. It reflects also how the Purāṇic Hinduism absorbed some of the features of the Buddhism in its fold and thereby it brings out the relevance of the Buddhism in religious and social matters.

REFERENCES & NOTES

1. On the causes of the decline of Buddhism in India vide Kane, P.V., *History of Dharmaśāstra*, Vol.V, Part II, Poona, 1962, pp. 1003ff; Ling Trevor, *Buddhist Revival in India: Aspects of the Sociology of Buddhism*, 1980, The Macmillan Press Ltd., pp. 24ff.
2. Bhatt G.H., *Viśva, nā Dharmo* (Gujarati), 1958, Baroda, P.71.
3. *Vide* Masih Yakub, *The Hindu Religious Thought, Delhi, 1983,* pp. *334ff.*
4. *Vide Suttanipāta*, SBE, Vol.10, verses 307-308; Masih Y, *op.cit*, p.335.
5. *Vide* SBE Vol. 2,p.154; Masih Y., *op.cit.*, pp.336ff.
6. *Vide Dhammapada* (ed. by Bhikkhu Dharmarakshita), Varanasi, 1959, pp.247ff; *Ambaṣthasutta*, p.122 (referred to by Masih Y., *op.cit.*, p.337).
7. pp. 120-121.
8. Kane, P.V., *op.cit.*, p.1701.
9. Ling Trevor,*op.cit.*, p.87.
10. Ling Trevor, *op.cit.*, p.87.
11. Ling Trevor, *op.cit.*,p.88.
12. Ling Trevor, *op.cit.*, p.90.
13. *Vide* Bechert H., Contemporary Buddhism as a major Factor of Social and Political Change, *Proceedings and Transactions of the All-India Oriental Conference*, 24th Session, Varanasi, October 1968 (published in 1972), pp.299ff.
14. Kane, P.V., *op.cit.*,p.1701.
15. *Vide* Shastri, K.K., *Śrī Vallabhācārya Mahāprabhujī*, (Gujarati), Baroda, 1977, Preface, p.10.
16. Kane, P.V., *op.cit.*, p. 947.
17. Parikh, Ramlal, Towards a Non-violent World-community, *Essays on Indology, Polity and Administration* in honour of Padmabhushan Sh. R.K. Trivedi (ed.by Dr. S.D. Trivedi), Vol.II, Delhi, 1989, p.415. On *ahiṁsā vide* Shah U.P., *Fundamental of the Practice of Ahiṁsā, op.cit.*, pp. 245ff.
18. *Vide, Kane, P.V., op.cit.*, pp. 993ff; Kantawala, S.G., *Cultural History from the Matsya-Purāṇa*, Baroda, 1964, PP.164ff.
19. *Vide* Kane, P.V.*op.cit.*, pp.950ff; Velankar, H.D., *Ṛgveda maṇḍala* VII, Bombay, 1963, Introduction, pp.i.ff.
20. *Vide* Kane, P.V., *op.cit.*, p.1025.
21. SBE. Vol.XI, p.127.
22. 23.1
23. *Vide* Kane, P.V., *op.cit.*, 1022ff.

Baroda

INDIVIDUAL AND SOCIAL IDENTITY: THE BUDDHIST APPROACH

Kewal Krishan Mittal

All those who are familier with Buddhist Philosophy do know that the doctrine of 'Non-Substantiality'(*Anātmatā*) is one of the core doctrines of the philosophy and the same denies the 'Identity' of the individual. It is the considered opinion of the author of this paper that the identity of a group or a society can also not be established, even though the same has not been so openly questioned, historically. Within the fold of Buddhism itself the Identity of one group, atleast it seems, that of the *Sangha* has obviously been taken for granted---as also, of course, of the *Buddha* and *Dharma*---by almost all except the well-known Buddhist philosopher Nāgārjuna.

Nāgārjuna boldly drew the implications of the dynamic World-view of Buddhist Philosophy in accordance with which the World (*Saṁsāra*) is marked by the three characteristics of Impermanence (*Anityatā*), Non - Substantiality (*Anātmatā*) and Suffering i.e. Decline and Death (*Duḥkhatā, Jarāmaraṇa*). No being in the world is such that having come into existence does not decline and meet with death. There is no moment at which it stays unchanged or is of the self-same character. *Nirvāna*, the highest state of being sought after, is not a goal beyond but a realization of the such-like character (or naturelessness) of every being of the world. It is a sort of living and enjoying the world in its Suchness (*Tathatā*), through going the Suchness-Way i.e. becoming *'Tathāgata'*. He (Nāgārjuna) gave expression to the idea, both positively and negatively, as follows---

"Whatever is the nature of the *Tathāgata* that too is of the World (*Jagat*);

Tathāgata does not have any nature, so also the world has no nature".

Tathāgato hi yat svabhāvastat svabhāvam idaṁ jagat;

Tathāgato niḥsvabhāvo niḥsvabhāvam idaṁ Jagat.

---*Mūlamādhyamikakārikā*, XXII. 16.

"Of the world from *Nirvāṇa* there is not the slightest difference;
Of *Nirvāṇa* from the World (*Saṁsāra*) there is not the slightest difference".

Na saṁsārasya nirvāṇāt kiñcidasti viśeṣaṇam;

Na nirvāṇasya saṁsārāt kiñcidasti viśeṣaṇam."

---*Ibid*. XXV. 19.

According to Nāgārjuna, all reality is free from the fourfold categorization, in term of being, non-being, both and neither (*Catuṣkoṭi-vinirmukta*). Nothing can be described as 'this', 'not-this', 'both this and not-this' or as 'neither this nor not-this'. He sums up such a characterization or rather non-characterizeability of reality in one word as *Śūnyatā* and is not shy of applying the same to the Buddha, *the Dharma* and *Saṅgha*. It is usual to translate *Śūnyatā* as 'emptiness', and some ununderstanding persons go to the extent of dismissing Nāgārjuna's thought as nihilistic, forgetting altogether his insistene that 'he is a *Mādhyamika,* the follower of the Middle-path that steers clear both the extremes of Eternalism (*Śāśvatavāda*) and Annihilationism (*Ucchedavāda)*'. The right translation of *Śūnyatā* must be 'Openness', 'Infinity', 'Limitlessness' or 'Relativity' which may indicate that, though indescribable in every sort of way, Reality is "All that is" *(Sarvamidam*)or 'All that is experinced' (*Vijñaptimātramidam sarvam*). We live through all the modes and moods of life those agree and disagree, go well or ill, are in accord and discord with each other. The flow of life continues in such a way that its preceding and succeeding phases may seem to contradict each other, contradictions emerge out and remerge into it making it took like a veritable mystery that is beyond words and ordinary understanding. It can be viewed in terms of all types of positions---albeit in a relative sort of way ruling out every kind of Absolutism and Ultimatism that shuts out one or the other position and militates against the richness and variety of the world experience.

Having understood the principle of world-process, its goings on (*Saṁsāragati*), we become calm and collected, nothing upsets us. We become capable of enduring and absorbing many shocks. We do not go by stereotypes and cliches but are always prepared to face reality as it is and as it is experienced, at any given moment, with a freshness of the outlook that rules out dullness and boredom of 'a fixed, unaltering (seemingly so, of course) routine' assumed or cultivated through the mechanism of habit-formation. Understanding puts us in a state of general 'Alertness (*Apramāda*)', the opposite that of sloth (*Pramāda*) that we are usually prone to under the stupifying influence of our passions such as 'attachment (*rāga*)', 'hatred (*dveṣa*)' and 'infatuation' (*moha*). The understanding (*prajñā*) is gained through the attainment of 'balanced-intellect (*samādhi*)' resulting from 'the moral practices (*śīla*)' enjoined by the Buddha through his fourth noble truth, that of the Way, in terms of the Noble *Eightfold path* consisting of the Right-view (*Samyak-dṛṣṭi*), Right-Resolve (*Samyak-saṅkalpa*), Right-speech (*Samyak-vāk*), Right-conduct (*Samyak-ācāra*), Right-livelihood (*Samyak-ājīva*), Right-Effort (*Samyak- vyāyāma*), Right-Mindfulness (*Samyak-smṛti*) and Right Balancing of the intellect (*Samyak-samādhi*).

Such an understanding does not only stand in the way of but also actually helps us to go on with 'indentifications' of individual things and persons as well as their groups and conglemorations. It engenders or generates a mentality informed by the apprehension that each one of such identifications is tentative, provisional, relative and yet practical in so far as it does fulfil the intended expectations in a given situation though not all of them, and always. It prepares us for all eventualities. A child with a naughty demeanour may develop into a youngman having a serious sombre nature or with a frivolous, jesting and happy go lucky attitude in life. Follies of youth may turn him into a wise-crack or into an old hack or into quite a different sort of old fellow. The vigour of the young gets changed into the tottering infirmities of old age yet the old age does have its own strength of character given to it by the ripening of the experience. One who thus understands the worldy life in its multifarious remifications can be well disposed to take to the advice of the great wayfarer, *Tathāgata-Buddha*, as found expressed in the following *Pāli* śloka:

"Lokasamaññam na atidhāveyya;
Parmattham na abhiniveseyya.

"Do not over-indulge in customs worldly;
Make not a Fetish of the Ultimate."

Buddhism, as a religious movement, in its initial stage, had two broad sets of followers: 1. Renunciates comprising of monks (*bhikṣūs*) and nuns (*bhikṣuṇīs*) and 2. Lay-followers consisting of male-devotees (*upāsakas*) and female-devotees (*Upāsikās*). The first group is expected to lead a life governed by a code of conduct marked by ten moral rules (*Daśa Śīla*) expressed as many abstensions. They are : 1. Abstension from violence (*Prāṇātipāta- Veramaṇī*). 2. Abstension from falsehood (*mṛṣāvāda-verāmaṇī*). 3. Abstension from stealing (*adinnā-dāna-veramaṇi*). 4. Abstension from wrong-indulgence in sex (*kāmeṣu- mithyācāra-veramaṇī*). 5. Abstension from consuming intoxicating drinks and drugs (*surā-merrya-madyapāna-veramaṇī*). 6.Abstension form partaking of food at a time transgressing the prescribed time (*vikāla-bhojana- virati*). 7. Abstension from singing, dancing and seeing and play-acting (*gāna, nṛtya, nāṭyādi-virati*). 8. Abstension from the use of perfumes and wearing of flower-garlands etc. (*gandhalepana mālādivirati*). 9. Abstension from using luxurious and lofty seats and bedspreads (*ucca sukhakara āsana śaiyyā-viratī*). 10. Abstension from accepting costly gifts of gold and silver etc. (*svarṇa-rajat-bahumūlya-vastudāna-grahaṇa-virati*). The monks and nuns are required to lead a life of voluntary poverty, sustain themselves on very little food, procured through begging, cover their bodies with a limited length of cloth of the course (rough) variety and of the unattractive earth like (*kaṣāya*) colour. This group is thus identified and distinguished from the other group of that of the lay followers, who are required to adhere to the first 'Five abstensions (*Pañcaśīla*)' only. The distinction between two groups is possible because of the diffence in their 'Identities'. During the course of more than twentyfive hundred and twentyfive years many changes have taken place in these formulations, though, theoretically the structure remains, broadly, the same. The order of nuns stands almost abolished. Among the monks, as also among the lay followers, there are two major divisions; one group comprising mostly of the Buddhists living in the countries to the North of India follows the *Mahāyāna* practices and the other group of them living in the countries situated to the South of India follows the *Hīnayāna* or the *Theravāda* practices. There is a considerable difference between them. The lay followers of Buddhism are hardly different from the lay followers of other religions who happen to be their co-citizens in a particular country, as their general socio-cultural and politico-economic behaviour as also their habits of food and dress are similar. When engaged in the activities of their normal work-a-day life, it is not possible to distinguish, say in Japan, a Buddhist from a Christian, and in India, from a Jain, an Ārya-samājist or a Sanatanist Hindu, We know any one to be one rather than to be the other when someone professes himself or herself to be a follower of such and such a Faith.

In accordance with the first of the abstensions, the Buddhists are not only expected to be pacifists in a general way, but also vegitarians in food habits. But what is strange, and seems to be positively shocking to those who have not properly understood the rationale of the law of life and the History of the spread of Buddhism in various countries, having varied traditions not only of socio-cultural modes of practices but also natural-geographical conditions determining---rather forcing particular kinds of food and dress neeeds and habits. Theoretically, some groups of Buddhists are expected to behave in a certain way but, practically, they are seen to behave in another, people have some stereotypes about them even though they are not altogether uninformed about the contrary behaviour of their neighbours. The stereotypes---biases and prejudices---contionously lead to the fallacy of non-observation. The contrary observations have occasionally been conveniently forgotten. The point may be illustrated by referring to two incidents happening with a gap of no less than that of twenty years yet, in terms of the continuity of strereotype, maintaining a similarity in their nature and purport. Late Justice Mohmed Ali Karim Chagla (who, besides having been an honourable Cabinet Minister and holding some other important Govt. offices had been a Retired Chief Justice of India) writes in his autobiography that once (sometimes in 1955 or so) when he was India's High Commissioner in Great Britain, His Holiness The Dalai Lama visited London, along with an entourage of his twenty companion monks. Justice Chagla was 'informed' by the officers of the Foreign Ministry from Delhi that 'His-Holiness avoided meeting women and would prefer having vegetarian food.' Justice Chagla, accordingly, instructed his female staff-members not to hold out their hands for a hand-shake with H.H. The Dalai Lama at reception---as per the usual diplomatic practice---but should greet the distinguished dignitory with a folded-hands' *Namaste*. But he and the women were surprised when H.H. The Dalai Lama himself held out his own hand for the hand-shake with each one of them also, as in the case of the male members of staff of the Commisionary. Taking hint, Mr. Chagla asked His Holiness as to what he and his companions would like to have in breakfast. The dishes that His Holiness mentioned were all meat and egg preparations. Almost a similar incident, in a way,was repeated exactly after twenty years when H.H. The Dalai Lama, with his companions, once again visited England. He and his party were invited at a Christian seminary for 'a dialogue to be followed by lunch'. At lunch the hosts had laid separate sets of tables---for the guests (The Dalai Lama and party), the tables with vegetarian food and for themselves (the hosts), the tables with non-vegetarian food. When invited to partake lunch, The Dalai Lama and his companions went over to the tables having non-vegetarian food and the hosts were thus left for resorting to the tables with the vegetarian food instead. Someone from among the hosts rather jocularly remarked, "We were in for the exchange of ideas but not for the exchange of lunch as well."

Such or similar discrepancies between expectations and actual happenings are going on and shall go on. What is needed to meet the situation more effectively is the widening of the horizon of our understanding by grasping it fully so that we are prepared for all eventualities. The same, I am sure, can be achieved through following the Buddhist approach to the question of 'Individual and Social Identity'. If we do so, we shall learn to take things calmly and quietly without being shocked or surprised.

Delhi

B.R. AMBEDKAR'S RELIGIOUS LEGACY

Sanghasen Singh

The advent of Bhimrao Ambedkar on the Indian scene has made enormous difference in the social, political and religious aspects. His crusade against untouchability and social segregation of the so-called low born Indians is the great landmark in the social history of our country. In his conversion to Buddhism, the social and religious change made a new mark as it had never been before. The concept of mass conversion from one religion to the other is also a new phenomenon in our social and religious history. All this could happen only under the leadership of a great revolutionary and social reformer, Bhimrao Ambedkar.

On perusal of the writings of B.R. Ambedkar particularly his books entitled 'Who were the Shudras', 'The Untouchables,' 'Annihilation of Caste,' 'The Buddha and His Dhamma' and many of his research papers, one is led to find the following facts about B.R. Ambedkar---(a) Ambedkar was a rational man who was well-trained in the scientific research methodology of the west. (b) His method of research is well evinced by his asking critical questions in the beginning of all his research books and then to investigate and answer them. (c) His major field was finance and law but he was a voracious reader in the field of sociology, anthropology, philosophy and comparative religion.

His conversion to Buddhism in the last phase of his life had led many scholars to investigate the causes that led to that stage. It is a false conception prevalent among anti-Ambedkar groups that he had a political and material cause behind his conversion. But on the contrary, the study of Ambedkar's books reveals religious, social and spiritual reasons. Ambedkar's researchful mind was fully convinced by the logical, empirical, humanistic and pragmatic teachings of the Buddha which are generally not found in the other religions of the world. One can find behind his conversion, an intensity of religious feeling, acute study and observation, and deep spirit of benevolence and compassion to liberate the downtrodden and the oppressed. His conversion to Buddhism in 1956 was the result of gradual evolution from 1935, when he declared to give up his parent religion. He had declared at that time that though he was born a Hindu, he would not die a Hindu. In order to remove any misunderstanding, he had very emphatically proclaimed after his conversion to Buddhism, "My religious conversion is not inspired by any material motive. There is hardly any thing which I cannot achieve even while remaining an untouchable. There is no other feeling than that of the religious feeling underlying my religious conversion." In fact it was since 1935 he had been constantly thinking and searching the most appropriate form of humanistic religion, which he found in Buddhism and hence embraced it with the core of his heart. Apart from his prime motive, there may have been many conditions such as incurable nature of Hindu caste system, political depression, unscientific nature of theological religions of the world, the idea of South-East Asian unity etc. which straightened the process of evolution. But it appears beyond all resonable doubts that Ambedkar was a religious man, who discarded hierarchal system of Hinduism and some other religions.

It is generally believed that Ambedkar disagreed with traditional Buddhist doctrines. In this context, one would say that this happened due to the fact that he had a rational mind, which made him reluctant to accept any thing which contradicts reason. He was also fully convinced with the fact that the Buddha was a rationalist and would not teach any thing which was irrational, unempirical and unverifiable. Ambedkar's survey and study of Buddhism forced him to criticize the following five traditionally accepted doctrines of Buddhism :

(1) The doctrine of the Four Noble truths is non Buddhistic and pessimistic.

(2) The nature of re-birth does not mean reincarnation but transformation.

(3) The cause of Buddha's renunciation is not in seeing the dead body etc. but a clash between Sakyas and Koliyas.

(4) The ritualism (prayers etc.) is non Buddhistic.

(5) The role of monks is not to dominate but to serve the society.

Baba Saheb Ambedkar always emphasized upon the communal harmony among various communities of the country. He propagated religious tolerance in the same spirit in which Gautama Buddha had taught seven rules of state welfare in the famous *Mahāparinibbāna Sutta* of the *Dīgha Nikāya*. Among them, the most relevant and beneficial today in the Indian contest is the one which preaches respect for the shrines of all religious communities. The politicians and religious leaders who propagate demolition and desecration of the shrines of the Buddhists, Muslims, Christians, Sikhs etc. are not following the true spirit in which Baba Saheb Ambedkar had taught religious tolerance. Baba Saheb was aware of the fact that many of the Buddhist shrines in the country were occupied by the non-Buddhists but he did not make them prestigious issues lest the religious communities in the country start fighting over the possession of such shrines.

Baba Saheb Ambedkar was a great champion of democracy and constitutionalism but at the same time he was of the opinion that if provisions of the given constitution come in the way of the amelioration of the sufferings of the oppressed people, the people should not hesitate to remove them. Thus it appears that Ambedkar was a humanist to the core and hence there is no exaggeration when people at large call him a Bodhisattva.

Delhi

SOME LEGAL PROBLEMS AND THEIR REMEDIES IN BUDDHIST LITERATURE*

Abha Kulshreshtha

The Buddhist period shows that there was a well codified legal system and procedure prevailing for general conduct of *Bhikkhus*, *Bhikkhunīs*, citizens and the members of the public. Not only this, the remedies for preventing crime were also provided. Lord Buddha enacted constitution which was later known as *Vinaya Piṭaka*. This was not only a legal book but it also had importance in religious aspects. The first three decades of Buddhist religion were full of criticism and conflicts over *Vinaya Piṭaka*.

After the *Nirvāṇa* of *Śāstā*, the conflict arose amongst the *Bhikkhus* regarding the rules as embodied in *Vinaya Piṭaka*. *Vinaya Piṭaka* is seen to have very vital and important role in *Dharma- Sādhanā* of Buddhist religion. The disciple of Lord Buddha, namely, Devadatta had strong views regarding incorporation of strict rules in the *Vinaya Piṭaka*. He had raised revolution against leniency in the rules of *Vinaya Piṭaka*. A reference is seen where Lord Buddha was constrained to leave the *Saṁgha* for misbehaviour by *Bhikkhus* of Kauśāmbī and Lord Buddha had proceeded to *Ekāntavāsa*. After the formation of *Saṁghas* for *Bhikkhus* and *Bhikkhunīs*, there was a need to have external rules to manage the *Saṁghas* as well as the *Bhikkhus* and *Bhikkhunīs* who were *Asaṁyanta* and *Avairāgyavān*. Under the said circumstances, Lord Buddha made the rules of *Vinaya Piṭaka* through his proclaimations.

In case of minor wrong-doings, Lord Buddha used to warn the *Bhikkhu* concerned and the things used to become normal. Such *Bhikkhus* were not to be disciplined since they were listening to Lord Buddha's warnings.

* This paper was presented at the viii International Congress of the International Association of Buddhist Studies held at California University, Berkeley, U.S.A. in August, 1987.

From the very beginning, Lord Buddha used to preach his people not to do sin acts and he used to teach them to have self-control and to do rightful acts. To make the preachings and proclaimations more clear for his disciples and other followers, Lord Buddha brought to light his preachings and teachings in such a manner that it included *Vinaya Piṭaka* in itself, which was not codified and in written form till this time. The said codification can be ascertained by a reference of *Theragāthā*. For instance in *Theragāthā* where statement of Sarabhaṅga appears as "I used to pluck *Sarkaṇḍās* and make my hut *(kuṭi)* for living and accordingly. I was named as Sarabhaṅga but now I must not pluck *sarkaṇḍas* since Lord Buddha had codified rules and laws for us."[1]

The statement of Sarabhaṅga shows that by this time, Lord Buddha had codilied the law for his disciples and followers. On account of this, it appears that the general awareness regarding codified laws, rules and limitations to do or not to do an act was generated.

For instance, certain provisions of *Vinaya Piṭaka* were as follows :

(i) Management of *Buddha Saṁgha.*

(ii) Day-to-day activities of *Bhikkhus* and *Bhikkhunīs.*

(iii) Rules regarding uniform and restrictions on eating food taken by way of *Bhikṣā.*

(iv) Rules regarding running of *Saṁgha.*

(v) Rules regarding unity of the *Saṁgha.*

Vinaya Piṭaka was enacted and codified in Pāli language which was prevalent in the time of Lord Buddha. Lord Buddha enacted and codified 227 conduct rules which can be categorised as under :

(a) Pārājika

It consists of four types of offences :

(i) Ravishing of a woman.

(ii) To steal an article which is not offered.

(iii) To praise murder or suicide.

(iv) To pose to have acquired wisdom and knowledge with intent to attract a female when no such wisdom or knowledge was actually acquired.[2]

These offences were mentioned under the head *Pārājika* according to Lord Buddha since these offences brought about defeat to a *Bhikkhu*. If any *Bhikkhu* committed any of the abovementioned four offences, he ceased to be disciple of Lord Buddha. He was considered to have fallen from his goal and was to be thrown out of the *Saṁgha* since there was no provision for pardoning such *Bhikkhu*. Lord Buddha proclaimed such a *Bhikkhu* as comparable to a leaf which had fallen down from a tree and could never reunite with that tree.

(b) Saṁghādideśa

It consisted of 13 types of offences which were considered to be graver type of offences. If a *Bhikkhu* had committed any of the thirteen offences mentioned under this head, by way of punishment, such *Bhikkhu* could be thrown out of the *Saṁgha* temporarily for six days during which period he had to be alone and perform *Tapa*. Only thereafter, he could join the *Saṁgha* again. The offences under this head are summarised herein below :

(i) Knowingly and intentionally destroying sperms.

(ii) Touching a woman with sexy intent.

(iii) Discussing and gossipping with a woman with intent of sex.

(iv) To attract a woman for mal-intentions by way of self-praise.

(v) To have marriage negotiations or to arrange meeting of a lover with his beloved.

(vi) To build a *Vihāra* for self use without obtaining permission from the *Saṁgha*.

(vii) To get built a *Vihāra* bigger than the size prescribed which had no open space on all sides.

(viii) To blame a *Bhikkhu* without any reason, out of anger.

(ix) To blame a *Bhikkhu* of *Pārājika* offence when the offence committed by *Bhikkhu* was not of *Pārājika* type but similar to it.

(x) To destroy the unity of the *Saṁgha* inspite of repeated warnings for the same.

(xi) To help the persons destroying the unity of the *Saṁgha*.

(xii) To trespass in the house of any family without permission.

(xiii) Not to listen to the co-*Bhikkhus* and directions of the *Saṁgha* inspite of repeated warnings for the same.

(c) Aniyatȧ

Aniyata means uncertainty according to Lord Buddha. *Aniyata* has been categorised in two types of offences :

(i) If a *Bhikkhu* is talking to a female in a lonely place and a disciple *Bhikkhunī* accuses the said *Bhikkhu* of committing of *Pārājika*, *Saṁghādideśa* or *Pācittiya* offence, and the *Bhikkhu* admits the committing of the said offence, then he is to be punished for such guilt.

(ii) If a *Bhikkhu* is talking to a female in open place but using objectionable words and a female disciple accuses him of committing offence and he admits the same, then he is guilty.

(d) Nissaggiya Pācittiya

These are the offences for which after confession of the guilt, provision has been made for *prāyaścitta*. These offences mainly relate to clothes etc. and the article relating to the offence was to be taken away from such *Bhikkhu*.

(e) Pācittiya

This is a type of offence where *Bhikkhu* is exonerated of the offence after *Prāyaścitta*. This head prescribes the following :

(i) *Bhikkhu* has to take meals only once in a day.

(ii) To be cautious and careful while preaching a *Bhikkhunī*.

(iii) To maintain dignity of *Bhikkhus*.

If a *Bhikkhu* committed any of such offences, he had to take a pledge that he would not repeat the same in future. These offences were related to telling lie, abusing, use of intoxicating articles etc.

(f) Paṭidesania

Asking for a pardon was very important for offences under this head. These offences related to acceptance of food from an unknown *Bhikkhunī*, to accept food from a family man without invitation and to call a family man at a place and accept food from his hands.

(g) Sekhiya

These offences were related to general code of behaviour. There were rules regarding clothing, laughing loudly, covering body with clothes in a proper way etc. If anybody broke such conduct rules, he had to be given teaching and preaching.

(h) Adhikaraṇasamatha

Seven rules were prescribed for maintaining peace in the *Saṁgha*. They were :

(i) *Sammukha-Vinaya* (hearing face to face)

(ii) *Smṛti-Vinaya*

(iii) *Amūḍha-Vinaya*

(iv) *Pratigyātakaraṇa*

(v) *Yadbhūyasika*

(vi) *Tatpāpīyasika*

(vii) *Tiṇavattāaraka*

General rules of conduct were also provided for *Bhikkhunīs* regarding behaviour and day-to-day routine acts.

Reference is also found where it is said that cases of dispute must be settled before a duly constituted meeting of the *Saṁgha* and in presence of the accused person.[3]

Another reference is seen where *Bhikkhunī* Mettiyā had blamed Mallian. Other *Bhikkhus* told that she had bitter intentions of causing Mallian's fall and that it was a groundless charge and breach of morality. Mallian was declared innocent and he had to be acquitted after he had requested the *Saṁgha* for the same. The reference is also there where five requirements were to be fulfilled for an acquittal. These were:

(i) Bhikkhu must be innocent and without offence.

(ii) Others must have construed him.

(iii) He must ask the *Saṁgha* for acquittal as being conscious of innocence.

(iv) Saṁgha must grant it.

(v) *Saṁgha* must be duly held and duly constituted.

A reference is also found where *Bhikkhus* assembled in *Saṁgha*, became violent, quarrelsome and disputative and kept on wounding one another with sharp words. As they were unable to settle the disputed question, the matter was told to the Blessed one. He allowed *Bhikkhus* to settle the dispute by the vote of majority. *Bhikkhu* possessing five qualifications had to be appionted as taker of voting tickets. The qualifications were:

(i) Who does not walk in partiality.

(ii) Who does not walk in medicine.?

(iii) Who does not walk in folly.

(iv) Who does not walk in fear.

(v) One who knows that what votes have been taken and what have not been taken.

A reference can be seen where *Bhikkhu* Khanna forced his way into the apartments of *Bhikkhunīs*. The Blessed one said that there are four kinds of legal questions that require formal settlement by *Saṁgha*:

(i) Legal questions arising out of disputes.

(ii) Legal questions arising out of censure.

(iii) Legal questions arising out of offence.

(iv) Legal questions arising out of business.

Legal questions regarding censure included morality, conduct, opinion and livelihood. Legal questions regarding business included resolution, proceedings etc.

References are also seen to show that Jury and Commission were also appointed. A *Bhikkhu* could be appointed as a Jury if he possessed the following ten qualifications :

(i) He must be virtuous.

(ii) Living enclosed by restraint of rules of *Pātimokkha*.

(iii) Upright in life.

(iv) Trained according to precepts.

(v) Taking precepts upon himself with a sense of danger.

(vi) Must be vested in the tradition.

(vii) A custodian of the tradition.

(viii) A storehouse of tradition.

(ix) Set forth the higher life.

(x) He must have well divided, well established, well investigated *sutta* by *Sutta* the *Pātimokkhas*.

It was also prescribed that Jury must be expert in *Vinaya*, capable of pointing out the right course for friends and foes. He must be clever in judging. He must understand legal questions.

One can also see that Justices, lawyers, rehearsers of law maxims, council of representatives etc. were there, who could acquit the accused. Consul had to award punishment according to the Book of Precedents. Tables of Law were also there.

In Buddhist literature, one can also find as to what were property rights, matrimonial rights and trade rights in those times.

We can see that no individual had right of bequest even to the extent of deciding the shares of his own family. All such matters were settled by custom, by general sense of community as to what was right and proper. Very often a family, on the death of a householder, would go on as before under the superintendence of the eldest son. If the property were divided, the land was equally divided among the sons. Eldest son used to receive an extra share. Law book of Gautama gives a statement that the youngest son of the family also received an extra share. But later law books do not show the prevalence of such a practice. The women too had their personal property of jewellary and clothes. Daughters inherited from mother. No individual could acquire either by purchase or inheritance any exclusive right in any portion of the common grassland or woodland. Tax used to be paid. Through village headman, all Government business was carried on and he had both opportunity and power to represent the case to the higher officials. There was security and independence. There were no landlords and paupers.

If we go through references of matrimonial aspect, it is seen that customs of endogamy and exogamy (choosing a husband or a wife outside a limited circle of relationship and inside a wider circle) were universal. There were restrictions on remarriage.

References show that there was a body of five persons to enquire when and how births and deaths occur with a view not only of levying a tax, but also in order that births and deaths among high and low may not escape cognizance of Government.

Another body of five persons was there to superintend trade and commerce. The memebers had charge of weights and measures. They had to see that the products in the season are sold by public notice. None was allowed to deal in more than one kind of commodity unless he paid a double tax. Another group supervised manufactured articles sold by public notice. New articles were sold separately from the old ones. There was a fine for mixing the two. Another class collected one tenth of prices of articles sold. Fraud in payment of this tax was punished with death.

References show that silver coins were used. There were instruments of credit. Promisory notes were also there. References of 18% interest per annum are also seen. Loans used to be advanced on personal security. No banking facilities were there. Money was hoarded in house or burried in jars in the ground or deposited with a friend, a written record of transaction being kept.

Reference regarding gambling is also seen. Separate hall was to be provided by the King. Earning part used to go to the treasury.

Regarding law and order situation, it is seen that jungles were infested from time to time by robbers and runaway slaves. The Koliyan Central authorities were served by a special body of persons or police distinguished by a kind of uniform. These men had bad reputation for extortion and violence. The Mallas had similar officials. Subordinate servants were also provided.

If one sees Buddha's legal system and the same is compared with our codified legal system prevalent now-a-days, many similarities would be seen. It looks like that our jurists have borrowed certain things from the ancient legal system. Examples can be seen as the Criminal Procedure Code provides the types of offences and their respective procedures in The Court of Law. Indian Penal Code specifies the offences for which punishments are also provided *e.g.* Section 375 of Indian Penal Code speaks about the offence for rape for which punishment is provided in Section 376 of IPC. Similarly, Section 300 of IPC deals with murder and its punishment is provided in Section

302 of IPC. Punishment may be life term with fine or death sentence. Similarly, Sections 171A to Section 171-I deal with offences relating to elections and we see that in Buddhist literature also, election procedure was prescribed for *Saṁgha*. Similarly, offences regarding weights and measures are seen in Buddhist literature and we also find the same in Indian Penal Code occurring in Sections 264 to 267.

Moral aspects are embodied in Sections 292 to 294-A of Indian Penal Code. Restrictions were imposed on *Bhikkhus* and *Bhikkhunīs* regarding their general code of conduct.

One can see the reference that *Bhikkhus* accused of theft were guilty. Theft provisions are incorporated in Sections 378 to 382 of Indian Penal Code. Offences regarding Extortion are embodied in Sections 383 to 389 of Indian Penal Code. Sections 441 to 462 of Indian Penal Code talk about offences of criminal trespass. We find references of criminal trespass in Buddhist literature also. We also get references of remarriage etc. in Buddhist literature and such offences are mentioned in Indian Penal Code in Sections 493 to 498.

Similarly, we find references of division of property and its succession after the death of the householder in Buddhist literature. *Vinaya Piṭaka* was exhaustive to the extent that it consisted of various aspects of life including succession of property. Our legal system has been divided into various branches, *e.g.* the concept of property is discussed in Indian Succession Act and Hindu Succession Act.

We find that *Vinaya Piṭaka* was very exhaustive, where all types of offences, their remedies, life style of people, code of conduct etc. were incorporated and dealt with in a compact manner and the same was self-sufficient for the need of that time. One comes to an undisputed fact that Lord Buddha was aware of human tendency, psychology, and he was so big a jurist that he codified all the important provisions in a single book called *Vinaya Piṭaka*. One can not feel hesitant in saying that Lord Buddha was not only a competent preacher, teacher and thinker but also a very competent jurist.

Lord Buddha's disciples, followers, *Bhikkhus* and *Bhikkhunīs* are still seen in all parts of the world still following the preachings and teachings of Lord Buddha. They still follow the norms, procedures, rules etc. laid down by Lord Buddha though they are centuries old.

The Buddhist culture still prevails all over the world. Lord Buddha had made rules and principles which were sufficient to maintain law and order in the society and the same have been preserved till date with the same vigour, force and spirit. It is the need of the hour to promote research in Buddhist and other cultures to bring about National & International solidarity and integrity among the countries of the world.

The departments of Culture in various countries have still preserved all these concepts which have been suggested, implemented and codified by Lord Buddha to give a set pattern to his disciples and followers to mend and spend their lives. The Department of Culture, Ministry of Human Resource Development, New Delhi, India is playing a vital role by providing facilities to scholars of various categories to bring to light different aspects of culture prevailing in different countries.

REFERENCES & NOTES

1. *Theragāthā* (Hindi translation), p. *138*.
2. *Mahāvagga*, IV, 16,12 & C.
3. *Vinaya* Texts, Vol.I, p.68, Rule of procedure called *Sammukha Vinaya* (proceeding in presence) is one of the seven modes of settling disputes.

Delhi

HUMANITY AND WORLD PEACE THROUGH BUDDHISM

Subhra Barua Pavagadhi

Today, Humanity is faced with a very challenging dilemma - War or Peace.War means the extermination of the human race, the end of our civilization, the worst sufferings for mankind. Peace means the survival of our planet, new progress and achievements for our civilization, smiles and hopes for our younger generation.

From the very inception of history, human civilization has strived for peace. A human being by nature is a mixture of good and evil. The evil in man if not checked turns him to a devil. Throughout the entire course of human history, mankind has struggled with the evil forces. When he has successfully controlled the evil, he has been able to create a glorious epoch in history. In fact, human civilization reaches its climax when there is an era of peace.

In today's world, science has made tremendous progress in increasing comforts for the people, but it has miserably failed to ease the prevalent threats to their destruction.

Man has practically achieved everything to make living comfortable but, on the other hand, a dark future seems to have set in. Man's own created tools have put a big question mark on the very existence of human race itself. Now there is arms race in the whole of the world to procure more and more sophisticated nuclear weapons. Its repercussions we have seen in the recent Gulf War. Fear has crippled the entire human civilization. The adverse result of modernization has changed the very concept of human values as also their behaviour. All this has put the world in peril. Consequently, there is a bewildered cry for peace in the world.

Buddhism historically has been a great source of inspiration for the establishment of peace. It follows the path of love and service to the suffering humanity. Violence has always been discarded and peace has always been welcomed in Buddhism.

Buddhism is based on the cardinal principles of universal love and friendship. It preaches the gospel of love and compassion. The ethical doctrine of Buddhism is humanistic. It is entirely devoted to the well-being of mankind.

The Buddha, throughout his forty-five years of teaching the *Dhamma,* preached on suffering and the end of suffering. The Buddha advocated eternal peace while the world desires peace amongst material gains. The former is a permanent bliss while the latter is transitory. The cause of this difference is ignorance of the truth. The Buddha stressed the need for removing the ignorance of the truth. He stressed the need for removing the ignorance which is the root of all evils. He discovered a path through which ignorance can be removed and peace can be achieved in the world. The Enlightened One asked his disciples to go forth to preach the *Dhamma* for the welfare of mankind. In the words of the Buddha, "Oh, *Bhikkhus,* you should go forth for the welfare of the many, for the happiness of the many, out of compassion for the world, for the advantage, for the welfare, for the happiness of deities and human beings."[1]

Buddhism is dedicated towards peace, peace among human beings, peace among all creatures and ultimately peace in the world. It stands for *Bahujanahitāya Bahujanasukhāya* (for the welfare of many and for the happiness of many).

The Buddha pinpointed the sufferings prevalent among human beings as the root cause of all unrest. His Four Noble Truths, namely, suffering (*Dukkha*); the origin of suffering (*Dukkha-Samudaya*); the cessation of suffering (*Dukkha- Nirodha*); and the path leading to the cessation of suffering (*Dukkha-Nirodhagāminī-Paṭipadā*) are the foundations of Buddhism.

The First Noble Truth is that of *Dukkha* which means suffering, sorrow or dissatisfaction in life. All life, to one who sees deeply, is suffering. All living beings are subject to birth, and consequently to decay, disease, and death. No one is exempt from these four inevitable causes of suffering. In brief, the body itself is a cause of suffering and is hence, *Dukkha*. We must recognise this truth so that we may not come to grief later on.

The Second Noble Truth is about the origin of *Dukkha*. It arises from craving *(Tañhā)*. This craving, gross or subtle, which leads to repeated births and deaths is the cause of all the ills in life. It is three-fold—*Kāma-Tañhā* or craving for enjoyment of sensual pleasures; *Bhāva-Tanhā* or craving for the various dogmas, faiths, views, ideologies, religious or secular, pertaining to the will to live over which rival individuals or groups dispute, wrangle or fight, which hardens or closes the mind to truth concerning wholesome ways of life now and here; and *Vibhāva-Tanhā* or craving for dogmas, views and ideologies pertaining to the will to annihilate life here or hereafter instead of seeking and adopting the wholesome way of life.

These cravings invariably rise in the presence of ignorance or *avidyā* with the help of three defilements–greed (*Lobha)*, hatred (*Doṣa)* and ignorance *(Moha)*. These defilements are the root of all evils and can be rooted out by knowing fully well that everything is impermanent, unsatisfactory and unsubstantial *(Anicca, Dukkha and Anatta*).

The Third Noble Truth is about the cessation of *Dukkha* which is achieved by the total eradication of all forms of craving. It is *Nibbāna,* the *summum bonum* of Buddhism, which can be attained. This Third Noble Truth, though dependent on oneself, is beyond logical reasoning and is superamundane. Unlike the first two which are mundane, it is purely a realisation. It should be noted that the mere cessation of suffering or the mere destruction of craving is not *Nibbāna*. In *Nibbāna,* nothing is annihilated because Buddhism denies the existence of a permanent soul or *Ātmā*.

The Third Noble Truth has to be realised by developing the Noble Eightfold Path (*Ariya Aṭṭhaṅgiko Maggo)* which is the Fourth Noble Truth. This is the Via Media-Golden Mean, *i.e.*, the Middle Path (*Majjhima Paṭipadā)*. It consists of Right View (*Sammā-Diṭṭhi*) which means to rid oneself of all superstitions, animism and primitive rites; Right Thought (*Sammā-Saṅkappo*) which leads towards clear thinking; Right Speech *(Sammā-Vācā)* which entails refraining from falsehood, slandering and harsh words; Right Action *(Sammā-Kammanto)* which deals with abstinence from killing, stealing and sexual misconduct; Right Livelihood *(Sammā-Ājīvo)* which suggests refraining from trade in arms, human beings and flesh; Right Effort *(Sammā-Vāyāmo)* which is the endeavour to discard evil that has already arisen, the endeavour to prevent the arising of fresh evils, the endeavour to develop unarisen good, and the endeavour to promote good which has already arisen; Right Mindfulness *(Sammā-Sati)* which is the attention paid to the activities and weaknesses of one's body and mind; and Right Concentration *(Sammā-Samādhi)* which is one-pointedness of mind. Of these constituents of the Noble Eightfold Path, the first two are grouped under wisdom *(Paññā)*, the next three under morality *(Sīla)*, and the last three under concentration *(Samādhi)*.

Thus Buddhism provides a complete way to nurture goodness by eradicating evils which cause unrest in the world.

Noble are the Four Great Truths, Noble is the Eightfold Path. Out of these sublime truths, Lord Buddha evolved a genuine code of ethics and morality—the practical side of this philosophy, in the form of a simple yet practical system of true human life. The code of *Pancasīla* or the five noble precepts enjoin us not to kill, not to steal, not to tell lies, not to live immoral life and not to consume intoxicants. It is this code of ethics that Lord Buddha promulgated for the gradual upliftment of the common man without going into the complications of multi Gods and varied beliefs. What makes the world wonder about the success of this simple philosophy is the gift of the great human who after penetrating deep into the root cause of human suffering discovered this panacea over 2,500 years ago. Its glory and effects remain afresh even after hundreds of generations.

Buddhism discards constantly brooding on the ills of life. Rather it advocates a doctrine of joy, happiness and hope. It does not make its followers morbid but rather inspires them to live a fuller and nobler life.

The main hindrances to peace are anger, cruelty, jealousy, attachment to the pleasurable and aversion to the non-pleasurable. These vices are inherent in man. In order to subdue these, the Buddha asked his followers to practise the modes of sublime state, i.e., the four *Brahmavihāras*. They are loving kindness *(Mettā)*, compassion *(Karuṇā)*, joy *(Muditā)* and equanimity *(Upekkhā)*.

Mettā is loving kindness. This attitude is not confined only to the human beings but also to the entire animal and sub-animal creations. This is a sincere wish for the welfare and happiness of all living beings.

Karuṇā means great compassion towards all beings. Lord Buddha takes a vow not to enter *Nibbāna* until all suffering beings destroy their sufferings and realise *Nibbāna*. This is the image of the Buddha as the incarnation of *Mahā-Karuṇā*, the great Compassionate One.

Muditā is the third *Brahmavihāra*. The meaning of *Muditā* is to be happy in the happiness of others. This is a great quality of noble beings. This virtue unfolds itself into sympathetic joy.

Upekkhā is the fourth *Brahmavihhāra*. This is a mental state rather difficult to attain. It is the equanimity between the opposites such as happiness and sorrow, gain and loss, etc. This is known as the state of *thiti-paññā* in Pāli. One has to remain in this condition unabsorbed and equal.

In brief, the true practice of all these sublime states makes a good ground for the proclamation of peace everywhere in the world by removing all the ills of man.

We know that happiness is based on peace. Peace is the result of the absence of conflicts. Conflicts, according to the Buddha, are the cause of various kinds of tensions that we face in everyday life. There are tensions within each one of us as individuals, tensions emanating from the strife of social, political, racial, religious and language groups, within states and societies. Then there are international tensions and also economic tensions between the haves and have-nots. These manifold tensions create fear and hatred which lead to all kinds of discriminations.

With goodwill and understanding, the problems confronting mankind can be solved. For this, the noble qualities of goodwill and brotherhood have to be cultivated. Thus if *Mettā* or universal love is practised in its true spirit, it could prove a panacea for all problems in the world and lay the foundations for a happy human family. The path of non-violence as enunciated by the Buddha and the founders of other religions has been appreciated by many great personalities for its validity as a valuable instrument of social transformation. *Karuṇā* or unconditional compassion, the positive force behind the doctrine of non-violence, should be the motive for our acting together to achieve the goal of peace in our time. It should also give birth to the wisdom and means of enabling us to work together through all difficulties, slowly binding us into a world of peace and love.

The call for disarmament which is necessary for the survival of mankind must come from us all together, or else it is bound to fail.

Thus, today our ardent need of the hour is peace - personal, social, national and international. To live and let live. The way to achieve this peace and the solution to get rid of the present vexing problems of life, political or spiritual, lies in adapting the sublime potentialities of Buddhism.

According to the *Dhammapada*, "Never by hatred does hatred cease here; it ceases by love, this is the eternal law."[2]

REFERENCES & NOTES

1. I. B. Horner, *The Book of the Discipline*, Vol. IV, p.28
2. *Dhammapada, Yamaka Vagga*, verse 5

Delhi

THE SOCIAL BEHAVIOUR OF MAN AS REFLECTED IN THE PĀLI NIKĀYA

Krishna Kant Trivedi

The relation between the man and the society has got prime importance in the *Pāli Nikāya*. A study of the passages quoted in it, exhibits that a society without man and a man without society can not be imagined. After all, a man of qualities and character provides favourable condition for the growth of social relation or behaviour. It is only the treacherous person who destroys the entire social entity. Therefore, the *Nikāya* recommends some rules which are supposed to be followed before we connect ourselves to the main stream of society. A man who lives without self and shares the sufferings of our people is considered to be fit for the social behaviour. Torture and violence should not take place in society. In fact, exploitation and the betrayal of trust are sufficient to bring about total decay to our social relations. According to the *Nikāya*, a society where the citizens are not tortured and harassed by the notorious persons is fit for mankind. It is our duty to provide equal opportunities to all citizens without considering their cast or creed. Hence, a person must be practical rather than theoretical.

Generally it comes to our notice that the property running under the control of different human groups is snatched away by treachery. Such acts are committed by all and not confined to a particular community. Lust for self is seen in each and every citizen. For the sake of wealth, people misbehave even with their parents and relatives and sometimes they attack them and torture them also. All such inhuman acts happen due to the lust for pleasure.[1]

A man is admired when he thinks for the goodness of the entire mass. There are examples to show that a man of qualities receives help and assistance from his relatives and friends.[2] Rendering service in the interest of society is contributory to our personality.[3]

When we look into the social relation, let us keep our mind enlightened and alert. The spirit of confidence should run and not to be broken without sufficient cause. If a minor mistake is committed by a person, he should not be held for punishment. Do not impose penalty because it brings upon him a lot of sorrow and miseries. Anger and enmity must be avoided in order to normalise the situation. A guilty man at first should be requested to get rid of his bad habits. After sometime, try to insturct him for good things.[4] Practically a man learns every thing from society and if he differs on some points, an attempt should be made for solution. He may enter into a council of the elders where an appropriate answer should be given to him. Sitting together may end all differences. A man should not be publicly abused for his mistake, on the contrary, the real cause of his failure should be disclosed to him.[5]

We become an integral part of society only after realising the real cause of sufferings. As a rule , the sufferings are not without reason and these are experienced throughout life.[6] In society, act of violence should never be encouraged. Enmity can be brought under control by spirit of non-enmity. Death is inevitable and if it is understood, our life will remain without violence.[7]

Both male and female citizens contribute in giving shape to our social behaviour. But there should be no place for anger and jealousy in human behaviour.[8] Our seniors deserve our due respect and courtesy. Food and robe should be offered to the wandering *śramaṇas*. A person, who offers nothing is considered to be miser and rustic.[9] In view of the Buddhist thinkers, the society runs because we enquire about the sufferings of mankind and work together in order to remove it. We help the helpless persons and examine our good and bad habits. Sometimes, we should meet to discuss the real cause of sufferings and also to find out the ways to get rid of the worldly sorrow.[10] When a male or female member helps in time, he deserves our obligation. Such spirit of co-operation must exist throughout the entire social domain.[11]

Since birth, man is associated with the society. He has to face struggle for his existence. Society never permits him to commit suicide.

According to the Buddhists, it is a crime against humanity. In spite of such prohibition, suicide is never without reason. A depressed and helpless person is sometimes forced to commit suicide. Therefore, he needs our love and sympathy.[12] The *Nikāya* also tells us that a person whom the right path of life is shown, can do better for the progress of humanity, but when he adopts wrong views, the common cause is destroyed.[13] Some people are found to have indulged themselves in conspiracy against their own people. Such acts take place due to the urge for self, which is mostly acquired by illegal methods.[14]

Again the *Nikāya* declares that the society is nothing but a unified form of relations which are established between the individuals and remain till the mutual confidence is there. In case of betrayal of trust, the society will plunge into disorder.[15]

We have at our disposal two types of councils : *Sama* and *Viśama* (Favourable and unfavourable). It depends on a person as to which counil he joins? The *sama* council according to the *Nikāya,* teaches us the *vinaya* (discipline). The nature of the *viśama* council is quite different. It brings disorder in public life.[16] A council may be formed by various groups of people and if it runs swiftly, it unites the nation as well as the society.[17]

Sensibility in man prevails since the beginning of civilization. Though different in outlook, each and every person learns things for his subsistence. The *Nikāya,* on psychological basis, refers to three types of persons who used to influence the social order. A person possessing good conduct *(śila),* acquiring the *Dhamma* with devotion and leading life without anger and jealousy is fit for social behaviour.[18]

The framework of the society is collapsed due to the unsocial activities of man. Sometimes, the living beings are attacked by some notorious people. In fact, due to such cruelty, the *Grāma, Nigama, Nagara* and *Janapadas* are left without their glamour and beauty. Virtually, such places of the human population are transformed into a barren piece of land.[19] The *Nikāya* makes it clear that the greediness and wrong views are menace to our society.[20] The improper acts against the living beings are caused by our body, soul and speech.

Human rights should not be disturbed. Punishment (*Daṇḍa*) is effective to check the criminal acts of those people who intentionally snatch the property and other means of livelihood belonging to the major section of our society. It is the duty of each person to maintain peace in society. If we fail to check the antisocial activities, our society will perish. Hence, it is necessary to give up bad habits. For social co-operation, the acts which are against the welfare of man, should not be promoted by us.[21] According to the *Nikāya,* there are four types of persons living together with their own specific behaviour : Those do not do better either for self or for others; those who do better for the benefit of the mass and never think for self; those who always look for self and never think for the welfare of others. The fourth and the last category comprises those persons who take notice of self and also care for the progress of the entire community.[22]

A man of virtues (*satpuruṣa*) tries to impress the society while a bad man (*asatpuruṣa*) kills the living beings and also indulges himself in stealing, illicit sexual contact, wine drinking and in different acts which are basically not social. A good man keeps himself away from all kinds of violent acts and warns the people against the evil deeds. Not addicted to drinking, he leads a pious life and presents a lot of ideals before the people.

After becoming a householder, one must grant charity to the poor. The *Nikāya* recommends five types of gifts which are made for the welfare of society.[23] A person who is honoured by the people should care for their progress and prosperity. The *Nikāya* compares such persons to a big tree where birds from all corners come to find their shelter and food.[24]

According to Buddhist thinkers, a person acquires greatness and fame when he averts sufferings of the mankind.[25] More precaution is needed when we look for the social contact. According to the *Nikāya,* some persons are found suitable to us, while some of them remain quite indifferent to us. There are five types of families (*kulas*) which are supposed to be unfavourable to us. It is safe to remain isolated from the contact of such families but if it becomes necessary to visit them, no seat should be taken there.[26] Each and every citizen requires our respect and honour but priority should be given to the righteous only.[27]

Unity and co-ordination are highly recommended for our social life because these not only preserve our interests but also bring progress and prosperity to our nation. Let us talk together and find solution to our differences. Paying honour to our tradition and due respect and courtesy to the elders will enable us to achieve progress and prosperity.[28] In social domain, anger is not permitted. An angry person loses support of his friends and relatives.[29]

The *Pāli Nikāya* supplies a list of acts to be done for the welfare of the common man. Priority should be given to gardening, forestry, bridge-construction and other works related to our material progress.[30] King Aśoka declares in his inscription that he had planted herbs and shady plants on both side of the highways in order to provide medical aid for man and animal. Besides these works, wells were dug out to serve water to all living beings.[31]

Uttering sweet words is another quality of a person which enables him to form harmonial social relations. The *Nikāya* makes it clear that it is the *Dhamma* which contributes much to mankind. Sweet words uttered are neither abusive nor destructive in nature. They give satisfaction to our soul and mind. The truth is immortal and ranks as *Sanātana Dhamma*. Again, it forms the basis of the *Artha* (Wealth) and *Dhamma*. Further, it leads us towards the *Nirvāṇa*.[32] A place hit by famine should not be visited. Even the monks were not allowed to visit such places.[33] The society should run without sinful acts. It should not be overlooked that a sinner at last gets no good results. A faultless person, it abused or insulted, is not confronted with troubles but it is the sinner who is destroyed.[34]

The society requires universal brotherhood which provides relief and assistance to all people.[35] Due courtesy extended, always pays in the long run. We should not expect pleasure at the cost of insult to the citizens.[36] Our social relations are inspired by good and spotless character. Hence, lust for illicit sexual contact is not good for any member of the society. A fearless life is not possible if one has not given up such bad habits.[37]

There is an exchange of ideas between man and society. Since the creation, the spirit of co-operation exists between different human groups. But in view of the *Nikāya*, it depends on a person whether he co-operates or is not willing to offer something in the interest of others. It is praiseworthy if a person offers much to and takes very little from the society.[38] Hence, mutual help and co-operation is needed for social existence. A person is benefited by his own supporters and this is the spirit which combines them together.[39] Inflicting harassment on the living beings invites sufferings in this and the other world.If a man extends love and affection to the depressed, he is adorned with admirable personality. A righteous person teaches the doctrine of the *Dhamma* to his own friends and relatives. In fact, a desireless person has the natural spirit of co-operation.[40] When we have surplus amount of wealth at our disposal, we should behave politely and not be proud of our prosperity, glamour and highbirth. According to the Buddhist thinkers, a proud man forgets even his parents and misbehaves with honourable persons too.[41]

It is the limbs of our body which produce good and bad results in this world. A person makes his limbs weak and less useful by doing harm to others but when he performs something good to others, his limbs become strong and more useful . In fact, it comes to mobilize our *Kamma*. Hence, a person should keep strict control over his limbs.[42]

The *Nikāya* recommends high ideals of life. Exploitation of labour is not good. When the major part of wealth is grabbed by some notorious people, the society gradually plunges into disorder.[43] A place where persons are exploited is not good for us.[44]

By rendering service to mankind, a person is rewarded with profound achievements. One of the *Jātaka* declares "Be polite, when you behold a good man. Take your seat with a man of justice. Help those persons who are known for their equal treatment to one and all. Do not have trust in an unreliable person. Do not miss the equality when you look for the social relations.[45] The policy of forgiveness should be promoted throughout the life. When a dull a stupid man insults a noble person, no punishment should be inflicted upon him because he does not know what are the ways of behaviour? Differences may take place among the noble citizens but they unite soon while the stupids are broken like the earthen vessels. A gentle person feels no hesitation in confessng his sins. He forgives others and tries to avert differences by mutual conversation.[46] A person commanding full control over his senses is fit for social behaviour. Sometimes, a person changes his colour and behaves like a monkey.[47] The *Jātaka* also makes it clear that living with a man of polluted character mars our prestige and social status. A person never falls in distress when he is associated with men of qualities and high ideals.[48]

Merits and demerits are obtained through company of different types of citizens. It is easy to analyze how much loss and profit shall we have in future? A sinner and a lier is not fit for our friendship. Indulgence in non-Aryan acts renders one devoid of qualities and then it gradually converts a man into a worthless and unreliable citizen.[49]

A drunkard by his behaviour invites lots of problems. According to the *Jātaka*, a person addicted to wine-drinking loses his qualities. He wanders like an animal, sings and dances without occasion and moves in the lanes in the nude. Finally, wine-drinking turns a man into an idle and stupid person. He appears to be a puppet and when presents himself before the council of elders, he cannot talk properly. He takes no care even of an sovereign. In short, wine has done so much harm to our people that many prosperous families are shattered into pieces. It is quite natural to think that a drunkard abuses his parents even and cannot keep himself away from illicit sexual contact. He feels no hesitation in killing the righteous persons. Therefore, a person known for his truthfulness immediately turns into a lier just after taking a glass of wine. He is misled and fails to realise the real values of life. Even a reserved person, after taking some drops of wine, begins to speak loudly. Discussing the negative behaviour of a person, the Buddhist thinkers consider wine as a poisonous snake and warn the common men by telling some selected stories.[50]

Before encouraging any type of social relation, the practical aspect should not be ignored. The blind support may cause some serious problems. Enemies and greedy persons are not be believed. Try your best to earn confidence of a number of persons but do not trust them personally. Beware of persons whom you are not acquainted with. Whatever you think should not be disclosed to others.[51]

REFERENCES & NOTES

1. *M.N.I.*p 120
2. *Ibid*. II p. 397
3. *Ibid*. p. 449
4. *Ibid*. III p. 133-134
5. *Ibid*. III p. 47
6. *Ibid*
7. *Ibid*. p. 222
8. *Ibid*. p. 282
9. *Ibid*. p. 283-284
10. *Ibid*. p. 283, 284
11. *Ibid*. p. 339
12. *Ibid*. p. 353 ff
13. *A.N.I.* p. 32, 33
14. *Ibid*. p. 63
15. *Ibid*. p. 65
16. *Ibid*.
17. *Ibid*. p. 97
18. *Ibid*. p. 138
19. *Ibid* p. 148
20. *Ibid*. p. 187
21. *A. N.* II p. 79
22. *Ibid*. P. 100
23. *Ibid*. p. 306
24. *Ibid*. p. 308
25. *Ibid*. p. 434
26. *I. N.* III p. 158
27. *Ibid*.
28. *Ibid*. p. 163-164
29. *Ibid*. p. 227
30. *A. N.* IV p. 31
31. *Girnar Rock Edict* - II
32. *S.N. I* p. 188, 189
33. *S.N.* III p. 286
34. *Itivuttaka*, p. 240 ff
35. *Dhammapada*. *(Piyavagga)*, 219
36. *Ibid*. 291
37. *Ibid*. *(Nityavagga)*, 310
38. *Itivuttaka*, p. 226 ff
39. *Theragāthā 149, 150*

40. *Ibid*. p. 237, 238
41. *Ibid*. 240, 242
42. *Ibid*. 423-425
43. *Ibid*.
44. *Ibid*. 728, 729
45. *Jā*, II p. 33
46. *Ibid*. IV p. 188
47. *Ibid*. *II p. 403*
48. *Ibid*. III p. 207
49. *Ibid*. p. 312
50. *Ibid*. p. 472
51. *Ibid*. IV 257-258

Darbhanga

बौद्ध धर्म में यज्ञ की अवधारणा

उर्मिला श्रीवास्तव

कहा जाता है कि जगत् के प्रत्येक संचय या विस्तार काल में अथवा प्रत्येक उस काल में जो दो प्रलयों के मध्य का अन्तराल है, कुछ महातपस्वी, महायोगी अवतरित होते हैं। साधारण रूप से जीवों की सेवा में कालयापन करते हुए ये योगी संसार से विरक्त हो जाते हैं और मोक्ष की सिद्धि में प्रयत्नशील होते हैं यद्यपि उनके लिए पृथिवी लोक पर मानव शरीर के रूप में जन्म लेना आवश्यक नहीं है। वे योगीश्वर इच्छानुसार मोक्ष का वरण कर सकते हैं किन्तु संसार के समग्र जीवों के प्रति परोपकार की भावना से मोक्ष से विमुख होकर दूसरा जन्म धारण करना स्वीकार करते हैं। बौद्ध धर्म के विश्वास के अनुसार, वे महातपस्वी जो निर्वाण-प्राप्ति के अधिकारी होते हुए भी प्राणिमात्र के प्रति दया की भावना से एक और जन्म लेना स्वीकार करते हैं, बोधिसत्त्व[1] कहलाते हैं। जीवन्मुक्त बोधिसत्त्व शान्त और शिव का साक्षात्कार करके नैष्ठिक और अच्युत पद को प्राप्त कर लेते हैं, उनके लिए कोई कर्त्तव्य भी शेष नहीं रहता है तथापि वे दयालु अपनी मुक्ति की कामना न करते हुए लोकसंग्रह के लिए सतत प्रयत्नशील और अज्ञानी प्राणियों की मुक्ति के लिए निरन्तर चिन्तित रहते हैं। अन्तिम शरीर धारण करने पर वे ही बुद्ध[2] होते हैं। बुद्ध रूपी ज्ञान सूर्य, जगत् के मोहान्धकार को नष्ट करने के लिए उदित होते हैं।[3]

सिद्धार्थ के जन्म ग्रहण से लेकर बुद्ध बनने तक उन्हें बोधिसत्त्व की संज्ञा अनेक प्राचीन ग्रन्थों में दी गई है।[4] बोधि का अर्थ है मानवों के कल्याण का ज्ञान, कल्याण मार्ग से उद्धार के लिए निरन्तर प्रयासरत प्राणी (सत्त्व) बोधिसत्त्व कहलाता है। प्रारम्भ में सम्भवत: गौतम के जन्म ग्रहण से सम्बोधि ज्ञान की प्राप्ति होने तक यह विशेषण उनके लिए प्रयुक्त होता होगा, बाद में यह धारणा बन गई कि उन्होंने उस जन्म से पहले भी अनेक जन्म ग्रहण किए थे, उन पूर्वजन्मों में भी उनको 'बोधिसत्त्व' विशेषण से सम्पन्न किया गया।[5]

गौतम बुद्ध जगद्विख्यात महापुरुष थे। वे महान् धर्मप्रचारक तो थे ही, तत्कालीन हिन्दू धर्म के सुधारक भी थे। साधारणत: भारतीय समाज में एक धारणा प्रचलित है कि बुद्ध वेद के वचनों में विश्वास नहीं रखते थे, वे नास्तिक और वैदिक कर्मकाण्ड के घोर विरोधी थे। यज्ञ को समाप्त करने के लिए ही बौद्ध धर्म का आविर्भाव हुआ था। सत्य तो यह है कि भगवान् बुद्ध का दर्शन करुणा और अनुकम्पा से प्रेरित था। यह धारणा अनुपयुक्त है कि वे वेदों के विरोधी और यज्ञों के निन्दक थे। वे यज्ञों की विधियों की नहीं, यज्ञों में प्रचलित पशु-हिंसा की निन्दा करते थे।[6] वस्तुत: वेदों के प्रति उनमें पर्याप्त आदर भाव था। उनके भिक्षु-संघ में महाकात्यायन जैसे

वेद-पारङ्गत ब्राह्मण थे। उन्होंने किसी नए धर्म का निर्माण करने की इच्छा कभी अनुभव नहीं की थी। इसीलिए उन्होंने हिन्दू धर्म के उत्तम विश्वासों और श्रेष्ठ मान्यताओं को सदा स्वीकार किया और अपने उपदेशों में वेदों के प्रति सम्मान प्रकट किया। वे कहते थे कि वेद को जानने वाला विद्वान् इस संसार में जन्म या मृत्यु में आसक्ति का परित्याग करके, तृष्णा तथा पाप से रहित होकर जन्म और वार्द्धक्य से मुक्त हो जाता है।[7] वह सांसारिक दृष्टि और असत्य विचारादि से कदापि अहङ्कार को नहीं प्राप्त होता है। कर्म और श्रवण से भी वह दूषित मनोवृत्ति को प्राप्त नहीं होता है तथा सांसारिक भ्रमों से भी परे रहता है।[8]

महात्मा बुद्ध की मान्यता थी कि यज्ञ में प्राणिवध करने से यजमान कायेन-वाचा-मनसा अकुशल कर्मों का आचरण करता है, अतः यज्ञ अमङ्गल रूप है। इस सम्बन्ध में एक सुत्त प्राप्त होता है जिसका भाव इस प्रकार है—'भदन्त आनन्द के अनुरोध पर भगवान् ने उपदेश दिया 'जो यज्ञ के लिए अग्नि जलाता है और यूप स्थापित करता है वह तीन दु:खोत्पादक अकुशल शस्त्र उठाता है। वे शस्त्र हैं- चित्तशस्त्र, वाचाशस्त्र और कायशस्त्र। जो यज्ञ को आरम्भ करता है उसके मन में यह अकुशल विचार आता है कि अधिकाधिक पशुओं की हत्या की जाए, इस रूप में वह सर्वप्रथम दु:खोत्पादक अकुशल चित्तशस्त्र उठाता है। फिर वह अपने मुख से इन प्राणियों की हत्या का आदेश देता है, इस रूप में वह दु:खोत्पादक अकुशल वाचाशस्त्र उठाता है। इसके पश्चात् उन प्राणियों को मारने के लिए प्रथम स्वयं शस्त्र उठाता है, इस रूप में वह दु:खोत्पादक अकुशल कायशस्त्र उठाता है।'[9]

निश्चित रूप से कहा जा सकता है कि बुद्ध के काल में धार्मिक विचार एवं व्यवहार प्रमुखतः दो भागों में विभक्त थे। प्रथम, देवों के प्रति याज्ञिक विधानों से उपलक्षित और द्वितीय आत्मनिग्रह एवम् आध्यात्मिकता की प्राप्ति से समन्वित। बुद्ध नैतिकता एवं सदाचार के पक्षपाती थे, उनके अनुसार महत्त्वपूर्ण था-बुद्ध-ज्ञान की प्राप्ति द्वारा व्यक्ति का चिन्ता एवं दु:ख से छूट जाना। निवृत्ति-प्रधान जीवन (निर्वाण) उनकी दार्शनिक विचारधारा का लक्ष्य था। वे अन्धश्रद्धा के प्रतिकूल थे। प्रत्येक को आत्मविश्वास की शिक्षा देते थे और सत्य का साक्षात्कार स्वयं करने का उपदेश करते थे। वे व्यक्ति को सत्य की ओर उठने वाली अभिलाषा की ओर प्रेरित करते थे तथा सत्य को ही शिव और सुन्दर मानते थे। वे आस्तिक्य बुद्धि से वेद और यज्ञ के सत् सिद्धान्तों में आस्था रखते थे किन्तु यज्ञों में पशुहिंसादि निर्दयतापूर्ण अनैतिक कृत्यों में उनकी सहमति नहीं थी।

गौतम बुद्ध के शिष्यों तथा अनुयायियों ने उनकी विचारधारा का अनुचित अर्थ निकाला और वेदविमुख हो गए। वैदिक विधियों से पराङ्मुख समाज यज्ञ-याग आदि धार्मिक कृत्यों से भी दूर हो गया। इसके दो कारण थे-एक तो ये यज्ञादि व्ययसाध्य होने के कारण साधारण व्यक्ति की पहुँच के बाहर थे, दूसरे उन यज्ञों में कृषिकार्य में उपयोगी असंख्य पशुओं का वध किया जाता था। फलस्वरूप सामान्य जन-मानस में यज्ञों के प्रति अरुचि एवं श्रमणों के उपदेशों में रुचि बढ़ रही थी। अतः श्रमण-संघों का उत्कर्ष स्वाभाविक था।

महात्मा बुद्ध के काल में संघों, आरामों और मठों में प्रवचन तथा पूजा के लिए चैत्यों के निर्माण की प्रवृत्ति ने भी यज्ञ को क्षति पहुँचाई। बुद्ध के जीवन की एक घटना इस विषय में उद्धरणीय है-'भदन्त आनन्द ने

तथागत से पूछा कि निर्वाण के पश्चात् आपका शरीर जला दिए जाने पर अवशिष्ट राख का क्या होगा ? बुद्ध ने उत्तर दिया- चार मार्गों के मुहाने पर शरीर के ऊपर स्तूप बनाया जाए ।'[10] बुद्ध के इस कथन का निर्वाह उनके अनुयायियों ने किया । निर्वाण-प्राप्ति के अनन्तर बुद्ध के शरीर की शेष भस्म को आठ भागों में विभक्त कर उस पर स्मारक रूप में स्तूप बनाए गए ।

सम्राट् अशोक सर्वधर्म-समन्वयी थे तथापि बौद्ध होने के कारण बौद्ध धर्म के प्रति उनका विशेष पक्षपात था । अशोक द्वारा स्तूप-निर्माण की बृहद् योजना ने यज्ञ को विध्वंस की कगार पर ला खड़ा किया । मौर्यकाल में यज्ञ की निरर्थकता सम्बन्धी विचारधारा ने अधिक विस्तार पाया तथा पहाड़ों तक में अनेक बौद्ध चैत्य निर्मित हुए । प्राचीन बुद्ध के रूप में मान्य कनकमुनि द्वारा स्थापित स्तूपों का पुनरुद्धार किया गया । सह्याद्रि पर्वतमाला की सभी गुहाओं को स्तूप के आकार में बनाया गया । काष्ठ शिल्प का प्रयोग भी इसी क्रम में उल्लेख्य है । स्तूप पवित्र भावना एवं पूजा के मूल आधार हो गए । स्तूप की पवित्रता को बनाए रखने के लिए वेदिकाओं तथा तोरणों का निर्माण किया गया । बौद्ध सम्प्रदाय की हीनयान शाखा[11] ने इस परम्परा को और आगे बढ़ाया ।

इतिहास साक्षी है कि बौद्ध सम्प्रदाय की स्थापना के अनन्तर बुद्ध की प्रतिमाओं से ही प्रतिमा-पूजन का विकास हुआ है । फारसी भाषा का बुत (बुद्ध) शब्द प्रतिमा-पूजन से सम्बन्ध स्मरण कराता है । बुद्ध की प्रतिमाओं के निर्माण तथा पूजन की प्रक्रिया ने भी यज्ञ को मिटाने में सहायता दी यद्यपि बौद्ध सम्प्रदाय की स्थापना तथा विकास और बुद्ध की मानवाकार प्रतिमा, इन दोनों घटनाओं के मध्य लगभग छः सौ वर्षों का अन्तर है । इस दीर्घ कालावधि में बौद्ध मतानुयायियों के मानस ही में बुद्ध आराधना-बिन्दु रहे । निर्वाण प्राप्त निराकार तथागत को प्रतिमा के माध्यम से पुनः रूपायित करने की कल्पना अनुद्भूत ही रही किन्तु भावुक हृदय के लिए शून्य में निराकार बुद्ध की कल्पना करके ध्यान केन्द्रित कर पाना कठिन हो रहा था फलतः बौद्ध सम्प्रदाय की महायान शाखा[12] ने प्रतीकों का निर्धारण किया । ये प्रतीक बुद्ध के जीवन की घटनाओं से निकटतम सम्बद्ध थे तथा जीवन की महत्त्वपूर्ण तिथियों को उपलक्षित करते थे । प्रतीक ही जनता के श्रद्धा-केन्द्र हुए । स्तूप के चारों ओर की वेदिकाओं पर इन्हीं प्रतीकों से बुद्ध के जीवन की कथावस्तु अलङ्कृत की गई । इस सज्जा के मूल में भावना थी कि जनता बौद्ध धर्म की ओर आकर्षित हो । प्रतीकों के अङ्कन की इस पद्धति में सफेद हाथी,[13] कमल, [14]घोड़ा,[15] बोधिवृक्ष,[16] वज्रासन,[17] गन्धकुटी,[18]भिक्षापात्र,[19]उष्णीष,[20]प्रभामण्डल,[21] धर्मचक्र,[22] पदचिह्न,[23] त्रिरत्न[24] तथा स्तूप [25] का प्रयोग किया गया ।

बौद्ध धर्म का प्रचार-प्रसार राज्याश्रय प्राप्त होने के कारण मौर्यकाल में पर्याप्त मात्रा में हुआ । अशोक ने बौद्धधर्म को स्वीकार कर उसे परिवर्धित रूप दिया । सम्राट् अशोक के विशाल साम्राज्य में पश्चिम में काबुल से लेकर पूर्व में गङ्गा के विलय तक तथा उत्तर में हिमालय से लेकर दक्षिण में विन्ध्यपर्वतमाला तक बुद्ध धर्म के सिद्धान्त प्रसारित किए गए । भारत के सभी भागों में धर्मप्रचारकों को भेज कर बुद्ध के उपदेशों का प्रचार किया गया । राजा एवं धनिकों की कृपा से स्थान-स्थान पर संघारामों का निर्माण हुआ । राजसाधनों से बौद्ध धर्म को विश्वधर्म बनाने का प्रयत्न किया गया । श्रीलंका, बर्मा, चीन, जापान, तिब्बत, थाईलैण्ड आदि पड़ोसी देशों में

धर्म-प्रचार-हेतु बौद्ध भिक्षु भेजे गए। अशोक के पुत्र महेन्द्र को लंका में बौद्धधर्म का प्रधान बनाया गया, पुत्री संघमित्रा भी प्रचार-हेतु दूसरे देशों में गई। वातावरण में तथागत के उपदेश गूँजने लगे, अगत्या वेदों के पठन-पाठन पर प्रहार हुआ, वेदार्थ विस्मृत हुआ, वेद के आध्यात्मिक रहस्य दुर्बोध हो गए। वेदों का ऐसा ह्रास हुआ कि वे अपनी खोई प्रतिष्ठा को पुनः प्राप्त नहीं कर सके। अनेक वैदिक अध्वर जो पशु-आलभन से सम्पृक्त थे, लुप्त हुए। उनके साथ अन्य यागों का सम्पादन भी समाप्त हुआ।

मौर्यकाल के पतन के साथ ही शुंग वंश का उदय हुआ। शुंगवंशी राजा बौद्ध धर्म के विरोधी थे। ब्राह्मणधर्म के समर्थक पुष्यमित्र शुंग को अयोध्या के एक शिलालेख में 'द्वि अश्वमेधयाजिनः' कहा गया। दो अश्वमेध यज्ञों का अनुष्ठान बौद्ध धर्म के उन्मूलन का प्रयास था। गुप्तवंशीय राजाओं के समय में यज्ञों को पुनः प्रतिष्ठित करने का प्रयत्न किया गया। समुद्रगुप्त के अश्वमेध यज्ञ का वृत्तान्त मदुरै में उपलब्ध शिलालेख से प्राप्त होता है। चन्द्रगुप्त द्वितीय ने भी अश्वमेध यज्ञ किया। किन्तु इन यज्ञों का राज्यस्तर पर आयोजन भी वैदिक संस्कृति के प्रतीक यज्ञों को सर्वसाधारण में प्रचलित न कर सका। नित्यप्रति विधीयमान अग्निहोत्र और दर्शपूर्णमास आदि भी समाप्तप्राय हुए।

गुप्त राजाओं की अवनति के साथ सातवाहनों का प्राधान्य हुआ। सातवाहन नरेश ब्राह्मण एवं ब्राह्मण धर्मावलम्बी थे किन्तु उन्होंने तथा उनके क्षत्रपों ने बौद्ध धर्म के प्रति उदारता का परिचय दिया। इसके पश्चात् यवन शासकों का प्रादुर्भाव हुआ, गन्धार यवनों का मुख्य केन्द्र हुआ। गान्धार कला के विकास के परिणाम स्वरूप बौद्ध दर्शन में एक नई क्रान्ति आई जिसके अन्तर्गत बुद्ध की प्रतिमा का अभाव तीव्रता से अनुभूत होने लगा क्योंकि समाज की रुचि और प्रवृत्ति भक्तिवाद को अपना रही थी। ब्रजभूमि में भागवत सम्प्रदाय जड़ें जमा रहा था, कृष्ण बलरामादि की प्रतिमाएँ तथा मन्दिर अस्तित्व में आ रहे थे। तीर्थयात्राओं का प्रचलन बढ़ रहा था। केवल इतना ही नहीं, दूसरे नास्तिक् सम्प्रदाय जैन आदि ने भी तीर्थङ्करों की प्रतिमाएँ स्थापित कर ली थीं। ऐसी परिस्थितियों में बौद्धों का एक वर्ग अपने आराध्य के अङ्कन के लिए व्यग्र हो उठा किन्तु पूर्व प्रवाहित धारा की दिशा मोड़ना सरल नहीं होता है। ऐसा क्रान्तिकारी कदम राजा या शासन की ओर से ही उठाया जा सकता है। कुषाण काल में बौद्धों को सत्ता का वरद हस्त प्राप्त हुआ। तत्कालीन राजा कनिष्क ने अपने सिक्कों पर देवताओं के समान बुद्ध का चित्राङ्कन किया। ब्राह्मण धर्म के अनुकरण पर बुद्ध को महापुरुष के स्थान पर दैवी-प्रतिभा से आविष्ट मान लिया गया तथा भगवान् के स्तर पर प्रतिष्ठित किया गया। बुद्ध को भगवान् के पद पर आसीन कराने में भक्ति-भावना प्रधान रही। शरीरधारी सत्ता के प्रति भक्ति के वशीभूत हो कलाकारों ने प्रतीकों के स्थान पर बौद्ध प्रतिमा को मान्यता दी और कुछ ही शताब्दियों में भारतीय चित्र एवं मूर्ति कला बौद्ध प्रतिमाओं से ओत-प्रोत हो गई।

बुद्ध-प्रतिमा का प्रथम निर्माण इसी काल में हुआ, ऐसी मान्यता है किन्तु सभी विद्वान् इस मत के समर्थक नहीं हैं। वे मानते हैं कि मथुरा में बुद्ध की प्रतिमा का आविर्भाव स्वतन्त्र रूप से और गान्धार कला के उद्भव के पूर्व हो चुका था। ईसा पूर्व द्वितीय शताब्दी तक बुद्धभक्ति के विकास के साथ ही बुद्ध प्रतिमाओं का निर्माण भी

अधिक हुआ। एक बौद्ध परम्परा के अनुसार जब तथागत त्रायस्त्रिंश लोक गए थे तब प्रसेनजित् ने उनकी गोशीर्ष-चन्दन की प्रतिमा बनाई थी जो प्रथम बुद्ध-प्रतिमा थी। यह प्रतिमा जैतवन में बहुत दिनों तक रही।[26] प्रतिमा-निर्माण में सम्भवतः अङ्गविद्या में वर्णित महापुरुष-लक्षण, हृदय में बुद्ध के प्रति पूर्णभक्तिभाव तथा मस्तिष्क में रूपायित तथागत की ध्यान-मुद्रा—तीनों के समन्वित रूप ने सहायता प्रदान की होगी। बौद्ध प्रतिमाओं को क्रमशः अपार लोकप्रियता मिली और बुद्ध की विशालकाय मूर्तियों का बहुलता से निर्माण हुआ। भगवान् बुद्ध की ये प्रतिमाएँ विश्व की चिरन्तन कृतियों में गिनी गईं। बुद्ध-मूर्तियों के निर्माण की दृष्टि से कुषाणकालीन सारनाथ एवम् अजन्ता की गुफाओं की चर्चा करना भी अनिवार्य है।

इसी क्रम में एक और तथ्य स्पष्ट होता है कि यज्ञों के सम्पादन में केवल द्विजों का अधिकार था किन्तु बुद्ध के उपदेशों में, आध्यात्मिकता में मानव-मात्र का समान रूप से अधिकार माना गया। बुद्ध के इस वचन से भी समाज को वैदिक साहित्य और संस्कृति के प्रति अश्रद्धा हुई। फलस्वरूप वैदिकों ने यज्ञ-याग त्याग कर बुद्ध को पूजास्पद माना। आध्यात्मिक विचारधारा श्रुतिविहित यज्ञ से विरत हो मूर्ति पर केन्द्रित हुई। यज्ञ की जिस वेदी पर अदृश्य वरुण देवता को हवि प्रदान की जाती थी, उस पर वरुण का मूर्तिकरण होने लगा। कारण कि यज्ञों से उदासीन व्यक्ति ध्यान की ओर आकृष्ट हो चुका था और ध्यान शून्य में केन्द्रित करना कठिन है। मन को केन्द्रित करने का उत्तम उपाय मूर्ति-प्रयोग में देखा जा सकता है।

निष्कर्ष रूप में कहा जा सकता है कि बुद्ध ने वातावरण को सत्य एवं कल्याणकारी आचरण के गौरवपूर्ण उद्घोष से मण्डित किया। उन्होंने समाज को बताया कि धनी एवं सवर्णी तथा निर्धन एवं निम्नजातीय सब एक हैं। न तो उच्च वर्ण में जन्म लेने से कोई ब्राह्मण है और न नीची जाति में जन्म लेने से शूद्र। व्यक्ति अपने कर्मों से ब्राह्मण या शूद्र होता है। यज्ञ-सदृश किसी पद्धति विशेष का उपयोग करके पूर्णता को नहीं प्राप्त किया जा सकता है। शुभ कर्मों से कोई भी व्यक्ति पूर्णता प्राप्त कर सकता है। आवश्यकता है स्वयम् अपना दीपक बनने की, सत्य को दृढ़ता के साथ पकड़े रहने की, उसी में जन्म की सार्थकता है, उसी में बुद्धत्व की प्राप्ति है।

सन्दर्भ-सङ्केत

1. बोधिसत्त्व का अर्थ है ज्ञानसम्पन्न सन्त।
2. बुद्ध का अर्थ है प्रकाश देने वाला।
3. ते ह नाकं महिमानः सचन्त यत्र पूर्वे साध्याः सन्ति देवाः॥ ऋग्वेद 10.90.16
4. पालि वाङ्मय के प्राचीनतम ग्रन्थ सुत्तनिपात में कहा गया है कि—

   सो बोधिसत्तो रतनवरो अतुल्यो।
   मनुस्सलो के हितसुखाय जातो।
   सक्यानं गामे जनपदे लुम्बिनेय्य॥
5. बौद्ध संघाचा परिचय, पृ० 154

6. कवि जयदेव ने गीतगोविन्द में कहा है—

   निन्दसि यज्ञविधेरहह श्रुतिजातम् ।
   सदयहृदयदर्शितपशुघातम् ।
   केशवधृतबुद्धशरीर जय जगदीश हरे ॥

7. सुत्तनिपात,1060
8. सुत्तनिपात,846
9. अंगुत्तरनिकाय,सुत्तनिपात
10. आनन्द—कथं मयं भन्ते तथागतस्स सरीरे परिपज्जामाति ।

    बुद्ध—चातुम्महापथे रञ्ञो चक्कवतिस्स थूयं करोति ।

    एवं चातुमहापथे तथागतस्स थूयो कातब्बो ॥
11. बौद्ध दर्शन एवं बौद्ध साहित्य में प्रतिपादित सिद्धान्तों में विश्वास रखने वाला सम्प्रदाय हीनयान है ।
12. सुधारणावादी महासांधिक बौद्धों का सम्प्रदाय महायान है ।
13. माता के गर्भ में बुद्ध के प्रवेश करते ही माता को श्वेत हस्ति के दर्शन हुए थे ।
14. सद्योजात बुद्ध सात पग चले थे,प्रत्येक पग के नीचे एक कमल खिला था ।
15. कुमार सिद्धार्थ ने घोड़े पर बैठ कर गृहत्याग किया जो महाभिनिष्क्रमण कहलाया ।
16. बिहार राज्य के गया नामक स्थान में एक पीपल के वृक्ष के नीचे कुमार सिद्धार्थ ने बोधि प्राप्त की और 'बुद्ध' कहलाए ।
17. बोधिवृक्ष के नीचे जिस चबूतरे या पत्थर पर बैठ कर सिद्धार्थ बुद्ध हुए,उसे वज्रासन कहा गया ।
18. बुद्ध का निवास-कक्ष गन्धकुटी है ।
19. बुद्ध द्वारा प्रयुक्त भिक्षापात्र ।
20. कुमार सिद्धार्थ का शिरोवस्त्र उष्णीष है ।
21. बुद्ध के मस्तक के पीछे दृश्यमान अलौकिक तेज प्रभामण्डल है ।
22. बुद्ध द्वारा सञ्चालित बौद्धधर्म-प्रवर्तन का कार्य धर्मचक्र है ।
23. बुद्ध के चरणचिह्न ।
24. बौद्धमत की मूलभूत आधारशिलाएँ त्रिरत्न—बुद्ध, धर्म, संघ ।
25. बुद्ध के मृत शरीर के अवशिष्ट अंश की समाधि स्तूप है ।
26. लेग फाश्येन,पृ.56-57

इलाहाबाद

SECTION III

Buddhist Philosophy

THE PROBLEM OF EXISTENCE AND NON-EXISTENCE IN BUDDHISM

Sanghasen Singh

One of the most debated problems during the period[1] of the Buddha was the question of existence and non-existence. It was debated whether the soul and the world are eternal (*Sassata* or *Śāśvata*) or are subject to decay and annihilation. There appears to have been two clear-cut schools of thought in this context during the period in question—the *Sassatavāda* (eternalism) and *Ucchedavāda* (annihilationism). The *Upaniṣadic, Jaina,* etc. fall under the former category, while *Lokāyata* and other materialistic schools of thought belong to the latter. The Buddha is reported to have kept himself aloof from the above-mentioned categories and resorted to the middle course. Though He propagated the non-soul doctrine, but still he believed that the life does not end with the death or passing away and continues even after that. Thus He accepted the continuity of life-process which lasts only when one attains the *Nibbāna* or *Nirvāṇa, i.e.,* the cessation of all sufferings and sorrows and the complete stopage of the cycle of life and death. In the context of the *loka* or the world, He thought that it was an endless process in whose case no one can specify its beginning and end (*anamataggo'yaṁ loko*). He accepted its changing nature and so also that of all elements related with the *loka* whether mental or material.

While emphasizing the real nature of the world, the Buddha described it to be subject to incessant change and in a state of constant flux. Thus everything in this world whether material or immaterial is impermanent and is constantly changing. To quote his own words *'Sabbe saṅkhārā aniccā', 'Aniccā vata saṅkhārā'*, etc., which tantamount to saying that all conditional things are phenomenal process, mental as well as material, that go to make up Saṁsāric plane of existence, are transient or impermanent.

The problem in question entails a detailed discussion on the definition and nature of impermanence and other related questions like common varying points of the theory of impermanence as defined in various Buddhist schools of thought and also its nature with the other two theories of *dukkha* or sufferings and *anattatā* or *anātmatā* or non-soulness. Finally, the justification for the aspirations to achieve *Nirvāṇa* in the wake of the fact that everything is imparmanent according to the Buddha needs a thorough probe in the light of the related problems that crop up in relation to the problem in question.

The Buddha is reported to have delivered His *First Sermon* designated to be the *Dhamma-cakka-pavattana Sutta* or the Discourse Revolving the Wheel of Law at Isipatana Migadāva indentified with a place at Sarnath near Varanasi. In His First Sermon, He clearly put forth the cardinal principles of His teaching and these are– *Dukkha* or Sufferings, *Dukkha-samudaya* or Cause of Sufferings, *Dukkha-nirodha* or Cessation of Sufferings and *Dukkha-nirodha-magga* or the Path Leading to the Cessation of Sufferings. These principles were designated as the Four Noble Truths *(Cattāri Ariya-saccāni* or *Catvāri Āryasatyāni*) by the Buddha Himself. Later in course of centuries detailed philosophical discussions and speculations developed on the very principles and thus the whole edifice of Buddhist Philosophy was created by those who professed Buddhism as their fundamental faith and by those who opposed it as the views of the heretical teacher/teachers.

The Buddha after the enlightenment realised that the very essential conditions of life, human as well as sub-human, without any exception were fraught with misery. Birth, old age, disease, death, sorrow, grief, wish, despair, in short, all that is born of attachment, is misery.[2] The discovery of this Truth on the part of the Buddha has been termed as a sort of *Pessimism* by the western critics of the Indian Philosophy (including the Buddhist Philosophy), but this is not an exception to Buddhism alone. Many Indian Philosophers have emphasized the role of *dukkha* or unpleasantness and consider it to be the basic truth of life. It is, however, a different matter that the Buddha, though realised it as a basic truth, yet at the same time sought and propagated the path leading to its cessation. Thus he turned pessimism into an optimism of the sort that led thousands and millions of Buddhists all over the world to renounce their households and lead the life of Buddhist mendicants.

The Buddha admitted that there exist both pleasures and pains, but he felt that the worldly pleasures appear as such only to the short-sighted people. Their transitoriness, the pains felt on their loss and the fears experienced lest they should be lost, and other evil consequences, make pleasures lose their charm and turn them into positive sources of fear and anxiety.

The diagnosis of this malady of suffering has been given by the Buddha in an altogether different way. He explains the origin of the life's evil in the light of His special conception of natural causation, *i.e.*, the *Pratītyasamutpāda*. According to it nothing is unconditional. That is to say the existence of everything depends on some conditions. As the existence of every event depends on some conditions, there must be something which being there our sorrow comes into existence. According to the Buddha, life's sufferings (old age, death, despair, grief, etc.) are there, because there is birth (jāti). If a man were not born, he would not have been subject to these miserable states. Birth again has its condition. It is the will to become (*bhava* or 'the disposition for becoming'), the force of the blind tendency or predisposition to be born, which causes our birth. The cause of the tendency to be born lies in our mental clinging to or grasping (*upādāna*) the objects of the world. This happens to be the condition responsible for our desire to be born. This clinging again is due to our thirst (*taṇhā* or *tṛṣṇā*) or craving to enjoy objects—sights, sounds, etc. We would not have any desire for objects, had we not tasted or experienced them before. Previous sense-experience, tinged with some pleasant feelings (*vedanā*), is, therefore, the cause of our thirst or craving. But sense-experience could not arise but for contact (*phassa or sparśa*), *i.e.*, contact of sense-organs with objects. This contact again would not arise, had there not been the six organs of cognition, the five senses and *manas* or mind (*ṣaḍāyatana*). These six again depend for their existence on the body-mind organism (*nāma-rūpa*), which constitutes the perceptible being of man. But this organism could not develop in the mother's womb and come into existence, if it were dead or devoid of consciousness (*viññāṇa*). But the consciousness that descends into the embryo in the mother's womb is only the effect of the impressions (*saṁskāra*) of our past existence. The last state of the past life, which initiates our present existence, contains in a concentrated manner the impressions of effects of all our past deeds. The impressions which make for rebirth are due to ignorance (*avidyā*) about truth. If the transitory, painful nature of the worldly existence were perfectly realized, there would not arise in us any *karma* resulting in rebirth. Ignorance, therefore, is the root cause of impressions or tendencies that cause rebirth.

To be precise, then (1) suffering in life is due to (2) birth, which is due to (3) the will to be born, which is due to (4) our mental clinging to objects. Clinging again is due to (5) thirst or desire for objects. This again is due to (6) sense-experience which, is due to (7) sense-object-contact, which again is due to (8) the six organs of cognition. These organs are dependent on (9) the embryonic organism (Composed of mind and body), which again could not develop without (10) some initial consciousness, which again hails from (11) the impressions of the experience of past life, which lastly are due to (12) ignorance of Truth.

In this way the twelve links in the chain of causation have been explained in the Buddhist scriptures. The order and number of the links are not always the same in all the sermons of the Buddha, but the above has come to be regarded as the full and standard account of the matter. It has been popularized among the Buddhists by various epithets, such as the twelve sources (*dvādaśa nidāna*), the wheel of rebirth (*bhava-cakra*)[3] and so on.

Some later Buddhist philosophers like Aniruddhācariya[4] interpreted the twelve links to cover the past, the present and the future life which are causally connected, so that present life can be conveniently explained with reference to its past condition and its future effect. The twelve links are, therefore, arranged with reference to the three periods in the following way preceeding from cause to effect:

(1) Ignorance (*avidyā*) (2) Impressions (*Saṅkhāra* or *saṁskāra*)	**Past Life**

(3) The initial consciousness of the embryo (*viññāna or vijñāna*)
(4) Body and mind, the embryonic organism (*nāma-rūpa*)
(5) Six organs of knowledge (*saḍāyatana*)
(6) Sense-contact (*phassa* or *sparśa*)
(7) Sense-experience (*vedanā*)
(8) Thirst (*taṇhā* or *tṛṣṇā*)
(9) Clinging (*upādāna*)

} **Present Life**

(10) Tendency to be born (*bhava*)
(11) Rebirth (*jāti*)
(12) Old age, death, etc. (*jarā-maraṇa*)

} **Future Life**[5]

The Third Noble Truth that there is cessation of suffering, follows from the Second Truth that misery depends on some conditions. If these conditions are removed, misery would cease. When the perfect control of passions and constant contemplation of Truth lead a practioner through the four stages of concentration to perfect wisdom, he is no longer under the sway of worldly attachment. He has broken the fetters that bound him to the world. He is, therefore, free, liberated. He is said then to have become an Arahanta or Arhat or Perfect or Liberated Person. The state is known as *Arahatta* or *Arhatva* Arahantaship. This is described in early Buddhist scriptures as the sumum bonum of life. But, it appears, in due course of time another term was coined which is known as *Nibbāna* or *Nirvāṇa* (the extinction of passions and, therefore, also of misery) which became very popular subsequently and thus newer and newer meanings and interpretations were added to the original concept.

It should be very clearly noted here that the specific methods and practices have been prescribed by the Buddha for the attainment of *Nibbāna* or *Nirvāṇa*. It is essential that for the attainment of perfect, clear and steady knowledge of the Fourfold Truth one has to withdraw all his attention from outside and even from other ideas within, and concentrate it wholly on repeated reasoning and contemplation of the Truths in all their aspects. But once wisdom has been permanently achieved, through concentrated thought, the liberated person should neither always remain rapt in meditation nor wholly withdraw from active life.[6]

Thus it is evidently clear that *Nibbāna* or *Nirvāṇa* does not mean extinction of existence. The etymological meaning of *Nibbāna* is devoid of passions or desires *(Ni+bāna)* and that of *Nirvāṇa* is 'blown out'. The metaphor of a 'blown out light' has been used and the liberated one is sometimes compared to it.

Nibbāna or *Nirvāṇa* is a guarantee that rebirth, whose conditions have been destroyed, will not occur. *Nibbāna* also positively means that one who has attained it enjoys perfect peace even in this very life so long as he lives after the attainment of *Nibbāna*. This peace is not like any of the pleasures born of the fulfilment of desires. It is, therefore, said to be beyond worldly pleasures and pains. It is, in fact, a state of serenity, equanimity and passionless self-possession. It cannot be described in terms of ordinary experiences. The best way of understanding it in the light of our imperfect experience is to think of it as a relief from all painful experience from which we suffer. This may be understood, though in a limited way, because all of us have experience at least of temporary feelings of relief from some pain or other, such as freedom from disease, debt, slavery, imprisonment.[7] Nāgasena, one of the later teachers of Buddhism did explain the nature of *Nirvāṇa* to his disciple, Greek King Menander (Milinda). He conveyed to him the idea of the blissful character of *Nirvāṇa* with a series of metaphors: *Nibbāna* is profound like an ocean, lofty like a mountain peak, sweet like honey, etc.[8] But all these, as Nāgasena points out, can scarcely convey to the imperfect man the idea of what that thing is. Reasoning and metaphor are of little avail for convincing a blind man what colour is like.

The Fourth Noble Truth, as seen already, lays down that there is a path (*magga* or *mārga*) – which the Buddha followed and others can similarly follow – to reach a state free from misery. Clues regarding this path are derived from the knowledge of the chief conditions that cause misery. The path recommended by the Buddha consists of eight steps or rules and is, therefore, called the Eightfold Noble Path (*Ariyo Aṭṭhaṅgiko Maggo*)[9]. This gives in a nutshell the essentials of Buddhist Ethics. The noble path consists in the acquisition of the following eight lofty steps of sanctification—

Right Views (*Sammādiṭṭhi* or *Samyagdṛṣṭi*): As ignorance, with its consequences, namely, wrong views (*mithyādiṭṭhi*) about the self and the world, is the root cause of our sufferings, it is natural that the first step to moral reformation should be the acquisition of right views or the knowledge of Truth. Right View is defined as the correct knowledge about the Four Noble Truths. It is the knowledge of these truths alone, and not any theoratical speculation regarding nature and self, which, according to the Buddha, helps moral reformation, and leads us towards the goal, *i.e.*, *Nibbāna* or *Nirvāṇa*.

Right Determination (*Sammāsaṅkappa* or *Samyakasaṅkalpa*): A mere knowledge of the Truths would be useless unless one resolves to reform life in their light. The moral aspirant is asked, therefore, to renounce worldliness (all attachment to the world), to give up ill-feeling towards others and desist from doing any harm to them. These three constitute the contents of right resolve.

Right Speech (*Sammāvācā* or *Samyagvāk*): Right Resolve should not remain a mere pious wish, but must issue forth into action. Right Resolve should be able to guide and control our speech, to begin with. The result would be right speech consisting in abstention from lying, slander, unkind words and frivolous talk.

Right Conduct (*Sammākammanta* or *Samyakkarmānta*): Right Resolve should end in right action or good conduct and not stop merely with good speech. Right conduct includes the Five *Sikkhāpadas* (*Śikṣāpadas*), *i.e.*, the five vows for desisting from killing, stealing, sensuality, lying and intoxication along with the rest of the Five *Sikkhāpadas*, *i.e.*, vows for abstaining from after-noon meal, merry-making (like dancing, singing, playing musical instruments, etc.), self-beautification (use of scents, ointments, cosmetics, etc.), use of high and costly seats, berths, etc. and acceptence of silver and gold.

Right Livelihood (*Sammā-ājīva* or *Samyagājīva*): Renouncing bad speech and bad actions, one should earn his livelihood by honest means. The necessity of this rule lies in showing that even for the sake of maintaining one's life, one should not take to forbidden means but work in consistency with good determination.

Right Effort (*Sammāvāyāma* or *Samyagvyāyāma*): Whie a person tries to live a reformed life, through right views, determination, speech, action and livelihood, he is constantly knocked off the right path by old evil ideas which were deep-rooted in the mind as also by fresh ones which constantly arise. One connot progress steadily unless he maintains a constant effort to root out old evil thoughts, and prevent evil thoughts from arising anew. Moreover, as the mind cannot be kept empty, he should constantly endeavour also to fill the mind with good ideas, and retain such ideas in the mind. This Fourfold constant endeavour, negative and positive, is called right efffort. This rule points out that even one high up on the path cannot afford to take a moral holiday without running the risk of slipping down.

Right Mindfulness (*Sammāsati* or *Samyaksmṛti*): The necessity of constant vigilance is further stressed in this rule, which lays down that the aspirant should constantly bear in mind the things he has already learnt. He should constantly remember and contemplate the body as body, sensations as sensations, mind as mind, mental states as mental states. About any of these he should not think, "This am I", or "This is mine".[10] This difficult excercise has to be constantly done as false ideas about body, etc. have become so deep-rooted in us and our behaviours based on these false notions have become more or less instinctive. If we are not mindful, we behave as though the body, the mind, the sensations and the mental states are permanent and all-abiding. Hence there arises attachment to such things and grief over their loss, and we become subject to bondage and misery. But contemplation on the frail, perishable, loathsome nature of these, helps us to remain free from attachment and grief. This is the necessity of constant mindfulness about Truth.[11]

Right Concentration (*Sammāsamādhi* or *Samyak-samādhī*): One who has successfully guided his life in the light of the last seven steps or rules and thereby freed himself from all passions and evil thoughts is fit to enter step by step into the four deeper and deeper stages of concentration that gradually take him to the goal of his long and arduous journey, *i.e.*, the cessation of suffering. He concentrates his pure and unruffled mind on reasoning (*Vitakka* or *Vitarka*) and investigation (*Vicāra*) regarding the Truths, and enjoys in this state, joy and ease born on detachment and pure thought. This is the first stage of intent meditation (*Jhāna* or *Dhyāna*).

When this concentration is successful, belief in the fourfold truth arises dispelling all doubts and, therefore, making reasoning and investigation unnecessary. From this results the second stage of concentration, in which there are joy, peace and internal tranquility born of intense, unruffled contemplation. There is in this stage a consciousness of this joy and peace too.

In the next stage attempt is made by him to initiate an attitude of indifference, to be able to detach himself even from the joy of concentration. From this results the third deeper kind of concentration, in which one experiences perfect equanimity, coupled with an experience of bodily ease. He is yet conscious of this ease and equanimity, though indifferent to the joy of concentration.

Lastly, he tries to put away even this consciousness of ease and equanimity and all the sense of joy and elation he previously had. He attains thereby the fourth state of concentration, a state of perfect equanimity, indifference and self-possession – without pain, without ease. Thus he attains the desired goal of cessation of all suffering, he attains Arahantaship or *Nibbāna.*[12]

To sum up the essential points of the Eightfold Path it may be noted first that the Path consists of three main things — Conduct (*Sīla*), Concentration (*Samādhī*) and Trancendental Wisdom (*Paññā* or *Prajñā*) harmoniously cultivated. The Buddha explicitly states in one of his discourses that virtue and wisdom purify each other and the two are inseparable.[13] In the Eightfold Path one starts with 'Right Views'– a mere intellectual apprehension of the Fourfold Truth. The mind is not yet purged of the previous wrong ideas and the passions or wrong emotions arising therefrom; moreover, the old habits of thinking, speaking and acting also continue still. Repeated contemplation of what is true and good, training of the will and emotion accordingly, through steadfast determination and passionless behaviour, gradually achieve the harmonious personality in which thought and will and emotion are all thoroughly cultured and purified in the light of the Truth. The last step of perfect concentration is thus made possible by the removal of all obstacles. The result of this unhampered concentration on the Truth is perfect insight or wisdom, to which the riddle of existence stands clearly revealed once for all. Ignorance and desire are cut at their roots and the source of misery vanishes. Perfect wisdom, perfect goodness and perfect equanimity-complete relief from suffering — are simulteneously attained, in *Nibbāna* or *Nirvāṇa.*[14]

After the description of the Four Noble Truths, the four cardinal principles which the Buddha is reported to have taught in His First Sermon itself, it becomes all the more imperative to analysise the philosophical implications of these Truths, particularly the Second Truth which may be defined as the Theory of Dependent Origination or Conditional Existence of Things.

The Second Truth, i.e. *Dukkha-samudaya* as it has been already evident culminates in Theory of *Paṭiccasamuppāda* or *Pratītyasamutpāda*. According to this theory, there is a spontaneous and universal law of causation which conditions the appearance of all events, mental and physical. This law (*Dhamma* or *Dharma*) works automatically without the help of any conscious guide. In accordance with it, whenever a particular event (the cause) appears, it is followed by another particular event (the effect). "On getting the cause, the effect arises". The existence of everything is conditional, dependent on a cause. Nothing happens fortuitously or by chance. This is called the Theory of Dependent Origination (*Paṭiccasamuppāda* or *Pratītyasamutpāda*).[15] This view, as per the Buddha's own words, avoids two extreme views – on the one hand, eternalism or the theory that some reality eternally exists independently of any condition and, on the other hand, nihilism (annihilationism) or the theory that something existing can be annihilated or can cease to be. The Buddha claims to hold the middle view,[16] namely that everything that we perceive possesses an existence but is dependent on something else, and that thing in turn does not perish without leaving some effect.

The Buddha had designated the *Paṭiccasamuppāda* the *Dhamma*, as he atteched so much importance to the understanding of this theory. He is reported to have remarked, "Let us put aside questions of the Beginning and the End. I will teach you the *Dhamma* (*Paṭiccasamuppāda*): That being thus, this comes to be. From the coming to be of that, this arises. That being absent, this does not happen. From the cessation of that, this ceases". He further asserted, "He who sees the *Paṭiccasamuppāda* sees the *Dhamma*, and he who sees the *Dhamma* sees the *Paṭiccasamuppāda*."[17] On another occasion the Buddha compared the *Paṭiccasamuppāda* to a staircase, by mounting which one can look round on the world and see it with the eyes of a Buddha.

The Buddha traces the cause of all troubles in one's failure to grasp this standpoint.[18]

The theory of *Karma* (Deed, Action) plays very important role in Buddhism. It is, in fact, only an aspect of the doctrine of *Paṭiccasamuppāda*. The present existence of an individual is the effect of its past and its future would be the effect of its present existence. This has been already seen very clearly in connection with the explanation of the origin of suffering in the light of the theory of Dependent Origination. The Law of *Karma* is only a special form of the more general law of causation as conceived by the Buddha. This law has been considered so profound by Him that it is supposed to control and guide all affairs of the humankind. Its position in Buddhism is as profound as the position of a Supreme Diety in theistic religions.

The *Paṭiccasamuppāda* or the Theory of Dependent Origination also yields the Buddhist theory of transitory nature of things. All things, according to the teachings of the Buddha, are subject to change and decay. As everything originates from some condition, it disappears when the condition ceases to be. Whatever has a beginning has also an end. Hence the Buddha's words, "Know that whatever exists arises from causes and conditions and is in every respect impermanent."[19] On another occasion the Buddha remarked, "That which seems everlasting will perish, that which is high will be laid low; where meeting is, parting will be; where birth is, death will come".[20]

It will not be out of place here, I believe, to elaborate the point regarding transitoriness of life and worldly things which the Buddha is reported to have logically perfected into the doctrine of impermanence. The later Buddhist teachers and philosophers developed it further into a theory of momentariness (*Kṣaṇikavāda*) which means not only that everything has conditional and, therefore, non-permanent existence, but also that things last not even for short periods of time, but exist for one partless moment only. This doctrine of momentariness of all things is suppported by later writers with elaborate arguments. The following may be cited as one of them – The criterion of the existence (*sattā*) of a thing is its capacity to produce some effect.[21] A non-existent thing, like a hare's horn, cannot produce any effect. Now, from this criterion of existence, it may be deduced that a thing having existence must be momentary. If, for example, a thing like a seed be not accepted to be momentary, but thought to be lasting for more than one moment, then we have to show that it is capable of producing an effect during each moment it exists. Again, if it really remains the same unchanging thing during these moments, then it should be able to produce the same effect at every one of those moments. But we find that this is not the case. The seed in the house does not produce the seedling which is generated by a seed sown in the field. The seed in the house cannot then be the same as that in the field. But it may be said that though the seed does not actually produce the same effect always, it always has the potentiality to produce it, and this potentiality becomes kenetic in the presence of suitable auxiliary conditions like earth, water, etc. Therefore, the seed is always the same. But this defence is weak, because then it is virtually confessed that the seed of the first moment is not the cause of the seedling, but that the seed modified by the other conditions really causes the effect. Hence the seed must be admitted to have changed. In this way it may be shown regarding everything that it does not stay unchanged during any two moments, because it does not produce the identical effect during both moments. Hence everything lasts only for a moment.

Though almost all authors of Buddhist Philosophy clearly and unequivocally admit that *Kṣaṇikavāda* or the theory of momentariness is a later development, yet they are of the view that it has really brought out the real idea contained in the theory of impermanence. They assert that the incessant change spoken of is a change occuring in every moment. That is to say, all phenomena of the world, mental and non-mental, undergo changes every moment. As regards the motive power behind this universal change, the Buddha is reported to have said that all things are endowed with four characteristics, namely *utpāda* or origination, *sthiti* or staying, *jarā* or decay (*i.e.*, advancing in age) and *nirodha* or destruction. It is said that a thing cannot continue to exist in the same condition for two consecutive points of time and undergoes changes in an endless series.

Though a lot has been said in favour or against the theory of momentariness, but one fallacy merits mention here. This fallacy lies in the fact that the doctrine of momentariness presupposes the existence of even the smallest point of time (designated as *Kṣaṇa*) which in itself is contrary to the basic idea of *Anicca* doctrine (*i.e.*, the doctrine of Universal Flux). The *Anicca* doctrine as taught by the Buddha speaks of continuous process, where there is no scope of any pause or halt even for the slightest point of time which may be defined or which may elude all attempts of fixing any particular definition. Thus to derive the doctrine of momentariness from *Aniccavāda* is misplaced and untenable.

It has been observed and conclusively proved beyond any doubt that the law of change is universal; neither man, nor any other being, animate or inanimate, is exempt from it. Thus consistently with His theories of conditional existence and universal change, the Buddha denies the existence of soul. The Upaniṣadics, Jainas, etc. believe that in man there is an abiding substance called the soul *(ātmā)*, which persists through changes that overcome the body, exists before birth and after death, and migrates from one body to another. Here, in this context the point worth notice is the fact that though the Buddha did not accept the existence of such an abiding substance in the body, yet he held the continuity of a person through different births, or even through the different states of childhood, youth and old age. Though denying the continuity of an identical substance in man, the Buddha does not deny the continuity of the stream of successive states that compose his life. Life is an unbroken series of states: each of these states depends on the condition just preceding and gives rise to the one just succeeding it. The continuity of the life-series is, therefore, based on a causal connection running through the different states. This continuity is often explained with the example of a lamp burning throughout the night. The flame of each moment is dependent on its own conditions and different from that of another moment which is dependent on other conditions. Yet there is an unbroken succession of the different flames. Again, as from one flame another may be lighted, and though the two are different, they are connected causally, similarly, the end-state of this life may cause the beginning of the next. Rebirth[22] is, therefore, not transmigration, *i.e.*, the migration of the same soul into another body: it is the causation of the next life by the present one. The conception of a soul is thus replaced here by that of an unbroken stream of consciousness.[23] As the present state of consciousness inherits its characters from previous ones, the past in a way continues in the present, throught its effect. Memory thus becomes explicable even without a soul. This theory of the non-existence of soul *(Anattavāda)* plays a very important role in making the teachings of the Buddha as clear and understandable as an *āmalaka* fruit on the palm of a hand.[24] He, therefore, repeatedly exhorted his disciples to shun and give up the false view about the self. He made it clear that those who suffer from the illusion of the self, do not understand the reality. It is out of their sheer ignorance that they proclaim that they love the soul and go in for propitiating soul by way of making the soul happy through the attainment of the so-called salvation. He likened this act of the person with the falling in love with the most beautiful maiden in the land though she had never been seen nor known.[25] Or, it is like building a stair-case for mounting a palace which has never been seen.[26]

The man or the human personality for that matter is only a conventional name for a collection of different constituents[27] technically known as *khandha-s* or *skandha-s* (*upādāna khandha-s* to be more precise). These *khandhas* are five in number, but are broadly divided into two parts, *i.e.*, *rūpa* and *nāma* (the meterial qualities and the consciousness along with its associates or *saṅkhāra-s*). These five *khandha-s* constitute the human form in the same way as wheels, axles, shafts, etc. constitute a chariot.[28] The existence of man depends on this collection and it dissolves when the collection breaks up. The soul or the ego denotes nothing more than this collection of different units which are undergoing constant change. To sum up, the man, as perceived from without and within, is analysable into a collection of the following five groups (*panca-khandhas*) of the changing elements namely (1) *rūpa* (form) consisting of the different factors which we perceive in this body having form, (2) *vedanā* (feelings of pleasure, pain and indifference), (3) *saññā* or *sañjñā* (perception including understanding and naming), (4) *Saṁkhāra-s* or *Saṁskāra-s* (predispositions or tendencies generated by the impressions of past experience, and (5) *viññāna* or *vijñāna* (consciousness).

In the whole analysis of the mind and matter (*nāma* and *rūpa*) one more factor merits mention, which plays important part in the harmonious functioning of the same. It is the Theory of Relations. The mind and matter are, in fact, the *Dharma-s* (states) which are opposite in nature. They, however, function together harmoniously in accordance with the Law of Relations.

In the later development of the Buddhist Philosophy, the role of the *Sarvāstivādins* and the *Vātsīputrīyas* have a direct bearing on the problem in question. According to the *Sarvāstivādins,* the things are substantially permanent and the change relates to modes or qualities which do not affect its intrinsic unity. Change is, in fact, acceptable to the *Sarvāstivādins,* but their views differ substantially and considerably. To cite an example, it may be stated that several sub-schools of the *Vaibhāṣika,* a sect of the *Sarvāstivāda* hold the view that the three divisions of time–past, present and future–are also existent and as such the things are also ever-existent. Accordingly the *Sarvāstivāda Ācāryas* have distinguished and defined four theories of change and these are as under–

1. *Bhāvānyathātva* (A Change of Existence):

Ācārya Dharmatrāta was of the view that past, present and future have to be differentiated on account of the non-identity of *Bhāva* (existence) and not of *dravya* (object).

2. *Lakṣanānyathātva* (A Change of Aspects):

Bhadanta Ghoṣaka held the view that the *Dharmas* (states) in their transition from past to present and present to future manifest changes in characteristics only.

3. *Avasthānyathātva* (A Change of Condition):

According to Ācārya Vasumitra, the past, present and future of a *Dharma* (state) are shown by the difference in condition. There is only a change of conditions and not a change of objects.

4. *Anyonyānyathātva* (A Change of Relative Existence):

Ācārya Buddhadeva held the view that an element in the course of time receives this or that denomination on account of its relation to the former and the next moment.

The *Vātsīputrīyas* represent a sect of Buddhism on the one hand and a school of Buddhist Philosophy on the other. They held the view that the Buddha admitted the existence of an impermanent soul quite different from the Upaniṣadic soul, which is eternal and changeless. The *Vātsīputrīyas* designated their changing soul as *'Pudgala'*, which differs from the *'Anatta, (Anātman)* of the doctrine of

Anattavāda of the Buddha. Thus it appears that the *Pudgalavādins* do preserve the essence of the *Anatta*-doctrine apart from their assertion that the *Pudgala* exists. They were, however, careful enough in defining the relation of *Pudgala* to the *skandha-s* in such a way that an erroneous belief in a self was put aside. They made it categorically clear that the person is neither identical with the *skandhas*, nor different from them. Thus the essence of the Buddha's teachings on *Anattavāda* has been preserved by the *Pudgalavādins*.

REFERENCES & NOTES

1. It is generally believed that the Buddha whose family name was Siddhattha or Siddhārtha and Gautama being the name of his clan, was born in a royal family of Kapilavastu on the foothills of the Himalayas now located in southern part of Nepal. According to the historians, he flourished in the 6th-5th Centuries B.C, Two dates are ascribed to the event of his birth. These are 563 B.C. and 567 B.C. The Simhalese tradition on the other hand holds that He was born on the fullmoon day of Vesākha in the 624th year before the birth of Christ.
2. Cf. *Dīghanikāya* (*Sutta* No.22).
3. Some devout Buddhists particularly of Tibetan Buddhism remind themselves of this teaching of the Buddha by turning wheels which are made to symbolize the wheel of causation. This forms a part of their daily prayers in the same manner as some resort to the practice of telling beads.
4. Vide *Abhidhammatthasaṅgaho*, 8.6.
5. It may be pointed out here that the Buddha had made a great contribution in establishing that the external phenomenon of life or the living organism is due to an internal impetus of desire, conscious or unconscious. The impact of this assertion of the Buddha may be traced negatively and positively in both Darwinians and anti-Darwinians respectively. For further detailes see the writings of French philosopher Bergson.
6. *Nibbāna* or *Nirvāṇa* is attainable in this very life. In fact, two types of *Nibbāna* have been described in Buddhist scriptures. These are *Sopadhisesa Nibbāna* (during the present life) and *Nirupadhisesa Nibbāna* (after the expiry of the body). It is also evident form the life of the Buddha Himself. Even after the attainment of *Nibbāna,* He continued an active life of forty-five years and passed away at the age of eighty. During the period since He attained *Nibbāna* and the moment of His passing away He established His order of monks and taught the Law to His disciples.
7. Vide *Sāmaññaphala Sutta* (*Dīghanikāya*).
8. Vide *Milindapañha*.
9. For full discussion See *Dīghanikīya* (*Sutta* No.22), *Majjhimanikāya, Dhammapada* *(Magga-vagga),* etc.

10. Vide *Majjhimanikāya*, Part one.
11. The Buddha's detailed instructions as to how such contemplation is to be practised is given in *Dīghanikāya, Sutta* No. 22.
12. For detailed treatment of the *jhānas* see *Poṭṭhapāda Sutta* and *Samaññaphala Sutta* of the *Dīghanikāya*.
13. Cf. *Soṇadaṇḍa Sutta* of the *Dīghanikāya*.
14. The four stages, progressively attained by the initiate, on the path or stream leading to *Nibbāna* or *Nirvāṇa* are distinguished as the following stages of (1) a *Sotāpanna* or *Śrotāpanna* (one who has entered the stream, the path), (2) a *Sakadāgāmī* or *Sakṛdāgāmin* (one who will return only once again to this world), (3) an *Anāgāmī* (one who will not return to this world), and (4) an *Arahanta* or *Arhat* (Liberated or perfect Person).
15. cf. *Visuddhimaggo*, Chapter XVII. Etymologically *pratītya*=getting (some thing), *samutpāda*= origination (of something else).
16. Vide *Saṁyuttanikāya*, XXII.
17. *Cf. Mahānidāna Sutta.*
18. *Ibid.*
19. Vide *Mahāparinibbāna Sutta.*
20. Vide *Dhammapada.*
21. *Arthakriyākāritva-lakṣaṇam sat.*
22. Rebirth is, in fact, not the proper or suitable word to express the idea of re-becoming (*punabbhava* or *punarbhava*) in Buddhism. The idea of *punarjanma* or rebirth or transmigration of an identical or same soul is, therefore, ruled out in the Buddhistic perspectives.
23. William James holds the same view in this context. It is quite likely that he derived the tenets of his philosophical thoughts from the Buddhist scriptures. It is a known fact that William James happened to be one of the pioneers of Sanskrit/Pali studies among the European scholars.
24. *Hastāmalakavat.*
25. *Cf. Poṭṭhapāda Sutta* of *Dīghanikāya.*
26. *Ibid.*
27. *Ibid.*
28. *Cf. Milindapañha.*

Delhi

PHILOSOPHIC ROOTS OF THE CONCEPT OF TOLERANCE* (WITH SPECIAL REFERENCE TO BUDDHIST PHILOSOPHY)

Kewal Krishan Mittal

To anyone who throws even a cursory glance on the known History of India, the fact is obvious that Tolerance of the opnions of others, different from one's own, comes very natural to the Indian mind and behaviour. We, as a nation, have practised tolerance as a matter of habit, throughout all the centuries gone by, a history of which is known to us today. But what may not be so obvious and needs a little bit of investigation is the fact as to what has been the reason of the emergence of Tolerance as a trait of Indian character. The reason, to me it seems, is not far to seek. We are bound to find it if we care to look at the philosophic roots of the concept of Tolerance.

On analysis, the Concept of Tolerance is seen to be embedded in the idea of unity in diversity, that is a recognition of difference together with a common basis of some sort and the same, in my considered opinion, is the deliverence of each one of the ancient systems of Indian philosophy . That, of course, is so if we understand Indian philosophy properly and do not go by the oversimplifications indulged into even by the greatest of our philosophers to show that Indian philosophy is an Absolutism of some sort, under the influence of the western orientalists. I have urged against that tendency at length in my book *Materialism in Indian Thought*. The very opening paragraph of which has a reference to the same. I quote that passage, "Some Modern Scholars, Indian as well as Western have created an

This paper was presented at a Seminar on "The Concept of and the Role of Tolerance in Indian Culture"organised By The Dr.Radha Krishnan Institute For Advanced Study In Philosophy, University Of Madras, Madras From March 2-5, 1983.

impression that Indian thought is pre-eminently spirtiual or idealistic in its outlook and charater."Philosophy in India is essentially spiritual," says Radhakrishnan, for example. And it is so, he thinks, because 'the spiritual motive dominates life in India.' "The Indian mind," he goes on to add, "has been traditionally exercised over the questions of the nature of the Godhead, the end of life and the relation of the individual to the Universal Soul." Again, 'in India, the interest of philosophy is in the self of man.' "The speculative mind is more synthetic...the brooding East, frequently employed as a term of ridicule, is not altogether without its truth." "If we put the subjective interest of the Indian mind alongwith its tendency to arrive at synthetic vision, we shall see how monistic idealism becomes the truth of things," he concludes.

I have taken the liberty to do the most unusal thing of quoting from my own writing in order to show that I am aware of 'the fact that the idea of unity in Diversity' is delivered by each one of the accredited systems of thought in each one's own characteristic way. Here, for the purpose of this paper, as a contribution to this seminar, I will breifly lay down the arguement on behalf of Buddhist philosophy. But before doing so, let me state in a sentence or two each the position, as I see, obtains in the case of *Vedānta, Sāmkhya Yoga, Jaina* Philosophy, *Nyāya-Vaiśeṣika* and the *Cārvāka Darśana.* In the case of *Vedānta,* one needs to remember four important statements. One from the *Ṛgveda---'Ekam sad viprāḥ bahudhā vandanti....'* (Truth is one but is described by the learned in various ways); Second from the *Upaniṣads "Tadaikṣat bahu syām..."* (That one thought, let me be many); The third from the *Brahmasūtra,* with the clear understanding that the very word Brahma used for describing the ultimate reality has been derived form the root 'Brih' to grow *'Janmādi asya ataḥ....'*(form which are birth etc.); and the forth, again, from the *Upaniṣads* (*Bṛhadāraṇyakopaniṣad* V.i.i.): *'Oṁ Pūrṇamadaḥ Pūrṇamidaṁ Pūrṇātpūrṇamudacyate; Pūrṇasya Pūrṇamādāya Pūrṇamevāvaśiṣyate,* (*Oṁ,* This is infinite, that is infinite, from the Infinite arises the infinite; Taking out the infinite from the infinite, the infinite itself remains).' It is in the light of these four statements that we should understand the various vedāntic positions of *Ajātivāda, Advaita, Śuddhāvaita, Viśiṣṭādvaita, Dvaitādvaita, Acintyabhedābheda, Dvaita* and the like. Any way, the idea of Unity in Diversity as delivered by *Vedānta* is too obvious to need further argument.

In *Sāṁkhya-yoga,* this idea can be delivered from their *Pradhāna-Kāraṇavāda* wherein *prakṛti* with the three *guṇas* of *Sattva, Rajas* and *Tamas* being Constitutive properties, the very epitome of Unity in diversity is made reponsible for all the affairs of the world. As for the aim of *mokṣa* or *Kaivalya* for each of the infinite number of puruṣas is concerned, we need not here discuss the same. So I will be content to bring out that the same does not in any way militate against the status and nature *(svabhāva) of Prakṛti.*

It is too well known to be argued that the *Jaina* thought with its exmphasis on *Anekāntavāda* (Open-endedness) and *Syādvāda* (realativity of desscriptions) does promote the idea of unity in diversity, a clear statement which we can find in the utterence of kundakundācārya; *'Je egam jānai se sabbe jānai; je sabbam jānai se egam jānai'* (One who knows one knows all and one who knows all knows one).

In the *Nyāya Vaiśeṣika* thought, the unity of all the multiple beings of the world in their manifold variety can be seen as emerging through a combination of just nine basic substantive factors. *Cārvāka Darśana,* though unlike the already mentioned philospophies does not have room for soul as one of the basic substances but its position does not seem to be substantially different form that of the *Nīyāya-Vaiśeṣika* in so far as it explains all diffences in terms of a unity of earth, water, air and fire yet it scores over the former by positioning the unity as due to not any external forces like a blind potency of *Karmas (Adṛṣṭa)* and God but due to an 'internal-go' *(Svabhāva)* of the elements themselves as also on the count of placing happiness as the goal of human endeavour, to be achieved through the harmony of the elements, accepting thus only the *Abhudaya* of the *Nyāya-Vaiśeṣika* thinkers and saying no to their *Nihśreyas* that to it is unattractive in as much as that amounts to be a realization of soul without consciousness.

Buddhist philosophy is the only philosophy among the various systems of Indian philosphy that accepts a thoroughly dynamic view of the world as the *saṁsāra* (world), according to the Buddhists, is characterised by *Anityatā* (Impermanence), *Anātmatā* (non- sustaniality) and *Duḥkhatā* (suffering) analysed into *jarā-maraṇa* (decline and death), *maraṇa* not being treated as the final end. Any being that dies may pass into either *parinirvāṇa* state about which nothing whatsover is said whether one lives, does not live, both lives and does not live or neither lives nor does not live after death; or into *jāti* i.e. birth or rebirth wherein one is to go through *jarā* and *maraṇa* again leading to next being or doing and so on i.e. through the law of *Karma*, in accordance with the principle of dependent origination (*Pratītya-Samutpāda*). This universal flux has been, in Buddhism, ontologically understood in three possible ways:

1. Objectively or realistically, in which every present moment of becoming is rich with the past and pregnant with the future, a position which is described by the statement *Sarvam Idam* (this is all) or *Sarvasti* (all is) and can be best understood through the example of a youngman who carries his childhood in the form of past influence that shapes him into what he is at any given moment as also shadowed rather moulded by the coming events of his future life.

2. Sunjectively or idealistically, in which being or becoming is understood in terms of experience itself and is described by the statement *vijñaptimātram idam sarvam* (All this is experiential) and examplified through a dream experience which is taken as the paradigm for all experience, for, it is in dream experience that the spontaneous, quicksilver sort of changing non-substantial aspect of reality shows itself in the best possible manner.

3. The third way of understanding being or becoming is the one that transcends both the realistic as well as the idealistic modes of doing so and is described by the statement: *Śūnyamidam* (It is *Śūnya*). *Śūnya* stands for that which is free of all determinism in terms of the four known categories of 'it is', 'it is not', it is and is not', and 'it neither is nor not', (*catuskoṭi-vinirmukta*) and can be excamplified by any 'item' of being or becoming where the item is placed under quotes to indicate its being only relatively so. All views, according to it, are *mithyā dṛṣṭis*. I will not dare to translate *mithyā* as false, as in general is done, as I have not translated *śūnya* as void or empty, for, then *Nāgārjuna*, the great Buddhist, would not have said 'the *Buddha* is *Śūnya*, 'the *Saṅgha* is *Śūnya* and the *Dharma* is *Śūnya*.'

I may rightly be questioned as to what this all has to do with the concept of Tolerance that I have claimed as having roots in Indian Philosophy inclusive of Buddhist Philosophy. My answer is quite simple and the same is that let one accept any attitude whether that of *Sarvāsti* or *Vijñaptimātratā* or *Śūuyatā*- Tolerance would emerge for him or her. If one is a *Sarvāstvādin* he can at once recognize the realistic objectivity of all views liked or disliked by one and shall definitely be tolerent towards the disliked. If one is a *vijñānavādin,* he will not fail to realize that dreams dreamt by him are as subjective as of anybody else. There is a spontaneity with which anything or person may become any other thing or any other person standing in the shoes of someone else and looking at the things from another's point of view has no difficulty for him for he realizes that what is another's idea can as well be his own. If one is a *śūnyavādin,* he is impartial towards all views, regarding them equally *mithyā*. Does not that amount to a toterance of a sort?

I Conclude by qouting three statements attributed to the Buddha, from *Cullaviyūha sūtta* of *Sūttanipāta* :

1. " One who does not tolerate another's view, is a fool, a dolt and stupid."

2. "If they argue that their own view (alone) is right, then the disputants are fools."

3. "The truth is indeed one and the knower of it does not dispute it."

Delhi

THE RELATION BETWEEN PRATĪTYASAMUTPĀDA AND ŚŪNYATĀ

T.R. Sharma

Dependent origination (*pratītyasamutpāda*) stands for causation in Buddhist philosophy. It offers a satisfactory link between cause and effect working at various levels. In the beginning it was mainly considered from the moral point of view, but the later Buddhist philosophical works widened its scope and intensified its working in a more dynamic manner. The law of dependent origination helps us in knowing the causes and conditions of the phenomenal world in a very subtle way. After analysing these causes and conditions of the phenomenal world, what is achieved in the transcendental sense, is nothing but emptiness (*śūnyatā*). After this we reach a stage, which may be called a phenomenal vacuum, which is *śūnyatā*. On the one end is the dependent origination and on the other end is the *śūnyatā;* and in between there is the existence of the whole of the phenomenal world. The discovery of the law of dependent origination was an attempt to analyse the mundane world and what is ultimately achieved by this process is known as the *Sāṁvṛtika satya*. At the other end process led to the concept of *śūnyatā,* which at level of the *pāramārthika satya* may be designated as the phenomenal vacuum. This stage may be interpreted as silence, *i.e.,* beyond which our intellect can no longer work. The purpose of this paper is to analyse this relation betwen dependent origination and *śūnyata* from the points of view of *sāmvṛtika satya* and the *pāraṃārthika satya*.

The law of causation is the central point in the Buddhist philosopical thought. Right in the beginning, it was conceived mainly in the domain of moral philosophy, but later on its scope was widened by the philosophers at a subsequent age. It may be pointed out that the law of causation was primarily based in the human experience in general. The early philosophers, when they first became confronted with the human experience, discovered the four major characteristics of the law of causation, *i.e.*, objectivity (*tathatā*), (ii) causal nexus (*avitathatā*), (iii) invariability (*anaññathatā*) and (iv) conditionality (*idapaccavatā*).[1] These four characteristics of the law of causation were basically observed in connection with the human experience. Even before the advent of the law of causation, there existed a number of theories of causation such as self causation, which implied the prior existence of the effect (*satkāryavāda*) and the idea of external causation which accounted for a previously non-existent effect (*asatkāryavāda*). The discovery of the law of causation brought out a revolution in philosophical cricles. It may be pointed out here that this law of causation had no ontological status. This law tried to find out the causes and conditions of the mundane world in a general manner. Kalupahana observes, "For them causation had no ontological status; it was purely epistemological category belonging solely to the description of human experience."[2] It must also be clearly understood that the law of causation was nothing but an attempt to analyse the mundane phenomena with regard to the happenings of the day-to-day life in relation to their causes and conditions. In other words, we may say that this was a methodological way of analysis of the things of the world of human experience based on certain generalisations. This methodological device had no ontological status. Nathmal Tatia opines, "But this is only a methodological device and should not be interpreted as an exhaustive ontological analysis."[3]

The early Buddhism tried to find out the causes and conditions of the phenomenal world. It was the *Sarvāstivāda* school that appears to have distinguished between cause (*hetu*) and condition (*pratyaya*). But it is also true that both cause and condition were used synonymously in early Buddhism also. Kalupahana says, "Therefore, we may conclude that early Buddhism as embodied in the *Pāli Nikāyas* and the Chinese *Āgamas*, as well as the later *Theravāda* and *Vijñānavāda* school, did not recognise a difference between 'cause' and 'condition' and that both words cause (*hetu*) and condition (*pratyaya*) did not denote such distinction."[4] Thus, we see that there is always a nexus between cause and effect. As far as the working of this law is concerned, it may be pointed out that a cause may give birth to dissimilar effect. The cause may or may not be similar to effect. Curd is produced out of milk and they are different in character. A paddy grain produces paddy and a barley gain produces barley. It should, therefore, be borne in mind that a cause is always a combination of conditions, which is called an assemblage of conditions (*pratyayasāmagrī*).

Nāgārjuna in a *Kārikā* (24.18) observes that dependent origination is emptiness by saying. " What is originating co-dependently, we call emptiness. It is designation based upon (some material). Only this is the Middle Path."[5] It is clear here that according to Nāgārjuna, dependent origination and emptiness are one and the same thing. According to Candrakīrti also they are equal and synonymous but he points out to another main important factor, *i.e.*, the dependent origination, if understood in the empirical sense, simply refers to a mere nomenclature. This fact is further explained by Candrakīrti saying the wheels (of a chariot) being the components of a chariot, thus this whole structure is designated as a chariot in the worldly sense. The chariot has no independent status and since it originates dependently, it lacks its own nature. Now, these very components are by their nature unproduced. According to him, this very non-production of the components of the wheel etc., is emptiness (*śūnyatā*). Such a *śūnyatā*, whose characteristic is non-production, is also designated as the Middle Path.[6] Mcreover, according to Candrakīrti's explanation *śūyata*, nomenclature (*upādāya prajñapati*) and the Middle Way (*Madhyamā pratipad*) are considered to be "different names"(*viśeṣa saṁjñā*) of the dependent origination (*pratītyasamutpāda*).[7] As far as the meaning of the two terms is concerned, Candrakīrti says at another place that whatever is the meaning of dependent origination (*pratītyasamutpāda*), is the meaning of emptiness (*śūnyatā*).[8] The term nomenclature based on some material (*upādāya prajñapti*) is also interpreted by various scholars in different ways. Venkatramanan translates this term as "derived name."[9] Gadjin M. Nagao translates it as "a designation based upon (some material)".[10] When we try to analyse this *Kārikā* (24.18), we find that first of all, we are confronted with normal functioning of the world, which consists of causes leading to some effect(s). This is direct way of analysis of the mundane world without denying it because this represents the ordinary worldly life. This leads to the conclusion that people are living in this mundane world without any awareness of its true nature as *śūnyatā*. This *śūnyatā* always assumes some nomenclature, which in Buddhist philosophy is called *prajñapti*. Thus, it finally leads to the middle path which is free from the two extremes of existence and non-existence. The *madhyamāpratipad* is also free from the two extremes of eternalism and annihilationism. The middle way is to see the things as they are. In the whole of the *Kārikā*, there are four *padas viz.*, *pratītyasamutpāda*, *śūnyatā*, *upādāya-prajñapti* and *maddhyamāpratipad*. As a matter of fact, all the four have some logical sequence in them. According to Gadjin M. Nagao, all these four *padas* are associated with each other in some way, are considered equal.[11] Thus the whole sequence can be put as follows :

pratītyasamutpāda=śūnyatā

=upādāya-prajñapti

=madhyamāpratipad.

As far as the working of the law of dependent origination is concerned, Candrakīrti adds another dimension to it. According to him, all such imperative verbs like 'go', 'do', 'cook', 'read',and 'stay'[12] being wordly usages are also based on the law of dependent origination. Here it may be noted that this type of usage of dependent origination in relation to the imperative verbs is certainly a new innovation found out by Candrakīrti.

With regard to the relation between dependent origination (*pratītyasamutpāda*) and emptiness (*śūnyatā*), Nāgārjuna has already stated that dependent origination is emptiness; it is a designation based on some material (*vijñapti*), it is middle path (*madhyamāpratipad*).[13] *Śūnyatā* is the central theme of the *Mahāyāna* philosophical system. This term has been used in the *Mādhyamika* system to denote a stage where all viewpoints with regard to the real nature of mundane world are totally rejected. In other words, we may say that to have a viewpoint is to cling to a position and there can be various types of positions with regard to the real nature of things. According to the *Mādhyamika* philosophical system, all points of view are endowed with some faults. Even if there is no fault in different views, they are all mutually conflicting. This, in turn, is the criticism of points of view with regard to the real nature of things. It demonstrates the hollowness of views in a dialectical way and itself is dialectics, and dialectics is *śūnyatā*.

Candrakīrti alongwith Nāgārjuna also states that whatever is the meaning of dependent origination (*pratītyasamutpāda*), is the meaning of emptiness (*śūnyata*).[14] From the study of the *mādhyamakaśāstra* and the commentary of Candrakīrti, it appears that the concept of *śūnyatā* was grossly misunderstood in the sense of metaphysical category of non-existence (*abhāva*). That is why Nāgārjuna had to say that *śūnyatā*, if misunderstood by a man of weak intellect, would destory him,[15] just like a snake, mishandled and the knowledge wrongly acquired. Candrakīrti uses three different words in this context, *i.e.*, emptiness (*śunyatā*), meaning of *śunyatā* (*śunyatārtha*) and purpose of *śunyatā* (*śūnyatāprayojana)*; and he counters the arguments of his opponent by saying that all these three have not been properly understood by him (opponent), and hence unjustified.[16] Likewise, the opponents of Candrakīrti had misunderstood the concept of *śūnyatā* in the sense of non-existence (*abhāva*); whereas this is not the import of *śūnyatā* according to Candrakīrti.[17] The meaning of *śūnyatā* is dependent origination (*pratītyasamutpāda*). He makes very interesting remarks about *pratītyasamutpāda* and *śūnyatā*. He says as if somebody riding a horse, has forgotten the horse itself and thereby denying it, is blaming others, likewise, you (opponent), riding the horse of the philosophy of *śūnyatā*, having the characteristics of dependent origination (*pratītyasamutpāda*), aggressively, without getting it (horse), are blaming us.[18] To this dimension of *śūnyāta*, another dimension is added by Bhāvaviveka. According to him, *śūnyatā* derived from the group of elements (*skandha*) is different from the *śūnyatā* of group of elements. Moreover, he says that the group of elements(*skandha*) exists in *śūnyatā* and vice versa; *śūnyatā* exists in the group of elements.[19] It may be noted that the *Mādhyamaka* philosophical system devoid of self-being (*niḥsvabhāva*) is also considered as equivalent to *śūnyatā*. So Candrakīrti emphatically declares that whosoever realises well the *śūnyatā* of self-being (*svabhāva*) being endowed with dependent origination (*pratītyasamutpāda*), realises the four noble truths in the right perspective.[20]

In the above lines, we have made a detailed study of the two concepts *i.e., pratītyasamutpāda* and *śūnyatā*. Apart from this study, we have also examined the working of the law of dependent origination in relation to the mundane nature of things in general. In this process we have observed that the law of dependent origination tries to analyse the basic constituents of the things of mundane world. We have realised that everything in the world is basically dependent upon something else for its existence. This interdependence of things in relation to cause and effect is nothing but *pratīyasamutpāda*. To go beyond this interdependence of things in relation to cause and effect is nothing but *śūnyatā*. To bifurcate cause and effect as different entities exsisting in different times is really the basic function of the law of dependent origination. This only shows that the mundane nature of things is unreal in themselves and they entirely depend upon so nothing else for their exsistence. So nothing is independent or real. We may say that the law of dependent origination (*pratītyasamutpāda*) has been interpreted in *Mādhyamika* system as *śūnyatā*. Murti says, "The entire Buddhist thought revolves on the pivot of *pratītyasamutpāda*; the *Mādhyamika* system is interpretation of *pratītyasamutpāda* as *śūnyatā*."[21] In the *Mādhyamika* philosophical system name has been designated as *prajñapti*, a derived name or a designation based upon some material. A very interesting remark is made with regard to name by Bhāvaviveka in *Prajñāpradīpa*, where he says that when there is the desire to designate something in the world and beyond this world, the term *prajñapti* is used and this is also the middle way.[22] To conclude, we can say that as far as the exact relation between *pratītyasamutpāda* and *śūnyatā* is concerned, it is of priority and posteriority in relation to each other working at different places and times having no connection with each other in a single frame work. Cause may be priority and the effect may be posteriority as far as time frame work is concerned, but they stand wide apart from each other. This type of analysis at the empirical level leaves nothing but a phenomenal vacuum and this vacuum leads to *śūnyatā* at the transcendental level in a conceptual way. In other words, we may say that we have always a desire to go beyond the conceptual analysis of the things which brings us to the level of *śūnyatā*, beyond which our intellect fails. Venkatramanan says, "To these three may be added another import of *śūnyatā*, *viz*., the sense of beyond, the thrust for the real, the thrust for fulfilment, which is the seat and spring of all the activities of man."[23] The significance of the identity relation between *pratītyasamutpāda* and *śūnyatā* lies in the recognition of a philosophical fact, *i.e.*, the law of dependent origination operates at the mundane level giving rise to *śūnyatā* at the transcendental level.

To put it other way, the law of dependent origination is a metaphysical ladder to reach the high pedestal of *śūnyatā* at the transcendental level.

REFERENCES AND NOTES

1. *Visuddhimagga*, Vol. III, Varanasi, 1972, pp. 1174-75.
2. Kalupahana, David J.; *Causality: The Central Philosophy of Buddism*, Honululu 1975,p.202.
3. Tatia N., *'Paticcasamuppāda'*, The Nava Nalanda Mahavihar Research Publication Vol. I. ed. Satkari Mukerji. Patna, 1957 p. 188.
4. Kalupahana, David J.;*op.cit*.p.66.
5. *Mādhyamakaśāstra*, (24.18) Ed. D.D. Shastri, Varanasi, 1983, p. 220.
   yaḥ pratīyasamutpādaḥ śūnyatāṃ tāṃ pracakṣmahe/
   sā prajñaptir upādāya pratipat saīva madhyamā//
6. *Cf*.Candrakīrti, *Prasannapadā on Mādhyamakaśāstra*(24.18) p. 220.
   yā ceyaṃ svabhāvaśūnyatā sā prajñaptir upādāya, saiva śūyatā upādāya prajñaptir iti vyavasthāpyate. Cakrādīny upādāya rathāṅgāni rathaḥ prajñāyate tasya vā. Saivāṅgānyupādāya prājñaptiḥ. Sā svabhāvenānutpattiḥ yā ca svabhāvānānutpattiḥ sā śūnyatā. saiva svabhāvānutpattilakṣaṇā madhyamā pratipat iti vyavasthāpyate.
7. *Cf. Ibid.*: *tad evam pratīyasamutpādasyaivaitā viśeṣasamjñaḥ śūnyatā upādāya prajñāptiḥ madhyamā pratipad iti.*
8. *Cf.* Candrakirti on *Mādhyamakaśāstra* (24.7) p.215.
   pratītyasamutpādaśabdasya yo, arthaḥ sa eva śūnyatāśabdārthaḥ
9. Venkatramanan K., *Nāgārjuna's Philosophy*, Delhi, 1978 p.339 (a).
10. Nagao, Gadjin M., *'From Mādhyamika to Yogācāra, An Analysis of MMK 24.18* and *M.V. (Madhyāntavibhāga)*, 1.1.2, Journal of International Association of Buddhist Studies, Vol. 2, No.1. Wisconsin, 1979 p.31.
    Cf. also Mervyn Sprung "I understand *prajñapti* to be a non-cognitive, guiding term which serves to suggest appropriate ways of coping with the putative realities on which it rests for its meaning and to which it lends meaning----A *prajñapti* is a guiding notion, a notion which a long tradition of successful teaching finds effective in helping students towards the clarity of mind that marks the wise man."
    Lucid Exposition of the Middle Way, London, 1979, pp.17- 18.
11. *Ibid.* p.31 (It may also be pointed out here that in the Sino-Japanese tradition, according to the Tien-tai school, all the three except the *pratīyasamutpāda* constitute the so-called 'threefold Truth", the truth of the empty (K'ung), the provisional (chia) and the middle (chung). *Cf.* Takakusu, *The Essentials of Buddhist Philosophy* (Honolulu Office Appliance Co., Third Ed. p.129 (quoted by Gadjin M. Nagao, p. 42).
12. *Cf.* Candrakīrti on *Mādhyamakaśastra (24-35), p. 224:*
    api ca sarva eva hyete 'gaccha' kuru, paca, paṭha tiṣṭha
    ity evamādaya laukika vyavahārāḥ pratīyasamutpannāḥ.
13. *Mādhyamakaśāstra*, 24.18.

14. *Cf.* Candrakīrti on *Mādhyamakaśāstra* (24.7), p.215.
evam pratītyasamutpādaśabdasya yo' rthah sa eva śūnyatāśabdārthaḥ.

15. Cf. *Mādhyamakaśāstra* (24.11), p.216;
vināśayati durdṛṣṭā śūnyatā mandamedhasam/
sarpo yathā durgṛhīto vidyā vā duṣprasādhitā/

16. *Cf.* Candrakīrti on *Mādhyamakaśāstra* (24.18) p.218.
śūnyatā, śūnyatārtham śūnyatāprayojanaṃ ca yathāvat abuddhvā upakṣiptaḥ. so' smākam śūnye śūnyatāvāde nopapadyate.

17. *Cf. Ibid:*
abhāvārthaṃ hi śūnyatārthaṃ adhyāropya prasaṅga udbhāvito bhavati. na ca vayam abhāvārtham vyācakṣmahe. Kim tarhi. pratītyasamutpādārthaṃ.

18. *Cf.* Candrakīrti on *Mādhyamakaśāstra (24.15), p.219:*
yathā hi kaścit yam evāśvamāruḍhas tam eva vismṛtaḥ san tadapahāradoseṇa parānupālabhate, evam eva bhavān pratītyasamutpādalakṣaṇaśūnyatādarśanāśvamārūḍha eva atyantavikṣepāt tam anupalambhamāno' samān parivadati.

19. *Cf.* Bhāvaviveka, *Prajñāpradīpa* on *Mādhyamakaśāstra, 24.10 (Mādhyamakaśāstra* Vol. II. ed. Raghunath Pandeya, Delhi, 1989 p.196.
skandhānāṃ śūnyatā skandhebhyośūnyatā anyā. śūnyatāyāṃ skandhā vidyante. skandheṣu śūnyatā vidyate.

20. *Cf.* Candrakīrti or *Mādhyamakaśāstra (24.10), p.225.*
yo hi sarvadharmapratīyasamutpādalakṣṇāṃ svabhāvaśūnyatāṃ samyak paśyati sa catvāri āryasatyāni paśyati yathābhūtāni taitvataḥ

21. Murti, T.R.V., *Central Philosophy of Buddhism,* London, *1980.p.166.*

22. *Cf.* Bhāvaviveka, *Prajñāpradīpa* on *Mādhyamakaśāstra (24.18)*,p.202.
lokaś ca lokato' tikrāntasya vyavahartum icchayā upādānaṃ pratītya prajñaptir bhavati. Saiva madhyamā pratipad.

23. Venkatramanan K., *op. cit.*, p. 339 (a).

Delhi

प्रारम्भिक बौद्धमत और उपनिषद्

चन्द्रकान्त शुक्ल

बौद्ध दर्शन के प्रतिष्ठापक गौतम बुद्ध के समय सनातन धर्म अपनी चरम पराकाष्ठा पर पहुँच गया था, परन्तु इसी के परिणाम-स्वरूप इसमें कुछ दुर्गुण भी आने लगे थे और सनातन धर्म में भी कुछ ऐसे साहित्य का सर्जन प्रारम्भ हो गया था जो इन दुर्गुणों की ओर लोगों का ध्यान आकृष्ट करने लगे थे। कुछ आस्तिक दार्शनिक सम्प्रदाय भी प्रकारान्तर से ऐसे दुर्गुणों का विरोध करने लगे थे अथवा उनके प्रति उपेक्षा की भावना अभिव्यक्त करने लगे थे। वैदिक कर्मकाण्ड के बाद उससे संलग्न होकर ही ज्ञानकाण्ड भाग को आधार बनाकर उपनिषदों की रचना हुई, और उनमें कर्मकाण्ड से सम्बन्धित दुर्गुणों के प्रति उपेक्षा की भावना परिलक्षित हुई। सांख्य, योग तथा वेदान्त दर्शनों ने भी इस ओर ध्यान दिया, किन्तु इन सबने स्पष्ट रूप से कर्मकाण्ड का विरोध नहीं किया, लेकिन गौतम बुद्ध ने अपने सिद्धान्तों के द्वारा खुले तौर पर कर्मकाण्ड का विरोध करना प्रारम्भ कर दिया। दूसरी दृष्टि से विचार करने पर हम पाते हैं कि उनके सामने सनातन धर्म की एक विस्तृत और समृद्ध परम्परा थी, अत: वे निश्चित रूप से इनसे प्रभावित भी हुए। इस क्रम में वे सर्वाधिक प्रभावित उपनिषदों से ही हुए। उन्होंने उपनिषदों का नाम्ना उल्लेख नहीं किया है, परन्तु उनके उपदेशों में सर्वत्र ज्ञान-सम्बन्धी ऐसी बातों का सङ्केत मिलता है जो उपनिषदों में पहले से ही विद्यमान थीं।

अनुश्रुति के अनुसार राजकुमार गौतम ने रोगी, वृद्ध और मृत व्यक्ति को देखा और उन्हें संसार से विरक्ति हो गयी। इसी कारण उनके सिद्धान्तों पर दुःखवाद का प्रभूत प्रभाव है। उपनिषदों में भी स्थान-स्थान पर ऐसे विषयों का हमें दर्शन होता है। उदाहरणस्वरूप कठोपनिषद् के उस प्रसङ्ग को देखा जा सकता है जहाँ नचिकेता सांसारिक पदार्थों को क्षणभङ्गुर मानता है और सांसारिक जीवों को वृद्धावस्था के दुःख से युक्त और उन्हें मरणधर्मा मानता है—

श्वोभावा मर्त्यस्य यदन्तकैतत्
सर्वेन्द्रियाणां जरयन्ति तेजः।
अपि सर्वं जीवितमल्पमेव
तवैव वाहास्तव नृत्यगीते ॥

अजीर्यताममृतानामुपेत्य
जीर्यन् मर्त्यः क्वधस्थः प्रजानन् ।
अभिध्यायद् वर्णरतिप्रमोदा-
नतिदीर्घे जीविते को रमेत ।।[1]

सुत्तपिटक के धम्मपद में भी हम उपर्युक्त तथ्यों का दर्शन करते हैं—

पस्स चित्तकतं बिम्बं अरुकायं समुस्सितं ।
आतुरं बहुसङ्कप्पं यस्स नत्थि धुपं ठिति ।।
परिजिण्णमिदं रूपं रोगनिड्डं पभङ्गुरं ।
भिज्जति पूतिसन्देहो मरणन्तं हि जीवितं ।।
यानिमानि अपत्थानि अलाबूनेव सारदे ।
कापोतकानि अट्ठीनि तानि दिस्वान का रति ।।[2]

बौद्ध धर्म मूलतः वैदिक कर्मकाण्ड के विरोध में ही उत्पन्न हुआ । इसके सिद्धान्तो में सर्वत्र कर्मकाण्डीय परम्पराओं के प्रति घृणा का भाव अभिलक्षित होता है । उदाहरणस्वरूप मुण्डकोपनिषद् के उस प्रसङ्ग को देखा जा सकता है जहाँ कहा गया है कि इष्ट तथा पूर्त कर्मों को जो श्रेष्ठ मानते हैं वे श्रेय को नहीं जानते हैं और स्वर्गलोक में जाकर भी वे जन्म-मरण के चक्र में पड़े रहते हैं—

इष्टापूर्तं मन्यमाना वरिष्ठं नान्यच्छ्रेयो वेदयन्ते प्रमूढाः ।
नाकस्य पृष्ठे ते सुकृतेऽनुभूत्वेमं लोकं हीनतरं वा विशन्ति ।।[3]

डॉ. राधाकृष्णन् भी उपर्युक्त तथ्य को स्वीकार करते हुए लिखते हैं—"कर्मकाण्ड के प्रति घृणा उनमें और उपनिषदों में एक समान है ।"[4]

विविध उपनिषदों में अविद्या-तत्त्व[5] का यत्र-तत्र उल्लेख प्राप्त होता है जो अज्ञान का अर्थ द्योतित करने वाला है अथवा विद्या का विरोधी है । बौद्ध दर्शन के पालि भाषा के ग्रन्थों में इसे ही अविज्जा कहा गया है । सुत्तपिटक के ही मज्झिमनिकाय में उपनिषदों के सिद्धान्तों के समान ही संसार को क्षणभङ्गुर और दुःखमय स्वीकार करते हुए अविज्जा का निरूपण किया गया है । उसके अनुसार इस दुःख के विषय में अज्ञान, इसकी उत्पत्ति के विषय में अज्ञान, इस दुःख को दूर करने के सम्बन्ध में अज्ञान और इसको दूर करने के साधनों के सम्बन्ध में अज्ञान, ये चार अविज्जा हैं ।[6] इस तथ्य पर विचार करते हुए एस.एन. दासगुप्त ने लिखा है—"इस दुःख के सम्बन्ध में अज्ञान (चतुर्बद्ध अज्ञान) ही चार प्रकार की अविज्जा है । यह चार प्रकार की अविज्जा ही चार दृढ़ सत्यों के समझने में बाधक है । इन चार सत्यों को आर्य सच्च कहा गया है जो इस प्रकार वर्णित है—दुःख, दुःख की उत्पत्ति का कारण, दुःख का मोचन और दुःख को मिटा़ने का साधन ।"[7]

सुत्तपिटक के ही अंश उदान में उस अज्ञात लोक का वर्णन करते हुए कहा गया है—

यत्थ आपो च पठवी, तेजो वायो न गाधति।
न तत्थ सुक्का जोतन्ति, आदिच्चो नप्पकासति ॥
न तत्थ चन्दिमा भाति, तमो तत्थ न विज्जति।
यदा च अन्त नावेदि, मुनिमोनन ब्राह्मणो ॥
अथ रूप अरूपा च, सुखदुक्खा पमुच्चति ॥[8]

उपर्युक्त सन्दर्भ पर पूरी तरह से उपनिषदों में प्राप्त होने वाले निम्नलिखित श्लोक का प्रभाव है—

न तत्र सूर्यो भाति न चन्द्रतारकं
नेमा विद्युतो भान्ति कुतोऽयमग्निः ।
तमेव भान्तमनुभाति सर्वं
तस्य भासा सर्वमिदं विभाति ॥[9]

उपनिषदों के अनुसार संसार के समस्त कार्य अर्थात् दृश्यमान जगत् कारणों की श्रृंखला के कारण उत्पन्न है जिनका न आदि है और न ही अन्त । प्रारम्भिक बौद्धमत भी इसी सिद्धान्त का पोषक है और वह भी मानता है कि सम्पूर्ण संसार कारणों के द्वारा ही नियन्त्रित है । बाद में चलकर बौद्ध दर्शन में इसी सिद्धान्त को प्रतीत्यसमुत्पाद के अन्तर्गत विवेचित किया गया । इसके अनुसार एक वस्तु की उत्पत्ति दूसरी वस्तु पर अवलम्बित है । बौद्ध मत के अनुसार परिवर्तन ही किसी वस्तु के अस्तित्व को बोधित करता है । यह क्रमशः एक दूसरे के पीछे चलने वाली दशाओं की श्रृंखला है । उसके अनुसार सत् पदार्थ में परिवर्तन की क्षमता नहीं हो सकती है, अतः सभी वस्तुएँ असत् हैं । उपनिषदों का सिद्धान्त 'ब्रह्म सत्यं जगन्मिथ्या' भी लगभग इसी तथ्य को प्रतिपादित करने वाला है । अन्तर यही है कि वहाँ एक तत्त्व ब्रह्म को सत् माना गया है ।

जगत् की अस्थिरता का जो सिद्धान्त हमें उपनिषदों में मिलता है वही प्रारम्भिक बौद्धमत में भी दृष्टिगत होता है । जगत् की क्षणभङ्गुरता की चर्चा उपनिषदों में भी आयी है और उसी का विकसित रूप परवर्ती बौद्धमत में क्षणिकवाद के रूप में प्राप्त होता है ।

त्रिविध दुःखों से आत्यन्तिक विमुक्ति दिलाना ही उपनिषदों का भी लक्ष्य है और बुद्ध के अनुसार भी दुःखों से मुक्ति ही निर्वाण है । जिस तरह उपनिषदों में दुःख से छुटकारा पाने के लिए स्वार्थपरता को त्यागने का सन्देश देते हुए 'तेन त्यक्तेन भुञ्जीथा मा गृधः कस्यस्विद्धनम्'[10] का उपदेश दिया गया है उसी तरह मज्झिमनिकाय के आरम्भिक अंश में बुद्ध ने स्वार्थपरता को छोड़ने के सम्बन्ध में उपदिष्ट किया है । जिस तरह उपनिषदों ने त्यागपूर्वक उपभोग की शिक्षा दी है उसी तरह बुद्ध ने भी मध्यम मार्ग अपनाने की शिक्षा देते हुए कहा है कि सभी प्रकार की अति और पराकाष्ठाओं को छोड़ देना चाहिए । वे मिलिन्दपञ्ह में एक कथा के माध्यम से कहते हैं कि जिस तरह घाव के हो जाने पर हम उसकी देख-भाल करने के लिए उस पर पट्टी आदि तो बाँधते हैं, किन्तु उस

घाव से प्रेम नहीं करते हैं "उसी तरह तपस्वी लोग अपने शरीर में आसक्ति नहीं रखते हैं फिर भी उसे धारण किये रहते हैं। वे इस शरीर को इसलिए धारण किये रहते हैं, क्योंकि वे धार्मिक जीवन में शरीर रूपी साधन को लेकर आगे बढ़ सके।"[11]

यदि उपनिषदों के प्रतिपाद्य विषयों पर प्रामुख्य की दृष्टि से विचार किया जाए तो वह विषय होगा आत्मतत्त्व। सभी उपनिषदों ने विस्तार से इस आत्मतत्त्व का विवेचन किया है, जबकि स्वयं बुद्ध इस तत्त्व के सम्बन्ध में मौन का अवलम्बन करते हैं। बुद्ध के समय में ही उनके शिष्य आत्मवाद का अभिप्राय जानना चाहते थे और बुद्ध इस विषय पर मौन हो जाते थे—"बुद्धैर्नात्मा न चानात्मा कश्चिदित्यपि देशितम्।"[12]

आत्मा के विषय में बुद्ध के मौन के दो अभिप्राय हो सकते हैं—प्रथम प्रश्नकर्ता की अयोग्यता और द्वितीय आत्मा की अनिर्वचनीयता। प्रथम विकल्प स्वीकरणीय नहीं है, क्योंकि बुद्ध के अनेक शिष्य अत्यन्त विद्वान् और कुशाग्रबुद्धि थे। अतः द्वितीय विकल्प ही विचारणीय है। ऐसा प्रतीत होता है कि बुद्ध का मौनावलम्बन इसीलिए था, क्योंकि आत्मतत्त्व वाणी का विषय नहीं है, वह अवर्णनीय है। उपनिषदों में भी ब्रह्म अथवा आत्मतत्त्व को अवर्णनीय कहा गया है—"यतो वाचो निवर्तन्ते।"[13]

नागार्जुन के टीकाकार चन्द्रकीर्ति बुद्ध के इस मौन पर विचार करते हुए कहते हैं कि कुछ लोग आत्मा को मानते हैं और कुछ लोग नहीं मानते हैं। भगवान् बुद्ध ने बीच का मार्ग अपना कर 'मध्यम मार्ग' की स्थापना की है। नागार्जुन लिखते हैं—

सर्वं तथ्यं न वा तथ्यं तथ्यं चातथ्यमेव च।
नैवातथ्यं नैव तथ्यमेतद् बुद्धानुशासनम्॥[14]

जिस आत्मतत्त्व या ब्रह्मतत्त्व को "स एष नेति नेत्यात्मा"[15] के द्वारा प्रतिपादित किया गया है, उसे ही बौद्ध दर्शन निम्नलिखित रूप में अभिव्यक्त करता है—

अनिरोधमनुत्पादमनुच्छेदमशाश्वतम्।
अनेकार्थमनानार्थमनागमनिर्गमम्॥[16]

आत्मा के सम्बन्ध में बुद्ध के मौन पर विचार करते हुए डॉ. राधाकृष्णन् लिखते हैं—"एक और कारण है जिसने बुद्ध को आत्मा के विषय में मौन रहने की प्रेरणा दी, यह था कि उन्हें विश्वास था कि साधारण आत्मा को स्वीकार करने की जो मूल प्रवृत्ति है वही सब आत्मिक पाप की छिपी हुई जड़ है। जीवात्मा सम्बन्धी अहंकार का जो प्रचलित भ्रान्त विचार है वे उसका खण्डन करते हैं और आत्मा की यथार्थता को अस्वीकार करते हैं। आत्मा के विषय में जितने असत्य विचार हैं उन सब का वे प्रतिवाद करते हैं। वे पदार्थ जिनके साथ हम अपने को एकरूप बताते हैं, सत्य आत्मा नहीं है।"[17]

इस तरह बुद्ध बार-बार यह तो बताते हैं कि अमुक वस्तु आत्मा नहीं है, यह आत्मा नहीं है, वह आत्मा नहीं है, किन्तु आत्मा वस्तुत: है क्या, इस पर मौन साध लेते हैं । इससे ऐसा प्रतीत होता है कि वे किसी न किसी रूप में आत्मतत्त्व को मानते अवश्य हैं । हाँ, उसका वे विवेचन नहीं करते हैं ।

ओल्डनबर्ग के अभिमत का उल्लेख करते हुए डॉ. राधाकृष्णन् लिखते हैं—"यदि बुद्ध आत्मा का निषेध करने से बचते हैं तो इसलिए कि एक दुर्बलात्मा श्रोता के मन में आघात न पहुँचे । आत्मा के अस्तित्व एवं निषेध सम्बन्धी प्रश्न से बचने के द्वारा यह उत्तर मिल गया कि आत्मा नहीं है, क्योंकि बौद्ध उपदेशों में पूर्वावयव (प्रतिज्ञा) की प्रवृत्ति साधारणत: इधर की ओर ही है' । हम इस विचार से सहमत नहीं है कि बुद्ध ने जानबूझ कर सत्य को गुप्त रखा ।"[18]

उपनिषदों के अनुसार आत्मा अमर है और वह मृत्यु के बाद फिर अलंग देह को धारण कर लेती है । प्रारम्भिक बौद्धमत में भी पुनर्जन्म को स्वीकार किया गया है । किन्तु बुद्ध के द्वारा आत्मा के सम्बन्ध में मौन का अवलम्बन प्रश्नचिह्न उपस्थित कर देता है । अभिधर्मकोष के अनुसार कर्म की निरन्तरता विद्यमान रहती है और मनुष्य का कर्म ही अथवा उसका चरित्र अगले जन्म में भी साथ रहता है ।

दु:खों से आत्यन्तिक छुटकारा पाने को ही उपनिषदों में मोक्ष या मुक्ति कहा गया है जबकि बुद्ध ने उसे निर्वाण संज्ञा से अभिहित किया है । निर्वाण का शाब्दिक अर्थ है—बुझ जाना अथवा ठंडा हो जाना । श्वेताश्वतर उपनिषद् में भी परमात्मा को ऐसी अग्नि कहा गया है जिसका ईंधन नि:शेष हो गया है—**दग्धेन्धनमिवानलम्** ।[19]

प्रारम्भिक बौद्धमत में साधारणत: संसार के कारणीभूत समग्र क्लेशों का सम्यक् रूपेण प्रहाण ही निर्वाण है । यह निर्वाण भी दो प्रकार का माना गया है—सोपाधिशेष और निरुपाधिशेष । पहले में मनुष्य की केवल वासनाएँ लुप्त होती हैं और दूसरे में पूरा अस्तित्व विलुप्त हो जाता है । सोपधिशेष निर्वाण की दशा में सास्रवपञ्चस्कन्ध विद्यमान रहते हैं जो पूर्व में कृत कर्मों के द्वारा प्रक्षिप्त होते हैं । निरुपाधिशेष निर्वाण में स्कन्ध की परम्परा विच्छिन्न हो जाती है । ऐसी स्थिति आने पर बुद्ध के अवतरण की धारा समाप्त हो जाती है । बुद्ध के अनुसार दूसरी दशा में भी निर्वाण अथवा परिनिर्वाण का अभिप्राय नितान्त अभाव नहीं है । यह भी चेतना की निर्दोष अवस्थाओं के प्रवाह के अतिरिक्त और कुछ नहीं है । प्राचीन बौद्धों के निर्वाण की स्थिति पर विचार करते हुए डॉ. राधाकृष्णन् लिखते हैं—"हमें ऐसा प्रतीत होता है कि कतिपय प्राचीन बौद्धों की दृष्टि में निर्वाण का अर्थ है—सत्य की पूर्णता, अनन्त परमसुख (कैवल्य) अर्थात् सांसारिक सुखों व दु:खों से बहुत ऊँचे पद का परम आनन्द ।"[20] धम्मपद में भी निर्वाण को परम सुख कहा गया है—"निब्बाणं परमं सुखं ।"[21]

जिस तरह प्रारम्भिक बौद्धमत में निर्वाण को सुखस्वरूप माना गया है, उसी तरह तैत्तिरीय उपनिषद् में भी ब्रह्मप्राप्ति रूप मोक्ष को आनन्दमय ही कहा गया है—"एष ह्येवानन्दयति । यदा ह्येवैष एतस्मिन्नदृश्येऽनात्म्येऽनिरुक्तेऽनिलयनेऽभयं प्रतिष्ठां विन्दते । अथ सोऽभयं गतो भवति ।"[22]

समासतः, मैक्समूलर और डॉ. राधाकृष्णन् के शब्दों के साथ सहमति रखते हुए हम कह सकते हैं—"उपनिषदों के बहुत से सिद्धान्त निःसन्देह विशुद्ध बौद्ध धर्म के ही सिद्धान्त हैं, अथवा इसे यों कहना अधिक सङ्गत होगा कि अनेक विषयों में बौद्ध धर्म ने ठीक-ठीक रूप में उन्हीं सिद्धान्तों को क्रियात्मक रूप दिया जो उपनिषदों में प्रतिपादित किए गए थे। बुद्ध स्वयं को किसी नवीन व्यवस्था का संस्थापक न समझ कर केवल प्राचीन मार्ग का पुनरुद्धारक समझते थे, और वह मार्ग उपनिषदों का था।"[23]

सन्दर्भ-सङ्केत

1. कठोपनिषद्-1.2.26 तथा 28
2. धम्मपद, जरावग्गो-147-149
3. मुण्डकोपनिषद्-1.2.10
4. भारतीय दर्शन (डॉ. राधाकृष्णन्) खण्ड-1, पृ.332
5. ईशावास्योपनिषद्-9-11, कठोपनिषद्-1.2.4-5 तथा मुण्डकोपनिषद्-1.2.8-9
6. मज्झिमनिकाय, प्रथम अध्याय, पृ.54
7. भारतीय दर्शन का इतिहास (एस. एन. दासगुप्त), भाग-1, पृ.112
8. उदान-पृ.72
9. कठोपनिषद्-2.2.15, मुण्डकोपनिषद्-2.2.10 तथा श्वेताश्वतरोपनिषद्-6.14
10. ईशावास्योपनिषद्-1
11. मिलिन्दपञ्ह-पृ.73
12. माध्यमकशास्त्र-18.6
13. तैत्तिरीय उपनिषद्-2.9
14. माध्यमकशास्त्र-18.8
15. बृहदारण्यकोपनिषद्-3.9.26
16. माध्यमकशास्त्र-1.1
17. भारतीय दर्शन, खण्ड-1-पृ.354
18. वही-पृ.355
19. श्वेताश्वतर उपनिषद्-6.19
20. भारतीय दर्शन, खण्ड-1, पृ. 413
21. धम्मपद, सुखवग्गो-203
22. तैत्तिरीय उपनिषद्-2.7
23. भारतीय दर्शन, खण्ड-1-पृ.434

रॉंची

भारतीय चिन्तनधारा में भगवान् बुद्ध के कार्य एवं महत्त्व

वीणा गौड़

वेद विश्व-साहित्य के प्राचीनतम अवशेष हैं । बौद्ध विचारधारा, जिसका उदय ईसा से 500 वर्ष पूर्व हुआ था, सम्पूर्ण वैदिक साहित्य को स्वीकार करती है । बौद्ध ग्रन्थ त्रिपिटक समाज के सामान्य मानव के दैनिक जीवन का दर्पण हैं जिसके अन्तर्गत तत्कालीन समाज के सभी वर्गों का सामाजिक चित्रण निहित है । भगवान् बुद्ध ने चारिकाएँ करते हुए जो उपदेश दिए उनका संग्रह त्रिपिटक के रूप में बाद में किया गया । उनकी चारिका बहुजन हिताय, बहुजन सुखाय[1] तथा लोक कल्याणार्थ होती थी जिससे दुःख-विमुक्ति का मार्ग प्रशस्त हो सके । बुद्ध-वचनों का प्रयोग जन-साधारण के लिए हुआ जिसमें अशिक्षित भी शामिल थे । इसीलिए इनका प्रचार-प्रसार लोक-भाषा के माध्यम से लोक कथाओं के द्वारा अधिक हुआ । फलस्वरूप बुद्ध की शिक्षा अधिक सरल व बोधगम्य हो सकी थी ।

भारतीय चिन्तनधारा से हमारा अभिप्राय विचारधारा के 'दार्शनिक पक्ष' से है । सांसारिक पदार्थों का वर्गीकरण एवं विश्लेषण करके उनका युक्ति-युक्त विवेचन प्रस्तुत करना ही 'दार्शनिक-पक्ष' है । बुद्ध-चिन्तन का मनन करने के अनन्तर जो आधार परिलक्षित होते हैं वे 'आचार-पक्ष' और 'दार्शनिक-पक्ष' के रूप में दिखाई देते हैं । दोनों ही पक्षों में भगवान् बुद्ध ने "मध्यम प्रतिपदा" का आविष्कार करके लोक-कल्याण में योगदान किया । किसी भी विचार-धारा के अध्ययन-हेतु निम्नलिखित प्रमुख पक्ष दृष्टिगत होते हैं—

विचार पक्ष, आचार पक्ष, साधना और उपासना पक्ष तथा पुराण एवं विश्वास पक्ष ।

प्रथम श्रेणी के अन्तर्गत विचारधारा का *'चिन्तन-पक्ष'* (दार्शनिक-पक्ष) आता है । दर्शन, विचारधारा का प्राणभूत तत्त्व व आधारशिला है । जिस प्रकार आधार अर्थात् नींव के बिना किसी भव्य-भवन का निर्माण सम्भव नहीं है, उसी प्रकार इस आधारशिला के अभाव में कोई भी विचारधारा एक विधि-निषेधों का समूहमात्र है । अतएव 'विचार-पक्ष' के अन्तर्गत सभी दार्शनिक और आध्यात्मिक तत्त्वों का समावेश है । बौद्ध दर्शन में 'प्रतीत्यसमुत्पाद' के माध्यम से दार्शनिक पक्ष को निर्दिष्ट किया गया है जिसका अर्थ अन्योन्याश्रित अर्थात् एक दूसरे की अपेक्षा से परस्पर उत्पत्ति बताई गई है ।

आचार-पक्ष विचारधारा का 'व्यावहारिक पक्ष' है। यह मानव समाज को नियन्त्रित करने वाला तत्त्व है। तात्कालिक समाज में आचार-पक्ष में प्रायः दो प्रकार के लोग थे। प्रथम वे जो प्रवृत्ति मार्ग से हटकर घोर तपस्या के द्वारा शारीरिक कष्ट के पक्षधर थे तथा द्वितीय वे जो सांसारिक सुखों में निमग्न होकर ही जीवन की इतिकर्त्तव्यता समझते थे। भगवान् बुद्ध ने इन दो अतियों अर्थात् **अत्तकिलमथानुयोगः** तथा **कामेसुकामसुखल्लिकानुयोगः** को छोड़कर 'अष्टांगिक[2] मार्ग का आविष्कार किया जो कि 'मध्यम प्रतिपदा' के नाम से विश्वविश्रुत है।

साधना तथा उपासना के अन्तर्गत दो भाग हैं — साधना और उपासना। अमरत्व तथा मोक्षप्राप्ति की प्रयत्न-पद्धति को साधना कहते हैं तथा उस प्रयत्न के आन्तरिक समर्पण को उपासना कहते हैं। उस समर्पण से पूर्व किए जाने वाले बाह्य उपचारों को 'पूजा' की संज्ञा से अभिहित किया गया है। यह विचारधारा का 'धार्मिक पक्ष' है।

प्रत्येक पद्धति में कुछ ऐसी सामान्य बातों का समावेश अवश्य होता है जिससे कि उसका प्रभाव जनसाधारण के मानस-पटल पर शीघ्र होता है। फलस्वरूप वह जनमानस को सरलता से बोधगम्य हो जाती है। वे सामान्य बातें (तत्त्व) ही '**विश्वास**' और '**पुराण पक्ष**' के अन्तर्गत आते हैं। इन्हीं का समन्वित रूप विचारधारा है।

रायस डेविड्स ने अपने विचार व्यक्त करते हुए कहा है[3]— भागवान् बुद्ध ने अस्तित्व के धर्म को जान लिया है तथा उसके कारण और निरोध को भी भली प्रकार पहचान लिया है। 'अभिधर्म कोश' में बुद्ध ने स्वयं आजीवकों के साथ विवाद करते हुए कहा है कि प्रत्येक वस्तु का अस्तित्व है। आजीवकों ने पूर्वकर्मों तथा नियति के प्रभाव का स्पष्ट निषेध करते हुए कहा- क्योंकि वे भूतकालिक हैं और उनकी कोई सत्ता नहीं है। अतः पूर्व कर्म हमारी नियति को प्रभावित नहीं कर सकते। भगवान् बुद्ध ने वस्तु की सत्ता में 'द्वादस निदान' का समावेश[4] किया है। उन्होंने नैतिक उत्तरदायित्व को महत्त्व दिया और संस्कार-समूह में परिवर्तन की भावना को जागृत किया जिन्हें 'पञ्च-स्कन्ध' (रूप, वेदना, संज्ञा, संस्कार तथा विज्ञान) के द्वारा जनमानस को बताया। वस्तुतः इन्हीं स्कन्धों की अनुभूति एवं कार्यावस्था को ही 'धर्म' कहा गया। रायस डेविड्स ने बौद्धमत का स्पष्टीकरण करते हुए कहा है कि आत्मादि की स्वीकृति ही भ्रमोत्पादक है[5]। इच्छाओं, आशाओं और सांसारिक पदार्थों के प्रति आसक्ति व्यर्थ है। ये सभी वस्तुएँ दुःख व मोह उत्पन्न करने वाली हैं।

कार्य तथा महत्त्व— इन दोनों शब्दों में बौद्ध विचारधारा को संक्षिप्त रूप में ही प्रस्तुत करने का प्रयास किया है। 'कार्य' से अभिप्राय उन नियमों और परम्पराओं से है जो उनके द्वारा प्रचलित किए गये थे तथा जो अपना विरोध होते हुए भी समाज द्वारा स्वीकृत व वन्दनीय थे। 'महत्त्व' से अभिप्राय है कि आचरणों का समाज में क्या प्रतिक्रियात्मक रूप रहा? तथा उसके बाद के क्या परिणाम हुए? उनके कार्यों में 'बुद्धिवादिता' प्रथम महत्त्वपूर्ण सोपान कहा जा सकता है।

बुद्धिवादिता— तात्कालिक समाज में प्रचलित प्रभावपूर्ण 'ब्राह्मण पद्धति' को बाह्य आडम्बर और अन्धविश्वास का पोषक बताकर उसका विरोध किया तथा उसमें श्रद्धा न रखते हुए बुद्धिवादिता का समावेश करना इनका सर्वप्रथम कार्य माना जा सकता है। भगवान् बुद्ध ने अपनी विचारधारा में अन्धविश्वास के प्रति की जाने वाली श्रद्धा को तर्क के रूप में परिवर्तित किया तथा वेदवाणी व गुरुवचन में अनास्था प्रकट कर व्यक्ति के स्वतन्त्र चिन्तन को अवसर प्रदान किया। यज्ञ-याग आदि में देवों की परिकल्पना और उनकी पूजा-अर्चना के प्रति इन्होंने सदैव विरोध प्रकट किया। इसके विपरीत यह उद्घोषणा की कि साधक को 'युक्तिशरण' होना चाहिए 'पुद्गलशरण' नहीं[6]। तथागत ने अपने शिष्यों को सदा यही कहा— स्वयं अनुभव के पश्चात् ही मेरे वचनों को ग्रहण करो, केवल 'मैंने कहे हैं' इस आधार पर नहीं।

अनात्मवाद— 'अनात्मवाद' बुद्धधर्म की दार्शनिक भित्ति है जिस पर समग्र आचार-विचार अपने आश्रय के निमित्त अवलम्बित है। सुगत ने आत्मवाद का खण्डन अत्यन्त अभिनिवेश के साथ किया है। उनका कथन है कि आत्मवादी पुरुष आत्मा के स्वरूप को बिना जाने उसके मङ्गल की कामना कर अनेक प्रकार के सत्कर्म और दुष्कर्म उसी प्रकार करता है जिस प्रकार कोई व्यक्ति देश की सबसे सुन्दर स्त्री के रंग-रूप तथा गुणों को देखे बिना ही उससे प्रेम करता है। ऐसे पुरुष का आचरण लोक में उपहासास्पद होता है। सत्ताहीन पदार्थों की प्राप्ति का उद्योग परम मूर्खता का सूचक है। उसी प्रकार असत् आत्मा के मङ्गल के लिए नाना प्रकार के कर्मों का सम्पादन है[7]। बुद्ध के मतानुसार आत्मा की सत्ता स्वीकारना केवल बालधर्म है।[8] वे नित्य, ध्रुव आत्मा के अस्तित्व के मानने से पूर्णतः पराङ्मुख हैं।

अनीश्वरवाद— अनात्मवाद के सदृश ही वे ईश्वरीय सत्ता को निर्मूल समझते थे। उन्होंने ईश्वर, जीव, ब्रह्म तथा प्रकृति इत्यादि दस विषयों को अव्याकृत की श्रेणी में परिगणित किया। अपने उपदेशों में अपनी अनीश्वरवादी भावना को स्पष्ट शब्दों में व्यक्त किया है। दीघनिकाय[9] में ईश्वर को भी अन्य देवताओं के तुल्य एक सामान्य देवता कहा है। 'तेविज्जसुत्त' में इन्होंने ब्रह्मा की सलोकता को प्राप्त कराने वाली विचारधारा को तुच्छ बतलाते हुए त्रैविद्यब्राह्मणों के कथन को "अन्धवेणी" तुल्य बताया है।[10]

देवों के प्रति अनास्था— भगवान् बुद्ध ने देवताओं की पूजा का विरोध पूर्णरूप से नहीं किया है अपितु देवताओं पर आश्रित रहकर मनुष्य में उत्पन्न होने वाली अकर्मण्यता को दूर करने का प्रयास किया है।[11] पालि साहित्य में अनेक स्थलों पर इन्द्रदेव का भगवान् बुद्ध के सम्मुख हाथ जोड़कर खड़े रहना देवताओं के महत्त्व की अल्पता को दर्शाता है।

गुरुवाद एवं मठवाद के प्रति अनास्था— बौद्धों ने गुरुवाद और मठवाद को विशेष महत्त्व नहीं दिया क्योंकि समाज में धर्मगुरुओं द्वारा धर्म का विकृत रूप प्रस्तुत किया जाता था। अतएव फलाभाव के कारण मानव को स्वयं मार्ग निर्मित करने का साहस प्रदान किया।

समस्त संसार अनित्य है । अपने निर्वाण के लिए प्रमादरहित होकर यत्नशील रहो । 'अत्तदीपा[12] विहरथ' अर्थात् 'तुम अपने लिए स्वयं दीपक हो, दूसरे का सहारा न ढूँढो' । ऐसे स्वावलम्बी विचार बुद्ध के महत्त्व को स्थापित करते हैं ।

भगवान् बुद्ध की विचारधारा आदर्श अथवा दोषों का ही उल्लेख करती है, ऐसी बात नहीं है अपितु उन दोषों के निराकरण का सरलतम मार्ग भी प्रशस्त करती है । यही स्थिति आदर्श और यथार्थ का सङ्गम है । उन्होंने आन्तरिक संशुद्धि पर बल दिया । उनका विश्वास था कि मनुष्य को व्यर्थ के तर्क-वितर्क में न पड़कर सरल, स्वाभाविक तथा सदाचार पूर्ण जीवन व्यतीत करना चाहिए । उनकी धारणा श्रमणमार्गी थी । वे श्रमण थे किन्तु कर्मों का उनकी दृष्टि में अत्यन्त महत्त्व था । वे कर्म को ही नियति का अभिधान देते थे । पालिग्रन्थ 'मिलिन्दपञ्ह' में नागसेन के वक्तव्य के माध्यम से कर्म की महत्ता को दर्शाया गया है ।

भगवान् बुद्ध महान सुधारक, योगी, सुसंस्कृत तथा अहङ्कारहीन थे । उन्होंने आडम्बरयुक्त, वर्णत्रस्त समाज के कल्याणार्थ अनेक कार्य किए । उनकी दृष्टि आचार-प्रधान थी । वे महान नैतिकवादी भी थे । 'धम्मपद' में बुद्ध-शासन के रहस्य को तीन शब्दों में ही स्पष्ट रूप से व्यक्त किया गया है—

सब्बपापस्स अकरणं कुसलस्स उपसम्पदा ।
सचित्त-परियोदपनं एतं बुद्धान सासनं ।।[13]

अर्थात् सब पापों का न करना, पुण्य का सञ्चय तथा अपने चित्त की परिशुद्धि- यही बुद्धोपदेशसार है ।

सन्दर्भ-सङ्केत

1. 'चरथ भिक्खवे, चारिकं बहुजनहिताय बहुजनसुखाय लोकानुकम्पाय अत्थाय हिताय सुखाय देवमनुस्सानं' । (महावग्गो-1,2,5,1)
2. सम्यक दृष्टि, सम्यक् सङ्कल्प, सम्यक् वचन, सम्यक्-कर्म, सम्यक् आजीव, सम्यक् व्यायाम, सम्यक् स्मृति और सम्यक् समाधि ।
3. दी सेंट्रल कन्सेप्शन ऑफ बुद्धिज़्म, प्रो. शेर वात्स्की, पृ० 51
4. अविद्या, संस्कार, विज्ञान, नाम-रूप, षडायतन, स्पर्श, वेदना, तृष्णा, उपादान, भव, जाति और जरामरण । इसे ही 'भव-चक्र' कहा जाता है ।
5. मेक्स वेबर, दी रिलीजन ऑफ़ इन्डिया, पृ० 206-207
6. बौद्ध दर्शन मीमांसा, पृ० 53
7. दीघनिकाय (हिन्दी अनुवाद), पृ० 73

8. 'अयं भिक्खवे, केवलो परिपूरो बालधम्मो', (मज्झिम निकाय, पृ० 1,1,2.)
9. पाथिक सुत्त, दी.नि, 3/1, केवट्ट सुत्त-11
10. तेविज्ज सुत्त, दी.नि., 13
11. सी. इलियट, हिन्दूइज़्म एण्ड बुद्धिज़्म, भाग-1, पृ० 20
12. बौद्ध धर्म तथा दर्शन (आचार्य नरेन्द्र देव), पृ० 11
13. धम्मपद, 14.5

दिल्ली

SECTION IV

Buddhist Literature & History

PRINCIPAL SENTIMENT IN THE NĀGĀNANDA

N.P. Unni

We can see that the plot of the *Nāgānanda* of Śriharṣa has two parts; the first deals with a charming love affair and the second with an exciting and magnanimous sacrifice. In both, Jīmūtavāhana plays the role of a hero. Now the question arises as to what is the principal sentiment in the play.

Being a drama either *Śṛṅgāra* or *Vīra* has to be delineated as the principal sentiment. Apparently, here both are well delineated. The treatment of *Śṛṅgāra* is appropriately and very effectively carried out in the first part of the story. The first three acts have enough scope for being considered as a drama on its own right. It is the last two acts which introduce *Vīra* to be exact the variety called *Dayāvīra*. The rules of Indian dramaturgy prescribe that only one of the two shall be principal; the other sentiments shall only be subordinated. What sentiment is the principal one in the present play? This is a difficult question to answer. If *Śṛṅgāra* were the principal one, the last two acts have no purpose. On the other hand, if *Vīra* delineated in the last acts is the chief sentiment then the delineation of *Śṛṅgāra* in the first part is predominantly clear. Thus in fact there is a little incongruity on the part of the dramatist. Let us consider the various sentiments that appear as predominant in the play one by one.

Śṛṅgāra as the principal one

The *Nāgānanda*[1] is conceived as drama enacted at an autumn festival. The stage-director informs the audience through his announcement that "today in the festival held in honour of Indra, I was cordially invited and told by the assemblage of princes who had arrived from several countries in different quarters to put on the *Nāgānanda*." It may appear proper to the occassion to put on a drama having the erotic sentiment at an autumn festival.

In the drama at hand we have the erotic sentiment delineated appropriately and boldly. Of the total of five acts, the first three contain an elaborate treatment of *Śṛṅgāra*. In other words, a major portion of the plot deals with *Śṛṅgāra* as the main sentiment. One cannot say that delineation is subtle. On the other hand there is enough scope for the full *Rasa* here.

In the first act, the *Vidūṣaka* forces a meeting of the timid lovers, when an ascetic from the hermitage arrives to take the heroine away. In Act II, Malayavatī who is love-sick, rests on a stone-seat in the garden. The King enters the same garden and shows his torments of love. He declares his love for the heroine and hints at the pangs of separation. Mitrāvasu comes to offer his sister's hand and the prince refuses it without knowing the identity of the lady. This makes the heroine desperate and she tries to hang herself. Her friends call for help and the hero saves her from the calamity and to his surprise learns that his sweetheart is none other than the sister of Mitrāvasu. The hero and the heroine are soon married. In the third act, after a comic interlude, we find the hero and the heroine enjoying the pleasures of life. Thus the first three Acts contain a beautiful love story. There is no hint at all for the theme to be described in the last two acts---at least to any appreciable extent.

In dealing with this part, it seems the dramatist has conceived it as a compact story, it appears. The sentiment of *Śṛṅgāra* is gradually developed passing through the usual and prescribed stages of delineation. There is nothing sudden or incongruous. In treating the sentiment of love, he delineates it from the first suggestion of an innocent mind to the perfection of passion depicting the various stages of love in consonance with the rules of Hindu dramaturgy. There is the feeling of union and anxiety of separation. The course of love is not smooth. The obstructions are overcome before the final union is achieved. All this will tempt a reader to consider *Śṛṅgāra* as the principal sentiment of the play.

But a careful perusal of the play as a whole will force one to abandon this view. The title of the play *Nāgānanda* itself will stand against such a proposition. The title literally means "the joy of the serpents." In the first three acts, there is no sufficient material to justify the title. Only in the later part of the story the idea is mooted and developed. The hero has to make the serpents happy by his benevolent acts. Then only the title becomes appropriate. The pious and magnanimous hero saves the race of *Nāgas* from utter destruction by offering his own life at the alter of sacrifice. According to some critics the story has some social significance too. *Nāgas*–a clan of snake-worshippers, whose name survives in the city of Nagpur represent the oppressed class for whom Jīmūtavāhana gave a timely help for survival.

Further, the Buddhistic elements in the play also deserve notice. The story is of a Boddhisattva and it is drawn by the dramatist from *'Vidyādharajātaka'* and recorded in the *Kathā* literature like *Bṛhatkathā* and *Kathāsaritsāgara*. To do full justice to the source, the great qualities of Jimūtavāhana are to be brought out in vivid details. It is only in the act of sacrifice that this worthy aspect is boldly pointed out. Hence the whole of the drama is to be considered before concluding as to what *Rasa* is delineated therein.

The *Śṛṅgāra* delineated in the first three Acts is clearly to bring out the general nature of the hero and the early history of his activities. Hence the delineation becomes subsidiary. *Vīra*---the heroic sentiment is the one intended by the poet thought it is not so much evident in the early part of the drama.

Vīra forms the principal sentiment

A careful examination of all aspects of the story forces one to conclude that *Vīra* is the main sentiment of the drama. The hero is a *Dhīrodātta* considering his many noble qualities and actions. Authorities on dramaturgy classify *Vīra* into three varieties. The first variety is called *Yuddhavīra* which is found in the actions of heroes like Śrīrāma. *Dānavīra* noticed in the actions of Paraśurāma is the second variety while the third one called *Dayāvīra* is exemplified through the actions of characters like Jīmūtavāhana. His bravery is not of the conventional type though he is not at all afraid of death. Real bravery consists in the endurance under the severest trials. The pain inflicted by Garuḍa is no cause for worry to Jīmūtavāhana. He does not feel the pain since his heart is compassionate towards the *Nāgas* who are mercilessly destroyed by Garuḍa preying on them everyday. His own pain is overshadowed by the pleasure of self-sacrifice. His act of bravery even causes Garuḍa to change his cruel outlook and habits and forces him to choose the path of *Ahiṁsā*. It is this self-sacrifice that distinguishes Jīmūtavāhana from the conventional heroes met with in Sanskrit dramas. Life is considered worth living if only it could be used for the service of others. It is this idea that is sought to be explained throughout the course of the play.

Dhanika, the author of the *Avaloka* commentary of Dhanañjaya's *Daśarūpaka* has dealt with these aspects in detail. He cites Jīmūtavāhana of the *Nāgānanda* as an instance of a *Dhīrodātta* type of hero and establishes the point adducing evidence from the play.[2] Dhanañjaya has defined *Dhīrodātta* as :

महासत्त्वोऽतिगम्भीरः क्षमावानविकत्थनः ।
स्थिरो निगूढाहङ्कारो धीरोदात्तो दृढव्रतः ॥[3]

This is explained by his commentator illustrating Jīmūtavāhana as the best example. Dhanika further adds that the hero of the *Nāgānanda* excells others since he showed his magnanimity by endangering his life for the sake of another fellow creature. He observes:

जीमूतवाहनादिस्तु प्राणैरपि परार्थसम्पादनाद् विश्वमप्यतिशेते, इत्युदात्ततमः ।[4]

He admits that in common with Buddha, the hero of the Nāgānanda has the quality of being pious. Still, there is a subtle difference. Dhanika continues :

बुद्धजीमूतवाहनयोस्तु कारुणिकत्वाविशेषेऽपि सकामनिष्कामकरुणत्वादिधर्मत्वादभेदः । अतो जीमूतवाहनादेर्धीरोदात्तत्वमिति ।[5]

Thus, it may be seen that Jīmūtavāhana is a *Dhīrodātta* hero beyond a shadow of doubt. It is also evident that *Dayāvīra*---one of the three divisions of *Vīra,* is the dominant emotion of the play. The delineation of the other sentiments only heightens its charm. This is the view that found acceptance at the hands of Indian literary critics.

Śāntarasa and the *Nāgānanda*

It is to be noted that the *Dhvanyāloka* school of critics hold *Śānta* as the dominant *Rasa* in the *Nāgānanda*. The delineation of *Śānta* ultimately leads to the sacrifice of his body by the hero. It is brought out by the first three stanzas spoken by the hero beginning with *"rāgasyāspadam ityavaimi"* etc. But before *Śṛṅgāra* is introduced, there is a subtle touch of the sentiment of wonder to act as a bridge in between. It is held that *Śānta* and *Śṛṅgāra* are not mutually incompatible, provided some other *Rasa* intervenes suitably. Ānandavardhana has permitted such delineation when he says :

विवक्षिते रसे लब्धप्रतिष्ठे तु विरोधिनाम् ।
बाह्यानामङ्गभावं वा प्राप्तानामुक्तिरच्छला ॥[6]

Once the intended leading sentiment has been established on a secure footing, there will be no defect in including even hindrances provided that these come as ancilliaries. Thus, *Śānta* is introduced first. Then the feeling of wonder intervenes to pave way for the introduction of a different sentiment. It is only then the emotion of *Śṛṅgāra* makes its appearance. It is gradually developed upto the end of the third act. *Hāsya* now appears to relieve the monotony before the next feeling is introduced. It is then the sentiment *Vīra* is adopted. The sentiment disappears giving occasion for Śānta which again asserts itself and continues upto the end of the play. This is how the view of the above theorists is elaborated.

The above view is opposed by some critics pointing out several reasons. First, it is held that according to the early school of rhetoricians, *Śānta Rasa* itself is not recognised. They point out that this particular *Rasa* is not enumerated by Bharata in his *Nāṭyaśāstra* since according to him it has no purpose to serve in drama which is composed to generate pleasure in the audience. Kālidāsa, the greatest of the dramatists has only alluded to eight sentiments and it is almost certain that he did not approve of *Śānta* in a dramatic composition.[7]

Dhanika who commented on the *Daśarūpaka*, criticises the propriety of introducing *Śānta* in dramas. He cites the *Nāgānanda* and observes that only *Vīra* can be accpted as the principal sentiment there. He states :

यत्तु कैश्चिन्नागानन्दादौ ़गमस्य स्थायित्वमुपवर्णितं, तत्तु मलयवत्यनुरागेणाऽऽप्रबन्धप्रवृत्तेन विद्याधरचक्रवर्तित्वप्राप्त्याविरुद्धम् । अतो दयावीरोत्साहस्यैव तत्र स्थायित्वम् ।

Thus Dhanika has established that *Śānta* could not be taken as the principal sentiment in the play.

Thus it is a matter of dispute as to what is the principal sentiment. Sentiments like *Śṛṅgāra, Vīra* and *Śānta* stake their claim for the status. Each view can be entertained to a certain extent pointing out situations in the play. The last one is eliminated on the ground that Bharata has not accepted it in dramas. Regarding the other two, the first appears more prominently in a major portion of the text. But then it ends rather abruptly towards the end of the third Act. Hence, it too cannot be given the status of the principal emotion. On the other hand, *Vīra* has an overall pervasion though subtle in appearance in the early part of the play. There again *Vīra* is not of the bold type. It is the variety known as *Dayāvīra* that suits the tenor of the play. Hence, it may be concluded that *Vīra* is the principal sentiment in *Nāgānanda*.

REFERENCES & NOTES

1. *Nāgānanda* of Śrīharṣa with *Vimarśinī* commentary of Śivarāma; Ed. Dr. N.P. Unni, Nag Publishers; Delhi, 1989.
2. *Daśarūpaka* of Dhanañjaya with the commentary *Avaloka* of Dhanika, Motilal Banarasidass, Delhi, 1979, p. 139.
3. *Ibid*. p. 137.
4. *Ibid*. p. 140.
5. *Ibid*. p. 141.
6. *Dhvanyāloka*, III, 20.
7. *Vikramorvaśīya*, II. 17.

मुनिना भरतेन यः प्रयोगो
भवतीष्वष्टरसाश्रयो नियुक्तः ।
ललिताभिनयं तमद्य भर्ता
मरुतां द्रष्टुमनाः सलोकपालः ।

Trivendrum

CAMPĀ MAHĀNAGARA'S CONTRIBUTION TO THE DEVELOPMENT OF EARLY BUDDHISM

K.T.S. Sarao

When Ānanda had a discussion with the Exalted One about a suitable place for *Mahāparinibbāna*[1] befitting the latter's position, Ānanda suggested the names of six *mahānagaras* so that many wealthy nobles, brāhmaṇas and heads of families may pay due honour to the remains of the Tathāgata.[2] Campā is named by Ānanda as one of these six *mahānagaras*.[3] In this paper, an attempt is made to study the contribution made by Campā in nursing Buddhism in its nascent phase.

The word "*Mahānagara*" literally means "Great City" but may be translated as metropolis. Settlements of this category were not only the real representatives of hardcore urban culture, but also controlled the fortunes of other urban settlements in more than one way.[4] Campā, was also known by other names like Campāmālinī, Campānagara and Kālacampā.[5] It was the capital of Aṅga mahājanapada and was situated on the eastern bank of river Campā.[6] It is identified with modern Campanagar situated at 25^0 15′ Lat.N and 86^0 58′ Long. E i.e. 24 miles from Bhagalpur in Bihar.[7] The Buddha's bathing-robe was deposited here after the *Mahāparinibbāna*.[8] Sages from the Himālaya came to this settlement in order to procure salt and condiments.[9] This settlement is said to have been "full of life, grassland, woodland, water and corn."[10] We are told that this place was fortified as it had gates and watch-towers,[11] a fact which is testified by the archaeological records.[12] Campā was an important centre of trade from where merchants travelled to far off places like Suvaṇṇabhūmi.[13] Evidence of extensive craft activity is provided by the archaeological finds of gold and stone ornaments as well as jeweller's moulds from about the NBPW phase till the Gupta period.[14] In all probability, it was the colonists from Campā who named one of their most important settlements in Indo-China after this famous old settlement.

Campā was the place where on the banks of the Gaggarāpokkharṇī, *Suttas* like the *Soṇadaṇḍa,*[15] *Dasuttara,*[16] *Kandaraka*[17] and the *Kāraṇḍava*[18] were preached besides the various regulations that were laid down here regarding the validity and invalidity of various formal acts of the *Saṃgha* as *Piṭaka.*[19] On one occasion, when the Buddha was sojourning here, Sāriputta approached him with a large number of the inhabitants of Campā and asked him questions about the efficacy of giving alms.[20] On another occasion, on the banks of the Gaggarāpokkharṇi, Vaṅgīsa alongwith a large number of monks and lay-followers, praised the Buddha in a song, pointing out how the Buddha outshone them all.[21] On the same spot, the *Dasuttara Sutta,* the last (34th) *Sutta* of the *Dīgha Nikāya* was preached by Sāriputta in the presence of the Buddha. It consists of groups of doctrines---ten single doctrines, ten two-fold doctrines, and so on up to ten tenfold.[22] At the end of the discourse 500 monks are said to have attained arhanthood.[23]

Soṇa-Kolivisa Thera was possibly the most important personality contributed by Campā to early Buddhism. He was a squire (*Paddhagu*) of Aṅga.[24] The day he was born, the whole city of Campā kept festival. He proved very lucky for his father as right from the day of his inception his father's income, who was a banker, started to increase. He got his name from the fact that his body was like burnished gold because he had presented an expensive ring in his previous birth to a pacceka Buddha. He lived in great luxury and his hands and feet were soft like *Bandhujīvaka* flowers, and a fine dawn grew upon them. King Bimbisāra, hearing of him, sent for him, and Soṇa Kolivisa went with 80,000 Campā-residents. While in Rājagaha, he heard the Buddha preach and entered the Order after having obtained his parents' permission. After having meditated for a long time at Sitavana, he could not win any attainment and this drove him to despair. The Buddha helped him by preaching to him the *Vinūpamovāda Sutta,* taught him the art of tempering energy with calm. After this Soṇa-Kolivisa made fresh effort and attained arhanthood.[25]

Soṇadaṇḍa was a learned Brāhmaṇa of Campā who lived in a royal domain given to him as a royal gift by King Bimbisāra. Once, while the Buddha was in Campā, Soṇadaṇḍa visited him on the banks of the Gaggarāpokkharṇi despite the protests of his colleagues and friends. After the conversation, which is recorded in the *Soṇadaṇḍa Sutta,* the elderly Brāhmaṇa expressed appreciation of the Buddha and his doctrine as well and invited the Buddha and his monks to a meal. Soṇadaṇḍa, at the end of the meal apologized to the Buddha for simply saluting him instead of having made humble obeisance in the presence of other Brāhmaṇas.[26] On the basis of this, it has been conjectured that perhaps Soṇadaṇḍa's conversion was partial,[27] yet his soft corner for Buddhism must have helped it immensely.

Jambugāmika Thera was born at Campā and he became an arhant after realizing his imperfections through a verse sent by his father.[28] The Buddhist texts mention three kings who ruled from Campā. One was Aṇga who fought a protracted war with the king of Magadha, with fluctuating fortunes. In the end, Aṅga lost the war, was slain and his country annexed into Magadha.[29] The second king was Dhataraṭṭha, who was the contemporary and vassal of king Reṇu.[30] The third king was Asama, who was the father of three brothers viz. Upasāla, Sāla and Paduma Buddha, the eighth of the twentyfour Buddhas.[31] Besides Paduma Buddha, Bodhisatta Susīma, who became an ascetic of great fame, was also born at Campā in the time of the Atthadassī Buddha.[32]

Nandaka Thera and Bharata Thera were two brothers from Campā, who had renounced household life after having heard that Soṇa-Kolivisa had renounced the world. Bharata, after having acquired six-fold *abhiññā,* gave a discourse on insight to his slow-witted brother. When Bharata was discoursing to Nandaka, a caravan passed by. A bull unable to pull the cart through the boggy place, fell down. The caravan leader had the bull fed with grass and water, after having him released. Now the bull was able to pull the cart. Nandaka's attention was drawn by Bharata to this incident, and the former, making this topic his subject of meditation, soon attained arhanthood[33].

Pessa, who was an elephant trainer by profession, was a man of great understanding. He is said to have once visited the Buddha at Gaggarāpokkharṇī and the conversation that took place between the two is recorded in the *Kandaraka Sutta.*[34] In this *Sutta,* the Buddha enumerated to Pessa and Kandaraka the four kinds of people in the world; those who torment themselves, torment others, torment both themselves and others, and , those who torment neither, dwelling beyond appetites, in bliss and holiness. But before the Buddha could further elaborate on the four categories of men, Pessa went away.[35] It was also on the bank of Gaggarāpokkharṇī in Campā that in response to a query from a monk called Bāhuna, the Buddha enumerated the ten conditions from which the Tathāgata is released and emancipated.[36] The *Kāraṇḍava Sutta* was also recited by the Buddha on the banks of the Gaggarāpokkharṇī at Campā.[37] As per this *Sutta*, a monk charged by his colleagues with an offence, reviled them. The Buddha hearing of this, insisted that the monk should be expelled from the Order forthwith, lest the rest of the community should suffer by his presence. He illustrated his argument with various similes among them that of an owner of the barley-field who, on seeing a diseased plant which failed to ripen, would uproot it and thow it away lest the other plants should be affected.

Vajjiyamāhita, a householder of Campā and a devout follower of the Buddha, was held by the Buddha to the monks as an example of a good householder who was capable of profitable discussion with followers of other persuasions.[38] Once in the Paribbājakārāma near the Gaggarāpokkharṇī, he refuted the allegations of the Paribbājakas that the Buddha ridiculed all forms of asceticism and austerity. He silenced them by maintaining that the Buddha declared what was good and what was bad, and that the truth of his teachings could be proved. The Buddha praised him for this good work and intellect.[39]

It may be interesting to note that as many as 173 urban settlements are mentioned in the *Pāli Vinaya* and *Sutta Piṭakas* and there are as many as 4682 references to these settlements in the two *Piṭakas*.[40] Campā is referred to 46 times in these texts, which makes about 1% of the total references. The break up of the references to Campā is as follows:

Text	Frequency
Dīgha Nikāya	17
Vinaya Piṭaka	12
Aṅguttara Nikāya	06
Jātakas	05

Buddhavaṃsa	02
Saṃyutta Nikāya	02
Majjhima Nikāya	01
Cariyāpiṭaka	01

Of the 2426 men and women mentioned in the *Pāli Vinaya* and *Sutta Piṭakas,* the settlement background of 1379 can be determined.[41] Out of these, 13 came from Campā which also makes about 1% of the total manpower that contributed towards the development of early Buddhism.

REFERENCES & NOTES

1. See *Mahāparinibbāna Suttanta, Dīgha Nikāya* (Ed.T.W. Rhys Davids & J.E. Carpenter, 3 vols, London: PTS, 1890-1911). II: 72-159.
2. *Dīgha Nikāya.* II.146.
3. The other five *mahānagaras* were Rājagaha, Sāvatthī, Sāketa, Kosāmbī and Bārāṇasī.
4. For detailed discussion see K.T.S. Sarao; *Urban Centres and Urbanisation as reflected in the Pāli Vinaya and Sutta Piṭakas,* Ph.D. dissertation submitted to the University of Cambridge, May 1989: 35-52.
5. K.T.S.Sarao; *Urban Centres and Urbanisation as reflected in the Pāli Vinaya and Sutta Piṭakas,* Delhi; Vidyanidhi, 1990: 57-58,122.
6. *Jātakas* (Ed.V.Fausboll, 6 vols, London: Trubner & Co, 1877-1897). IV.454.
7. A.Cunningham; *The ancient geography of India,* I, London: Trubner & Co. 1871: 546.
8. *Buddhavaṃsa* (Ed.N.A.Jayawickrama,London, 1974). XXVIII.9.
9. *Jātakas.*VI.256.
10. *Dīgha Nikāya.* I.112.
11. *Jātakas.*VI.32.
12. See for archaeological information, *Indian Archaeology: A Review,* New Delhi, 1969-70; 2-5; 1970-71: 4-5; 1972-73: 6-7; 1974-75: 8-9; 1975-76: 7; 1976-77: 11-12.
13. *Jātakas.* VI.539.
14. *Indian Archaeology: A Review,* 1974-75:9.
15. *Dīgha Nikāya.*I.111.
16. *Ibid.* III.272.
17. *Majjhima Nikākya* (Ed.V. Trenckner & R. Chelmers, 3vols, London: *PTS, 1888-1896). I. 339.*
18. *Aṅguttara Nikāya* (Ed.R. Morris & E. Hardy, 5 vols, London: PTS, 1885-1900).IV. 168.

19. *Vinaya Piṭaka (*Ed.H.Oldenberg, 5vols, London: *PTS, 1879-1883). 1.312ff, II.307.*
20. *Aṅguttara Nikāya.* IV. 59ff.
21. *Saṃyutta Nikāya.* I.195; *Theragāthā.* v.1252.
22. *Dīgha Nikāya.III.272ff.*
23. *Sumaṅgala-vilāsinī* (Ed.T.W. Rhys Davids, J.E.Carpenter & W. Stede, 3 vols, London; PTS, 1886-1971). III.1064.
24. *Theragāthā* (Ed.K.R.Norman & L.Alsdorf, London: PTS, 1966).v.632.
25. *Vinaya Piṭaka.* I. 179ff; *Theragāthā.* v.632-44; *Apdāna* (Ed.M.E. Lilley, 2 vols, London; PTS, 1925-27).I.24.
26. *Dīgha Nikāya.* I.111ff.
27. G.P. Malalasekera; *Dictionary of Pāli Proper Names;* Delhi: Orient Reprint, 1983, vol.2: 1297.
28. *Theragāthā.* v.28.
29. *Jātakas.* IV. 453.
30. *Dīgha Nikāya.* II.235.
31. *Buddhavaṃsa.* IX.9,21; *Jātakas.* I.36.
32. *Jātakas.* I. 39; *Buddhavaṃsa.* XV. 9f; *Maddhuratthavilāsinī* (Ed. I.B. Horner, London: PTS; 1946). 180.
33. *Theragāthā.* 173 f.
34. *Majjhima Nikāya.* 1.339ff.
35. *Ibid.*
36. *Aṅguttara Nikāya.* V. 151f.
37. *Ibid.* IV. 168ff.
38. *Ibid.* III.451, V.189ff.
39. *Ibid.*
40. See.K.T.S. Sarao (1990); Op. Cit. Appendix:I.
41. See K.T.S. Sarao; *The origin and nature of ancient Indian Buddhism,* Delhi: Eastern Book Linkers, 1989, Appendix: V.

Delhi

FROM PASSION TO SALVATION : NANDA'S JOURNEY TO ENLIGHTENMENT

S.M.P.N. Singh Shahi

The story of Gautama Buddha's enlightenment is well-known to all but what is least known is the pain that the Seer took to enlighten others with His own knowledge of the Supreme Truth. The Tathāgata's main endeavour was to make people understand that the worldly pleasures were the root cause of all sorrows in life. One who remained devoted to the objects of the senses derived a false pleasure at the cost of the real pleasure that could come to one only on observance of the Law that the Seer preached. Even if it was not possible for someone to adopt the wandering life (the life that the Buddha Himself led), he could reduce his passion to a minimum in order to ensure for himself a life of happiness, plenty and virtue. And those who remained absorbed in a life of passion invited doom for themselves.

No doubt, the spell of Buddha was such that people readily accepted Him as their spiritual guide and adopted the path paved by the great passion-free Seer. Even his father, the lord of the earth, became His disciple and prostrated himself before Him as before a *guru*. Describing the conversion of the King to Buddhism, Aśvaghoṣa says :

नृपतिस्ततः प्रथममाप फलममृतधर्मसिद्धयोः ।
धर्ममतुलमधिगम्य मुनेर्मुनये ननाम स यतो गुराविव ॥[1]

The king obtained the First Fruit for the fulfilment of the immortal Law and thus entered into possession of the unparalleled Law of the Seer. He then prostrated himself before Lord Buddha as before his spiritual guide.

Thereafter many young nobles of Kapilavastu took on themselves to observe the restrictions (as advised by Lord Buddha) till death and kept them with all their hearts. Even those, earlier occupied with the sensual objects now took delight in almsgiving, in the Rule and abstinence. In short, they now lived a blissful life :

अपि च स्वतोऽपि परतोऽपि न भयमभवन्न दैवतः ।
तत्र च सुसुखसुभिक्षगुणैर्जहृषुः प्रजा कृतयुगे मनोरिव ॥[2]

Now they were free from dangers from themselves, from others or from fate. They enjoyed a life of happiness, plenty and virtue as people did in the age of Manu.

Thus Buddha, the Enlightened, had not only gained complete control over Himself but also over the people He preached. But whereas almost all the townsmen of Kapilavastu, including the king and his kinsfolk, followed the path shown by Him, His half-brother, Nanda, paid no heed to the Law of the Seer. He remained in his palace absorbed in love with his mistress, Sundarī. They loved each other too passionately to care for whatever was happening outside the palace. Most of the times they engaged themselves in sportively intoxicating each other by way of various love-plays.

One day, while Nanda was thus taking delight inside his palace, the Tathāgata entered there for begging alms. But His arrival remained unnoticed not only by Nanda and Sundarī but also by the maids employed for their enjoyments. After waiting for a while, Buddha departed from there without obtaining any alms. It was then that He was noticed by one of the maids who informed Sundarī about the Holy One's departure from the palace. On learning this, Nanda was shaken from within and expressed his desire to immediately leave for paying reverence to the great Seer. The very thought of her separation from Nanda, even though temporary then, stirred Sundarī from within and she clasped him trembling as a creeper stirred by the wind clasps a *śāla* tree. With tearful eyes, she took a promise from Nanda that he would return to her before the sandalwood paste on her body dried up. Nanda then hurried to see His Holiness but so long Sundarī was within his sight he was moving "like a royal goose pressing forward on the waves".

After making obeisance to the Seer, Nanda begged apology for not having seen Him at his palace and humbly prayed Him to take His mid-day meal at his palace. But the Blessed One made a sign to show that He felt no need of food. Nanda again made obeisance to the Sage and decided to go home. But Buddha had probably gauged his inner self which was yearning to rush to his beloved, Sundarī. The Seer could easily perceive that the passion of the sins was fierce in Nanda and that he was inclined to sensuous indulgences. And, it all was there because Nanda was weak of knowledge, knowledge which is the origin of salvation. Hence, what was required first was to purge Nanda of his sins, the sin of passion in particular. So he asked him first to hold His begging bowl. But despite holding the Holy bowl, Nanda wanted to go home. He, however, could not do it, for the Sage confounded him by blocking his movement. Nanda, helpless now, followed the *Guru* , but all the time thought of his wife who, he fancied, must be waiting for him eagerly. The Enlightened One then led him to the monastery famed as the pleasureground of knowledge in which pleasure in woman was destroyed.

The Compassionate One could understand that Nanda was writhing from grief for not being able to rush to his wife. He pitied Nanda's wretchedness and softening Himself in His dealings with him He caressed his head with His hand, the palm of which bore the wheelmark, and then advised him not to run after the illusory pleasure, the pleasure derived from passionate loving of a woman, or from the acquisition of riches, for while sensuous pleasure is unsubstantial, the accumulation of wealth invites troubles instead of giving enjoyment. Adding to it the Buddha said :

हितस्य वक्ता प्रवरः सुहृद्धो धर्माय खेदो गुणवान् श्रमेभ्यः ।
ज्ञानाय कृत्यं परमं क्रियाभ्यः किमिन्द्रियाणामुपगम्य दास्यम् ॥[3]

The best friend is one who speaks what is advantageous, the most meritorious of all labour is the exertion made towards Righteousness; the highest of actions lies in the effort made to gain knowledge; what is gained in being a slave to the senses?

Admonishing Nanda thus, the Seer warned him to prepare himself to face death fearlessly and in a tranquil state of mind, for no one knows its definite date of arrival to an individual. Likewise, nobody can retain youth for ever : one inevitably grows old which surely robs one of one's beauty; similarly, nobody can keep away from disease which brings nothing but calamity with it, and then nobody can avert death which is the most dangerous of all dangers on earth. Whereas affection makes us bonded, desire results into destruction, and love (sensuous love) is more dangerous than fire. One would surely lead a tranquil life if these three did not exist in one's life. The Sage further said that separation from one's dear ones makes one grief-stricken, and if one does not keep restraint over oneself, one is sure to lose self-control. It requires wisdom and courage to put an end to existence. If one can attain indifference and conquer the illusions of the world, grief cannot strike him. Death does not come as a baffling experience to one who is well-practised in *yoga* and has arrived at the Ultimate Truth.

The Tathāgata, after having addressed Nanda thus, thought that the latter would now take to the path shown by Him and so asked Ānanda, his disciple, to initiate him into the mendicant's life. But Nanda, not yet free from his passionate desires, refused to become a mendicant. The Buddha having come to know of Nanda's state of mind once again persuaded him to abandon the snare of delusion, namely, his mistress, if he wanted to win over the sufferings of the world. Though it may be disagreeable to him, the Seer added, but his alone can make him holy and pure. Just as a doctor's pills are not always savoury to the patient's tongue but he has to take it if he wants to be cured of his illness. Nanda should also carry out *yoga* even though it may seem to be an unpleasant task to him. Upon this, Nanda agreed to act as advised by Buddha.

The Sage of Videha got Nanda's head shaved and dressed him as a mendicant. But Nanda still brooded over his mistress, and the task of accomplishment appeared too difficult to him under such a state of mind. Much more frustrating was the fact that while on the one hand his passionate self drew him towards his mistress again and again; on the other, his reverence for th *Guru*, the Buddha, did not let him disobey Him. He felt as if he were placed between the two wheels of a cart.

Lamenting thus over his plight, Nanda recalls instances of sages like Vasiṣṭha, Parāśara, etc., who went astray through women, obviously in order to excuse himself for being prone to excitement and devoid of self-restraint. And since it went against the dictates of Buddhism, Nanda finds no sense in putting on a mendicant's robe without having taken off the robe of passion. He finally determines to give up the mendicant's robe and get back home at once. A certain disciple of Buddha then tries to dissuade him from his decision. Nanda expresses his aversion to the joys of the forest-life and honestly confesses that he took no pleasure in the practice of the Law and found no more contentment without his mistress than a king could when deprived of his sovereign power. The disciple admonishes Nanda and advises him not to deviate from the Holy path. But Nanda's mental darkness, obviously resulted from his sinful disposition to passion, keeps him still obsessed with the thoughts of Sundarī. The disciple tries to convince him about the detriments of passion :

> यथोपयुक्तं रसवर्णगन्धवद्वधाय किंपाकफलं न पुष्टये।
> निषेव्यमाणा विषयाश्चलात्मनो भवन्त्यनर्थाय तथा न भूतये ॥[4]

Despite its taste, colour and fragrance being good, a *kiṁpāka* fruit if eaten causes death and gives no nourishment. Similarly, inclination towards sensual objects takes the man of unbalanced mind to doom and brings no properity.

But despite such convincing arguments of the mendicant, Nanda remained irresolute about adopting the path of Salvation. The mendicant then reported the matter to the Buddha, the Knower of the Truth.

The Blessed One summoned Nanda with a view to rescuing him from the darkness called 'wife', who have enveloped his mind and body. Nanda, ashamed of his failure to take the path of Salvation but resolute about going back to his mistress, appeared before Him. The Buddha grasped his hand and flew up into the sky and took him to the heaven. Nanda was amazed to see the charming *Apsarasaḥ* engaged in various sports in the heaven. Their beauty inflamed his passion to the extent that he forgot all about his wife now. The Enlightened One knew that 'great beauty eclipses minute beauty', and a passionate being like Nanda would certainly turn away his mind from his wife if he saw the charming and beautiful *Apsarasaḥ*. And, the Sage succeeded in His aim. When asked by the Buddha, Nanda confessed that the *Apsarasaḥ* were far more superior to his wife in beauty. Nanda now realised that overmuch passion could burn a being as he was feeling at the moment. The blaze of passion became unbearable for him and he himself prayed the Sage to cast the water of His voice on him before he could be consumed by the fire of passion. He then vowed to take refuge in Him. But the Seer, aware of Nanda's greatest weaknes (of passion), could realise that he was still not all free from passion though his attention had now shifted from Sundarī to the *Apsarasaḥ*. He thought it better to dissuade him completely from his passion for his wife first and then, in course of the practice of His Law, from all passions including that of the *Apsarasaḥ*. The Sage, therefore, said that the women of paradise, the *Apsarasaḥ*, could be obtained not by force (as mighty men do on earth), or by other labours, but only by abiding diligently in the observances. Nanda took a vow to abide by the advice of Buddha who then flew down to the earth with him.

Nanda began to carry out his vow with all sincerity but only with his body, for his mind, though free from the passion for his wife, had shifted to the *Apsarasaḥ* now. When Ānanda could learn of it, he pointed out the absurdity of Nanda's aim and said :

यथासनार्थं स्कन्धेन कश्चिद्गुर्वीं शिलां वहेत् ।
तद्वत्त्वमपि कामार्थं नियमं वोढुमुद्यतः ॥[5]

Your striving to assume self-control for the sake of passion is just like a man's carrying about a heavy stone on his shoulder to sit down on it.

Ānanda advised Nanda to apply his mind to the delight of inner self if he wanted true happiness. External delight could be obtained in various ways but nothing equals the inner delight, for this alone is both tranquil and free from sin. Inner delight does not require any aids like music, women or ornaments; it can be enjoyed alone and at one's own will. Contrary to it, desire breeds suffering because it never dies. Ānanda warned that Nanda's desire to obtain the *Apsarasaḥ* will ultimately lead to his suffering, for even if he reaches paradise after performing a number of difficult tasks he cannot deem his sojourn in paradise permanent: the moment he deviates from the right path, the path of virtue, he is sure to fall from there only to face disgrace on the earth. Paradise, therefore, is to be recognised as transitory and in no way an abode for the men of wisdom. If one wishes to lead a happy life, a life beyond all fears (of disease and death), one should attempt to lead a holy life, and it can be achieved only by adopting the path of the Law.

Upbraided thus by Ānanda, Nanda felt highly abashed. Agitated in his mind, he went to the Buddha, narrated Him his recent realisation, and requested Him to explain the Supreme Law to him so that he could endeavour to reach the Supreme State. The *Guru* felt pleased at Nanda's change of heart and advised him to have faith in the Law first, for "the Law grows with faith as a tree grows with its root":

श्रद्धाङ्कुरमिमं तस्मात्संवर्धयितुमर्हसि ।
तद्वृद्धौ वर्धते धर्मो मूलवृद्धौ यथा द्रुमः ॥[6]

In other words, faith was the root of salvation, and therefore, stronger it was, greater were the chances of further advancement on the path of salvation.

When the Tathāgata found Nanda thoroughly fortified by the faculty of faith. He asked him to perfect discipline, for the ladder of salvation started from it. And, the best way to do it was to control the activity of the senses as also the dirt.

Self-controlled thus in both mind and body, a *yogin* should avoid sleep and devote all his time in the practice of *yoga* shaking off all drowsiness. And, then the practice of *yoga* should be started with a pure mind and senses kept under control.

The next step the Seer advises Nanda to follow, while moving on the Holy path, is to develop awareness of the actions of the body. The Tathāgata advances reasons behind :

शरव्यः स तु दोषाणां यो हीनः स्मृतिवर्मणा ।
रणस्थः प्रतिशत्रूणां विहीन इव वर्मणा ॥[7]

As the enemy makes the unarmed man a target on the battlefield, the vices make those their target who lack the armour of attention.

Besides these controls of mind and body, the selection of place for meditation was also important, which should obviously be free from all disturbances. After having guided Nanda in the preliminary preparations for meditation, the Buddha begins to teach him the process of it.

The first and the foremost step of *yoga* is the concentration of mind. The Seer warns that in most human beings there remains a latent tendency towards passions like a fire covered up with ashes, and hence, the mendicant's first aim should be destruction of the passions by destruction of the latent tendencies. Evil thoughts must not be cherished in the heart since they breed disaster alike for oneself and for others. Much more important than all these is the detachment from all worldly objects and relationships. It is nothing but delusion that causes the attachment of one person to another. To Buddha, all relationships are relationships of convenience. Hence, thoughts of relatives or kinsfolk should not obsess Nanda. Likewise, he should also be aware of the fact that death in inevitable and invincible. And, since there is no relying on (the continuance of) life, man breathes in and immediately after breathes out again :

प्रश्वसित्ययमन्वक्षं यदुच्छ्वसिति मानवः ।
अवगच्छ तदाश्चर्यमविश्वास्यं हि जीवितं ।।[8]

In view of this wonderful fact of life, Nanda is advised by the Tathāgata to obtain mastery over attention with regard to in- and out-breathing.

What was most remarkable about Budddha , the Teacher, was not only his convincing capability but also the instances he cited from the day-to-day happenings around us, and He did it with such conviction that even subtler aspects could be easily grasped by the listeners. We come across one such instance when, in course of imparting the finer nuances of *yoga* to Nanda, He compares a *yoga*-adept with a goldwasher and a goldsmith. He says that a goldwasher first eliminates the grosser pieces of dirt and then the finer ones for its cleansing, and having cleansed it, he retains the particles of gold. Similary, one who has concentrated his mind for the sake of emancipation, first eliminates the groser vices and then the subtler ones to cleanse his mind, and having cleansed it, retains the constituent of the Law. Again, just as the goldsmith gradually separates the dirt of gold by washing it with water and heating it in the fire, so does the *yoga*-adept cleanse his mind from the vices in order to separate it completely from the worldly sins. It is thus that he brings his mind to tranquillity and concentrates it. Further, just as the goldsmith reduces the gold in many ways so that it may be easier for him to give it the desired shape while making ornaments, the mendicant after cleansing his mind and havaing secured control of the supernatural sciences, reduces it to tranquillity and then employs it as and where he wants to.

Buddha's teachings cast its spell on Nanda. He diligently practised whatever the *Guru* advised him to do for the former's betterment. When the Seer got assured that Nanda had cleansed himself of all his vices. He began to expose him to the subtler elements of the Law. He said that if the *yogin* succeeded in attaining the four trances through the immobility of his mind, he would spontaneously acquire the five supernatural sciences : (a) wit, (b) various magic powers, (c) awareness of others' thoughts, (d) remembrance of past births, and (e) pure and heavenly sight and hearing. One of the most important steps that a *yoga*-adept should follow then was to understand the four Noble Truths as expounded by Buddha, in order to overcome the infection of passion etc. and attain tranquillity. These Truths are: (1) *Dukkha* (suffering), (2) *Dukkha-samudaya* (cause of origin of suffering), (3) *Dukkhanirodha* (cessation or suppression of suffering), and (4) *Dukkhanirodhagāminīpaṭipadā* (the path leading to the cessation of suffering).

Nanda is advised by Buddha to penetrate to the core of these Noble Truths in order to attain *Nirvāṇa*, a stage if attained, would exhaust him of all his vices and take him to peace. The *Guru* further says that birth is the casue of all suffering and the cessation of suffering is possible only when one is not reborn. In order to reach such a stage, the *yoga*-adept must extirpate the vices with respect to all his dispositions and become completely passionless. The following verse makes the point amply clear :

दोषक्षयो जातिषु यासु यस्य वैराग्यतस्तासु न जायते सः ।
दोषाशयस्तिष्ठति यस्य यत्र तस्योपपत्तिर्विवशस्य तत्र ।।[9]

Satischandra Chatterjee and Dhirendramohan Datta in their incisive study on *'The Buddha Philosophy'* mention twelve links in the chain of suffering. They observe: "(1) Suffering in life is due to (2) birth, which is due to (3) the will to be born, which is due to (4) our mental clinging to objects. Clinging again is due to (5) thirst or desire for objects. This again is due to (6) sense-experience which is due to (7) sense-object-contact, which again is due to (8) the six organs of cognition; these organs are dependent on (9) the embryonic organism (composed of mind and body), which again could not develop without (10) some initial consciousness, which again hails from (11) the impressions of the experience of past life, which lastly are due to(12) ignorance of truth."[10]

The path leading to cessation of suffering is called the Eightfold Noble Path in the Buddha philosophy. "It consists in right views, right resolve, right speech, right conduct, right livelihood, right effort, right mindfulness, and right concentration", observes Bimal Churn Law.[11]

The Eightfold Noble Path propounded by Buddha is straight, noble and incorruptible, and by following this path one could reach a state free from misery. In other words, this path takes one to the supremely blessed stage known as *Jñāna* or *samādhi*. And, if the mind is rightly liberated, that is, if the *yogin* succeeds in destructing complaisance and passion, he needs nothing to accomplish further.

Dr. Keith finds the Eightfold Noble Path, variously known as the Middle Path or the Golden Mean, as a "well-tested method of attaining the internal purity of the self."[12] He represented it as a way to freedom or path to salvation. The underlying spirit of the doctrine of the 'Golden Mean' in Buddhism is well expressed in verse 141 of the *Dhammapada* :

न नग्गचरिया न जटा न पङ्का नानासका थण्डिलसायिका वा।
रजो च जल्लं उक्कुटिकप्पधानं सोधेन्ति मच्चं अवितिण्णकङ्खं ॥[13]

Unless one has gone beyond doubt, one cannot purify oneself either by nakedness, or by plaited hair, or by dust, or by fasting, or by lying on the bare ground, or by rubbing with dust, or by sitting motionless.

Having made Nanda understand the significance of four Noble Truths and the Middle Path, the Awakened One asks him to take care of the time chosen and the method adopted for practising *yoga*. Choice of subjects of meditation was no less important a factor. Equally significant was the need for rooting out evil thoughts through study, action, or if possible, through elimination. The Seer reminds Nanda that much energy and courage are required to practise *yoga* and attain salvation through it, but one should not get daunted at the beginning, for when streams, by ever running swiftly, wear away even mountains, why can't a man achieve salvation by uninterrupted practice of *yoga*.

Nanda thus, having received instructions from the Enlightened One entered the path of salvation. He paid his earnest reverence to the *Guru* and began to practise *yoga* in the forest on His guidelines. But the task was still not easy. Despite the zeal of his mind and the resolution of his soul to tread on the path of salvation, Nanda had to fight with passionate feelings and other evil thoughts which disturbed his mind. He, however, overcame them, and gradually reached the stage of the first fruit of the Law. By and by he obtained all the Four Truths and realised the four trances one by one. Ultimately,he succeeded in attaining Arhatship and thus became worthy of reverence. He was now free from all desires, all expectations; he was no more troubled by hope, fear, grief, conciet or passion. Outwardly the same though, he was a thoroughly changed person now from within :

अर्हत्त्वमासाद्य स सत्क्रियार्हो निरुत्सुको निष्प्रणयो निराशः।
विभीर्विशुग्वीतमदो विरागः स एव धृत्यान्य इवाबभासे ॥[14]

Nanda was a true *yogin* now : He had attained the stage of salvation. His journey from passion to salvation was quite torturous but when he had completed it under the blessed quidance of the Enlightened One, he felt the ecstasy of reaching the peace of *Nirvāṇa*. He paid his obeisance to Buddha thus :

तं वन्दे परमनुकम्पकं महर्षिं
मूर्धाहं प्रकृतिगुणज्ञमाशयज्ञं।
संबुद्धं दशबलिनं भिषक्प्रधानं
त्रातारं पुनरपि चास्मि संनतस्तं ॥[15]

I pay my reverence to Him, the Supreme Seer, the Compassionate One, Who knows all, the Enlightened One, the Holder of ten powers, the Chief of physicians, the Saviour. Again I do Him obeisance.

Nanda, enlightened now, went to see Buddha Who was equally eager to see him, for his attainment of salvation was not a matter of pride and satisfaction for him alone but for Buddha as well since His toil had been fruitful. Nanda expressed his gratitude to the Seer and explained to Him his disjunction from all mundane phenomena and his realisation of the Supreme Truth. He then sought His advice as to what he should do next with his new-found knowledge. Buddha directed Nanda to practise compassion and extend a helping hand to people (even if they were his enemies) in distress. A true saint enlightens others with his knowledge and hence Nanda should teach the lessons of tranquillity to others. The Saviour said:

इहोत्तमेभ्योऽपि मतः स तूत्तमो य उत्तमं धर्ममवाप्य नैष्ठिकं ।
अचिन्तयित्वात्मगतं परिश्रमं शमं परेभ्योऽप्युपदेष्टुमिच्छति ॥[16]

The best among the best in this world is one who, after obtaining the Supreme Ultimate Element, desires to teach this tranquillity to others without caring for the troubles involved in it.

Having received the command of Buddha, Nanda began to preach the law to the people in Kapilavastu making them astonished and probably remark: "Look, this is a miracle that he who was addicted to passion now tells the tale of final emancipation!"

REFERENCES & NOTES

1. E.H. Johnston; *The Saundarananda of Aśvagoṣa* (Delhi: Motilal Banarasidass), Ist edition, Rpt.1975,III : 27.
2. *Ibid.*, III: 41.
3. *Ibid.*, V: 25.
4. *Ibid.*, IX: 48.
5. *Ibid.*, XI: 24.
6. *Ibid.*, XII: 41.
7. *Ibid.*, XIV: 38.
8. *Ibid.*, XV: 57.
9. *Ibid.*, XVI: 24.
10. Satischandra Chatterjee & Dhirendramohan Datta; *An Introduction to Indian Philosophy* (Calcutta: Calcutta University Press), 2nd edition, 1944,p.139.
11. Bimal Churn Law; *Concepts of Buddhism*, p.10.
12. Dr.A.B. Keith; *Buddhist Philosophy*, p. 119.
13. *Dhammapada, 141*, Delhi University Publication, *1977*.
14. E.H. Johnston; *op.cit.*, XVII: 61.
15. *Ibid.*, XVII: 73.
16. *Ibid.*, XVIII: 56.

Ranchi

BUDDHISM IN INDIA

Priyasen Singh

It is paradoxical to believe that Buddhism which originated, flourished and branched off in different parts of pre and post 1947 India, became one of the dead religions except in a few pockets in the Himalayan regions of India and Nepal. Buddhism had enriched every aspect of Indian culture from its very beginning. It gave India one of the richest philosophies. Its literature is the richest in its depth and vitality. It had been the religion of the ruling class of India for a number of centuries, but when it started declining, it shrunk to smaller and smaller pockets,say, the Himalayan kingdoms and parts of Magadha, Gauda and Banga regions. In this context, it may be suggested that the study of decline of Buddhism in India remains to be one of the most fascinating and illuminating studies in the field of Buddhological sciences. Almost all the scholars worth their names have spoken on this aspect in their writings and comments, but only a few systematic studies may be cited which throw sufficient light on this problem. T.S. Elliot, Mahapandita Rahul Sankrityayana, R.C. Mitra, L.M. Joshi and Trevor Ling may be mentioned as those who had made major contributions on the subject. Those scholars who have studied ancient and medieval Indian History have offered a number of factors leading to the decline of Buddhism in the main land India. These factors need to be studied and examined thoroughly before a conclusion is drawn to establish the theory of decline of Buddhism in India. The problem may be approached in two broad sets of factors--Internal and External. In the case of the former, the Moral Degradation of the members of the Buddhist Order, the presence of Sectarianism of the highest order among the Indian Buddhists, Esoteric nature and practices of Buddhism and the lack of cooperation and coordination between the laity and the members of the Buddhist Order, while the external factors mainly confine to the following---Lack of Royal partronage, Royal and Brahmanic persecution, Revival of Brahmanism and the process of unification and assimilation of Buddhists and other religious systems into their fold and lastly stray foreign invasions.

The scholars in the field had very rightly pointed out the moral degradation of the members of the Buddhist Order as one of the major factors leading to the final decline of Buddhism. But this and other factors should not be taken in isolation because none of the factors may be cited as the main factor, but all the factors mentioned above have contributed their bit in the sum total of decline of Buddhism. As regards the moral degradation, in fact, it has started from the period of Buddha himself and we have examples to suggest that within a span of 110 years after the passing away of the Buddha, unvinayic practices had become common at least in a section of Buddhist Order. The travel accounts of Chinese pilgrims (Fa-hien, Huan-tsang, I-tsing etc.) and the references in *Mṛcchakaṭika* of Śūdraka, *Mālavikāgnimitra* of Kālidāsa, *Daśakumāracarita* of Ḍaṇḍin, *Mālatīmādhava* of Bhavabhūti, *Rājataraṅgiṇī* of Kalhaṇa etc. are some of the evidences which amply suggest that there had been gradual decline in the moral standard of the Buddhist monks and nuns which culminated during the period when Buddhism became the most vulnerable to all sorts of onslaughts and thus finally succumbed to its total disappearance. The monks and nuns started deserting the order, leading household life, accumulating property in the *Vihāras* and transforming them to individual control, taking active participation in political affairs of the states, in their administration and war, and playing the role of go-between are some of the instances to substantiate the point.

It is a common knowledge that Buddism had developed a number of sects in itself which were inimical to each other and instead of carrying on healthy competition among themselves, those sects succumbed to hostile rivalries and at times cut across each other's interest. This tendency had become quite common in the later period, particularly after the fall of the Pāla dynasty. At that stage the normal, philosophical and ecclesiastical differences turned into aggressive and hostile points of controversies.

Most of the authors dealing with the later Buddhism are of the opinion that the populistic approach of Mahāyāna Buddhism was more responsible for the decline of Buddhism in India than somewhat conservative nature of Hīnayāna Buddhism. There are evidences to suggest that during and by the end of the 7th centruy A.D. the Mahāyāna Buddhists became more or less worshippers of Bodhisattvas and reciters of Mahāyāna Sūtras. The so-called great vehicle laid emphasis on the image worship, prayer and incantations, pompous ceremonies and rituals, folk-beliefs, accommodation of the emotional demands of laity and so on. And thus the distinguishing marks between Buddhism and Hinduism became totally dim. The common man found very little difference between the worship of Viṣṇu and Buddha, of Śiva and Avalokita and of Tārā and Pārvatī.

The excessive emphasis on Bodhisattvayāna by the Mahāyānists led to the weakening of the institution of recluseship and mendicancy among the Buddhists, as according to Mahāyāna it was not essential to renounce the world to embrace Bodhisattvacaryā. There happened to be Pravrajita and Gṛhastha Bodhisattvas in large numbers. The examples were set by the Vaitulyakas/Vaipulyakas in this regard, who even made provisions of sexual indulgence (*maithunodhammo*) under special conditions. In this regard, it may not be farfetched to conclude that this peculiar nature of religious practices became the source of the doctrine of co-efficiency of female element in the Tantra.

The Vajrayāna texts are full of examples to suggest that the Buddhist ascetics were associated with their female partners. The Guhya-Samāja-Tantra even goes to the extent of declaring "rāgacaryā kulaputra yadut bodhisattvacaryā". The examples of 84 Siddhas of Tantric Buddhism can also be cited in this regard, most of whom either married or had espoused yoginīs, The Indian Tantricism during the later period developed in such a way that Hindu and Buddhist Tantricism almost intermingled with each other. This led to the obliteration and narrowing down of the distinction and difference between popular Hinduism and Buddhism. The pristine purity of Buddhism evaporated in the Tantric practices of the later period. The Buddhist Tantras though claimed to have been proclaimed by the Buddha himself led to the process of virtual replacement of ethical values of Buddha to occult practices of all sort. It is also to be pointed out here that there are some scholars who have refuted the stand of those scholars who ascribe some role to excessive and degenerate tantric practices among Buddhists to its final decline in major parts of India. They argue that similar development in Hinduism did not cause its decline. But they fail to appreciate the point that the basic nature of both religions had been totally different, while practices of the sort referred to were quite admissible in the broader spectrum of Hinduism but the same had no place in Buddhism whatsoever.

A close study of the words of the Buddha enshrined in the *Tripiṭaka* indicates that the laity was not within the direct purview of the Buddha's scheme of things. He probably concentrated on the members of the Order alone with a view to train and discipline them to be ideal mendicants to lead exemplary life for the rest of the society. Mahapandita Rahul Sankrityayana has opined in this context that the Buddha had derived the model of his Order from any of the then existing social orders. Thus the laity was not given full attention so far as his training and discipline were concerned. Barring a few discourses ascribed to the Buddha, we find that almost the whole of the teachings of the Buddha were directed towards the upliftment of the moral and spiritual attainment of the Buddhist monks and nuns. In view of this fact the laity was almost free to practise any ritual suited to him. Thus the relation between the Buddhist laity and the members of the Order was very loose and informal. Though we find some instances here and there to suggest that a section of the laity felt concerned whenever there arose any dispute or schism in the Order, but by and large they remained aloof and unconcerned. Secondly the religious and ecclesiastical duties were prescribed to the members of the Order, but the Buddhist laity, unlike the Jain laity, had no role to play in that respect. The result was that even at a time when external dangers loomed large before the *Saṁgha* the laity felt the least concerned and by and large did not find ways and means to come forward to their rescue. One of the most typical instances in this respect may be cited from the history of Nālandā Mahāvihāra itself as mentioned by Dharmasvāmin in his records. According to him, when a few horsemen of Bakhatiyar Khilji raided the Mahāvihāra, the laity in the villages around the Mahāvihāra did not come forward to the help of the inmates of the Mahāvihāra.

The external factors affecting the decline of Buddhism in later period are equally important in analyzing the causes of decline of

Buddhism. It will not be out of place to mention here that to search for immediate causes for the decay of Buddhism will be far-fetched in arriving at the correct picture of the whole problem. Whatever causes that worked for the decline of Buddhism were active since very long time, say, for centuries till almost total decline of Buddhism. The Royal patronage is cited as one of the factors which accelerated the pace of fast growth of Buddhism in its early period. Once the patronage by the nobility and the class that associated itself with the nobility took up the cause of Buddhism,it continued with it for centuries and that is why even with the change of regimes much harm could not be done in the early and medieval periods. But at the later period, the nobility as well as the associated class seems to have deserted Buddhism altogether. That is why when the rulers hostile to Buddhism took over the power in various regions, Buddhism was the most-affected casuality. This truth is very evident. Even the hostile attitude of Puśyamitra Śuṅga, Mihirakula, Śasāṅka and a few other rulers during the early and medieval periods could not do much harm to Buddhism and it continued flourishing as is evidenced by the records of the Chinese travellers. But in the later period change of nobility affected the fate of Buddhism considerably as the class that supported it had switched over to popular form of Hinduistic beliefs and practices. This may be substantiated with the fall of the Pāla rulers and the rise of Sen rulers thereafter. It is a known fact that the Sen Dynasty was established by Ballālasena who hailed from South India and probably belonged to a community which was totally pro-Brahmanic. They persued a policy totally against Buddhism and thus it became weaker and weaker due to lack of patronage. It may also be put in another way that the weakening situation of Buddhism during that period made the then Sen rulers switch off their patronage totally from Buddhism and placed it to the service of Brahmanism or the popular Hinduism of the period. It may be possible, though there is dearth of very many evidences, that large scale persecution might have been carried through with the involvement of the then rulers knowingly or with their connivance.

Brahmanical penetration into the fold of Buddhism had been probably from the peridod of Buddha himself. All those disciples of the Buddha who hailed from Brāhmaṇa community were not true converts to the new faith propounded by Śākya Muni Buddha who himself was a Kṣatriya by birth. But there is no doubt about it that majority of them proved to be true Buddhists and contributed excellently to the sum total of the growth and development of Buddhism. There were many among them in the early and medieval period who had contributed a lot and had enriched Buddhist religion, philosophy and lore. But there are instances of some who were not true believers and they might have worked against the interests of their new-found faith. The story is recorded in case of the life of Kumārila, who had entered the Buddhist Order but later could not conceal his Brahmanical predilection. In this context, a number of instances of Brahmanical persecution of Buddhists and their large scale propaganda against Buddhism may be cited from a number of Brahmanical texts from the early to the late periods. Some of these instances suggest that this sort of persecution was not only on the academic plane alone but it had taken the form of physical oppression and annihilation of the Buddhists. The following are some of the instances in this regard :

1. The attitude of the Brāhmaṇas towards Buddhism had been hostile, since the Buddha's time. They considered the Buddha's view on the caste system as an affront to their superiority.

2. Particular references :

(a) Kauṭilya's *Arthaśāstra*---To see a Bhikṣu is inauspicious and hence be avoided.

(b) *Bṛhannāradīyapurāṇa*---A Brāhmaṇa should not allow a Bhikṣu to enter his house. It is a sin.

(c) *Mṛcchakaṭika*---It was considered inauspicious in Ujjayinī to see a Bhikṣu. He was hated upon.

(d) *Agnipurāṇa*---Śuddhodana's son enticed the Buddhist demons to bring them to his Order.

(e) *Vāyupurāṇa*---The Śūdra shavelings in reddish robes will perform religious ceremonies.

(f) *Viṣṇupurāṇa*---The Buddha is considered *'Mohaka'* who appeared to deliver teachings of *Ahiṁsā* and *Nirvāṇa* in order to change the customs and practices of the people. They will ultimately be crushed by the gods *(devas)*.

(g) The writings of Kumārila and Śaṅkara are full of disparaging passages to the Buddha.

3. The references of persecution cited above and thousand more written and unwritten were not the simple statesments used during debating bouts, they were the same which lead to physical fights where blood-bath was the necessary consequence. The Indian and Tibetan medieval texts are full of such direct and oblique references.

It appears that the approach of the Brāhmaṇa leaders in liquidating Buddhists had been two-pronged. On the one hand, they resorted to critical intellectual attack on the Buddhist leadership and scholarship and on the other, they started bringing them to their fold gradually through the process of persecution and assimilation. It is also to be noted in this context that during the course of time when the Brāhmaṇa leadership realized that the ascendency of Buddhism could not be curved through simple and straightforward way, they resorted to the method of deceit and calumny. They thought of setting their house in order through the process of resurgence of Brahmanism of the pre-Buddhistic period. The faith towards *Varṇāśrama* system, inculcation of values of householder's life, etc. were being vigorously re-established through the composition of new set of texts known as *Purāṇas* which partially replaced the teachings of the *Vedas* and partially supplemented them. According to the *Devībhāgavata Purāṇa*, the Śūdras, the women and the rest of the common people were given the advantage of *Purāṇas* since they had no right to read, recite and retain the Vedic scriptures. In this way, these texts of resurgence of Brahmanism (*Nava-Brāhmaṇavāda*) served the purpose of re-establishment of supremacy of householder's life, *Varṇāśrama* system, faith in the efficacy of the *Vedas* and so on and so forth. Thus the *Purāṇas* proved to be the main source of the resurgence of Buddhism. On the other hand, this gave a powerful jolt to Buddhism.

In this process, assimilation of Buddhism into the fold of Brahmanism or popular Hinduism also went on side by side. It was asserted that Buddhism was not different from Brahmanism and its propounder too was also one of the Avatāras/incarnations of Lord Viṣṇu. The Buddha was accepted as an *Avatāra* of Viṣṇu in the *Purāṇas*. The Buddhist pilgrim centres were adopted as Hindu pilgrim centres as well. Ācārya Śaṅkara who flourished in the 8th century A.D. went a step further in paying high tributes to the Buddha by calling him *"Yogināṁ cakravartī"*, i.e., the lord of the *Yogins*. He succeeded in establishing an order of Hindu mendicants on the same pattern as that of the Buddhists. It was in fact, a great innovation in the field of Brahmanism or popular Hinduism where the emphasis had always been on the supremacy of the *Āśrama* system.

A section of the Indian Historians attach too much importance to the foreign invasions in their analysis of the decline of Buddhism. They exaggerate the matter to the highest extent. Though it is difficult to rule out the foreign invasions of Huns, Arabs, Turks, Afghans and others in the process of weakening of Buddhist strongholds in India and the neighbouring countries, but to apportion total blame on them in decline of Buddhism seems to be misplaced and erroneous. It is suggested that they destroyed Buddhist monasteries, persecuted Buddhist monks and nuns, burnt their religious scriptures etc., which became primarily responsible for the downfall of Buddhism. But the argument does not seem to be tenable as the foreign invaders equally harmed the institutions of other religions as well, say, of Jainism, Brahmanism and so on. Since the religions other than Buddhism which were equally affected by the foreign invasions could withstand such invasions, why Buddhism could not be expected to withstand in the same manner. If they could survive the invasions why not Buddhism. Thus it appears that this argument is not convincing enough to be accepted as one of the major causes for the downfall of Buddhism. Secondly when the Turk and Afghan invasions took place in the 11-12th centuries A.D., Buddhism had already given way to other religions even in its own strongholds.

The next question that needs thorough investigation and a convincing explanation is to say whether the process of assimilation started by neo-Brahmanism did assimilate the Buddhists in their totality into their own fold. The answer to this question is in the negative. The Buddhists who were losing their grounds from 7-8th centuries A.D. onwards continued with their weakened strength and less popular support for a few centuries in the different pockets of the main land India and the vast section among them continued to remain outside the pale of Hinduism. In the absence of any central power and unifying agency among them, they had no option but to either lean towards Hinduism or to look for any other shelter. It was per chance that Isiam reached India about the same time in a big way. The Arab, Turk and Afghan invaders were by faith Muslims. But a large number of Muslim saints, scholars, travellers, traders, etc. had made their way into the Indian society even before the actual invasions. The *Ekeśvaravāda* (Tawhid) of Islam had a strong appeal to the Buddhists and ex-Buddhists who had the Buddha as the Supreme Lord into their faith. The moral and spiritual teachings of Buddhism and Islam had many similarities which proved to be an attraction to the Buddhists during their hard days. On the other hand, the proud self-respecting and conscientious section of the Buddhists did not like to join Hindu fold as they knew fully well that Brahmanism or popular Hinduism of the period had no scope for proselytisation as it was in the universally acclaimed religions like Buddhism, Christianity, Islam, Sikhism and so on. They knew fully well that entering the Hindu fold did mean accepting the status of Śūdras or even lower than the Śūdras. No Mleccha or an outsider was supposed to become a Brāhmaṇa or Kṣatriya. He was allowed to become a Śūdra alone, except perhaps forcefully as it was in the case of Kuṣāṇas, Śakas, Hūṇas and so on. If this way, the large populace of the period which professed Buddhism in one form or the other opted to become Muslim in large numbers. Mahapandit Rahul Sankrityayana in the Introduction to his *Buddhacaryā*, emphasizes the point by citing the example of large scale conversion of Buddists to Islam in the around all the strongholds of the Buddhists of the period. The Muslim majority areas of Bihar Sharif, Bhagalpur, Pataliputra, Visesaraganj of Benares, village Kosam of Kausambī and a host of others has been cited by him to prove his point.

Another very important question that crops up for discussion here is the fact whether such a wide-spread and powerful religion as Buddhism could be totally wiped out and replaced by other religions and faiths. What happened to their institutions,scriptures, literary texts, traditions and so on? An answer to this question may appear to be unpleasant to many amongst Hindus and Muslims, but the fact remains that both Hinduism and Islam in India today have raised their citadels over the ruins and graves of the Buddhists. Their monasteries were turned into Śiva or Viṣṇu temples and their scriptures were burnt and the conscientious Buddhists were forced to seek refuge primarily into countries of the bordering regions. It is not a coincidence to find that the Buddhist texts were totally lost and were not found anywhere on the plains of India, barring a few texts like *Pramāṇavārtika,* which were found in Jain *Granthāgāras* here and there. Some historians have tried to explain this phenomenon in terms of vagaries of nature which might have taken their toll considerably but to say that all texts were lost due to natural phenomena is, it seems, a travesty of facts.

So far as the Buddhist beliefs and practices are concerned, these were absorbed among Hindus and Muslims and others of specific regions. Many Buddhist communities are being discovered today which still survive in their truncated form. The Sarakas of Orissa and Bihar are one of them to cite as an example. The new researches being done in different parts of the country provide us ample information in this regard. According to one research, even the Jagannātha Temple of Purī was originally a Buddhist Temple. The Bodh-Gaya Temple needs no mention in this context. It is universally known to be the famous Historical Mahābodhi Temple of Bodh-Gaya. The Badrinath Temple of famous Badrinath pilgrim centre was originally a Buddhist Stūpa where the Buddhists of the region used to perform their *Pūjās* and offer ceremonial *stūpas* to the main shrine even till the British period. Late Mahapandita Rahul Sankrityayana published a booklet on the Badrinath shrine, but the same was proscribed by the British Government subsequently fearing communal trouble on that account.

A close analysis of Hinduism today may also reveal absorption of many Buddhist beliefs and practices. In fact the modifications of Hinduism today are full of remnants of Buddhism.

Delhi

संघमित्रा और बोधिवृक्ष—एक परिचय

संघमित्रा बौद्ध

मौर्य वंश के संस्थापक चन्द्रगुप्त थे। चन्द्रगुप्त के पश्चात् उनके पुत्र बिन्दुसार मगध के राजा बने। बिन्दुसार ने अट्ठाईस वर्षों (297-269 ई. पू.)[1] तक राज्य किया। बिन्दुसार की मृत्यु के बाद उनके पुत्र अशोक ने मौर्य साम्राज्य के राजसिंहासन पर अधिकार प्राप्त किया। बौद्ध साहित्य के अनुसार जब अशोक ने राजसिंहासन प्राप्त किया तो वे बहुत क्रूर और अत्याचारी थे। अशोक के अभिलेखों में केवल एक ही शस्त्र-विजय का उल्लेख मिलता है और वह थी उनकी कलिंग-विजय। उन्होंने कलिंग पर विजय तो प्राप्त की किन्तु युद्ध के क्रूर परिणामों से उनका हृदय हाहाकार कर उठा। युद्ध के परिणामस्वरूप उन्होंने अहिंसा का मार्ग अपनाकर बौद्धधर्म में दीक्षा ली तथा उनकी प्रवृनि चण्डाशोक से 'धम्माशोक' में परिवर्तित हुई।

संघमित्रा का जन्म एवं व्यक्तित्व

सम्राट् अशोक जब युवराज के रूप में थे तब उन्हें शासक बनकर उज्जयिनी जाना पड़ा। वहाँ पर विदिशा नामक नगर में देव श्रेष्ठी की कन्या विदिशाकुमारी देवी से उनका प्रणय हुआ[2] और वह देवी परिणीता के रूप में उनके साथ उज्जयिनी गई। उन्हीं 'देवी' से महेन्द्र कुमार का जन्म (284 ई. पू.)[3] हुआ। उसके दो वर्ष बाद देवी ने (282 ई. पू.)[4] एक पुत्री को जन्म दिया जिसका नाम 'संघमित्रा' रखा गया। दोनों बच्चों ने अपना बाल्यकाल वहीं व्यतीत किया। फिर बड़े होने पर वे अपने पिता के साथ मगध चले गये। उनकी ममता की छाया में इनकी शिक्षा का प्रबन्ध हुआ और रूप के साथ ये गुणों में भी अद्वितीय हो गये। सम्राट् अशोक ने अपने सुख और कल्याण की अपेक्षा संसार के सुख एवं कल्याण को सर्वोपरि स्थान दिया। उन्होंने अपने अनुभव से दूसरों को भी बौद्ध-धर्म से लाभान्वित करने के लिए सर्वप्रथम अपने पुत्र महेन्द्र और पुत्री संघमित्रा को बौद्ध-धर्म के प्रचारार्थ लंका भेजा। यह प्रथम सुअवसर था जब एक भारतीय धर्म गठित रूप में भारत की सीमा के बाहर प्रचारित हुआ।

युवती होने पर संघमित्रा का विवाह (268 ई. पू.) अशोक के भागिनेय अग्निब्रह्मा के साथ हुआ।[5] विवाह के पश्चात् उसने एक पुत्र को जन्म दिया, जिसका नाम सुमन रखा गया।[6] कुछ दिनों बाद अग्निब्रह्मा राजा अशोक से आज्ञा लेकर प्रव्रजित हुए।[7] उनकी प्रव्रज्या लोगों के महान् हित के लिए सम्राट् अशोक के अभिषेक के चतुर्थ वर्ष में हुई।[8] राजकन्या संघमित्रा ने भी अधिक समय तक गृहस्थ जीवन व्यतीत नहीं किया। उन्होंने

वैभव के उपकरणों में रहते हुए भी करुणा, ममता और शील पालन को आदर्श माना । सम्राट् अशोक की इच्छा एवं अपनी धर्मभावना से इन्होंने यौवन के द्वार पर कदम रखते ही समस्त वैभव को त्याग कर प्रव्रज्या को स्वीकार किया जिसका वर्णन महावंस में इस प्रकार वर्णित है—'बौद्धधर्म ग्रहण करने पर राजा अशोक ने बहुत से विहार बनवाये जिनमें पाटलिपुत्र का अशोकाराम मुख्य था । इसके बनने में तीन वर्ष लगे ।[9] विहार बन जाने पर राजा ने विहार-प्रवेश के समय खड़े होकर भिक्षु-संघ से पूछा—'भन्ते । क्या मेरे समान (त्यागी)धर्म का उत्तराधिकारी (दायाद) कहला सकता है ?'[10] धर्मधुरन्धर स्थविर मोग्गलिपुत्ततिस्स ने राजपुत्र महेन्द्र और राजकन्या संघमित्रा के भविष्य को जानकर उनके द्वारा धर्म का होने वाला हित देखकर, राजा को कहा, 'राजन् ! तुम्हारे जैसे महात्यागी को भी धर्म का दायाद नहीं कह सकते, दायक (दाता) ही कह सकते हैं । किन्तु जो अपने पुत्र अथवा पुत्री को धर्म में प्रव्रजित कराता है, वह धर्म का दायाद और दायक दोनों होता है' ।[12] तब राजा ने धर्म दायाद होने की प्रबल इच्छा से पास में खड़े पुत्र महेन्द्र और पुत्री संघमित्रा से पूछा—'क्या तुम लोग प्रव्रज्या ग्रहण करोगे ?' पिता के इस वचन को सुनकर उन दोनों ने कहा, 'देव ! यदि आपकी इच्छा हो, तो हम आज ही प्रव्रजित होंगे' ।[13] अतः दोनों भाई बहन प्रसन्नतापूर्वक अपनी स्वीकृति देकर पितृ-ऋण से मुक्त हुए । प्रव्रज्या ग्रहण करते समय महेन्द्र की आयु बीस वर्ष की थी और संघमित्रा की अट्ठारह वर्ष ।[14] संघमित्रा ने तो अग्निब्रह्मा की प्रव्रज्या के समय ही प्रव्रजित होने का संकल्प कर लिया था ।[15] अशोक के धर्मगुरु स्थविर मोग्गलिपुत्ततिस्स ने ही दोनों को बौद्धधर्म में प्रव्रजित किया ।[16]

उसी समय महेन्द्र की प्रव्रज्या और उपसम्पदा तथा संघमित्रा की प्रव्रज्या और शिक्षा-दान[17] हुआ । महेन्द्र के उपाध्याय मोग्गलिपुत्ततिस्स और प्रवज्या देने वाले महादेव स्थविर हुये ।[18] माध्यमिक स्थविर ने कर्मवाचा पढ़ा ।[19] महेन्द्र ने उपसम्पन्न होने के समय ही पटिसम्भिदा सहित अर्हत् पद प्राप्त किया ।[20] संघमित्रा की उपाध्याया प्रसिद्ध धर्मपाला और आचार्या आयुपाला हुईं । उपयुक्त समय शिक्षा-दीक्षा को पाकर संघमित्रा ने भी अर्हत् पद प्राप्त किया ।[21] इन दोनों की प्रव्रज्या राजा अशोक के शासन के छठे वर्ष में हुई । प्रव्रज्या के कुछ ही दिनों बाद संघमित्रा बौद्धधर्म-प्रचार-हेतु लंका में प्रथम धर्मप्रचारिका के रूप में गई । लंका द्वीप पर कृपा करने वाले महामहेन्द्र ने उपाध्याय के पास रहकर तीन वर्ष में तीनों पिटकों में निपुणता प्राप्त की । इस प्रकार भिक्षुणी संघमित्रा और भिक्षु महेन्द्र ने चाँद और सूर्य की तरह बुद्ध-धर्म रूपी आकाश को सुशोभित किया ।

संघमित्रा की लंका यात्रा

तथागत गौतम ने जिस वृक्ष के नीचे बोधि प्राप्त की, उसका बौद्ध धर्म में अत्यधिक महत्त्व है । बुद्ध द्वारा बताये गए निम्नलिखित चार स्थान महत्त्वपूर्ण हैं—तथागत का जन्मस्थल—लुम्बनी वन में शाल-वृक्ष के नीचे, तथागत ने जहाँ सम्बोधि प्राप्त की—उरुवेला में बोधि (पीपल) वृक्ष के नीचे, तथागत ने जहाँ धर्मचक्रप्रवर्तन किया—सारनाथ तथा जहाँ तथागत महापरिनिर्वाण को प्राप्त हुए—कुशीनारा में शाल-वृक्ष के नीचे । ये चारों स्थल दर्शनीय एवं वैराग्यप्रद है । ये बौद्ध धर्म के प्रमुख चार तीर्थ-स्थल है । इनमें से द्वितीय उरुवेला (वर्तमान

बोधगया) में स्थित बोधि-वृक्ष का विशेष महत्त्व है जिसके नीचे तथागत सम्यक-सम्बुद्ध हुए अर्थात् उन्होंने सर्वज्ञता (ज्ञान, बोधि) प्राप्त की। आज भी यह विश्व का सबसे प्राचीन ऐतिहासिक वृक्ष है एवं भारतवर्ष की सर्वाधिक मूल्यवान् सांस्कृतिक निधि है। बौद्ध धर्म में बोधिवृक्ष एक सजीव प्रतीक है, जो तथागत बुद्ध के जीवन, उनकी साधनाओं एवं सम्बोधि को दर्शाता है। इसी कारण से बौद्ध जगत् में इसका अद्वितीय स्थान है। इसके दर्शन एवं पूजनार्थ समस्त बौद्ध अनुयायी उत्सुक रहते हैं और इसके दर्शन से साक्षात् बुद्ध-दर्शन जैसा लाभ करते हुए स्वयं को पुण्यवान् एवं पवित्र मानते हैं। बुद्ध की सम्बोधि-प्राप्ति के कारण इस बोधि-वृक्ष को बोधिद्रुम, महीरुह, महारुक्ख, महाबोधि तथा महाबोधि-वृक्ष विशेषणों से अलकृत किया गया है। सर्वप्रथम इस वृक्ष की शाखा का आरोपण सम्राट् अशोकपुत्री संघमित्रा द्वारा लंका में किया गया।

लंकानरेश देवानां प्रिय तिष्य के अनुरोध पर थेर महेन्द्र ने अपनी बहन थेरी संघमित्रा को लंका में आमन्त्रित किया, साथ में बोधिवृक्ष-शाखा को लाने का भी अनुरोध किया। राजा तिष्य के मन में यह विचार आया कि बौद्ध धर्म के अनुयायियों की श्रद्धा बुद्ध के प्रति सदैव बनी रहे। अतएव एक ऐसा प्रतीक होना चाहिए जिसकी वे पूजा व उपासना कर सकें। इस पुण्य-कार्य की पूर्ति-हेतु थेरी संघमित्रा ने बोधिवृक्ष-शाखा-सहित लंका जाने का निर्णय किया। सम्राट् अशोक ने बोधिशाखाओं की रक्षा के लिए अट्ठारह क्षत्रिय परिवार,देवकुल, अमात्यों, ब्राह्मणों एवं व्यापारियों के आठ-आठ परिवार, ग्वालों, बढ़ई, बिन्दों, नागों, यक्षों के परिवार को बोधिशाखाओं के साथ भेजा।[22] ग्यारह थेरियों सहित संघमित्रा को तथा अरिट्ठ अमात्य आदि को नाव पर आरूढ़ किया। स्वयं सम्राट् अशोक अपनी सेना के साथ स्थल-मार्ग द्वारा विन्ध्य पर्वत के मार्ग से एक सप्ताह में समुद्र के निकट पहुँचे। सम्राट् अशोक बोधिशाखाओं को जाते हुए देखकर अश्रुपूर्ण नेत्रों सहित अपने नगर को लौट गए।[23] महाबोधिवृक्ष के लंका जाने का चित्रण साँची स्तूप की निचली तथा बीच की मेहराबों में किया गया है। इस प्रकार महावंस में वर्णित बातों को पुरातत्व के खोजपूर्ण परिणामों से भी समर्थन प्राप्त हुआ है।[24]

बोधिशाखाओं सहित थेरी संघमित्रा ने समुद्र मार्ग से लंका के लिए प्रस्थान किया और उनके मार्ग में अनेक विपत्तियाँ एवं विघ्न उपस्थित हुए। इन विघ्नों का काल्पनिक एवम् अलौकिक विवरण महावंस में प्रस्तुत हैं—'महाबोधि को लिए हुए नाव समुद्र में चली। चारों ओर योजन भर तक समुद्र की लहरें शान्त हो गईं। चारों ओर पाँच रङ्ग के कमल फूल निकल आये और आकाश में अनेक प्रकार के बाजे बजने लगे। देवताओं ने अनेक प्रकार से महाबोधि की पूजा करनी आरम्भ की और नाग उसे उड़ा ले जाने की चेष्टा करने लगे। छः अभिज्ञाओं में पारङ्गत संघमित्रा महाथेरी ने गरुड़ का रूप धारण करके उन महानागों को डराया। तब भयभीत होकर उन महानागों ने थेरी से याचना की और उसकी आज्ञा से महाबोधि को नाग-भवन ले जाकर, नाव में स्थापित किया'।[25] यद्यपि प्रस्तुत वृत्तान्त पूर्णरूपेण अतिशयोक्तिपूर्ण प्रतीत होता है तथापि इतना तो निश्चित है कि लंका में बोधिवृक्ष शाखा को लाने में थेरी संघमित्रा ने अनेक कठिनाइयों का सामना किया। इस प्रकार अनुराधपुर के महाविहार में बोधिवृक्ष-शाखा की स्थापना का महत्त्वपूर्ण कार्य इनके द्वारा सम्पादित किया गया।

बोधिशाखाओं का लंका में आरोपण एवं प्रातिहार्य

महाबोधि के आगमन पर प्रेम के आवेग से उत्साहित होकर लोगों ने जय-जयकार किया। सुविज्ञ राजा ने सोलह कुलों सहित गले तक गहरे पानी में प्रवेश करके महाबोधि को सिर पर रखकर किनारे पर लाकर सुन्दर मण्डप में रखा। तत्पश्चात् लंकेश्वर ने लंका के राज्य से महाबोधि की पूजा की। अपना राज्य उन सोलह कुलों को सौंपकर राजा ने स्वयं द्वारपाल के स्थान पर खड़े होकर तीन दिन तक विविध प्रकार से महाबोधि की पूजा कराई।[26] दशमी के दिन विज्ञ राजा ने वृक्षराज महाबोधि को सुन्दर रथ में रखकर पूर्व विहार के स्थान पर स्थापित किया। सब लोगों को संघ सहित भोजन कराया। महामहेन्द्र स्थविर ने राजा को इस स्थान पर नागों के दमन की कथा सुनायी। राजा ने स्थविर से सम्बुद्ध के उपवेशन आदि से पवित्र स्थानों की बात सुनकर सभी स्थानों पर स्मृति-चिह्न बनवा दिये।[27]

तत्पश्चात् राजा के द्वारा महाबोधि को तिवक्क ब्राह्मण ग्राम के द्वार पर रखवाकर स्थान-स्थान पर शुद्ध बालू बिछवाकर अनेक प्रकार के श्रेष्ठ फूलों एवं पताकाओं से मार्ग को सजवाकर, निरालस्य होकर दिन-रात महाबोधि की पूजा करते हुए चतुर्दशी के दिन अनुराध के समीप लाया गया।[28] वहाँ पर राजा ने राज अलङ्कारों से अलंकृत करके सोलह कुलों सहित महाबोधि को उठाया और आरोपित करने के लिए रख दिया। हाथ से दूर होते ही वह महाबोधि आकाश में अस्सी हाथ ऊँची चढ़ गई। वहाँ ठहरकर छः रङ्ग की सुन्दर किरणें छोड़ने लगी। लंका द्वीप में फैल कर ब्रह्मलोक तक पहुँचने वाली सुन्दर किरणें सूर्यास्त के समय तक रहीं।[29] इन प्रातिहार्यों को देखकर दस हजार लंकावासियों ने प्रसन्न हो, दिव्य-दृष्टि और अर्हत् पद को प्राप्त कर प्रव्रज्या ग्रहण की। तब सूर्यास्त के समय रोहिणी-नक्षत्र में उतरकर महाबोधि स्थापित हुई, उस समय पृथ्वी काँपी। महाबोधि के प्रतिष्ठित होने पर चारों ओर से आकर लोगों ने गन्धमाला आदि पूजा की सामग्री से महाबोधि की पूजा की। मेघवृष्टि तथा हिमगर्भ शीतल बादलों ने महाबोधि को ढक लिया। लोगों को आनन्दित करने वाली महाबोधि सात दिन तक उस हिमगर्भ मेघों में ही अदृश्य रही। सप्ताह की समाप्ति पर समस्त मेघ हट गये। उस समय छः रङ्ग की किरणों के सहित महाबोधि दिखाई दी। महामहेन्द्र स्थविर, संघमित्रा भिक्षुणी अपने अनुयायियों के सहित एवं राजा भी अपने प्रजाजनों सहित वहाँ आये। कजरग्राम और चन्दनग्राम के क्षत्रिय, तिवक्क ब्राह्मण एवं दूसरे लंकानिवासी जो महाबोधि-महोत्सव के लिए बहुत उत्सुक थे, देवताओं के प्रताप से वहाँ आ पहुँचे। इस प्रातिहार्य से विस्मित महासमागम में सबके देखते-देखते पूर्व की शाखा में से एक अखण्डित पका फल गिर पड़ा।'[30]

महाबोधि के उस गिरे फल को उठाकर स्थविर ने राजा को लगाने के लिए दिया। राजा ने उसे महासन के स्थान पर रखे हुए सुगन्धित मिट्टी से परिपूर्ण सोने के कड़ाहे (गमले) में लगा दिया। सबके देखते-देखते उसमें से आठ अंकुर निकल आये और वह बढ़कर चार-चार हाथ लम्बे बोधि के पौधे हो गये। राजा ने उन छोटे बोधि-पौधों को देखकर श्वेत छत्र से उनकी पूजा की और उनका राज्याभिषेक किया। एक-एक बोधि-पौधे को आठ स्थानों में स्थापित किया गया। शेष चार पके हुए फलों से उत्पन्न कुल बत्तीस बोधि-पौधों को चारों ओर योजन-योजन की दूरी पर यत्र-तत्र विहारों में स्थापित करवा दिया। इस प्रकार लंका-निवासियों के हित के लिये,

सम्यक् सम्बुद्ध के तेज से वृक्ष-राज महाबोधि की स्थापना होने पर अपनी मण्डली सहित अनुलादेवी ने संघमित्रा थेरी से प्रव्रज्या ग्रहण करके अर्हत् पद प्राप्त किया ।[31]

संघमित्रा का बोधिवृक्ष से लगाव

भिक्षुणी संघमित्रा ने विहार में निवास करते हुए धर्म के कार्य और लोगों का हित-साधन किया । महासिद्ध महामति संघमित्रा महाथेरी ने उनसठ (59) वर्ष की अवस्था में, उत्तिय राजा के नौवें वर्ष में हत्थाल्हक विहार में रहते हुए परिनिर्वाण प्राप्त किया ।[32] राजा उत्तिय ने एक सप्ताह तक उनकी देह का उत्तम पूजा-सत्कार किया । लंका को पूर्ण अलंकृत करके सप्ताह की समाप्ति पर उनके शरीर का नगर से बाहर, स्तूपाराम के पूर्व, चित्र शाला के समीप, महाबोधि के सामने थेरी के अपने बतलाये हुए स्थान पर अग्नि-कृत्य किया । फिर राजा ने उस स्थान पर स्तूप बनवाया ।[33]

संघमित्रा का लंका में योगदान

भिक्षुणी संघमित्रा और स्थविर महेन्द्र का लंका में बौद्ध धर्म की नींव स्थापित करने में महत्त्वपूर्ण योगदान है । इनके सम्मिलित प्रयासों के परिणामस्वरूप वहाँ बौद्ध धर्म अंकुरित एवं पल्लवित हुआ । संघमित्रा का व्यक्तिगत जीवन नितान्त सादगीपूर्ण, त्यागमय और शीलयुक्त था । विदिशा नगरी में जन्मी इन महान् विभूति ने जीवन के प्रत्येक पक्ष को कर्तव्यनिष्ठा से निभाया । शैशवावस्था से ही बौद्ध धर्म के प्रति दृढ़ श्रद्धामयी होने से इन्हें अट्ठारह वर्ष की आयु में बौद्ध धर्म में प्रवेश करने का सुअवसर मिला । जिस समय बौद्ध धर्म का दायाद बनने के इच्छुक पिता (सम्राट् अशोक) ने इनसे प्रव्रज्या ग्रहण करने का अनुरोध किया, पिता की आज्ञा को शिरोधार्य कर इन्होंने इसे अमूल्य पुण्यावसर माना । इनकी प्रव्रज्या सम्राट् अशोक के शासन के छठे वर्ष में हुई थी ।[34] इस प्रकार इनका बौद्ध धर्म में पदार्पण एवं कार्य-क्षेत्र के लिए मार्ग विस्तीर्ण हुआ ।

भिक्षुणी संघमित्रा ने उपाध्याया धर्मपाला तथा आचार्या आयुपाला के संरक्षण में बौद्धविद्यार्जन किया । निरन्तर अध्ययनरत रहते हुए इन बहुश्रुत भिक्षुणी ने अर्हत्व पद प्राप्त किया । इन्होंने जीवनपर्यन्त लंका में रहकर बौद्ध धर्म का प्रचार-प्रसार करते हुए अपने शिष्यानुशिष्यों को भी तन्निमित्त नियुक्त किया । इस प्रकार लंका में बौद्ध धर्म के विकास में इनके योगदान का निरूपण प्रसङ्ग-प्राप्त है ।

भिक्षुणी-संघ-संस्थापिका

लंका में भिक्षुणी-संघ की स्थापना का मुख्य श्रेय भिक्षुणी संघमित्रा को प्राप्त है । स्थविर महेन्द्र द्वारा बौद्धधर्म के उपदेशों को सुनकर राजा तिष्य की बहन अनुलादेवी ने अपनी पाँच सौ सहचरियों सहित बौद्धधर्म में दीक्षित होने की इच्छा प्रकट की, किन्तु उसे निराश होना पड़ा क्योंकि भिक्षुओं को यह अधिकार नहीं था कि वे स्त्रियों को दीक्षा दे सकें । इस पुण्य-कार्य को यथार्थ रूप देने के उद्देश्य-हेतु भिक्षुणी संघमित्रा को लंका आने के लिए आमन्त्रित किया गया । इन आमंत्रण को स्वीकार कर उन्होंने अपने पिता (अशोक) से लंका जाने की

अनुमति माँगी जिसे सुनकर राजा अशोक ने कहा—'पुत्रि, मैं तुम से वियुक्त होकर कैसे रहूँगा'।[35] इस पर संघमित्रा ने कहा कि 'इस पुण्य-कार्य के लिए मेरा लंका जाना ज़रूरी है क्योंकि वहाँ पर प्रव्रजित होने वाली स्त्रियों की संख्या अधिक है'।[36] इस तर्क से सहमत होकर अशोक ने उन्हें स्वीकृति दी। और वे भिक्षुणी-संघ एवं बौद्धधर्म-प्रचार-हेतु लंका गईं। भारतीय इतिहास में यह प्रथम सुवर्ण अवसर था जब एक सम्राट् की कन्या धर्मप्रचारार्थ विदेश गई।

भिक्षुणी संघमित्रा के लंका आने तक अनुलादेवी तथा उसकी सहचरियाँ पवित्र काषाय वस्त्र धारण करके तथा दसशीलों का पालन करते हुए, प्रव्रज्या-प्राप्ति की इच्छा से भिक्षुणी के आगमन की प्रतीक्षा करती हुईं, विशेषतः भिक्षुणियों के लिए बनवाये विहार में रहने लगीं।[37] भिक्षुणी संघमित्रा ने लंका आने पर अनुला देवी तथा पाँच सौ स्त्रियों को अपनी अध्यक्षता में संघ में प्रविष्ट किया और थोड़े ही समय में उन सभी ने अर्हत् पद प्राप्त किया।[38] इस प्रकार भिक्षुणी संघमित्रा द्वारा लंका में भिक्षुणी-संघ की स्थापना हुई। भिक्षुणी संघमित्रा तथा दूसरी भिक्षुणियों के निवास-हेतु जो विहार बना, वह 'उपासिका-विहार' नाम से प्रसिद्ध हुआ।

इस प्रकार लंका में भिक्षुणी-संघ की स्थापना में संघमित्रा का योगदान अत्यन्त महत्वपूर्ण है। उन्हीं के प्रयत्नों के कारण भगवान् बुद्ध द्वारा प्रतिपादित अष्टांगिक आर्य मार्ग का लंका में प्रचार हुआ।

प्रथम धर्मप्रचारिका

बुद्ध द्वारा संघ में स्त्री-प्रवेश को अनुमति देना भारतीय साहित्य में एक नए अध्ययन का शुभारम्भ करता है। बुद्ध के जीवन-पर्यन्त बौद्धधर्म का प्रचार भारत तक ही सीमित रहा किन्तु उनके परिनिर्वाण के 218 वर्षों बाद बौद्ध धर्म का प्रचार भारत से बाहर अन्य देशों में भी हुआ। भिक्षुणी संघमित्रा बौद्धधर्म- प्रचार-हेतु लंका में प्रथम धर्मप्रचारिका के रूप में गईं जिसका बौद्ध इतिहास में एक विशेष महत्त्वपूर्ण स्थान है। इसलिए इन्हें लंका में बौद्ध-धर्म रूपी जड़ को स्थापित करने का श्रेय प्राप्त है। इस तरह कहा जा सकता है कि यदि राजा शुद्धोधन के पुत्र सिद्धार्थ ने राज-सुख को त्याग कर संसार के सुख के लिए बौद्ध धर्म की स्थापना की तो उस का विदेश में जाकर प्रचार करने का महत्त्वपूर्ण कार्य एक दूसरी राजपुत्री संघमित्रा ने पूर्ण किया। यद्यपि अन्य अनेक बौद्ध भिक्षुओं ने भी विदेश में जाकर इस धर्म का प्रचार किया, किन्तु इस राजकन्या ने राजमहल में प्राप्त सुखों को छोड़कर बौद्ध भिक्षुणी बनकर अनजान देश में जाकर धर्म के प्रचार में अपना समस्त जीवन उत्सर्ग कर दिया। न केवल स्वयं को अपितु अपने पति और पुत्र को भी बौद्धधर्म-प्रचारार्थ समर्पित किया, जो कि एक असाधारण बात है। यदि ध्यान से देखा जाए तो संघमित्रा का त्याग स्वयं अशोक की बौद्धधर्मप्रियता से भी बढ़कर प्रतीत होता है। इनके त्याग से प्रेरित होकर स्त्रियाँ लंका में ही नहीं अपितु संसार के सभी बौद्ध देशों में भी बौद्ध-धर्म में दीक्षित हुईं। अतः भिक्षुणी संघमित्रा आज भी बौद्ध धर्मप्रचारकों में प्रेरणास्रोत के रूप में जानी जाती हैं। उनका यह उत्सर्ग बौद्ध इतिहास में सदैव स्मरणीय एवं वन्दनीय रहेगा।

लंका को धार्मिक देन

लंका द्वीप में बुद्ध-शासन की प्रतिष्ठा भारत से हुई। बुद्ध-शासन की प्रतिष्ठा का अर्थ था, भारत से भिक्षुओं का आना, धर्म-प्रचार, लंका के निवासियों को प्रव्रजित तथा उपसम्पन्न करना, सर्वज्ञ (बुद्ध)-धातु (बुद्ध के शरीर अवशेष) को लंका लाना, भिक्षुणी-शासन की स्थापना, विहारों का निर्माण और देश-भर के लोगों को भगवान् बुद्ध के उपदेशों के अनुसार अपने जीवन-यापन करने की प्रेरणा देना।

संघमित्रा द्वारा लंका लाई गई बोधिवृक्ष-शाखा को अनुराधपुर के महाविहार में रोपा गया, जो बौद्ध संस्कृति का एक केन्द्र बन गया। देवानां प्रिय तिष्य द्वारा इस विशेष उद्देश्य के लिए ही महाविहार की स्थापना की गई, जो कि लंका का एक पवित्र धर्मस्थल है। इस महाविहार में बोधिवृक्ष के विद्यमान होने के कारण श्रद्धालुओं की संख्या में दिनोदिन वृद्धि हुई, बौद्ध जगत् में लंका को धार्मिक क्षेत्र में विशेष महत्ता प्राप्त हुई। इस धार्मिक महत्ता का श्रेय भिक्षुणी संघमित्रा को ही प्राप्त है। राजा देवानां प्रिय तिष्य ने भिक्षुणी संघमित्रा तथा दूसरी भिक्षुणियों के निवास हेतु 'उपासिका-विहार' की स्थापना की। यह लंका का प्रथम भिक्षुणी-विहार बना तथा एक अन्य 'हत्थाल्हक विहार' भिक्षुणियों के निवास हेतु बनावाया गया। इन भिक्षुणी-विहारों के बनने के पश्चात् लंका में भिक्षुणियों की संख्या में अत्यधिक वृद्धि हुई जिससे थोड़े समय में ही भारत की तरह लंकाद्वीप भी काषाय वस्त्रों से प्रकाशवान् हो गया।

इस प्रकार लंका में अनेक स्तूपों, विहारों एवं प्रतिमाओं आदि का उनकी शैली में उत्तरोत्तर विकास होता गया जिस कारण लंका ने शिल्प जगत् में महत्वपूर्ण स्थान प्राप्त किया। वस्तुतः लंका में बौद्ध-धर्म के प्रचार-प्रसार में इनकी महत्त्वपूर्ण भूमिका रही।

लंका को सांस्कृतिक देन

भिक्षुणी संघमित्रा द्वारा अनुराधपुर में रोपी गई उरुवेला (बोध गया) के बोधिवृक्ष की ही शाखा है, जो आज भी लंका की अमूल्य सांस्कृतिक निधि है। यह बोधिशाखा सर्वाधिक प्राचीन (ऐतिहासिक) है जिसकी पूजा लंकावासी अत्यधिक श्रद्धा से करते हैं। लंका में यह जयश्री महाबोधि के नाम से सुप्रसिद्ध है।[39] लंका में बोधिवृक्ष की पूजा एक महान् पूजा है क्योंकि इसकी पूजा सम्बुद्ध की पूजा के समान है। आज लंका में साधारण व्यक्ति भी बोधिवृक्ष के प्रति असीम श्रद्धा रखता है। इस वृक्ष का उनके व्यक्तिगत, धार्मिक एवं सामाजिक जीवन से घनिष्ठ सम्बन्ध है जैसे—नामकरण, विवाह, आशीर्वाद आदि अवसरों पर बोधिवृक्ष-पूजा एक अनिवार्य कर्म (क्रिया) है। बोधिवृक्ष के बिना वे अपना जीवन अपूर्ण मानते हैं।

भगवान् बुद्ध की धातुओं—हंसली की अस्थियों आदि को भिक्षुणी संघमित्रा-पुत्र श्रामणेर सुमन द्वारा भारत से लंका में ले जाया गया। उनके ऊपर निर्मित विशाल स्तूप, चैत्य आदि को भी लंका में विशेष आदरपूर्वक पूजा जाता है।

लंका में बौद्ध धर्म के प्रभाव की अभिव्यक्ति आज भी वहाँ पर मनाये जाने वाले उत्सवों, जुलूसों, झाँकियों आदि के द्वारा स्पष्ट होती है। बौद्ध उत्सवों में सबसे बड़ा उत्सव वैशाख-महोत्सव है। स्थविरवादी बौद्धों का विश्वास है कि वैशाखी पूर्णिमा के दिन सिद्धार्थ कुमार का जन्म, बोधि-प्राप्ति तथा बुद्ध का परिनिर्वाण हुआ था। इसलिए वैशाख-महोत्सव सुदीर्घ समय से निरन्तर मनाया जाता रहा है। इस प्रकार बौद्ध धर्म भारत और लंका के सांस्कृतिक इतिहास को मिलाने वाली एक महत्त्वपूर्ण कड़ी है। सिंहली कला, शिल्प, साहित्य, सङ्गीत, पर्व और उत्सव आदि सभी भारतीय देन हैं जिनको लंका में ले जाने का श्रेय भिक्षुणी संघमित्रा को ही प्राप्त है।

सन्दर्भ-सङ्केत

1. महावंस, पञ्चम परिच्छेद, पृ.22
2. वही, त्रयोदश परिच्छेद, पृ.68
3. अशोक परिशिष्ट 'क', पृ- 37
4. वही
5. वही
6. महावंस, पञ्चम परिच्छेद, पृ.34
7. वही
8. वही
9. वही, पृ.32
10. वही, पृ.33
11. वही
12. वही
13. वही
14. वही, पृ.34
15. वही, पृ.33
16. वही, पृ.34
17. 'विनय' के अनुसार स्त्री को उपसम्पदा पाने के पूर्ण दो वर्ष तक उम्मीदवार रहना पड़ता है। वही, पृ.34
18. वही
19. वही, भिक्षुओं की उपसम्पदा में एक क्रिया।

20. वही
21. वही
22. वही, एकोनविंश परिच्छेद, पृ.100
23. वही
24. वही, भूमिका, पृ.4
25. वही, एकोनत्रिंशपरिच्छेद, पृ.101
26. वही
27. वही, पृ.102
28. वही
29. वही
30. वही, पृ.103
31. वही
32. वही, विंश परिच्छेद, पृ.101
33. वही, पृ.109
34. वही, पञ्चम परिच्छेद, पृ.34
35. वही, अष्टादश परिच्छेद पृ.97
36. वही
37. वही, पृ.96
38. वही, एकोनविंश परिच्छेद, पृ.100
39. श्रीलंका, पृ.119

दिल्ली

SECTION V

Music In Buddhist Literature

जापान में संस्कृत सङ्गीत

लोकेश चन्द्र

1972 वर्ष की कड़कड़ाती ठण्ड में जापान में लेखक-सम्मेलन के लिए निमन्त्रित था। निमन्त्रण देने वाले नोबल- पुरस्कार-विजेता श्री कावाबाता, 'सात सोई सुन्दरियाँ' लिख कर स्वयं सो गये थे। हाराकिरी कर ली कि मैं वृद्ध हो गया, शरीर व्यर्थ हो गया और फिर से सप्त सुन्दरियों के समकक्ष अनुभव और कृति असम्भव हो गई। क्योतो में पहुँचा, तो कावाबाता के निधन में वातावरण क्षुब्ध पाया। मन्दिरों की घण्टियों के सान्ध्य स्वर वायु में लुप्त होते सुनाई देते-अनित्यता का अनुपम उदाहरण। सम्मेलन पूर्ण होने पर पर्वतांचलों के मौन में विराजमान कोयासान गया। यहाँ कई सौ मन्दिर हैं, प्राचीन स्मृति-चैत्य हैं और यह मन्त्रयान का मुख्य केन्द्र है। शून्य से 40 अंश नीचे का हड्डियाँ चीरकर घुसता हुआ शीत था। सायं बिजली के मेज के चारों ओर यामामोतो परिवार के साथ बैठकर पूछ रहा था कि ऐसे वातावरण में मूर्तियाँ कैसे शिल्पित की जा सकती हैं और पटचित्रों का आलेखन कैसे सम्भव है ? मिलने आए हुए थे-भिक्षु कोजुम् आराह। आराह बोले मैं आपको संस्कृत सङ्गीत सुनाऊँगा और शीत भाग् जाएगा। पूछा-कौन सा संस्कृत सङ्गीत ? बोले सुनिए। गाने लगे, ऊँचे, स्वर में, ध्यान में विलीन, शताब्दियों के भावों में मग्न। यह मङ्गलगाथाष्टक का पहिला पद्य था—

यन्मङ्गलं तुषित-विमान-गर्भाद्
आसीद् इहावतरतो जगतो हिताय।
सेन्द्रैः सुरैरनुगतस्य तथागतस्य
तन्मङ्गलं भवतु शान्तिकरं तवाद्य॥

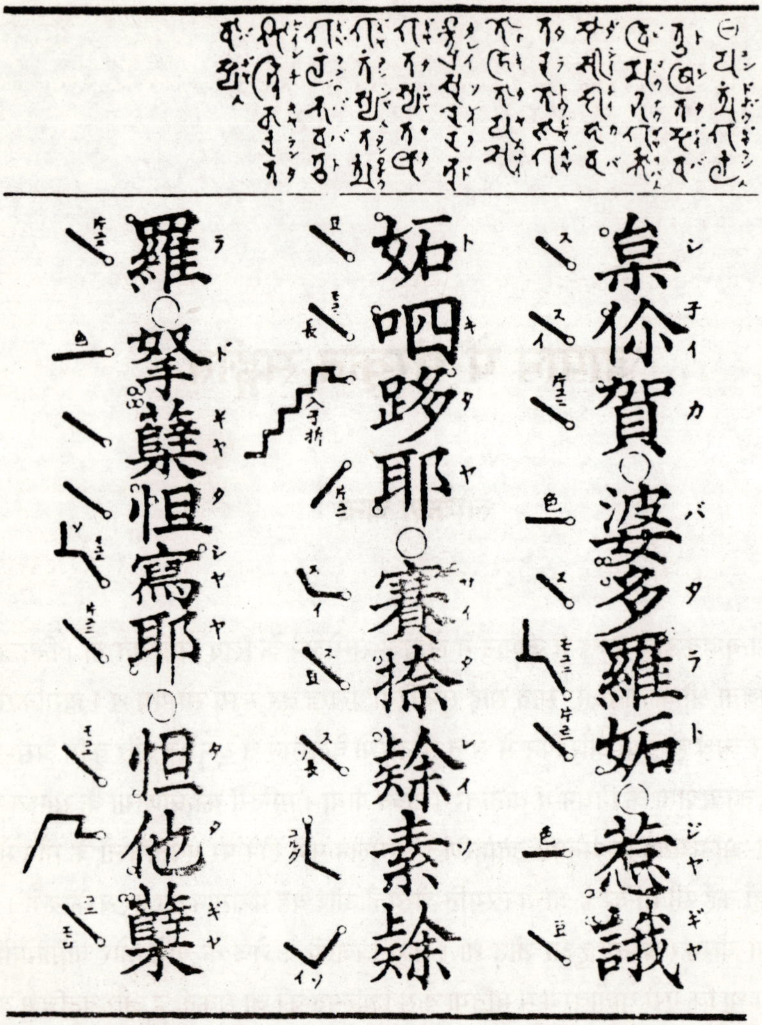

संस्कृत

चीनी लिप्यन्तर और पार्श्व में जापानी में उच्चारण । बाईं ओर स्वराङ्कन ।

जापानी गायन-ग्रन्थ में मङ्गल गाथा-संस्कृत, चीनी और स्वर, स्वरों के आलाप, विस्तार, उतार-चढ़ाव उनके पुष्पित-पल्लवित होने में आधा घण्टा लगा । मैं अस्थिवेधी शीत भूल गया और सोचने लगा कि क्या गा रहे हैं । संस्कृत का उच्चारण जापानी बन गया था और शब्दों का पहिचानना असम्भव था । भिक्षु आराह ने सिद्धनागरी से पूरा पद्य लिखा । यह नागरी का सातवीं शताब्दी का रूप है । पढ़ा और संस्कृत की प्रतीति होने लगी । पूछा क्या मुझे लिखकर दे सकते हैं ? अगले दिन पूर्ण गायन लिख कर ले आए-चीनी अक्षरों में संस्कृत, सिद्धनागरी में संस्कृत और प्राचीन स्वराङ्कन । भिक्षु जी से पूछा कि आपको इसमें कैसे रुचि हुई । बोले, मैं सड़कों की इंजीनियरिंग पढ़ा था, पर सोचा जनहित के लिए यान, मन्त्रयान अधिक आवश्यक है । सड़क-निर्माण छोड़

कर लोगों की आत्माओं का निर्माण करने में लग गया। इसके लिए संस्कृत-सङ्गीत सीखा और आगे भी सीख रहा हूँ। दुःख से बोले—यह विद्या हमारे देश से लुप्त हो रही है। कितना अच्छा होता कि हम भोगवाद की ओर अग्रसर न होते, और यह विद्या न खोई जाती। धन की अपेक्षा आत्मा का विकास मानव के लिए अधिक श्रेयस्कर है। यदि जापान आर्थिक दृष्टि से कम सम्पन्न होता, तो हमारी आध्यात्मिक चेतना अधिक परिपुष्ट होती। विचारों की सरणि को खण्डित करते हुए मैंने कहा-भिक्षु जी मुझे आपके सम्पूर्ण संस्कृत-गेय-पद, उनकी चीनी और सिद्धनागरी, तथा स्वराङ्कन चाहिए। आप इनको सङ्गीतबद्ध करेंगे और मैं भरूँगा। दस दिन में 50-60 पृष्ठ में कुछ सङ्कलन लाए और मैंने उनके यन्त्र पर ही सङ्गीत भर लिया। बीस वर्ष से यदा-कदा कुछ न कुछ भेजते रहते हैं और विपुल संग्रह हो गया है। सब पद्यों की संस्कृत ठीक कर ली है। इसके एक पृष्ठ का चित्र इस लेख में दे रहा हूँ। ये गीतबद्ध संस्कृतपद्य चीन होते हुए कोरिया और जापान पहुँचे। जापान में इनको बोम्बाइ अथवा शोम्यो कहते हैं।

चीन के सम्राट् वुति Wuti ने 138-126 ईसा पूर्व में चाङ्छयेन् को बर्बर जातियों को खोजने भेजा। चाङ्छयेन मध्य एशिया होते हुए भारत पहुँचा और देखा कि भारत की संस्कृति कितनी ऊँची है। भारतीय सङ्गीत, नृत्य और वाद्यों से इतना प्रभावित हुआ कि अपने देश 'महातुषार राग' ले गया। इस राग के आधार पर चीनी सम्राट् के जामाता और सेनापति ने 28 प्रयाण-गीत लिखे। तुषार राग आज भारत में केवल सिख गुरुग्रन्थ साहब में ही मिलता है। चाङ्छयेन् भारतीय सुन्दरियों के उड़ते उत्तरीय और उमड़ती यौवनभरी नृत्यकला से अभिभूत हो गये। चीन में लकड़ी की ढोलक और भारतीय नृत्य का प्रारम्भ किया।

सन् 192-232 में राजकुमार और कवि त्साओची ने बौद्ध स्तोत्रों को लोकप्रिय स्वरों में बाँध कर जनजन में व्याप्त किया। गन्धर्व पञ्चिक का सङ्गीत सुनने राजकुमार चीन के यू पर्वत पर जाया करते और लौटकर स्वर-रचनाएँ करते। दिव्य प्रेरणा से अनुप्राणित उन्होंने 3000 स्वरबन्ध किए।

अमिताभ बुद्ध के स्वर्ग का नाम सुखावती है। सुखावती का गगन अप्सराओं और वाद्यों से भरा है। ये व्योमबालाएँ सुखावती के सप्तरत्न सरोवर में स्नान करती हैं, माँस और मदिरा का उपयोग न कर, फूलों से मधु-संचय करती हैं और आकाश से पुष्प वर्षा करती हैं। जगत् को सुरभित और सङ्गीतमय बनाती हैं। कटि के ऊपर दिगम्बर, गगन में प्रवहमान उत्तरीयों में उड़ती रहती हैं। कुमारजीव ने पुण्डरीक सूत्र का सन् 416 में चीनी भाषा में अनुवाद किया था। इसमें लिखा है कि जब भगवान् बुद्ध ने अपने अग्रणी शिष्य शारिपुत्र को अनुत्तरा सम्यक्संबोधि कर वर दिया, तब उपस्थित देव, गन्धर्व आदि हर्षोन्मत्त नाचने लगे। अपने उत्तरीय उतारकर भगवान् को दे दिये। इसलिए अप्सराएँ उत्तरीय-हीन ऊपर दिगम्बरियाँ हैं। चीनी समाज में महिलाएँ अत्यधिक वस्त्र पहिनती थीं। भारत की कला का जब चीन में प्रचार होने लगा तब अनावृत वक्षःस्थल की व्याख्या चाहिए थी। पुण्डरीक सूत्र ने इसकी पूर्ति की।

सुखावती में अप्सराएँ वीणा लिए निरुत्तरीय नृत्य करती हुईं।

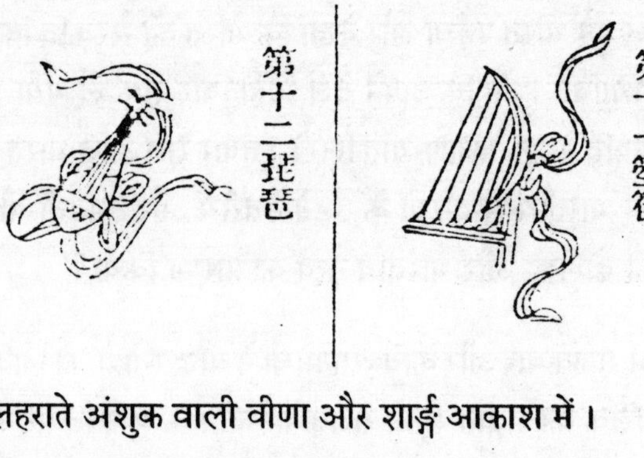

लहराते अंशुक वाली वीणा और शार्ङ्ग आकाश में।

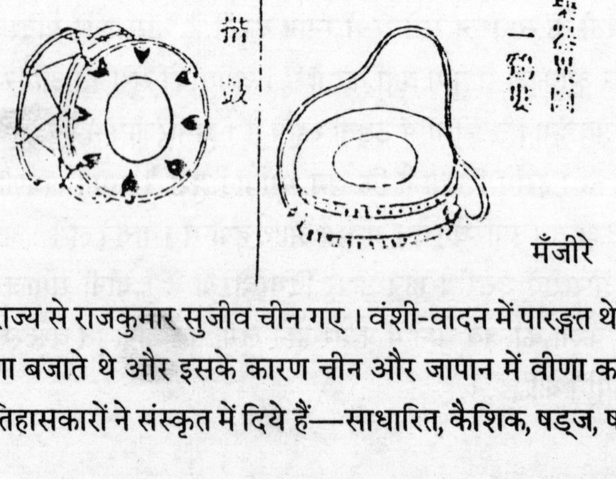

दुन्दुभि मँजीरे

सन् 568 में कूचा राज्य से राजकुमार सुजीव चीन गए। वंशी-वादन में पारङ्गत थे। चीन में सप्त-स्वरीय सङ्गीत प्रारम्भ किया। ये वीणा बजाते थे और इसके कारण चीन और जापान में वीणा का प्रवेश हुआ। सुजीव के सात स्वरों के नाम चीनी इतिहासकारों ने संस्कृत में दिये हैं—साधारित, कैशिक, षड्ज, षड्जग्राम, षाडव, पञ्चम, ऋषभ।

चीन से भारतीय सङ्गीत, कोरिया होता हुआ, जापान पहुँचा । आठवीं शताब्दी में जापान के सम्राट् शोमु (624-748) के काल में जापान में भारतीय सङ्गीत और नृत्य का प्रचार हुआ । आज भी राजप्रासाद में इनमें से कुछ परम्पराएँ सुरक्षित हैं । आचार्य बुत्तेत्सु और भारद्वाज गोत्र के बोधिसेन ने दाहआन्-जी विहार में अवतंसक, संस्कृत और सङ्गीत की शिक्षा दी । सङ्गीतमय नृत्यों में ऋग्वेद के अश्वराज- पेदु, भैरव और अम्बा, सहस्रशरदानन्द आदि हैं ।

जापान में सङ्गीत की गुरु-शिष्य परम्पराएँ इकट्ठी थीं । इनमें एक परम्परा सन् 650 से लेकर आज तक की है । काञ्ची के आचार्य नागार्जुन से आरम्भ होती है जो 650 के लगभग काञ्ची में तन्त्रों के महान् आचार्य थे । यह भारतीय सङ्गीत के इतिहास में प्राचीनतम निरन्तर अविच्छिन्न परम्परा है ।

जापान में वीणा को बीवा कहते हैं । इसमें चार तार होते हैं । अंगुलि से बजाते हैं । जब बाहर खींचते हैं तो 'बी' ध्वनि और 'वा' ध्वनि जब अन्दर की ओर । इसलिए इसका नाम बीवा है । वाद्य में स्वर्ग, पृथिवी और मनुष्य की त्रिवेणी है । इसके पञ्चाङ्ग पाँच गुणों के प्रतीक रूप हैं और इसके चार तार, चार ऋतुओं के द्योतक हैं । गुणों का निधान, ऋतुओं के सामंजस्य से शरीर की स्वस्थता और स्वरमाधुर्य से स्वर्ग को धरती पर लाता है । जापान के शोसोइन् भाण्डागार में सन् 657 की वीणा सुरक्षित है । यह संसार की प्राचीनतम वीणा है । सौ वर्ष पूर्व जापान के पथों पर प्रज्ञाचक्षु गायक, वीणा के मधुर स्वरों से स्तोत्र गाते थे । जापान में दुन्दुभि को 'तुदुमि' (त्सुजुमि) कहते हैं । वह भी भारत से गया है । शब्द भी संस्कृत का रूपान्तर है ।

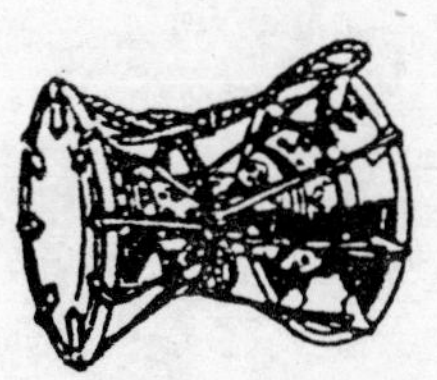

प्रज्ञाचक्षु गायक बेन्तेन्, सरस्वती वीणा लिए हुए, तुदुमि अर्थात् दुन्दुभि

जापान में वज्रलास्या, वज्रमाला, वज्रगीता और वज्रनृत्या देवियों का समावेश ध्यान-पट वज्रधातु-महामण्डल में है । भारत में नृत्य और सङ्गीत, साधना के अङ्ग हैं । परम कैवल्य आनन्द है, स्वरों की मूर्च्छनाओं और गतिलहरियों के पार की पारमिता है । सङ्गीत उस पारमिता का साधन है ।

वज्रगीता (जापान, नवीं शती)

वज्रनृत्या (जापान, नवीं शती)

दो सौ वर्ष पूर्व जापानी विद्वान् शिंगेन् की हस्तलिपि में वाराणसी के पुण्य-मङ्गल का आह्वान है ।

पुर्यां वाराणस-नदी-प्रतिमण्डितायां
तन्मङ्गलं भवतु शान्तिकरं तवाद्य ॥

यह नीचे जापानी काष्ठलिपि से उद्धृत है—

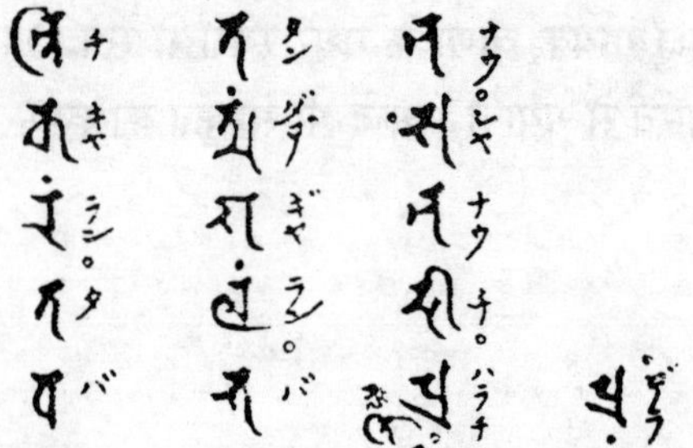

वाराणसी द्वारा मङ्गलकामना
(सिद्धनागरी और उसका जापानी लिपि में उच्चारण)

जापान की गहन मानसिकता में बसा है उसके नव-प्रभात का रहस्य । इस गहनता का मूल, श्रमणों के संस्कृत सूत्रों की चेतना है जो कभी-कभी और कहीं-कहीं संस्कृत पद्यों के गायन में फूट पड़ती है । युवा किग्यो मियाजिमा के शब्दों में यह देवता-योग है । वे भारत आकर मनुस्मृति का जीवन व्यतीत करना चाहते हैं, अदरक खाकर भी । मुझे अदरक खाते देखा और सोचा भारत में अदरक खाने का बहुत प्रचार है ।

नई दिल्ली

बौद्ध वाङ्मय में सङ्गीत

सुषमा कुलश्रेष्ठ

ललित कलाओं में सङ्गीत का महत्त्वपूर्ण स्थान है। 'गीतं वाद्यञ्च नृत्यञ्च त्रयं सङ्गीतमुच्यते'। सङ्गीत के अन्तर्गत गायन, वादन एवं नृत्य तीनों को परिगणित किया जाता है। वैदिक एवं लौकिक संस्कृत साहित्य सङ्गीत की सरसता तथा सङ्गीत के शास्त्रीय उल्लेखों से युक्त है। बौद्ध एवं जैन ग्रन्थों से भी तत्कालीन सङ्गीत कला का अच्छा ज्ञान प्राप्त होता है। बौद्ध ग्रन्थों में गायन, वादन एवं नृत्य के अनेकविध उल्लेख उपलब्ध होते हैं जो तत्कालीन सङ्गीतविद्या की उन्नति के परिचायक हैं। बौद्ध वाङ्मय में जो सङ्गीत उल्लिखित है, आगे चलकर उसकी अभिव्यक्ति भारत की प्राचीन शिल्प एवं चित्रकला में प्राप्त होती है जिसके आधार पर तत्कालीन गीत, वाद्य एवं नृत्य के स्वरूप का ज्ञान आसानी से किया जा सकता है।

अन्य विद्याओं की भाँति सङ्गीत विद्या का भी विधिवत् अध्ययन तत्कालीन सम्पन्न परिवारों में किया जाता था। स्वयं बोधिसत्त्व सङ्गीत तथा नाट्य कला के कुशल ज्ञाता थे। उनके परिवार की सब स्त्रियाँ भी कुशल सङ्गीतज्ञा थीं। ललितविस्तर में उल्लेख है कि बुद्ध की माता माया देवी कलानिपुण थीं। बुद्ध के भावी श्वसुर ने विवाह के पहले शर्त रखी थी कि उनकी कलानिपुण पुत्री के लिए अपने को योग्य सिद्ध करने के लिए भावी वर को सङ्गीतादि कलाओं की अपनी दक्षता प्रदर्शित करनी होगी।[1] सिद्धार्थ के लिए ऐसी वधू चाहिए थी जो गणिका के समान कलानिपुण हो—'शास्त्रे विधिज्ञकुशला गणिका यथैव'।[2] बुद्धचरित में उल्लेख है कि तत्कालीन अन्तःपुरों में महती वीणा, मृदङ्ग, पणव, तूर्य, वेणु आदि वाद्यों का वादन तथा गायन मनोरञ्जन के लिए किया जाता था। पितृपुत्रसमागम नामक कथा में वर्णन है कि भगवान् बुद्ध के जन्मावसर पर पाँच सौ वाद्यों का वृन्दवादन हुआ था।[3] इस प्रकार का वाद्यवादन आजकल विशिष्ट राजकीय समारोहों तथा चलचित्र-गीतों की रिकार्डिंग के अवसर पर देखने और सुनने में आता है।

बौद्ध युग में विद्याप्रदान का प्रमुख केन्द्र तक्षशिला था जिसमें अनेक अध्ययन विभाग थे यथा-वैदिक विद्यालय, अष्टादश विद्यालय, शिल्पविज्ञान विद्यालय आदि जिनमें पाँच-पाँच सौ विद्यार्थी अध्ययन करते थे।[4] शब्दविद्या, अध्यात्मविद्या, चिकित्साविद्या, हेतुविद्या और शिल्पविद्या नामक वैदिक पञ्च महाविद्या जातक युग में 'पञ्चयान' कहलाती थीं।[5] परोपहस्स जातक के अनुसार बोधिसत्त्व ने इसी विश्वविद्यालय में समस्त शिल्पों की शिक्षा प्राप्त की थी। इसी काल का एक दूसरा विद्याकेन्द्र था वाराणसी, जिसमें सङ्गीताध्यापन का स्वतन्त्र विभाग

था। नालन्दा, विक्रमशिला तथा ओदन्तपुरी सदृश दूसरे विश्वविद्यालयों में भी सङ्गीत का स्वतन्त्र निकाय था जिसमें अध्यक्ष के रूप में भारतप्रसिद्ध सङ्गीतज्ञ की नियुक्ति की जाती थी।[6] सङ्गीत के लिए 'गन्धब्ब वेद' अथवा 'गान्धर्ववेद' संज्ञा थी जिसके अन्तर्गत गीत, वादित्त, नच्च (नृत्य), अक्खानं आदि का सन्निवेश था। अक्खान के अन्तर्गत प्राचीन आख्यान तथा वीर गाथाओं का गायन सन्निविष्ट था।[7] इनकी गणना 'सिप्प' अथवा 'शिल्प' में की जाती थी।

वेद तथा वेदाङ्गों का जैसा अध्ययन वैदिक युग में प्रचलित था, ठीक वैसा ही जातक युग में भी था।[8] तेविज्ज सुत्त में साम के छान्दोग्य चरण का उल्लेख प्राप्त होता है। दीर्घनिकाय में छान्दोग्य चरण के आचार्यों को 'छान्दोक' कहा गया है। सेलसुत्त में शैल नामक ब्राह्मण का उल्लेख है जो तीनों वेद तथा वेदाङ्गों का कुशल ज्ञाता था और तीन सौ विद्यार्थियों का वेदाध्यापक था। वैदिक मन्त्रों की भाँति बौद्ध सुत्तों को भी सस्वर पढ़ने की प्रणाली उस समय वर्तमान थी।[9] पालि महावग्ग तथा उदान[10] में लिखा है कि गौतम की इच्छानुसार कोण कुट्टिकण्ण नामक भिक्षु ने अट्ठकवग्गिक (अर्थपाद) सूत्रों को सस्वर पढ़ा था—'सरेण अभासि'।[11]

जातक ग्रन्थों में उस काल के प्रचलित व्यवसायों की एक सूची प्राप्त होती है जिसमें निम्नलिखित वर्ग समाविष्ट हैं—नट, नर्तक, गायक, भेरीवादक एवं नाटककार आदि।[12] इनमें से प्रत्येक का सङ्गीत से कुछ न कुछ सम्बन्ध अवश्य है। इन सबके अनेक संघ होते थे तथा इनके लिए नगर में पृथक् उपनिवेश का प्रबन्ध था। उस काल में गणिकाओं एवं नर्तकियों को समाज में सङ्गीतज्ञा के रूप में विशिष्ट सम्मान प्राप्त था। गङ्गमाल-जातक में वर्णन है कि राजकुमारी के परिणयावसर पर 16,000 नर्तकियाँ गान तथा नृत्य प्रस्तुत करने के लिए निमन्त्रित की गई थीं (3.452)। सुमङ्गलविलासिनी ग्रन्थ के अनुसार काशी नरेश के अन्तःपुर में अनेक कुशल नर्तकियाँ नियुक्त थीं।[13] उस काल में गणिका को अन्य सामान्य वेश्याओं की तुलना में अधिक सम्मान प्राप्त था क्योंकि वह सङ्गीतकलाविदुषी हुआ करती थी। गणिका सङ्गीतादि अनेक शास्त्रों को जानती थी तभी तो ललितविस्तर में कहा गया है—'शास्त्रे विधिज्ञकुशला गणिका यथैव'। शासनकार्य को सुचारु रूप से चलाने के लिए प्रमुख पदाधिकारियों के अलावा जिन एकादश अङ्गों की आवश्यकता थी, उनमें गणिका का भी समावेश था (द्र. कुरुधम्म-जातक)। वेश्या का जनपद-कल्याणी के रूप में राष्ट्रीय सम्मान होता था और इनके लिए पञ्चशील की दीक्षा आवश्यक मानी जाती थी (द्र. दुम्मेध-जातक)।

बौद्ध युग में सङ्गीत एवं नाट्यकला अपनी उन्नत अवस्था में वर्तमान थी। सङ्गीत एवं नाट्यादि कलाओं के विकास के लिए राजसाहाय्य अत्यावश्यक है और यह राज्याश्रय इन कलाओं को उस काल में प्राप्त था। राजसभा में गायक, वादक एवं नर्तक-नर्तकियों की विधिवत् नियुक्ति की जाती थी। राजसभा में 16,000 नर्तकियों की नियुक्ति का उल्लेख मिलिन्दपञ्ह में है—'सोलस्सु नाटकीसहस्सेसु'।[14] जिस राजसभा में 16,000 नर्तकियाँ स्थायी रूप से नियुक्त हों, वहाँ के राजकीय साङ्गीतिक समारोहों की शोभा एवं भव्यता का सहज अनुमान किया जा सकता है। राजसभा के गायक, वादक और नर्तकों के रहने पर भी आवश्यकता पड़ने पर चतुर गणिकाओं को गायन, वादन एवं नृत्य के लिए निमन्त्रित किया जाता था।[15] उस काल के राजा तथा समाज के समृद्ध जन

बौद्ध विहारों को आर्थिक तथा अन्य सहायता सदा प्रदान किया करते थे। विहारों में आराधनार्थ नियुक्त आराधक कलाकारों को राज्य की ओर से अर्थ प्रदान किया जाता था। शासन का पूरा नियन्त्रण इन कलाकारों पर था। सरगुजा राज्य में प्राप्त गुम्फाभिलेख से ज्ञात होता है कि वहाँ के विहार में सुतनुका नाम की एक देवदासी थी। उसके एवं वहाँ के आराधक के मध्य प्रेम व्यवहार को देखकर दोनों को कठोर दण्ड दिया गया था।

बौद्धकालीन समाज में अनेक लोकोत्सव हुआ करते थे जिनमें गायन, वादन एवं नृत्य का समावेश होता था। फाहियान के यात्राविवरण में मगध में होने वाले ऐसे उत्सवों का स्पष्ट उल्लेख है। ये सामाजिक उत्सव 'समज्जा' अथवा 'समाज' संज्ञा से अभिहित होते थे। ऐसे सामूहिक उत्सवों का आयोजन नियमित रूप से होता था—इसके प्रमाण अशोक के अभिलेख हैं, विधुरपण्डित-जातक में एक समज्जा का चित्र अंकित है जिसमें सभी स्त्री पुरुषों के गीत, नृत्यादि में सम्मिलित होने का उल्लेख है।[16] ऐसे लोकोत्सवों के अवसर पर आख्यानों के गाने की भी परम्परा थी—यह सिगालोवाद सुत्तन्त से ज्ञात होता है।[17] जैसे वर्तमान युग में विशिष्ट सभागारों में भव्य उत्सव आयोजित होते हैं तथा विशिष्ट व्यक्तियों को निमन्त्रित किया जाता है, उसी प्रकार उस युग में ऐसे लोकोत्सव शैलशिखरों तथा पवित्र स्थानों पर आयोजित होते थे और नगर के माननीय प्रतिष्ठित लोगों को इनमें विशेष रूप से निमन्त्रण प्राप्त होता था।[18] विसुद्धिमग्ग में उल्लेख है कि उत्सव में 500 नर्तकियों को निमन्त्रित किया गया था।[19]

बौद्ध काल में नाट्य के लिए 'पेक्खा' अथवा 'प्रेक्षा' संज्ञा थी। नाट्य का दिग्दर्शक अथवा निर्देशक नटाचार्य कहलाता था। प्रमुख नट के लिए 'नटगामणि' अभिधान था। नट लोग जनता के सम्मुख रङ्गभूमि पर अनेकविध अभिनयों द्वारा उनका मनोरञ्जन करते थे—'यो सो नटो रंगमज्झे समज्जमज्झे सच्चालिकेन जनं हासेति रमेति'।[20] नाटक में नट के साथ नटी भी हुआ करती थी किन्तु समाज में नटी को सम्मान की दृष्टि से नहीं देखा जाता था क्योंकि वे सौन्दर्य-प्रसाधन तथा विविध-कला-कुशलता द्वारा शरीर-विक्रय भी किया करती थीं। कुसजातक में उल्लेख है कि राजा अपनी धर्मपत्नियों से संतान न होने पर उन्हें धर्मनटी बनाकर बाहर भेज देता था जिससे वे अभीष्ट पुरुष से गर्भधारण कराने में समर्थ हो सकें।[21]

विभिन्न वाद्यों द्वारा उद्भूत स्वर तथा लय का आनन्द वाद्य सङ्गीत अथवा वादन द्वारा प्राप्त होता है। साङ्गीतिक वाद्य चार प्रकार के माने गये हैं—तत, अवनद्ध, सुषिर और घन। आचार्य भरतमुनि के अनुसार—

ततं तन्त्रीकृतं ज्ञेयमवनद्धं तु पौष्करम्।
घनं तालस्तु विज्ञेयः सुषिरो वंश उच्यते॥[22]

बौद्ध वाङ्मय में इन चारों प्रकार के वाद्यों के अनेकविध उल्लेख उपलब्ध हैं। उङ्गलियों से छेड़कर (यथा स्वरमण्डल, तम्बूरा), कोण या त्रिकोण की सहायता से (यथा सितार, वीणा, सरोद), गज से रगड़ कर (यथा सारंगी, इसराज, दिलरुबा) तथा डण्डी से प्रहार कर (यथा सन्तूर) बजाये जाने वाले वाद्य तत वाद्य कहलाते हैं। बौद्ध साहित्य में तत वाद्यों में निम्नाङ्कित वाद्यों का नामोल्लेख प्राप्त होता है—परिवादिनी वीणा, विपञ्ची, वल्लकी, महती, नकुली, कच्छपी तथा तुम्बवीणा।[22] वास्तव में ये सब तरह-तरह की वीणाओं के ही नाम हैं। तारों की

संख्या तथा वादन-विधि के भेद से एक ही वीणा के अनेक भेद बन गए। इसी बात को सोमेश्वर ने अपने मानसोल्लास में लिखा है—'तन्त्रीभेदैः क्रियाभेदैर्वीणावाद्यमनेकधा'।[23]

नारदकृत सङ्गीत-मकरन्द में उन्नीस वीणाओं का नामनिर्देश उपलब्ध होता है। वे हैं—कच्छपी, कुब्जिका, चित्रा, वहन्ती, परिवादिनी, जया, घोषावती, ज्येष्ठा, नकुली, महती, वैष्णवी, ब्राह्मी, रौद्री, कूर्मी, रावणी, सारस्वती, किन्नरी, सैरन्ध्री एवं घोषका। बौद्ध वाङ्मय में उल्लिखित विभिन्न तत वाद्य वीणा के ही पृथक्-पृथक् भेद हैं। उस काल में तत वाद्यों के लिए 'वीणा' सामान्य संज्ञा थी। वीणा की तुम्बी के लिए बीलीफल का उपयोग किया जाता था। वीणा उस काल का सर्वाधिक प्रिय वाद्य रहा है। दीघनिकाय में उल्लेख है कि वीणावादन के साथ प्रस्तुत किये गये श्रुतिमधुर सङ्गीत ने बुद्धदेव सदृश वीतराग को भी प्रभावित कर दिया था। कथा कुछ इस प्रकार हैं। पंचसिख नामक एक गन्धर्व था जो प्रसिद्ध गन्धर्व तुम्बरु की कन्या सूर्यवर्चसा से प्रेम करने लगा। अपनी प्रेमसाधना में असफल होकर एक दिन वह वीणा पर कारुणिक गीत गा रहा था। वीणा-तन्त्री पर झंकृत स्वरों तथा करुणगीति के शब्दों का सामञ्जस्य कुछ ऐसा था जिसे सुनकर स्वयं भगवान् बुद्ध प्रसन्न हो गीत की प्रशंसा करने लगे—'अहो ! सङ्गीत का प्रभाव अक्षुण्ण है।' सङ्गीतादि कलाओं को राज्याश्रय प्राप्त था। राज्य की ओर से ही वीणावादकों की अनेक प्रतियोगिताएँ आयोजित की जाती थीं जिसमें विजेता को पुरस्कार एवं राज्याश्रय-प्राप्ति रूप सम्मान-लाभ होता था। उस काल में अनेक चतुर वीणावादक थे। मूसिल-जातक तत्कालीन वीणा-वादन-कौशल का स्पष्ट परिचायक है। कथा है कि उज्जयिनी के वीणावादक मूसिल तथा वाराणसी के राजवादक गु,त्तिल के मध्य ईर्ष्या पनप गई। यद्यपि मूसिल ने गुत्तिल से ही वीणा-वादन के गूढ़ रहस्यों को सीखा था तथापि वे उन्हीं को पराजित करने का प्रयास करने लगे। राजसभा में स्पर्धा का आयोजन किया गया। स्पर्धा के अन्तर्गत गुत्तिल ने वीणा के सात तारों में से एक-एक को तोड़कर बचे हुए तारों पर वीणा-वादन ज़ारी रखा। स्पर्धा के अन्तिम क्षणों में सभी तन्त्रियाँ तोड़ने के अनन्तर वीणा के दण्ड से ही ध्वनियाँ गूँजती रहीं। इससे यह निष्कर्ष निकलता है कि सम्भवतः उस समय वीणातन्त्रियों के कर्षण से एकाधिक स्वरों का वादन करने की प्रणाली प्रचलित रही हो। वीणा का वादन कोण द्वारा किया जाता था।

वे वाद्य जो भीतर से पोले तथा चमड़े से मढ़े हुए होते हैं और हाथ या किसी अन्य वस्तु के ताडन से शब्द उत्पन्न करते हैं, अवनद्ध अथवा आनद्ध कहलाते हैं। अवनद्ध वाद्यों में मृदङ्ग, पणव, भेरी, डिण्डिम तथा दुन्दुभि का उल्लेख जातकों में प्राप्त होता है। मृदङ्ग बजाने के लिए दण्ड का प्रयोग किया जाता था। कौशाम्बी, रामनगर, राजघाट, मथुरा तथा भीटा आदि स्थानों पर किये गए उत्खननों में कोण तथा वादनदण्ड प्रचुर मात्रा में प्राप्त हुए हैं। वे वाद्य जो ठोकर लगाकर बजाये जाते हैं, घनवाद्य कहलाते हैं। घनवाद्यों में घण्टा, जल्लली, झल्लरी तथा कांस्यताल का प्रचार था। मुख की वायु द्वारा बजाये जाने वाले वाद्य सुषिर वाद्य कहलाते हैं। सुषिर वाद्यों में शंख, तूर्य, कुराल, शृङ्ग आदि का नामनिर्देश उपलब्ध होता है। तूर्य वाद्य की ध्वनि अत्यधिक तेज़ एवं दिग्व्यापिनी थी।[24]

सङ्गीत के अन्तर्गत स्वर, ग्राम, मूर्च्छना के साथ रागों का प्रचलन भी प्रारम्भ हो चुका था। सुस्वर सङ्गीत पशु-पक्षि-जगत् को भी आकृष्ट कर सकता है—ऐसी जन-मान्यता थी। आज भी इस सम्बन्ध में अनेक शोधकार्य किये जा रहे हैं। गान में सुस्वरता तथा श्रुतिमधुरता परमावश्यक अङ्ग हैं। सुस्वरता से अभिप्राय साङ्गीतिक स्वरों के सही प्रयोग से है तथा श्रुति-मधुरता से तात्पर्य है गान का कर्णप्रिय होना। विस्वरता गान का बड़ा दोष है। दीर्घकालीन विस्वर गान की अपेक्षा अल्पकालीन सुस्वर गान श्रेयस्कर है—ऐसा तत्कालीन सङ्गीतज्ञों का विश्वास था।

निष्कर्षत: कहा जा सकता है कि बौद्ध काल में सङ्गीत की तीनों विधायें—गायन, वादन तथा नृत्य अपनी उन्नत अवस्था में वर्तमान थीं। लोग गान करते थे। गान के साथ विभिन्न वाद्यों के वादन की प्रथा थी। चारों ही प्रकार के वाद्यों का प्रचलन था। गायन और वादन के साथ नृत्य का भी पर्याप्त प्रचार था। कई कई सौ एवं हज़ार नर्तकियाँ विशिष्ट अवसरों पर नृत्यार्थ निमन्त्रित की जाती थीं। नाट्य में भी सङ्गीत का पर्याप्त प्रयोग होता था। सङ्गीत एवं नाट्यादि कलाओं को उचित राज्याश्रय प्राप्त था अन्यथा इन कलाओं को विकास का समुचित अवसर प्राप्त होना कठिन था। सङ्गीत का प्रयोग पारमार्थिक तथा शृङ्गारिक दोनों कार्यों के लिए किया जाता था। बौद्धों को वही सङ्गीत मान्य था जो उनकी आध्यात्मिक साधना में बाधक न बने। बौद्ध-विहारों में सङ्गीताराधन के लिए आराधकों तथा देवदासियों की नियुक्ति होती थी और इनके चारित्रिक व्यवहारों पर शासन का कठोर नियन्त्रण रहता था। सङ्गीत का सामूहिक अनुष्ठान गिरग्ग, समज्ज तथा नक्कत्तकीलं जैसे प्रसिद्ध लोकोत्सवों पर किया जाता था। इन अवसरों पर सङ्गीत के साथ नाट्य तथा आख्यानों का गायन भी हुआ करता था।

बौद्धकालीन सङ्गीत का एक संक्षिप्त विवरण यहाँ प्रस्तुत किया गया है। सङ्गीत की तीनों विधाओं का कैसा रूप उस काल में था, समाज में सङ्गीत तथा सङ्गीतप्रयोक्ताओं को किस दृष्टि से देखा जाता था, वैदिककालीन सङ्गीत का बौद्धकालीन सङ्गीत पर क्या प्रभाव पड़ा, आदि ऐसे अनेक विषय हैं जिन पर शोध किया जाना परमावश्यक है। इन सब विषयों पर किया गया शोधकार्य नूतन तथ्यों को प्रकाशित करेगा और बौद्ध वाङ्मय को और अधिक गौरवान्वित करेगा।

सन्दर्भ-सङ्केत

1. सोशल लाइफ़ इन एनशन्ट इण्डिया—चकलादार, पृ० 85
2. ललित विस्तर, 12, पृ० 139, चकलादार, पृ० 127, 139
3. अर्थपाद०, पृ० 152, बापट
4. जातककालीन भारतीय संस्कृति, पृ० 98

5. वही
6. एनशन्ट इण्डियन एजूकेशन, राधाकुमुद मुखोपाध्याय, पृ० 490
7. दीघनिकाय 1, पृ० 6
8. सेतकेतु-जातक, 337; जातकालीन भारतीय संस्कृति, पृ० 97
9. महावग्ग, 5, 13, 9
10. उदान, 5, 6,
11. अर्थपादसुत्त, भूमिका, पृ. 1 बापट
12. मिलिन्दपञ्ह, 331. बी.सी. लॉ, पृ० 66-67
13. लॉ कृत 'ट्राइब्स ऑफ़ एनशन्ट इन्डिया' 1943, पृ० 110
14. बी.सी. लॉ., पृ० 72
15. वही, पृ० 166
16. जातक, 6, 277
17. द्र. रिस डेविड्स, पृ० 83
18. वही
19. द्र. 1489, विमानवत्थुभाष्य, पृ० 62-74, 'ट्राइब्स ऑफ़ एनशन्ट इन्डिया', पृ० 218
20. गामणिसंयुत्त 4, पृ० 306, 'हिस्ट्री ऑफ संस्कृत पोयटिक्स,' काणे, पृ० 323
21. जातककालीन भारतीय संस्कृति, वियोगी, पृ० 14
22. नाट्यशास्त्र, 28, 2
23. मानसोल्लास, 3, 572
24. तेविज्जसुत्त, दीघनिकाय, 251, लॉ., पृ० 224

दिल्ली

GLIMPSES OF MUSIC IN THE BUDDHACARITA OF AŚVAGHOṢA*

Sushma Kulshreshtha

Aśvaghoṣa was a contemporary of King Kaniṣka and a predecessor of Kālidāsa. According to the Tibetan biographer of Aśvaghoṣa, he was an excellent musician who himself composed pieces of music and travelled about with a band of male and female singers in the bazars. He played and sang with his choir melancholy songs about the vanity of existence, and attracted by the beautiful melodies, the crowd stood still and listened. In this way he won many over to the Buddhist religion.

Chinese pilgrim I-tsing, who travelled through India in 671-695 A.D. praises Aśvaghoṣa. I-tsing mentions that at his time in India, among other songs which were chanted at Buddhist sanctuaries, there was a collection of sacred texts compiled by Aśvaghoṣa. He relates him also as a composer of songs of the *Sūtrālaṁkāra* and of the *Buddhacarita*.

Buddhacarita is an epic composition widely read and sung throughout India and the countries of the southern sea according to I-tsing. In the present paper, an attempt is made to show Aśvaghoṣa's knowledge of Music, Musical Instruments and Dance. He has made a number of references to different types of songs, *stutis*, dances and instruments like *Vīṇā, Parivādinī, Mahatī, Mṛdaṅga, Paṇava, Dundubhi, Tūrya and Veṇu* and the music of birds also.

Music and Dance occupy a prominent place in Fine Arts *'Gītaṁ vādyaṁ tathā nṛtyaṁ trayaṁ saṅgītamucyate.*[1] Music includes Music Vocal, Music Instrumental and Dance. Aśvaghoṣa has referred to all these

* This paper was presented on 23rd August, 1990 at the XXXIII ICANAS, International Congress of Asian and North African Studies held at University of Toronto, Toronto, Canada from 19th to 25th August, 1990.

three at a number of places in his *Buddhacarita* in the course of his narratives and descriptions as well as in the usage of similes and metaphors.

In the third canto entitled *Samvegotpattiḥ* of *Buddhacarita,* we come accoss a beautiful description of the forests. Prince Siddhārtha once happened to listen about these forests, which having a number of other good things were resounding with the songs and were possessed of the sweet notes of *Puṃskokila* :

Tataḥ kadācinmṛduśādvalāni
puṃskokilonnāditapādapāni.
Śuśrāva padmākaramaṇḍitāni
gītairnibaddhāni sa kānanāni[2].

In the fourth canto entitled *Strīnivāraṇa,* a beautiful lady in order to attract Siddhārtha towards herself, sang a sweet song with the presentation of gestures :

Madhuraṁ gītamanvarthaṁ kācitsābhinayaṁ jagau
Taṁ svasthaṁ codayantīva vañcitosītyavekṣitaih[3].

Among the animals, deer are very fond of listening to music. They are attracted by the deceitful music of the hunter. For their love of music, they give up their lives even :

Gītairhriyante hi mṛgā vadhāya
rūpārthamagnau śalabhāḥ patanti.
Matsyo giratyāyasamāmiṣārthī
tasmādanarthaṁ viṣayāḥ phalanti.[4]

When the *Dharma-cakra* (wheel of *Dharma*) set forth by Gautama Buddha started rotating in all the three worlds, human and divine beings started dancing and singing aloud on the earth, in the quarters and in heaven :

Ahinarasuraloke dharmacakraṁ yadedaṁ
tribhuvanasukhaśāntyai cāśu śubhraṁ cacāla.
Bhuvi diśi divi devā bhūtasaṁghāśca sarve
saha kusumanipātairnṛtyagītaṁ ca cakruḥ.[5]

Aśvaghoṣa has made reference to a number of *stutis,* eulogies also. When prince Siddhārtha approached on the Rājapatha, people offering him their respectful *stutis*. We may presume that these eulogies were in the form of musical compositions :

Taṁ tuṣṭuvuḥ saumyaguṇena keci-
dvavandire dīptatayā tathānye.
Saumukhyatastu śriyamasya keci-
dvaipulyamāśaṃsiṣurāyuṣaśca .[6]

When Siddhārtha attained *Buddhattva, Siddhas, Devas* and the *Maharṣis* started offering him their respectful eulogies, naturally in the form of musical composition and that too in high pitch :

Uccaistamīḍire'dṛśyāḥ siddhā devā maharṣayaḥ.
Āpatiṣyadvipatteḥ prāgiva mamlau tu manmathaḥ.[7]

Trividha saṅgīta (threefold music) is an art. Vātsyāyana in his *Kāmasūtra* referes to 64 arts,[8] out of which the following five are related to music :

(i) *Gīta*
(ii) *Vādya*
(iii) *Nṛtya*
(iv) *Udakavādya*
(v) *Vīṇāḍamarukavādya*

Kalās

Kalās (Arts) are meant for the attraction and recreation of others and self-recreation also. Aśvaghoṣa refers to different arts. In the harem of Siddhārtha, charming ladies tried to attract Siddhārtha through performance of various arts :

Vāgbhiḥ kalābhirlalitaiśca hāvai-
rmadaiḥ sakhelairmadhuraiśca hāsaiḥ.
Taṁ tatra nāryo ramayāṁbabhūvu-
rbhrūvañcitairardhanirīkṣitaiśca .[9]

Adeptness in the performance of arts is essential if a *Nāyikā* wants to attract a *Nāyaka* towards herself. Courtesans are particularly very expert in alluring *Nāyakas* through performance of different arts that include music and dance. King Śuddhodana permitted the courtesans who had expertise in arts to attend to prince Siddhārtha :

Snehācca bhāvaṁ tanayasya buddhvā
sa rāgadoṣānavicintya kāṅścit.
Yogyāḥ samāgyāpayati sma tatra
kalāsvabhigyā iti vāramukhyāḥ.[10]

Instrumental Music

Aśvaghoṣa seems to be familiar with all kinds of musical instruments which have been classified into four groups as follows :

Tataṁ tanrīkṛtaṁ jñeya-
mavanaddhaṁ tu pauṣkaram.
Ghanaṁ tālastu vijñeyaḥ
suṣiro vaṃśa ucyate.[11]

1. Tata Instruments (Cordophones)

Musical instruments using stretched strings, be they of grass, animal gut or metal wire and which are played by fingers (*e.g., Svaramaṇḍala, Tambūrā*) or by the help of *Koṇa* or *Trikoṇa* (*e.g., Viṇā, Sitāra* and *Saroda*) or *Gaja* (*e.g.*, Violin, *Sāraṅgī, Īsarāja* and *Dilrubā*) or stick (*e.g., Santūra*) are called *Tata* Instruments (cordophones or stringed instruments). Among the Tata instruments, Aśvaghoṣa has referred to *Viṇā, Mahatī* and *Parivādinī*.

Three types of *Vīṇā, Ekatantrī, Dvitantrī* and *Tritantrī* are mentioned in the *śāstras*. Lord Brahmā was the expounder of *Nāṭyaveda* and teacher of Bharatamuni. His *Vīṇā* was *Brāhmī*. The other names of *Brāhmī viṇā* are *Ghoṣa, Ghoṣaka, Ghoṣavatī* and *Ekatantrī*. We find detailed description of *Ekatantrī Vīṇā* in the *Saṅgītaratnākara* of Śārṅgadeva. *Ekatantrī* is considered to be the mother of all the *Vīṇās*. The very touch and holy *Darśana* of this bless the beholder with *Bhukti* and *Mukti*.

As there were no frets (*Sārikās*) in *Ekatantrī*, all the *Mūrcchanās* and *Śrutis* were always present there :

Śrutayo'tha svarā mūrcchanā nanāvidhāstathā.
Ekatantrīkaviṇayāṁ sarvametatpratiṣṭhitam.[12]

The *Viṇā* known as *Ghoṣaka, Ghoṣavatī* or *Brahmī* upto the times of Bharata, Mataṅga and Nārada came to be called as *Ekatantrī* during the times of Nānyadeva, Sudhākalaṣa and Śārṅgadeva. We get the reference of nineteen types of *Vīṇās* in the *Saṅgitamakaranda* of Nārada. They are *Kacchapī, Kubjikā, Citrā, Vahanti, Parivādinī, Jayā, Ghoṣavatī, Jyeṣṭhā, Nakulī, Mahatī, Vaiṣnavī, Brāhmī, Raudrī, Kūrmī, Rāvaṇī, Sārasvatī, Kinnarī, Sairandhrī* and *Ghoṣakā*. Originally, there was only one type of *Vīṇā* which was multiplied in different types of *Vīṇās*, with different number of strings in them and also with different ways of playing in due course of time. This fact is brought out by Someśvara in his *Mānasollāsa* :

Tantrībhedaiḥ kriyābhedairvīṇāvādyamanekadhā.[13]

In the fifth canto entitled *Abhiniṣkramaṇa* of *Buddhacarita*, we get beautiful account of how King Śuddhodana, father of Gautama, tries his best to get his son deviated from his supreme goal---attainment of *Buddhatva*. Gautama seeks permission form his father to repair to forest for the attainment of *mokṣa* whereas Śuddhodana makes large arrangements of security and various enjoyments and pleasures so that his son may not leave for the forest. Threefold music is a big source of delight. When Gautama entered his palace, a number of ladies came to attract him in different ways. Some had come there with musical instruments. They began to serve him with enchanting music played on the *Tūryas*. But, alas, Gautama could not get any pleasure in that music as he was aspirant of *Abhiniṣkramaṇa* :

Paramairapi divyatūryakalpaiḥ
sa tu tairnaiva ratiṁ yayau na harṣam.
Paramārthasukhāya tasya sādho-
rabhiniścikramiṣā yato na reme.[14]

Thus, those beautiful ladies became unsuccessful in their endeavour. When gods came to know the firm determination of Gautama, they put all those ladies into deep slumber. They were unaware of their garments and limbs etc. Some lady had come there to please and attract Gautama with her fine performance on *Vīṇā*. But by the grace of gods, she was put to sleep. Aśvaghoṣa has given beautiful description of this lady. She was enjoying sound sleep. She rested her cheek on her hand. She was keeping her beloved gold-plated *vīṇā* on her lap but, all of a sudden, she gave up the *vīṇā* as though she was enraged on her and plunged into deep sleep:

Abhavacchayītā hi tatra kāci-
dviniveśya pracale kare kapolaṁ.
Dayitāmapi rukmapaktracitrāṁ
kupitevāṅkagatāṁ vihāya vīṇām.[15]

Such a description of *vīṇā* on the part of our poet proves his very knowledge of this stringed instrument. He is aware of the fact that *vīṇā* is played keeping it on the lap.

Kālidāsa also describes his *Yakṣī* of *Meghadūta* placing her beloved *Vīṇā* on her lap in the following famous verse in which is given the best reference to *vīṇā* and playing on it :

Utsaṅge vā malinavasane saumya nikṣipya vīṇāṁ
madgotrаṅkaṁ viracitapadaṁ geyamudgātukāmā.
Tantrīmārdrāṁ nayanasalilaiḥ sārayitvā kathañci-
dbhūyo bhūyaḥ svayamapi kṛtāṁ mūrcchanāṁ vismarantī.[16]

The players of instruments have high regard and love for their instruments, hence the appropriate word *'dayitām'* by Aśvaghoṣa in the previous verse.

The composer of *Buddhacarita* refers to *Mahatī* and *Parivādinī* in the following verse :

Mahatīṁ parivādinīṁ ca kāci-
dvanitāliṅgya sakhīmiva prasuptā.
Vijughūrṇa calatsuvarṇasūtrā
vadanenākulayoktrakeṇa .[17]

Mahatī and Parivādinī are two different types of *vīṇās*. *Parivādinī* has been enumerated by Nārada in his *Saṅgītamakaranda*. It contained seven strings :

Saptabhiḥ tantrībhiḥ (vīṇā) dṛśyate parivādinī.[18]

Amarakośa says---

Vīṇā tu vallakī vipañcī sā tu tantrībhiḥ saptabhiḥ parivādinī.

No information regarding *Parivādinī* is available in the works of Bharata or Śārṅgadeva. Lexicons like *Yatimānapādakhaṇḍa* and *Abhidhānacintāmaṇi* do refer to it.

Some scholars are of the opinion that the very first reference to *Parivādinī vīṇā* has been made by Kālidāsa[19] in the *Raghuvaṁśa* in the following verse :

Bhramaraiḥ kusumānusāribhiḥ parikīrṇā parivādinī muneh.
Dadṛśe pavanāvalepajaṃ srjatī vāṣpamivāñjanāvilam.[20]

Kālidāsa uses the term *Parivādinī* for the *vīṇā* of sage Nārada whereas according to our *śāstras, Mahatī* is the *vīṇā* of sage Nārada. Hemādri, the famous commentator of *Raghuvaṁśa* quotes :

Viśvāvasostu bṛhatī tumbarostu kalāvatī.
Mahatī Nāradasya syātsarasvatyāstu kacchpī.[21]

The famous poet Māgha also refers to *Mahatī* as the *vīṇā* of Nārada in his *Śiśupālavadha* :

Raṇadbhirāghaṭṭanayā nabhasvataḥ
pṛthagvibhinnaśrutimaṇḍalaiḥ svaraih.
Sphuṭibhavadgrāmaviśeṣamūrcchanā-
mavekṣamāṇaṁ mahatīṁ muhurmuhuḥ.[22]

According to Nānyadeva, *Mahatī* was a *vīṇā* comprising twentyone strings. All the three scales and three *grāmās* were available on it and all the twentyone *Mūrcchanās* could be played on it :

Trigrāmasvarasaṅkhyābhistantrībhirmahatīti yā
nārado vādakastasya nāparo divi viśrutaḥ.
Atra vyaktāstrayo grāmāḥ sphuṭāḥ saptasvarā api
pratisvaraṁ pratigrāmaṁ mūrcchanāstvekaviṃśatiḥ.[23]

It is very strange that our poet uses *Mahatī* and *Parivādinī* in one single verse. He wants to convey that some lady wanted to attract Gautama by her able performance on *vīṇā* but all of a sudden, she plunged into deep sleep. It appeared as if she embraced her beloved *vīṇā* like her beloved female friend. What exactly is the idea, Aśvaghoṣa wants to express in the aforesaid verse is not very clear. If we say that the lady had come with two *vīṇās* - one *Mahatī* and the other *Parivādinī* and slept embracing her *vīṇās* like her beloved female friend, then the presence of two *vīṇās* does not sound proper. The only expression which can easily be drawn is that Aśvaghoṣa has used one word as the name of *vīṇā* and the other word for denoting *vīṇā* instrument. It means according to Aśvaghoṣa that the lady had come prepared to play on either *Mahatī* or *Parivādinī vīṇā* or we may come to the conclusion that *Mahatī* and *Parivādinī* were the same *vīṇās* because both are described as the *vīṇā* of the sage Nārada.

2. *Avanaddha or Ānaddha Instruments (Membranophones)*

The instruments hollow from inside and covered with the high of animals and which are played upon by hands or sticks are called *Avanaddha* or *Ānaddha* instruments. According to Bharatamuni, there were one hundred types of *Avanaddha* instruments but he has not given detailed description of each of them. The *Avanaddha* instruments referred to by Aśvaghoṣa in his *Buddhacarita* are *Mṛdaṅga, Dundubhi, Paṇava* and *Bherī*.

Mṛdaṅga

According to Sudhākalaṣa, Lord Śaṅkara was the expounder of *Mṛdaṅga* or *Muraja*. Initially, all the *Avanaddha* instruments were known by the term *Puṣkara* as *Puṣkara* was the foremost among the *Avanaddha* instruments. *Puṣkara (Mṛdaṅga)* had three *mukha-s* (drums) which were convered by animal hide. It was made of clay and hence the word *Mṛdaṅga*. In the later period, *Mṛdaṅga* was made of wood having two *mukhas* (drums) only.

In the second canto entitled *Antaḥpuravihāra* of *Buddhacarita*, we come across a graphic description of the royal palace which looked like Kailāsa. Beautiful music was being played there. The palace was resounding with the sounds of golden drums being gently beaten by the ladies and pretty damsel-like dancers were dancing there. It is noteworthy that the music was being perfomed by ladies only:

Kalairhi cāmīkarabaddhakakṣai-
rnārīkarāgrabhihatairmṛdaṅgaiḥ
Varāpsaronṛtyasamaiśca nṛtyaiḥ
kailāsavattadbhavanaṁ rarāja.[24]

In the fifth canto entitled *Abhiniṣkramaṇa*, Aśvaghoṣa refers to *Mṛdaṅga* thus :

Navapuṣkaragarbhakomalābhyāṁ
tapaniyojjvalasaṅgatāṅgadābhyam.
Svapiti sma tathāparā bhujābhyām
parirabhya priyavanmṛdaṅgameva.[25]

A pretty beauty had come to allure Gautama with her *Mṛdaṅga*. But instead of playing on *Mṛdaṅga* and attracting him, she plunged into deep slumber embracing with her arms the *mṛdaṅga* like her lover. Here and also in the previous illustration (V.48), it is remarkable that the poet combines music with erotics. There is one more peculiarity. Aśvaghoṣa referes to the playing of *mṛdaṅga* by ladies only.[26]

Dundubhi

Dundubhi is one of the oldest *Avanaddha* instruments of India. It is played generally by divine beings only on the auspicious occasions of celebrations of birth and marriage etc. We get the reference of *Dundubhi* in the *Ṛgveda, Atharvaveda, Taittirīya Brāhmaṇa, Śatapatha Brāhmaṇa, Vājasaneyī Saṃhitā, Kāṭhaka Saṃhitā, Śāṅkhāyana Śrautasūtra* and *Bṛhadāraṇyaka Upaniṣad*.

According to the *Saṅgītaratnākara, Dundubhi* is made of bronze and its *mukha* is covered by animal hide. it is beaten by a *koṇa* made of animal hide. Originally, there was only one drum in *Dundubhi* but in due course of time, there were two drums in it.

A beautiful description of the beating of *Dhundubhi* drum in the clear sky at the auspicious occasion of the birth of Kumāra Gautama is found in the *Buddhacarita* :

Kalaṁ praṇeduḥ mṛgapakṣiṇaśca
śāntāmbuvāhāḥ sarito babhūvuḥ.
Diśaḥ prasedurvimale nirabhre
vihāyase dundubhayo nineduḥ.[27]

The deep sound of the *Dundubhi* drum is often used as standard of comparison too. The pleasing voice of prince Gautama very much resembled with the sound of *Dundubhi* :

Pralambabāhurmṛgarājavikramo
maharṣabhākṣaḥ kanakojjvaladyutiḥ.
Viśālavakṣā ghanadundubhisvana-
stathāvidhopyāśramavāsamarhati.[28]

On the auspicious occasion of the attainment of *Buddhatva* by Siddhārtha, *Dundubhi* drums were beaten in the sky by the divine beings :

Buddhe tasmiñjughūrṇāsau
dharā matteva kāminī.
Siddhaiḥ saha diśo dīptā
nedurdundubhayo divi.[29]

Paṇava

Aśvaghoṣa refers to *Paṇava,* an old and important *Avanaddha* instrument in the following verse :

Paṇavaṁ yuvatirbhujāṁśadeśā-
davaviśraṁsitacārupāśamanyā.
Savilāsaratāntatāntamūrvo-
rvivare kāntamivābhinīya śiśye.[30]

A young lady had come with the intension of attracting prince Gautama by playing on the *Paṇava* but herself slept keeping the instrument in between her thighs like her lover at the end of sexual dalliance. Here also, poet has mingled the description of music with eroticism.

Bherī

Bherī was one of the foremost battle instrument. *Bherī* drums were beaten in order to arouse valour in soldiers. *Bherī* is two hands long and is made of metal. It has two *mukhas* which are covered with animal hide. It is beaten by a wooden stick on its right side and by hand on its left side.

We get a beautiful reference of the beating of *Bherī* drums in *Buddhacarita* where Siddhārtha declares that he is repairing to Vārāṇasī in order to beat the *Dharma-bherī* not for his own pleasure or fame but solely for the welfare of all the beings :

Bherīṁ nādayituṁ dharmyāṁ kāśiṁ gacchāmi sāmpratam.
Na sukhāya na yaśase cārtattrāṇāya kevalam.[31]

3. Suṣira Instruments (Aerophones)

Instruments that use air directly or indirectly to produce sound are called *Suṣira* (wind) instruments (Aerophones). In most of the wind instruments, air is made to vibrate and is the cause of tones. Aśvaghoṣa has referred to two *Suṣira* instruments. They are *Tūrya* and *Veṇu*.

Tūrya

In ancient times, playing of *Tūryas* was popular on the auspicious occasion of child-birth, marriage etc. and also at the time of battle for which we get different terms, *e.g.*, *'Maṅgala Tūrya'* and *'Yuddha Tūrya'*. There are *Yāma-turyās* also for the announcement of time. *Tūryas* are played in the temples of South India on the occasions of marriage and other celebrations. *Tūrya* looks like a modern *Śehnāi* instrument but is bigger than a *Śehnāi'*. It is made of wood and is 27″ long. It has seven holes for seven notes. There is an eighth hole also for the circulation of air. There are two side holes beneath the seventh hole and eighth hole also. It is played with the help of an apparatus called *Śivālī*.

The *Antaḥpura* palace of the prince Gautama was full of the pleasing notes of *Tūryās* being played by expert lady-musicians :

Tataḥ śarattoyadapāṇḍureṣu
bhūman vimāneṣviva rañjiteṣu.
Harmyeṣu sarvartusukhāśrayeṣu
strīṇāmudārairvijahāra tūryaiḥ.[32]

A number of young beautiful ladies approached the Prince who was like Devendra with their *Tūrya* instruments with the intention to attract him by their pleasing performance on *Tūryas* :

Tata uttamamuttamāṅganāstaṁ
nisi tūryairupatasthurindrakalpam.
Himavacchirasīva candragaure
draviṇendrātmajamapsarogaṇaughāḥ.[33]

But, alas! Gautama could get neither any happiness, nor any pleasure with the sounds of notes played on those *Tūryas* as he was desirous of attaining some higher goal and was willing to leave his house :

Paramairapi divyatūryakalpaiḥ
sa tu tairnaiva ratiṁ yayau na harṣam.
Paramārthasukhāya tasya sādho-
rabbiniścikramiṣā yato na reme.[34]

Tūryas were also used for the awakening of kings and princes in the morning. When Gautama leaves the house, his mother cries remembering again and again how her son will now be awakened who was accustomed of giving up his sleep with the pleasing sounds of *Tūryas* :

Śucau śayitvā śayane hiraṇmaye
prabodhyamāno niśi tūryanisvanaiḥ.
Kathaṁ bata svapsyati so'dya me vratī
paṭaikadeśāntarite mahītale.[35]

Veṇu

The other names of this instrument are *Vaṁśī, Bansī, Bānsurī* and *Muralī* etc. Lord Kṛṣṇa is famous for his *Vaṁśī*-playing. It has a very significant role to play in the musical theory in India. Besides the *vīṇā,* the *veṇu* was one of the early instruments to define the musical scale. *Nāradīyaśikṣā* (Ist cent. A.D.) gives us perhaps, for the first time, the relations of the vedic (descending) scale and that of the flute (ascending)[36]. It says :

Yaḥ sāmagānāṁ prathamaḥ sa veṇormadhyamaḥ svaraḥ.[37]

Veṇu is made of bamboo, white or red sandal wood, iron, bronze, silver or gold. The sizes are varied anywhere from 15cm to 60cm. There were nine holes in a *Vaṁśī* which was known by the name of *'Ekavīra'*. There were fourteen types of this *'Ekavīra Vaṁśī* based on the difference of distance between *Mukha-randhra* and the *Tārarandhra (Nādarandhra).*

In the *Buddhacarita,* a young lady keeping *veṇu* in her hands comes to the palace of Gautama but suddenly falls into deep sleep. Here also, it is noteworthy that *veṇu*-player is a female :

Vibabhau karalagnaveṇuranyā
stanavisrastasitaṁśukā śayānā.
Ṛjuṣaṭpadapaṅktijuṣṭapadmā
jalaphenaprahasattaṭa nadīva.[38]

4. Ghana Instruments (Idiophones)

The instruments which are played by striking with a stick or rubbing are called *Ghana* instruments (Idiophones). Any two pieces of solid struck or rubbed together can become an idiophone. These do not require any special kind of tuning and can be played as they are made. *Tāla, Kānsyatāla, Ghaṇṭā, Kṣudraghaṇṭā, Mañjīrā and Jalataraṅga* are the famous *Ghana* instruments.

Directly, we do not get reference to *Ghana* instruments in the *Buddhacarita,* but indirectly, we do get a few references.

Ghaṇṭā (Bells)

The commonest bells we come across are those of indefinite pitch and are struck. They have not been musical instruments to any significant extent, but have remained parts of the paraphernalia for worship in homes and temples. As one enters a Hindu temple, a row of suspended bells of varying sizes and shapes attract one's attention, and it it a sign of devotion to first ring them and then enter the sanctum. There are, of course, the bells of justice and the bell of victory as well as the cow-bells.[39]

In the thirteenth canto of the *Buddhacarita,* we come across a detailed description of *Bhūtagaṇas,*[40] the attendants of Māra. Some of them were wearing girdle-strings which had bells producing sound :

Śvetārdhavaktrā haritārdhakāyā-
stāmrāśca dhūmrā harayo sitāśca.
Vyālottarāsaṅgabhujāstathaiva
praghuṣṭaghaṇṭākulamekhalāśca.[41]

Kṣudraghaṇṭikā (Kiṅkiṇī, Ghungharū)

Description of *Kṣudraghaṇṭikā* or *Kiṅkiṇī* is found in the old musicological texts. In modern times, it is known by the name

'Ghungharū' or *' Ghungharā'*. These were made of gold, silver, bronze, iron, copper etc. and were used in dancing. Sometimes, these were adorned in the necks of animals so that they produced pleasing sounds when the animals moved.

In the *Buddhacarita*, Aśvaghoṣa describes the horse of Siddhārtha as wearing *kiṅkiṇī* in his neck thus :

Navarukmakhalīnakiṅkiṇīkaṁ
pracalaccāmaracāruhemabhāṇḍam.
Abhiruhya sa kanthakaṁ sadaśvaṁ
prayayau ketumiva drumābjaketuḥ.[42]

Nūpura and Kāñcī

Nūpura and *Kañcī* are two different ornaments worn by women in their foot and waist respectively. There are small *kṣudraghaṇṭikās* in *Kāñcī*. The sound of *nūpura* and the *kṣudraghaṇṭikā* of *kāncī* are very pleasing to the ears and resemble the sounds of the *Ghana* instrument *kṣudraghaṇṭikā*. Sanskrit poets have very often mentioned the pleasing sounds of *nūpura* and *kāñcī*. Aśvaghoṣa also refers to the musical sound of *nūpura* and *kāñcī* worn by ladies who were very keen to have a glimpse of Kumāra Siddārtha :

Prāsādasopānatalapraṇādaiḥ
kāñcīravairnūpuranisvanaiśca.
Vitrāsayanto gṛhapakṣisaṁghā-
nanyonyavegānśca samākṣipantyaḥ.[43]

Dance

Music includes dance also. Dance is an expression of rejoicing. All beings dance when in joy. We get several references of dance in the *Buddhacarita*. When Kumāra Siddhārtha was born, Brāhmaṇas requested King Śuddhodana to organize a big dance-festival in the celebration of his child's birth :

Samepsavo ye bhuvi santi sattvāḥ
putraṁ vinecchanti guṇaṁ na kañcit.
Tvatputra eṣo'sti kulapradīpo
ṇrtyosavaṁ tvadya vidhehi rājan.[44]

In the harem of Siddhārtha, there were beautiful young ladies who were like celestial nymphs and presented enchanting dances :

Kalairhi cāmīkarabaddhakakṣai-
rnārīkarāgrā bhihatairmṛdaṅgaiḥ.
Varāpsaronṛtyasamaiśca nṛtyaiḥ
kailāsavattadbhavanaṁ rarāja.[45]

One of the *Bhūtagaṇas* of the army of Māra also danced with *Triśūla* in his hand :

Nanarta kaścid bhramayanstriśūlaṁ
kaścidvipusphūrja gadāṁ vikarṣan.
Harṣeṇa kaścid vṛṣavannanarda
kaścitprajajjvāla tanūruhebhyaḥ.[46]

A beautiful description of dance by human and divine beings on the earth, in the quarters and in heaven is found in the fiteenth canto of the *Buddhacarita*. All these people danced when the *Dharma-cakra* set forth by Gautama started rotating everywhere :

Ahinarasuraloke dharmacakraṁ yadedam
tribhuvanasukhaśāntyai cāśu śubhraṁ cacāla.
Bhuvi diśi divi devā bhūtasaṃghāśca sarve
saha kusumanipātairnṛtyagītaṁ ca cakruḥ.[47]

Music of Birds and Animals

The world of birds and animals does enjoy the melody of music like the human beings. They themselves also produce music. Sanskrit literature is full of the references of the music of birds and animals. Aśvaghoṣa presents beautiful pictures of the music of birds and animals in his *Buddhacarita*.

There are several theories with regard to the origin of the seven musical notes. According to one theory, the seven notes of music originate from the sounds of seven different birds and animals thus :

Ṣadjaṁ vadati mayūraḥ punaḥ svaramṛṣabhaṁ cātako brūte
gāndhārākhyaṁ chāgo nigadati ca madhyamaṁ krauñcaḥ.
Gadati pañcamamañcitavākpiko raṭati dhaivatamunmadadarduraḥ
śṛṇi samāhatamastakakuñjaro gadati nāsikayā svaramantikam.[48]

Ṣaḍja, the very first note of music is originated from the sound of *mayūra* (Peacock, Pavo Cristatus), *ṛṣabha* from *cātaka* (the pied crested cuckoo, Clamator Jacobinas), *gāndhāra* from *chāga, madhyama* from *krauñca* (Anthropoides Virgo, Koonj), *pañcama* from *pika* (Cuckoo, Eudynamys Scolopacea), *dhaivata* from *dardura* (Toad)and *niṣāda* from *kuñjara* (Elephant, Elephas Indicus, Proboscidea Elephantidae).

Peacock is our national bird. *Ṣaḍja,* the very first note of music originates from the sound of peacock. The sound produced by peacock is called *'Kekā'*:

'Ke mūrdhni kāyanti dhvanantīti kekā mayūravāṇyaḥ.'
'Kekā vāṇī mayūrasya ityamaraḥ.'

Peacocks when in rejoicing mood, start producing *kekā* and dance. When they see the clouds in the sky and listen to the thunders of the clouds, they produce *kekā* and dance. When peacocks witnessed Gautama in the forest, they were so delighted as though they had seen the blue cloud and they at once started their *kekā* :

Hṛṣṭāśca kekā mumucurmayūrā
dṛṣṭvāmbudaṁ nīlamivonnamantaḥ.
Śaṣpāṇi hitvābhimukhāśa tasthu-
rmṛgāścalākṣā mṛgacāriṇaśca.[49]

Pañcama, the fifth note of music originates from the sound of *Puṃskokila* - male cuckoo. Sanskrit literature is full of the references of the music of *Puṃskokila*. Our poets were aware of the scientific fact that the sound of *Puṃskokila* is more pleasing and appealing than that of the *Kokilā* - female cuckoo. Aśvaghoṣa has made several references to *Puṃskokilanāda* in his *Buddhacarita*. Prince Siddhārtha once happens to know about a forest which is full of the pleasing notes of cuckoos :

Tataḥ kadācinmṛduśādvalāni
puṃskokilonnāditapādapāni.
Śuśrāva padmākaramaṇḍitāni
gītairnibaddhāni sa kānanāni.[50]

Cuckoos have great love for the mango tree. When the mango tree is full of the blossoms of its *mañjarīs* and the cuckoo, sitting there starts singing, it appears as if he is confined in a golden cage:

Paśya bhartaścitaṁ cūtaṁ
kusumairmadhugandhibhiḥ.
Hemapañjararuddho vā
kokilo yatra kūjati.[51]

It is peculiar to note that the cuckoo gets intoxicated by the sweet fragrance and taste of *āmra-mañjarī* in the spring season and starts singing aloud. When one cuckoo sings, the other cuckoos also join :

Mattasya parapuṣṭasya ruvataḥ śrūyatāṁ dhvaniḥ.
Aparaḥ kokilo'nvakṣaṁ pratiśrutyeva kūjati.[52]

Deer are very fond of music. Sometimes, they have to give up their lives even for their love of music :

Gītairhriyante hi mṛgā vadhāya
rūpārthamgnau śalabhāḥ patanti
Matsyo giratyāyasamāmiṣārthī
tasmādanarthaṁ viṣyāḥ phalanti.[53]

Thus, we find that Aśvaghoṣa had mastery over the knowledge of *Trividha Saṅgīta* - Music vocal, music instrumental and dance. He was well-versed in different types of musical instruments prevalent in his time. He had not only the theoretical knowledge of these instruments but also expertise in their practical performance, otherwise, he could not have successfully described minute intricacies of the various instruments and their playing. To understand the real meaning of various words used by Aśvaghoṣa in his *Buddhacarita* in the context of music, it is desirable to have an interpretation based on *saṅgītaśāstra* otherwise it is difficult to appreciate the poetry of Aśvaghoṣa in its true perspective.

REFERENCES & NOTES

1. *Saṅgītaratnākara* 1.2.
2. *Buddhacarita* III.1.
3. *Ibid.*, IV.37.
4. *Ibid.*, XI.35.
5. *Ibid.*,XV.67.
6. *Ibid.*,III.11.

7. *Ibid.*,XIV.96.
8. *Kāmasūtra* 1.3.15.
9. *Buddhacarita* II.31.
10. *Ibid.*, III.52.
11. *Nāṭyaśāstra* XXVIII.2.
12. *Bharatabhāṣya* (Nānyedeva) (Manuscript)
13. *Mānasollāsa* III. 572.
14. *Buddhacarita* V.46.
15. *Ibid.*,V.48.
16. *Meghadūta* II.25.
17. *Buddhacarita* V.55.
18. *Vādyaprakāśa 30, Tatavādyāni* (Manuscript) quoted in *Bhāratīya Saṅgīta Vādya:, p.46.*
19. *Bhāratīya Saṅgīta Vādya,* p.46.
20. *Raghuvaṁśa* VIII.35.
21. *Ibid.*,VIII. 35, p.755.
22. *Śiśupālavadha* 1.70.
23. *Bharatabhāṣya* (Nānyadeva), see *Bhāratīya Saṅgīta Vādya, p.48.*
24. *Buddhacarita* II.30.
25. *Ibid.*, V.50.
26. *Ibid.*, II.30;V.50.
27. *Ibid.*, 1.26.
28. *Ibid.*, VIII.53.
29. *Ibid.*, XIV.90
30. *Ibid.*, V.56.
31. *Ibid.*, XV.10.
32. *Ibid.*, II.29.
33. *Ibid.*, V.45.
34. *Ibid.*, V.46.
35. *Ibid.*, VIII.58.
36. *Musical Instruments of India* (B.C. Deva), p. 108.
37. *Nāradīyaśikṣā* V.I.
38. *Buddhcarita* V.49.
39. *Musical Instruments of India* (B.C. Deva), p. 49.
40. *Buddhacarita* XIII 18-27.
41. *Ibid.*, XIII.22.
42. *Ibid.*, V.3.
43. Ibid., III.15.
44. *Ibid.*, 1.32.
45. *Ibid.*, II.30.
46. *Ibid.*, XIII.26.

47. *Ibid.*, XV.67.
48. *Saṅgītadarpaṇa* 170-171.
49. *Buddhacarita* VII.5.
50. *Ibid.*, III.1.
51. *Ibid.*, IV.44.
52. *Ibid.*, V.51.
53. *Ibid.*, XI.35.

Delhi

MUSIC AND DANCE IN BUDDHIST LITERATURE*

Sushma Kulshreshtha

Music occupies a prominent place in Fine Arts---*gītaṃ vādyaṃ tathā nṛtyaṃ trayaṃ saṅgītam ucyate*. Music includes Music Vocal, Music Instrumental and Dance. Vedic and Classical Sanskrit literature is full of the sweetness of Music as well as the references of technical terms of Music. A number of references of Music Vocal, Instrumental and Dance are found in Buddhist Literature that bring to light the prominence of the art of music in those days. Music found in Buddhist Literature has been beautifully presented in India's ancient sculpture and paintings through which a thorough study of Music and Dance of those days can be done.

The Art of Music was learnt like other *vidyās* by the members of rich and well-to-do families. Bodhisattva himself was an expert in Music and drama. The ladies of his family were also expert musicians. We get a reference in *Lalitavistara* that Māyā Devī, mother of Buddha was expert in Fine Arts. Before marriage, the would be father-in-law of Buddha had placed a condition that in order to prove himself a worthy bridegroom for his daughter who was extremely expert in arts, he would have to demonstrate his expertise in Fine Arts.[1] Such a bride was required for Siddhārtha who was an expert in Fine Arts as a courtesan—*Śāstre vidhigyakuśalā gaṇikā yathaiva*.[2] *Buddhacarita* refers that the instruments like *mahatī, vīṇā, mṛdaṅga, paṇava tūrya, veṇu* etc. were played for entertainment in the harems. The stroy entitled *Pitṛputrasamāgama* refers to the presentation of an orchestra consisting of 500 instruments at the time of the celebration of Lord Buddha's

* This Paper was presented at the VIII International Congress of the International Association of Buddhist Studies held at California University, Berkeley, USA in August, 1987.

birth.[3] Such an orchestra now-a-days is heard at the great Govt. celebrations or the recordings of film music.

In Buddha age, Takṣaśilā was the Centre of Education where there were a number of teaching departments like *Vaidika Vidyālaya, Aṣṭādaśa Vidyālaya, Śilpavijñāna Vidyālaya* etc., where 500 students each used to study.[4] *Vaidika Pañca Mahāvidyā* consisting of *śabdavidyā, adhyātmavidyā, cikitsāvidyā, hetuvidyā* and *śilpavidyā* was known by the technical term *pañcayāna* in *Jātaka* age.[5] According to *Paropahassa Jātaka*, Bodhisattva had got the training of all the *śilpas* in this very University of Takṣaśilā. Another centre of education of the same age was Vārāṇasī where there was an independent department of Music. In other universities of Nālandā, Vikramaśilā and Odantapurī also, there were independent faculties of music where India-famed musicians were appointed as Deans and Heads of the departments.[6] *Gandhabba Veda* or *Gāndharva Veda* was the technical term denoting music which included *gīta, vāditta* and *naccha (nṛtya), akkhānam* etc. Singing of ancient *ākhyāna* and *vīragāthā* was included in *akkhāna.*[7] This was included in *'sippa'* or *'silpa'*.

The study of *Veda* and *Vedāṅgas* in *Jātaka* age was as popular as it was in Vedic age.[8] The *Chāndogya Caraṇa* of *Sāman* is referred to in *Tevijja sutta*. The *Ācāryas* of *Chāndogya Caraṇa* are called *'Chandoka'* in *Dīghanikāya*. A Brahmin named Sela is described in *Selasutta* who was an expert in the three *Vedas* and *Vedāṅgas* and who used to teach three hundred students. During those days, the tradition of reciting *Bauddha Suttas* with *Svara* like the *Vaidika mantras* was very much popular. *Pāli Mahāvagga*[9] and *Udāna*[10] refer that on the wish of Gautama, a Bhikkhu named Koṇa Kuttikaṇṇa had recited the *Suttas* of *Aṭṭhakavaggika(Arthapāda)---'Sareṇa abhāsi'.*[11]

We get a list of the means of livelihood prevalent in those days in *Jātaka granthas* which includes the following categories---*naṭa, nartaka, gāyaka, bherīvādaka and nāṭakakāra.*[12] All these are connected with music to some extent in one or the other way. All these had their own *saṅghas* and separate *upanivesas* were arranged for them in the town. In those days, courtezans and dancers commanded high respect in the society like an expert musician. *Gaṅgmāla Jātaka* describes that 16,000 female dancers were invited to present music and dance at the auspicious occasion of the marriage of Princess (III.452). According to a work, *Sumaṅgalavilāsinī*, a number of expert female dancers were appointed in the harem of Kāśīnareśa.[13] In those days, *gaṇikā* (courtezan) commanded higher respect in the society than the ordinary *veśyā* (prostitute) because she was expert in the art of music. *Gaṇikā* used to know a number of *Śāstras* which included music also---*Śāstre vidhigyakuśalā gaṇikā yathaiva.* For the efficient rule of the country, besides chiefs of departments, *Ekādaśa Aṅga* was also required which included *gaṇikā* (see *Kurudhamma Jātaka*). *Veśyā* commanded national respect in the form of *Janapadakalyāṇī*. The *Pañcaśīla-dīkṣā* was essential for her (see *Dummedha Jātaka*.)

The art of music and drama had a very high place in Buddha age. For the development of the art of music and drama, royal patronage is a must and the same was available to these arts in those times. Artists like musicians (vocalists), instrument players, and male and female dancers were formally appointed for the royal kingdom. *Milindapañha* refers to the appointment of 16,000 female dancers in a royal *sabhā (Solassu nāṭakīsahassesu)*.[14] In a royal *sabhā,* where 16,000 female dancers are permanently appointed, we can easily infer the beauty and grandeur of the royal musical performances which occur there. Although, there were permanent singers, instrument players and dancers in a royal *sabhā,* courtezans were specially invited to present music vocal, instrumental and dance when need be.[15] The kings and the distinguished personalities of those times used to support the *Bauddha vihāras* financially and in other ways too. Adequate finances were provided to the *ārādhaka* artists by the royal kingdom. They were appointed in the *vihāras* for *ārādhanā*. The royal kingdom had its full control over these artists. We come to know from a cave-inscription found in Saragujā state that there was a *devadāsī* named Sutanukā in the *vihāra* situated there. She had an affair with the *ārādhaka* of the *vihāra*. Both of them were given severe punishment for that.

There were a number of celebrations and festivities which included music vocal, Instrumental and Dance in the society of Buddha period. The travelogue of Fa-hi-yan clearly indicates such celebrations which took place in Magadha. These social celebrations were known by the term *Samajja or Samāja*. The incriptions of Aśoka provide ample proof that such group celebrations (*Samajja*) were regularly organised in the society. In *Vidhura Paṇḍita Jātaka,* we get a description of a *samajja* in which all men and women had presented music and dance.[16] We come to know from *Sigālovāda Suttanta* that *ākhyānas* were also sung in such social festivities.[17] As in the modern age, grand music concerts are organised in beautiful auditoriums and great personalities of the society are invited, similarly, in that age also, group celebrations were organised on the tops of mountains and other pious places and the respected members of the society were specially invited to attend those functions.[18] *Visuddhimagga* describes a celebration in which 500 female dancers were invited.[19]

Pekkhā or *Prekṣā* was the technical term for *Nāṭya* in Buddha age. The director of *Nāṭya* was called *Naṭācārya.* The epithet of *Naṭagāmaṇi* was used for the foremost *Naṭa.* The *Naṭas* used to entertain the audience with the presentation of different types of acting on the stage---*yo so naṭo raṅgamajjhe samajja-majjhe saccālikena janam hāseti rameti.*[20] In the presentation of a drama, *naṭī* was also there with the *naṭa. Naṭīs* did not command respect in the society because sometimes they indulged themselves in the business of their physique by way of decoration and their expertise in the arts of music and dance. We get a peculiar reference in *Kuśa Jātaka* where it is mentioned that the king having no projeny from his wives used to send them in the form of *dharmanaṭīs* to other males of their choice for conception.[21]

The enjoyment of a note (*svara*) presented by playing on an instrument is called instrumental music. According to Bharatamuni, musical instruments have been classified into four groups - *tata, avanaddha, suṣira* and *ghana* as follows :

Tataṃ tantrīkṛtaṃ jñeyam
avanaddhaṃ tu pauṣkaram.
Ghanaṃ tālas tu vijñeyaḥ
suṣiro vaṃśa ucyate.[22]

The references to all these four types of instruments are found in Buddhist Literature. Musical instruments using stretched strings---be they of grass, animal gut or metal wire and which are played by fingers (*e.g., svaramaṇḍala, tambūrā*) or by the help of *koṇa* or *trikoṇa* (*e.g., vīṇa, sitār* and *saroda*) or *gaja* (*e.g.,* violin, *sāraṅgī, isarāja* and *dilarubā*) or stick (*e.g., Santūra)* are called *tata* instruments (cordophones or stringed instruments). Among the *tata* instruments, the following are referred to in Buddhist Literature---*viṇā, parivādinī, vipañcī, vallakī, mahatī, nakulī, kacchapī* and *tumbaviṇā*. In fact, all these are the different types of *viṇās*.

We get the reference of nineteen types of *vīṇās* in the *Saṅgītamakaranda* composed by Nārada. They are *kacchapī, kubjikā, citrā, vahantī, parivādinī, Jayā, ghośāvatī, jyeṣṭhā, nakulī, mahatī, vaiṣṇavī, brāhmī, raudrī, kūrmī,rāvaṇī, sārasvatī, kinnarī, sairandhrī*, and *ghoṣaka*. Originally, there was only one type of *vīṇā* which was multiplied in different types of *vīṇās* with different numbers of strings in them and also with different ways of playing in due course of time. This fact is brought out by Someśvara in his *Mānasollāsa* :

Tantrībhedaiḥ kriyābhedair vīṇāvādyamanekadhā.[23]

The *tata* instruments referred to in Buddhist Literature are in fact different types of *vīṇās*. *Vīṇā* was the general term for *tata* instruments in those days. *Vīṇā* was the most popular instrument of that time. *Dīghanikāya* mentions that the music presented with the playing of *vīṇā* is so pleasant to the ears of the listener that even Buddhadeva, who had renounced the world, was attracted by it. The story runs thus : There was a Gandharva named Pañcasikha who fell in love with Sūryavarcasā, daughter of Tumbaru, a famous Gandharva. Depressed in his affair, one day, he was singing a pathetic song with the playing of *vīṇā*. The co-ordination and harmony presented by the notes produced by playing on *vīṇā* and the words of that pathetic song were such that compelled Lord Buddha to be pleased and applaud the music thus : Oh! The effect of music is imperishable.

Fine Arst like music etc., received royal partronage. A number of concerts and competitions of the *vīṇā*-players were organised in which winners had the privilege to receive awards and royal patronage. In those days, there were a number of expert *vīṇā*-players. *Mūsila Jātaka* presents testimony to the efficient playing of *vīṇā* in those days. There is a stroy that jealousy arose between two : Mūsila, the famous *vīṇā*-player of Ujjayinī and Guttila, the famous *vīṇā*-player of Vārāṇasī. Although, Mūsila had learnt the secret intricacies of *vīṇā*- playing from Guttila himself, but now he wanted to defeat him in *vīṇā*-playing. A competition between the two was organised in the royal assembly. Guttila started his grand performance on *vīṇā*. He, while playing on the seven strings of the *vīṇā,* broke its strings one by one and continued to play notes on the remaining strings. Druing the last moments of his performance, when all the strings had been broken, the notes were still resounding as if they were coming out from the *vīṇā-daṇḍa* itself. This brings to light the fact that the technique of producing more than one note at a time by the *karṣaṇa* of the strings of *vīṇā* was popular in those days. *Vīṇā* was played with the help of *koṇa.*

The instruments hollow from inside and covered with the hide of animals and which are played upon by hands or sticks are called *avanaddha or ānaddha* instruments (Membranophones). According to Bharatamuni, there were one hundred types of *avanaddha* instruments but he has not given detailed description of each of them. *Avanaddha* instruments referred to in Buddhist Literature are *mṛdaṅga, paṇava, bherī, ḍiṇḍima* and *dundubhi. Daṇḍa* was used for playing on *mṛdaṅga.* A number of *koṇas* and *vādanadaṇḍas* have been found in excavations carried at the following places: Kauśāmbī, Rāmanagara, Rājaghāṭa, Mathurā and Bhītā. The instruments which are played by striking with a stick or rubbing are called *ghana* instruments (idiophones). Any two pieces of solid struck or rubbed together can become an idiophone. These do not require any special kind of tuning and can be played as they are made. *Ghaṇṭā, jhallarī* and *kāṃsyatāla* were among the famous *ghana* instruments popular in those times. Instruments that use air directly or indirectly to produce sound are called *suṣira* (wind) instruments (Aerophones). In most of the wind instruments, air is made to vibrate and is the cause of tones, but in some cases, as in the harmoniam, air is only a means to vibrate a reed which gives out a note[22]. Among the *suṣira* instruments referred to in Buddhist Literature and *śaṅkha, tūrya, kurala, śṛṅga* etc. In ancient times, playing of *tūryas* was popular on the auspicious occasion of child-birth and marriages etc. and also at the time of battle for which we get different terms *e.g., maṅgala-tūrya* and *yuddha-tūrya.* There were *yāma-tūryas* also for the announcement of time. The sounds pleasing to the ear of auspicious *tūryas* could be heard not only on earth but also in the path of Gods.[25]

In the age of Buddha, besides *svara, grāma* and *mūrcchanā,* the singing of *rāgas* also came into being. It was the general opinion that sweet music can attract even animals and birds. A number of researches are being carried out these days in this regard. In Vocal and Instrumental Music, the presentation of the notes in their exact form and their sweetness are most essential. The presentation of notes in their exact form means the very correct use of notes and the sweetness means that the presentation of the notes of music should be pleasant to the ears of the listener. *Visvaratva* is a great defect of *gāna* or *vādana*. If a person presents *visvara* note, the effect of music vanishes. It was the firm belief of the musicians in those days that a short *susvara-gāna* (Song presenting exact notes) is far better than a long *visvara-gāna* (song presenting wrong notes).

To conclude, it can be said that all the three aspects of music *e.g.*, Vocal, Instrumental and Dance were in their developed stage in Buddha age. People used to sing. Singing was accompanied by the playing of numerous instruments. All the four types of instruments were played. Alongwith music vocal and instrumental, dance was also very popular. Hundreds and thousands of distinguished female dancers were specially invited on specific occasions for their dance-performances. Music had a peculiar place in drama also. Arts like music and drama received royal patronage for their development. Music was utilised for both the purposes : *pāramārthika* as well as erotic. Bauddhas favoured that music only which did not come in the way of their spiritual practices. For the worship of music *ārādhakas* and *devadāsīs* were permanently appointed in *Bauddhavihāras*. Royal kingdom had its full control over them. The group performances of music were organised on the auspicious occasion of the famous festivities like *giragga, samajja,* and *nakkattakīlam*. On these occasions, singing of the *nāṭya* and *ākhyānas* was also presented alongwith music.

Keeping in view the references found in Buddhist Literature pertaining to music and dance, it can be inferred that their authors were well-versed in vocal music, instrumental music and dance. They had sound knowledge of all the four types of instruments prevalent in their times. They had not only the theoretical knowledge of these instruments, but also expertise in their practical perfomance, otherwise, they could not have successfully described minute intricacies of the various instruments and their playing in their works. It appears that these authors had mastery over the knowledge of *trividha saṅgīta* (threefold music) and its various aspects such as occasion of playing particular musical instruments, their co-ordination with singing and dancing etc. To understand the real meaning of various words used by these authors in their works in the context of music, it is desirable to have an interpretation based on *Saṅgītaśāstra* (musicology) otherwise it is difficult to appreciate their works in its real perspective.

A brief account of the music pertaining to Buddhist Literature is presented here. During that period, what was the exact form of all the three aspects of music; did musicians and artists command high respect in the society; what was the influence of the music of Vedic age on the music of Buddha age; what was the influence of the music of Buddha age on the music of the Classical Sanskrit age etc., are some topics on which researches are urgently needed. Researches done on these topics will bring to light new facts which will highlight the importance of Buddhist Literature.

REFERENCES & NOTES

1. Chakladar, *Social Life in Ancient India,* p. 85.
2. *Lalitavistara,* 12, p. 139; Chakladar, p. 127, 139
3. Bapat, *Arthapāda,* p. 152.
4. *Jātakakālīna Bhāratīya Saṃskṛti,* p. 98.
5. *Ibid.*
6. Radhakumud Mukhopadhyaya, *Ancient Indian Education,* p. 490.
7. *Dīghanikāya* I, p. 6.
8. *Setaketu Jātaka,* 337; *Jātakakālīna Bhāratīya Saṃskṛti,* p. 97.
9. *Mahāvagga,* 5,13,9.
10. *Udāna,* 5,6.
11. Bapat, *Arthapādasutta,* Introduction, p.1.
12. *Milindapañha,* 331; B.C. Law, pp. 66-67.
13. Law, Tribes of Ancient India, 1943, p. 110.
14. B.C.Law, *op. cit.,* p. 72.
15. *Ibid.,* p. 166.
16. *Jātaka,* 6, 277.
17. See R. Davids, p. 83.
18. *Ibid.*

19. *Vimānavatthubhāṣya*, 62-74; *Tribes of Ancient India*, p. 218.
20. *Gāmanisanyutta*, 4, p. 306; Kane, *History of Sanskrit Poetics*, p. 323.
21. *Jātakakālīna Bhāratīya Saṃskṛti*, Viyogī, p. 14.
22. *Nāṭyaśāstra*, xxviii. 2
23. *Mānasollāsa*, III. 572
24. B.C. Deva, *Musical Instruments of India*, p. 103.
25. *Tevijjasutta*, *Dīghanikāya*, 251, Law, p. 224.

Delhi

SECTION VI

Jātaka-Studies

जातकमाला में बोधिसत्त्व की कल्पना*

कमलाकान्त मिश्र

जातकमाला के प्रधानपात्र बोधिसत्त्व प्राणियों के आर्तिनाशक हैं। जातकमाला का दूसरा नाम है—बोधिसत्त्वावदानमाला। अवदान का अर्थ है सुकर्म। इस प्रकार बोधिसत्त्वावदानमाला का अर्थ होगा—बोधिसत्त्व के अवदानों अर्थात् सुकर्मों की माला। बोधिसत्त्व ने अनेक पूर्वजन्मों में बुद्धत्व-प्राप्ति के लिए भगीरथ प्रयत्न किए। बोधिसत्त्व—यह मुख्यत: महायान की प्रकृष्टतम कल्पना है।

बौद्धधर्म की प्रारम्भिक अवस्था में 'अर्हत्' की भावना पायी जाती है। भगवान् बुद्ध को 'अर्हत्' कहा गया। साथ ही साथ चार आर्य सत्य एवम् अष्टाङ्गमार्ग के उपदेश प्राप्त करने वाले उनके शिष्यों को भी 'अर्हत्' पद से अभिहित किया जाने लगा। ऐसे लोग अष्टाङ्गमार्ग का अनुसरण कर तीनों आस्रवों (ऐन्द्रियिक सुख, सत्ता-प्रेम, अज्ञान) से रहित होते थे। 'ब्रह्मजालसुत्त' आदि पालि-ग्रन्थ के अनुसार 'अर्हत्' वह है जो मुक्त हो गया है, पुनर्जन्म के बन्धन से रहित है, जिसने अपने सारे भवबन्धनों को त्याग दिया है, जो पवित्र जीवन व्यतीत कर रहा है, जिसकी इच्छा एवं प्रवृत्ति अन्तिम मुक्ति के प्रति उन्मुख है, जो अपने मार्ग में एकाकी, उत्साहपूर्ण तथा अपना स्वामी स्वयं है।[1] अर्हत् स्वयं मुक्ति प्राप्त करके संसार के अन्य प्राणियों की मुक्ति के लिए बुद्ध के उपदेशों का प्रचार करता था। अर्हत् का जीवन मृत्युपर्यन्त सांसारिक जीवों के कल्याणार्थ अर्पित होता था। गौतम बुद्ध के परिनिर्वाण के तीन सौ वर्षों बाद तक 'अर्हत्' की यही धारणा रही। परन्तु धीरे-धीरे इस भावना में परिवर्तन होने लगा और ईसा पूर्व दो सौ वर्ष तक बौद्ध भिक्षु सांसारिक जीवों की दु:खनिवृत्ति एवं कल्याण से विमुख होकर अधिक स्वार्थलिप्त हो गये। वे अपनी ही मुक्ति के लिए प्रयत्नशील रहने लगे। सामान्य लोगों के उद्धार के लिए बुद्ध के उपदेशों के प्रचार करने का उत्साह उनमें नहीं रहा। जन-कल्याण के प्रति भिक्षुओं के उदासीन तथा उनके आत्मकेन्द्रित होने की भावना का उल्लेख परवर्ती पालि-साहित्य में अनेक स्थलों पर मिलता है। धम्मपद[2] में जहाँ एक ओर आत्मसंयम, ध्यान आदि की प्रशंसा की गई है, वहीं सामान्य-जन के कल्याण के प्रति उदासीनता की भावना भी परिलक्षित होती है। थेरगाथा[3] के अधिकांश कवियों ने वैयक्तिक मुक्ति पर ही ध्यान को केन्द्रित किया है, प्राणियों के कल्याण की बात वहाँ शायद ही कहीं आयी है। मिलिन्दपञ्ह[4] का कथन है कि 'अर्हत्' को अपने ही दु:खों से मुक्ति के लिए प्रयत्नशील होना चाहिए।

* आर्यशूरकृत जातकमाला—एक अध्ययन (डॉ. कमलाकान्त मिश्र), 1977 से साभार गृहीत।

उपर्युक्त संकीर्ण विचारों के विरोध में सभी जीवों की रक्षा एवं कल्याण के सिद्धान्त - रूप में बोधिसत्त्व की कल्पना का प्रादुर्भाव हुआ।

"The Bodhisattva doctrine was promulgated by some Buddhist leaders as protest against this lack of true spiritual fervour and altruism among the monks of that period".[5]

बोधिसत्त्व का मुख्य कार्य अर्हत् की आध्यात्मिक सङ्कीर्णता की आलोचना एवं निन्दा करना था।

"A Bodhisattva is emphatically and primarily one who criticises and condemns the spiritual egoism of such "Arhats" and Pratyeka-Buddhas."[6]

इस सिद्धान्त का अनुगामी संगठन महायान की संज्ञा से अभिहित किया गया।

बोधिसत्त्व की कल्पना महायान की सबसे बड़ी विशेषता है। बोधि का अर्थ है बुद्धत्व (*Enlightenment*) – ऐसा प्रायः सभी विद्वान् मानते हैं किन्तु सत्त्व का अर्थ विभिन्न विद्वानों ने विभिन्न ढङ्ग से समझा है और इस कारण बोधिसत्त्व शब्द की विविध व्याख्या की है। डॉ० हरदयाल ने अपनी पुस्तक *The Bodhisattva Doctrine in Buddhist Sanskrit Literature* में बोधिसत्त्व के अर्थ का निम्नलिखित ढंग से विश्लेषण किया है—

(1) सत्त्व (नपु.) का अर्थ मोनियर विलियम्स के अनुसार बुद्धि, चरित्र, ज्ञान तथा प्रकृति है। अतएव जिसे बोधि अर्थात् पूर्ण ज्ञान हो, जिसकी प्रकृति पूर्ण ज्ञानमयी हो, वह बोधिसत्त्व है।

(2) सत्त्व (पु.) का अर्थ है प्राणी (*Any living or sentient being*) । पालि 'सत्त' का अर्थ है—सजीव पदार्थ (*A living being, creature, a sentient and rational person*) यह अर्थ अधिकांश विद्वानों के द्वारा स्वीकृत है। इसी आधार पर समाधिराजसूत्रकार ने बोधिसत्त्व का अर्थ किया है—

'बोधति सत्त्वान् इति बोधिसत्त्वः'[8]

पी. घोष ने भी सत्त्व का अर्थ प्राणी ही किया है किन्तु समस्त पद बोधिसत्त्व की व्याख्या उन्होंने इस प्रकार की है—

'बोधिः स चासौ महाकृपाशयेन सत्त्वालम्बनात् सत्त्वश्चेति'।[9] इससे द्योतित होता है कि मनुष्य बोधि और सत्त्व दोनों ही है।

(3) सत्त्व का अर्थ है—आत्मा, मनस्, इन्द्रिय तथा चेतना। पालि में सत्त का अर्थ है—आत्मा। प्रज्ञाकरमति ने **बोधिचर्यावतार** की टीका में लिखा है—

'तत्र (बोधौ) सत्त्वम् अभिप्रायोऽस्येति बोधिसत्त्वः।[10]

पी. घोष ने भी एक व्याख्याकार का उल्लेख किया है जो सत्त्व का अर्थ अभिप्राय करते हैं—

'बोधौ सत्त्वम् अभिप्रायो येषां ते बोधिसत्त्वा:'[11]

तदनुसार बोधि पर जिसका मन, प्रवृत्तियाँ, विचार तथा इच्छाएँ केन्द्रित हों, वह बोधिसत्त्व है।

(4) सत्ता का अर्थ है— गर्भ, गुप्त, अज्ञात तथा अव्यक्त (मोनियर विलियम्स)। तदनुसार बोधिसत्त्व वह है जिसमें बोधि(ज्ञान) अव्यक्त रूप से निहित हो।[12]

(5)योगसूत्रानुसार सत्त्व का अर्थ पुरुषाश्रित मन तथा बुद्धि हो सकता है। यह ई. सेना के अनुसार है जिन्होंने बौद्ध धर्म पर योगदर्शन का प्रचुर प्रभाव माना है। किन्तु यह विचार बुद्धिग्राह्य नहीं हो सकता क्योंकि इसमें इतिहास की भूल (*Anachronism*) होगी। अधिकांश विद्वान् योगसूत्र का समय 300 ई. के आसपास मानते हैं जबकि 'बोधिसत्त्व' शब्द पालि निकायों में ही आता है[13] जिनका समय 5वीं-4थी शताब्दी ई. पू. माना जाता है।

एच. कर्न[14] ने 'बोधि' शब्द को सांख्य-योग के 'बुद्धि' शब्द का समानार्थी माना है। किन्तु यह अर्थ उपयुक्त प्रतीत नहीं होता क्योंकि बौद्धतत्त्व-मीमांसा के अनुसार 'बुद्धि' सत्ता के निम्नतर स्तर से सम्बद्ध है जबकि 'बोधि' का सम्बन्ध उच्चतम ज्ञान से है।

(6) मोनियर विलियम्स-कृत संस्कृत-अंग्रेजी-कोश में 'सत्त्व' का अर्थ है-शक्ति, बल तथा उत्साह।[15] तदनुसार जिस व्यक्ति की शक्ति बोधि (जागृति, ज्ञान) की ओर अभिमुख है। इस अर्थ में 'सत्त्व' शब्द क्षेमेन्द्र-कृत **अवदानकल्पलता** में अनेक बार प्रयुक्त हुआ है। यथा—

सत्त्वाब्धि:[16], सत्त्वोज्ज्वलं भगवतश्चरितं निशम्य[17], सत्त्वनिधि:[18], बोधिसत्त्व: सत्त्वविभूषित:[19]आदि।

बुद्धचरित (अश्वघोष-कृत) में भी यह शब्द प्रयुक्त हुआ है—

बोधिसत्त्व: परिपूर्णसत्त्व:।[20]

तिब्बती कोशकारों ने भी बुद्धि और उत्साह-सम्पन्नता पर बल दिया है। चीनी कोशकारों के अनुसार बोधिसत्त्व वह है जिसकी प्रकृति बोधि हो गयी है।

डॉ. हरदयाल का निष्कर्ष है कि पालि वाङ्मय में आये हुए 'बोधिसत्त' शब्द का सम्बन्ध वैदिक 'सत्त्वन्' (वीर, साहसी) शब्द से है जिसके अनुसार हम 'अध्यात्मवीर' के रूप में इसका अर्थ कर सकते हैं। वास्तव में 'बोधिसत्त्व' शब्द में दो भावनाएं अन्तर्निहित हैं-प्रथम सत्ता की भावना और द्वितीय संघर्षमय जीवन की। इस प्रकार दूसरों के कल्याण के लिए निरन्तर संघर्षशील रहकर, इस संसार में 'अध्यात्मवीर' की भूमिका का निर्वाह करने वाला व्यक्ति ही बोधिसत्त्व है। इसे महासत्त्व भी कहते हैं। बोधिसत्त्व के जीवन का लक्ष्य नितान्त उदात्त, महनीय तथा व्यापक होता है। उसके 'स्व' की परिधि में जगत् के समस्त जीव समा जाते हैं। उसके प्रधान गुण होते हैं—महामैत्री और करुणा।

बोधिसत्त्व को प्रथमतः बोधिचित्त ग्रहण करना होता है। उसके लिए वन्दना, पूजा, पापदेशना, पुण्यानुमोदना, अध्येषणा, बोधिचित्तोत्पाद तथा परिणामना—इस सप्तविध अनुत्तरपूजा का विधान है। बोधिसत्त्व में ही प्राणियों को मुक्त बनाने की योग्यता रहती है।

जातकमाला के सभी जातकों में प्रधानपात्र बोधिसत्त्व हैं। वे मनुष्य की योनि में कभी राजा[21], कभी आचार्य[22], कभी ब्राह्मण[23], कभी तपस्वी[24], कभी परिव्राजक[25], कभी श्रेष्ठि[26] तथा कभी नाविक [27]के रूप में प्रकट होते हैं। देवयोनि में देवताओं के अधिपति शक्र[28] होते हैं और पशु-पक्षियों की योनि में व्याघ्री [29], शशक[30], मत्स्य[31], मृग[32], कपि[33], हस्ती[34], वनमहिष[35]एवं हंस[36] होकर जन्म लेते हैं। जिस भी किसी योनि में उत्पन्न हों, वे बचपन से ही बहुत होनहार होते हैं। अल्पायु में ही सर्वगुण-सम्पन्न हो जाते हैं।

बोधिसत्त्व के जीवन का प्रधान लक्ष्य **भागवत** की इन पंक्तियों के उद्धरण में प्रायः प्रकट हुआ है—

न कामयेऽहं गतिमीश्वरात् परामष्टर्द्धियुक्तामपुनर्भवं वा।
आर्तिं प्रपद्येऽखिलदेहभाजामन्तःस्थितो येन भवन्त्यदुःखाः॥[37]

वे भूख की ज्वाला से व्याकुल होकर अपने सद्यःप्रसूत शावकों को खाने के लिए उद्यत बाघिन के आगे अपना शरीरोत्सर्ग कर उसकी प्राणरक्षा तथा धर्मरक्षा करते हैं।[38] वे सर्वस्वदान से ही सन्तुष्ट न होकर अपने शरीर का अवयव भी प्रसन्नतापूर्वक दे देते हैं।[39] दान-कर्म में भयानक विघ्न उपस्थित होने पर भी वे अपने कर्म से विचलित नहीं होते।[40] तपस्या-काल में जब वे केवल कमल-नाल खाकर रहते थे, लगातार कई दिनों तक इन्द्र के द्वारा उनका आहार लुप्त किए जाने पर भी उनके मन में विकार का उदय नहीं होता है।[41] मनुष्य का ताज़ा मांस और रुधिर चाहने वाले भूखे-प्यासे यक्षों को अपने ही शरीर से मांस के टुकड़े व रुधिर की धारा पिलाकर वे उन क्रूर-हृदयों में भी करुणा का संचार करने में समर्थ होते हैं।[42] शशक-योनि में उत्पन्न होने पर वे भूखे अतिथि के लिए अपने सुन्दर शरीर को ही अग्नि में डालकर अतिथि-सत्कार का अलौकिक दृष्टान्त उपस्थित करते हैं।[43] आजन्म आचरित अहिंसा के प्रभाव से वे समुद्र में सङ्कटापन्न जहाज के संत्रस्त यात्रियों की प्राण-रक्षा करने में समर्थ होते हैं।[44] वे अपने अमात्य की रूपवती पत्नी को देखकर मोहित होते हैं और अमात्य द्वारा अपनी पत्नी अर्पित की जाने पर भी उसे अस्वीकार करते हुए शीघ्र ही मोहमुक्त होकर सन्मार्ग का उपदेश करते हैं।[45] वे देवेन्द्र शक्र होकर मद्यपान में आसक्त राजा को मद्यपान से विरत करके राजा और उसकी प्रजा का कल्याण करते हैं।[46] विपत्ति में पड़े हुए प्राणियों को देखकर बोधिसत्त्व दया से द्रवीभूत हो उठते हैं और अपने अलौकिक पराक्रम से उनकी रक्षा करते हैं। उपकृत प्राणी कृतघ्नता या विश्वासघात करें, बोधिसत्त्व उनका उपकार ही करते हैं। वे रुरुमृग होकर प्रखर जलधारा में बहते हुए, जीवन से निराश मनुष्य को जान की बाज़ी लगाकर बचाते हैं, किन्तु वह कृतघ्न लोभवश उन्हें राजा से पकड़वा देता है। फिर भी वे पुनः उसकी प्राण-रक्षा कर दया का अद्‌भुत दृष्टान्त उपस्थित करते हैं।[47] शतपत्र पक्षी होकर वे कण्ठ में अस्थिखण्ड के अटक जाने से व्याकुल सिंह की प्राणरक्षा करते हैं। कालान्तर में वे क्षुधार्त होकर, आहार ग्रहण करते हुए सिंह के पास पहुँचने पर भी फटकार कर भगाये

जाते हैं। समर्थ होकर भी वे उसका बदला नहीं लेते हैं और उसे क्षमा कर देते हैं।[48] वे क्षान्तिवादी ऋषि होकर क्रोधी, हिंसक एवं कर्त्तव्यच्युत राजा के द्वारा अङ्ग-अङ्ग काट डालने पर भी क्षमाशील बने रहते हैं और उसके कल्याण की कामना करते हैं।[49] कुमार्गगामी हिंसक प्राणियों पर करुणा करते हुए वे सदुपदेश और सदाचरण के द्वारा उनका हृदय परिवर्तन कर उन्हे सन्मार्ग पर लाते हैं। वे क्रूर नरभक्षी सौदास को प्राणिहिंसा से विरत करते हैं।[50] वानरपति होकर वे अपने आश्रित वानरों को सङ्कट से बचाने के लिए स्वयं सेतु बनकर प्राणत्याग द्वारा भी परम सुख का अनुभव करते हैं।[51]

सुकर्मों द्वारा पुण्य-सञ्चय वे संसार रूपी कान्तार में फँसे हुए लोगों के उद्धार की भव्य भावना से ही करते हैं, न कि सांसारिक या पारलौकिक सुखसमृद्धि, यश या मोक्ष की प्राप्ति के लिए। लोकरक्षा ही उनका प्रधान लक्ष्य है और इसी के अनुष्ठान में वे सदैव यत्न करते हैं—

नायं यत्नः सार्वभौमत्वमाप्तुं नैव स्वर्गं नापवर्गं न कीर्तिम्।
त्रातुं लोकानित्ययं त्वादरो मे याच्ञाक्लेशो मा च भूदस्य मोघः ॥[52]

इस प्रकार बोधिसत्त्व के कर्म दिव्य और अद्भुत हैं। उनका जीवन अलौकिक और आदर्श है। उनके सदाचरण से हमें प्रेरणा मिलती है। हम भूखी बाघिन के आगे अपना शरीरोत्सर्ग न कर सकें, किन्तु भूखे प्राणियों, पशु-पक्षियों और मनुष्यों की वेदना से द्रवीभूत होकर उनकी भूख की ज्वाला शान्त करने के लिए कुछ उद्योग अवश्य करें। हम परोपकार सीखें। उससे प्राप्त होने वाला दिव्य आनन्द ही हमारा अपूर्व पुरस्कार होगा।

सन्दर्भ-सङ्केत

1. ब्रह्मजालसुत्त (दीघनिकाय-1, 1-46)
2. धम्मपद (28 वग्ग) 'पब्बतट्ठो व भूमट्ठे धीरो बाले अवेक्खत्तीति।'
3. (क) थेरगाथा सं.245, पृ.31
   यथा ब्रह्मा तथा एको यथा देवो तथा दुवे।
   यथा गामो तथा तायो कोलाहलं तत् उत्तरिन्ति ॥
   (ख) थेरगाथा सं.380, पृ.42
   यस्स कत्थाय पब्बजितो अगारस्मा अनगारियम्।
   सोमे अत्थो अनुप्पत्तो सब्बसंयोजनक्खयोति ॥
4. मिलिन्दपञ्ह-31 'किंतिं महाराज इदं दुक्खं निरुज्झाय अञ्ञञ्च दुक्खं न उप्पज्जेय्याति, एतदत्था महाराज अम्हाकं पब्बज्जा अनुपादापरिनिब्बानं।'

5. Hardayal, *Bodhisattva Doctrine*, P 3.
6. *Ibid.*, p. 31
7. M. Williams, *Sanskrit Dictionary*, P. 688 b.
'One who has Bodhi or perfect wisdom as his essence'
8. समाधिराजसूत्र,25a, 4
9. शतसाहस्रिकाप्रज्ञापारमिता, 1-XII अध्याय,टिप्पणी-2,पृ.2
10. बोधिचर्यावतारपञ्जिका,पृ.421
11. शतसाहस्रिकाप्रज्ञापारमिता,टिप्पणी-3, पृ.2
12. H.S.Gaur, *Buddhism*, p. XI
'In whom, knowledge is latent and undeveloped'.
13. मज्झिमनिकाय-1.17.6, 'मय्हं पि खो अनभिम्बुद्धस्स बोधिसत्तस्सेव'।
14. *Manual*, Note 5, p.65. 'personification of potential intelligence.'
15. M. Williams, *Sanskrit Dictionary*, p. 1052, strength, energy, vigour, power, courage.
16. अवदानकल्पलता-भाग 2, पद्य 42, पृ.713
17. वही,74, पृ.85
18. वही,21, पृ.945
19. वही,8, पृ.113
20. बुद्धचरित-9/30
21. शिबि - जातक,कुल्माषपिण्डी.,मैत्रीबल.,विश्वन्तर.,यज्ञ.,उन्मादयन्ती.,सुतसोम. तथा अयोगृह-जातक।
22. ब्राह्मण-जातक
23. बिस-जातक तथा चुड्डबोधि-जातक
24. अगस्त्य-जातक तथा क्षान्ति-जातक
25. महाबोधि-जातक
26. श्रेष्ठि.,अविषह्यश्रेष्ठि.,श्रेष्ठि (20)-जातक
27. सुपारग-जातक
28. शक्र-जातक तथा कुम्भ-जातक
29. व्याघ्री-जातक
30. शश-जातक
31. मत्स्य-जातक
32. शरभ-जातक तथा रुरु-जातक

33. महाकपि (24, 27 वाँ) - जातक
34 हस्ति-जातक
35. महिष-जातक
36. हंस-जातक
37. श्रीमद्भागवत - IX. 21.12
38. व्याघ्री-जातक
39. शिबि-जातक
40. श्रेष्ठि-जातक (चतुर्थ)
41. बिस-जातक
42. मैत्रीबल-जातक
43. शश-जातक
44. सुपारग-जातक
45. उन्मादयन्ती- जातक
46. कुम्भ-जातक
47. रुरु-जातक
48. शतपत्र-जातक
49. क्षान्ति-जातक
50. सुतसोम-जातक
51. महाकपि-जातक
52. जातकमाला-2/28

नई दिल्ली

IMAGE OF WOMAN AS REFLECTED IN JāTAKAS*

Harcharan Singh Sobti

There are number of stories contained in the *Jātakaṭṭhakathāvaṇṇaṇā,* which are woven in a single pattern denigrating woman, painting her licentious and cautioning the *Bhikkhus* to 'keep wide awake' as regards woman. At the same time, women are also eulogized as *therīs,* whose life-sketches in the form of the *Therīgāthā* form an integral part of the Buddhist canon. This means that 'woman is eligible to attain *Nibbāna*'. These two views involve contradiction. I propose to examine this very contradiction in this paper.

The *Jātakas* in Pāli language form a very vast literature containing the teachings of the Buddha. They are in the form of *555* main stories of the previous births of the Buddha (but the number of *Jātakas* available so far is *547*) and a number of interlinking stories of the *Bodhisattva* striving for the fulfilment of ten perfections *(Pāramitās)*[1], for the attainment of Buddhahood. The *Jātakas* in their original form were in verses *(gāthās)* and the number of verses contained in the available *547 Jātakas* is *2440*. The theme of teaching has been interwoven through these verses. The details about them were surviving in oral tradition in society.

Since the Buddhist tradition was alive in India for centuries, the people had no diffculty in understanding these verses in the background of the introductory material already available in oral tradition. In course of time, there was the chance of disappearence of the oral tradition. Therefore, Buddhaghoṣa (5th century A.D.), an eminent commentator of the words of the Buddha, understood the

* This paper was presented at the International symposium on 'Folklore in Slavonic Finno-Ugrian and Indian Literature' (FOLSFUIL) organised by Department of Slavic Studies, University of Delhi at its South Delhi Campus from 27ṭḥ to 31ṣṭ March, 1989.

psychological trends of the society and put all such materials into writing, rightly adjusting them with the theme of the verses. Thus, each *Jātaka* appeared in the form of one complete story of the deeds of the *Bodhisattva*. Of course, in many cases the story is further interwoven with a number of other stories connected with the theme. Every single *Jātaka* story consists of five component part *viz. (i) Paccuppannavatthu,* (ii)*Atītavatthu, (iii) Gāthā,* (iv) *Veyyākaraṇa* and (v) Samodhāna or in other words it passes through these five successive stages. Right in the beginning, one is made familiar with the context (*paccuppannavatthu*) which prompts the Buddha to narrate a *Jātaka* story; then a story of the previous birth of the Buddha (*atītavatthu*) when, actually he was *Bodhisattva,* is narrated; thereafter *gāthā* supported by *abhisambuddha-gāthā* is recited followed by a word for word commentory of the *gāthā* (*veyyākaraṇa*). The fifth and last component part of the *Jātaka* story is *Samodhāna.* Here the characters of the 'story of the present', are identified with those of the 'story of the past' alongwith it the psychological effect of the discourse on the minds of the hearers is described.[2] Our main concern, at present, is with *atītavatthu* and psychological effect on the minds of the hearers.

The *Jātaka* stories we have selected for an appraisal, in the background of the Buddhist tradition, are contained in the *Ithivagga* of *Jatakaṭṭhakathāvaṇṇanā.* These stories depict woman as "lustful, profligate, vile and degraded"[3] and are symbolized as "a sex composed of wickedness and guile, unknowable, uncertain as the path of fishes in the water,"[4] "given an opportunity, all women work iniquity"[5] and last but not the least, they are compared to "highways, rivers, courtyards, hostelries or caverns, which to all alike extend one universal hospitality."[6] The psychological effect of these stories on the minds of hearers is invariably that of renunciation of the household life in favour of entering into a state of homelessness. Rati Lal N.Mehta, while writing on 'Position of Woman' in his book *Pre-Buddhist India* (1939), based on *Jātaka* stories, is quite near to the truth when he opines that "these utterness are from, and for the ascetics—those who, perhaps, tired of their own weakness, and despaired of their failures want to run away from the world."[7] But, this tutored psychological effect involves wider issues that call for an analysis.

The Buddha was critical about woman. This unhappy conclusion is readily derived, mainly, from three canonical evidences. These evidences are : (i) the Buddha's reluctance to admit women into the *Saṅgha*, (ii) an institution of *aṭṭhagurudhamma* exclusively meant for *Bhikkhunīs* and (iii) the Buddha's advice to Ānanda 'to keep wide awake' in regard to woman. It seems to be a case of misreading of the canon. A misreading of the canon, whether intentional or otherwise, as history of religions tells us, creates problems. At times, a misreading stems from an outlook not rooted in the soil of the land. The alleged hostility of the Buddha against woman needs to be looked into in the background of the indigenous cultural heritage.

The Buddha's reluctance, in the present case, is rather revealing. Let us look into the circumstances in which the Buddha allowed admission of women into *Saṅgha*. While going through the text of *Cullavagga* (which is second sub-part of the *Khandhaka*, second book of *Vinaya Piṭaka)*, we learn that, when the Buddha was staying at Kpilavatthu, in the Nyagrodha park, Mahāprajāpati Gautamī, Gautama's aunt and later on his foster-mother, visited the Buddha and asked for his permission thrice 'to enter the homeless state under the doctrine and discipline proclaimed by the *Tathāgata*'. But to her utter dismay, the Buddha continued to remain adamant in not allowing women to enter the homeless state'.

If Gautama, the Buddha was adamant, Gautamī too was determined. The story continues. But, now we find the Buddha staying in Mahāvana at Vesālī. Imagine for a while Gautamī alongwith a number of ladies of the sākya clan, having her shaven head, wearing saffron-coloured robes, with swollen feet covered with dust, sad and sorrowful, weeping and in tears, arrives at Vesālī and is standing outside under the entrance porch of Mahāvana. The scene, so to say, is pathetic. Ānanda, the Chief Disciple of the Buddha, happens to be there. He is moved and enquires about their plight and consequently intervenes in the matter. Ānanda requests the Buddha for admitting Gautamī and other ladies of the Sākya clan into *Saṅgha*. Ānanda, repeats the request thrice, but, in vain. At the same time, Ānanda refuses to accept his defeat and changes his strategy. Now, Ānanda does not request but asks :

"Are women, Lord, capable—when they have gone forth from the household life and entered discipline proclaimed by the Blessed one—are they capable of realising the fruit of conversion, or of the second path, or of the third path, or Arhantship?"

They are capable, Ānanda,[9] The Buddha replies.

Hence, at this juncture, Ānanda reminds the Buddha of Gautamī's great service rendered to him, when as aunt and nurse she nourished him and gave him milk, and on the death of his mother suckled the Blessed one at her own breast. Ānanda seems to have sentimentalized the whole situation. When Gautamī, at one time, 'Suckled the Blessed one at her own breast', the Blessed one is not short of milk of human kindness. The Buddha's acceptance of 'capability' of woman and Gautamī's service rendered, prepared a ground for admission of women into *saṅgha*. The Buddha grants the permission, but, with a condition, thus :

"If then Ānanda, Mahāpajāpati, the Gautamī takes upon herself the Eight Chief Rules (*aṭṭhagurudhammā*), let that be reckoned to her as her initiation".[10]

In spite of woman's 'capability', the Buddha's reluctance to initiate woman is disturbing. Our primary concern, at the moment, of course, is to discuss the meanings of the Buddha's reluctance.

Every human being is bisexual combining both the masculine and feminine characteristics, irrespective of being man or woman. This psychological truth was discovered in India, long ago, and projected in the myth of *ardhanārīśvara* preserved in *Śivapurāṇa*."[11] The myth of *ardhanārīśvara* takes the form of masculinity and femininity, ingrained in human psyche. *Sakhisampradāya* of Swami Haridas that advocates the view that 'there is only one male and all others are females' has its roots in this very human psyche. The male adherents of this *sampradāya* dress themselves like woman and identify themselves with Rādhā and conduct themselves likewise. Those, who are attracted towards this kind of devotion to God in the form of Kṛṣṇa certainly imbibe disproportionate quantity of feminine traits in their psychic beings. It is a case of projecting femininity rooted in the male biological organism.

The fact of human beings imbibing composite psychic nature, is also acknowledged by Guru Nanak (1469-1539), the founder-Guru of Sikhism, when he says that :

"There is a woman in man

and man in woman

only the wise can discern it."[12]

Bisexuality as a psychic phenomenon is a subject of study in modern psychology, too. "Every individual" discovered Sigmund Freud (1856-1939)" displays a mixture of the character-traits belonging to his own and the opposite sex; and he shows a combination of activity and passivity whether or not these last character- traits tally with his biological ones"[13]. He identified activity in woman as a masculine trait and passivity in man as feminine one. Therefore, psychologically speaking every individual is to be viewed in this background.

The Buddha on the one hand was reluctant to admit woman into *Saṅgha* and on the other hand he endorsed the querry of Ānanda with regard to the capability of woman for realising 'the fruit of conversion' when 'entered the homeless state under the doctrine and discipline proclaimed by the Blessed one'. *'Woman is capable'*, here, woman is viewed as a psychological being that imbibes both the masculine and feminine character-traits. The capability of woman as a psychological being is directly linked up with 'the doctrine and discipline of the Buddha.' What is there in woman and doctrine and discipline, that goes well with each other? The basic thing in the doctine of the Buddha is that it is meditative in nature. In order to draw any benefit from the doctrine of the Buddha, it is imperative that it suits the temperament of the person concerned. In *theravāda* Buddhism, even an object of meditation needs to be selected, with the guidance of *Kalyāṇa-mitta,* according to one's temperament.[14] So it is temperament of the person pursuing religious discipline that works as a deciding factor. All humans are essentially bisexual. The *therīs* were more masculine than feminine in their temperament. Therefore, They were eligible for *Nibbāṇa*. But *Bhikkhuṇīs* are more average women and licentious. Only the latter are to be denied admission into the *Saṅgha,* not the former. Such an interpretation will remove the apparent contradiction regarding the position of women in the Buddhist *Saṅgha*.

As already stated, the Buddhist discipline is meditative (and not devotional) in its approach. Now, whether it suits masculine or feminine temperament, it is yet to be seen. Masculinity in its contents is through and through assertive, active and hence egoistic. It is difficult for a person havaing an overall masculine temperament to accept 'the other'. It is prerogative of feminine temperament alone to accept 'the other' and melt oneself therein. There is 'no other' in *Theravāda* Buddhism conducive as an object of devotion that feeds the feminine-self. Therefore, we can safely conclude that the way of the Buddha suits the person imbibing masculine temperament alone.

The Buddha's acceptance of 'capability of woman' to become *arhata* refers to the masculinity inherent in her being. Mrs. C.A.F. Rhys Davids in the introduction to *Psalms of the Sisters* (translation of *Therīgāthā* has made certain observations useful for our present discussion. While drawing a distinction between 'Indian Marys and their Christian sister's, she states that :

"But herein we note a sharp contrast between these Indian Marys and their Christian sisters. Where He, the Central figure, intervenes, and gratitude is blent with adoration, the little poem (*Therīgāthā*) reveals no word of quasi-amorous self-surrender to the person or image of the Beloved, such as characterizes not a little of that Christian literature for which the Song of Soloman---'I am my beloved's and my beloved is mine'—was a sacred archetype."[15]

Again, Mrs. Rhys Davids comments that: "The utmost length a *therī* presumes to go in relating herself to her Teacher, is to claim spiritual fatherhood in him......"[16]

To add further, Mrs. Rhys Davids holds the view "that of the four notorious Magdalens who found peace and purity in the order of *Bhikkhuṇīs*—Addhakāsī, Vimalā, Abhaya's mother and Ambapālī—not one expresses any deep feeling of personal attachment to the teaher."[17] The possibilities of imbibing feminine traits, such as, 'self-surrender' and 'deep personal attachment' by the *therīs* numbering 101, whose life-sketches and verses certifying the fact of having attained *arhatahood*, we find in *Therīgāthā*, are ruled out. These *therīs*, therefore,are exceptional women being dominantly masculine in their mental disposition. This is also borne by the fact that"life under the *Vinaya* was one of both active and contemplative discipline."[18]

Normally, woman is more feminine and consequently less masculine. The femininity inclines towards love that needs a partner. This resulted in the involvement between the *Bhikkhus* and *Bhikkhuṇīs*. After allowing woman's admission to *Saṅgha*, the Buddha told Ānanda that :

"If, Ānanda, woman had not received permission to go out from the house-hold life and enter the homeless state, under the doctrine and discipline proclaimed by the *Tathāgata*, then would the pure religion, Ānanda, have last long, the good law would have stood fast for a thousand years. But, since Ānanda, women have now received that permission, the pure religion, Ānanda, will not now last so long, the good law will stand fast for only five hundred years."[19]

The Buddha anticipated the decline of 'good law' and 'pure religion' on account of expressive femininity of woman. The 'good' and 'pure' refers to the basic Buddhist doctrine and discpline that envisages meditation demanding fullest expression of masculinity inherent in human psyche. We know that the 'good' and 'pure' declined in due course of time because of intermixing 'love' in it. Love made meditation 'bad' and 'impure'.

The Buddha's permission to woman was conditional demanding strictly observing *aṭṭhagurudhammā*. It is, in fact, the First Rule that caused much agitation in the minds of women for a just cause, in a way, and also for men only interested in painting the Buddha as anti-women. The First Rule reads:

"A *Bhikkhuṇī*, even if of a hundred years standing, shall make salutation to, shall rise up in the presence of,shall bow down before, and shall perform all proper duties towards *Bhikkhu*, if only just initiated...."[20]

It appears that the Rule commands subservience of *Bhikkhuṇīs* to *Bhikkhu* irrespective of the fomer's seniority. But, the matter is not that simple. The Rule ought to be looked into in the background of indigenous cultural heritage. We know as Indians the value of reverence shown by man and woman for each other, in day to day living. When a woman, (except wife, of course) shows reverence for man, due to any reason, the latter, is handicapped to forge any sexual relation with that woman. Since, when a man gets reverence from a woman, it feeds his ego. Inflow of sex leading to a relation costs man an ego and which he would rarely like to forego. The first Rule was simply to guard against an inflow of sexual feeling.[21] 'Salutation', 'rising up', 'bowing down'—all these amount to show reverence for the *Bhikkhus*.

How ironic it seems to be that Ānanda who once pleaded the case of woman's admission into *Saṅgha* should ask the Buddha as to how to conduct themselves with regard to women. The querries and its replies need to be examined in the background of Buddhist discipline. The dialogue between the Buddha and Ānanda dialating on the subject reads thus :

"How are we to conduct ourselves Lord, with regard to womenkind"?

"As not seeing them, Ānanda".

"But, if we should see them, what are we to do."?

"No talking Ānanda."

"But, if they should speak to us, Lord, what are we to do"?

"Keep wide awake, Ānanda."[22]

The reference to womenkind in this dialogue is generally construed to mean to denigrate women. If we emphasize upon the expression 'seeing' and 'talking', the conclusion cannot be otherwise. But, when viewed in the background of Buddhist doctrine and discipline, the emphasis should be on "Sati, *Ānanda, upaṭṭhāpetabbaṁ*" or 'keep wide awake'. The *Bhikkhu* is 'to keep wide awake' at all times and in all circumstances. The reference to women is incidental.

Thus, we come across three dimensions of woman in Buddhist canonical literature, such as, *therī*, who is exceptionally masculine and therefore has attained *Nibbāṇa; Bhikkhuṇī*, one who is on the path and an average woman who is painted licentious. The *Bhikkhu* is warned with regard to licentious woman, one of the very popular theme in folk literature. He is also guarded against his own inflow of sexual feelings by means of the First Rule binding on *Bhikkhuṇīs*. Buddhism is not prejudiced against woman as such, rather, it presents a balanced view of woman.

REFERENCES AND NOTES

1. These ten *pāramitās* are: almsgiving (*dāna*), goodness (*sīla*), renunciation (*neśkamma*), wisdom (*prajñā*), energy (*vīrya*), patience, (*khanti*), truth (*satta*), resolution (*sankappa*), friendliness (*mettya*) and equanimity (*uppekhā*). These *pāramitās* are beautifully illustrated in *Jātaka* No. 35.
2. Rati Lal N. Mehta, *Pre-Buddhist India*, Anmol Publications, Delhi, Reprinted 1985. p.xix.
3. E.B. Cowell, *Jātaka Stories* (Gen.Ed.) Pāli Text Society, London, 1973 (Ist published : Cambridge University, 1875) Vol. I+II, Vol. I, p.147.
4. *Ibid*. p. 155
5. *Ibid*. p. 151
6. *Ibid*. p. 161
7. Rati Lal N. Mehta, *op.cit.*, p. 289
8. *Cullavagga* X 1.2 to X 1.4
   T.W. Rhys Davids and Herman Oldenberg (trs.), *Vinaya Texts, Sacred Books* of *East Series* Part III, Motilal Banarsidass, Delhi, 1965, Reprint. (First published by Oxford University Press, 1885) pp. 320-322.
9. *Ibid*. X. 1.4., p. 322
10. *Ibid*. X. 1.5., p.324
11. *Śivapurāṇa : Śatarudrasaṁhitā*, chapter III cf. Gopinath T.A., Rao, *Elements of Hindu Iconography*, Indological Book House, Delhi, 2nd edition : 1971 (Ist edition : New York 1914) Vol. II Part I pp. 321-331. For statues of *ardhanārīśvara*, see plates No 95-98.
12. *Ādigrantha*, p. 879
13. James Strachey, *The Complete Psychological Works of Sigmund Freud* (Gen. Ed.), The Hograth Press, London, 1965 (First published in 1953) Vol. III, p. 220.
14. Bhikkhu Nyanmoli, *The Path of Purification*, translation of *Visuddhimagga*), Buddhist Publication Society, Kandy, Sri Lanka, Fourth edition, 1979 (First published in 1956), pp. 102 ff.
15. C.A.F. Rhys Davids, *Psalms of the Sisters-1* (Translation of *Therīgāthā*), Pāli Text Society, London, 1980. (First published in 1909) p. xxxii.
16. *Idem*
17. *Ibid*. p.xxxiii.
18. *Ibid*. p.xxxiv.
19. *Cullavagga* p. 256, Pāli Text Society, London.
20. *Viṇaya* Texts, *Cullavagga*, *op. cit.*, x.1.4
21. Rajneesh, *Ess Dhammo Sanatano*, Rajneesh Foundation, Poona, 1976, Vol.I, p.77
22. *Dīgha Nikāya*, Part II, Pāli Text Society, London, p. 141.

Delhi

THE STATUS OF WOMEN IN THE BUDDHIST JĀTAKA

Krishna Kant Trivedi

The Buddhist *Saṁgha* heighlights the moral character of male and female citizens. Dealing with the reality of life, the Buddhist writers are supposed not to have favoured the feeling of sex and caste in determining the status of women. From the Pāli canon, it becomes clear that during the Buddha's age, the position of women seems to have been slightly changed. The *Parivrājaka* who propagated a different philosophical system never denied the role of women in various fields and also stressed on the point that they are not merely an object of pleasure. It appears from most of the Pāli literature that the Buddha had not preached much about the social reforms of his time and he simply associated himself with the religious and philosophical problems. It may also be stated that the Buddhism in its early stage never indicates a radical change in the status of women. Although a slight change seems to have occurred in their social recognition. According to the Buddhists, an heirless person may attain the *Nirvāṇa*. But the Hindu faith did not favour such hypothesis.

Women in their social context were allowed to achieve freedom. Generally divorce was not favoured for those women who gave birth to girl child only. On the other hand, a person willing to have a son was allowed to marry another woman but in no case was he permitted to cut off his relation with the first wife. The *Dharmaśātra* criticises a barren woman for not offering an heir to her family. It is remarkable to note that the Buddhists did not favour the adoption of a child as successor. A daughter may be declared as all heiress. Most of the Jātaka stories testify the fact that a daughter was declared as an heiress by her father.

Briefly, it is to be pointed out here that the Buddhist view is against the basic importance of marriage. A person can lead his life alone. A son never becomes a way to *Nirvāṇa* to his father. Hence, a pious woman has all qualities of attainning *Nirvāṇa* similar to her male partner. There are some examples that women of highbirth did not prefer to marry and left their houses for getting an entry into the Buddhist order. When a woman was insulted by her husband or by other members of the family, she felt no hesitation to get entry into the *saṁgha*. Physical and mental torture of women was not uncommon. Even a housewife of a wealthy merchant was harassed by her husband. Tired of continuous negligence and torture, a woman seems to have got shelter in the *saṁgha*. Such act of women was not criticised by the Buddhists.[1]

The Jātaka states that the marriage at last forfeits our purpose. In spite of such negative statement, the Buddha recommends that a woman should marry in order to speed up the creation. But within the curtain, rights of women were challenged by most of the people.

According to the Buddhist view, a woman ranks as means of material prosperity. Therefore, she requires a reputed position among the domestic objects.[2] A woman of good character used to display her simplicity while a treacherous and disloyal woman plunged herself into sinful acts. Mutual understanding and co-operation was necessary to bring stability in domestic affairs. A housewife proved to be indifferent to her husband but according to the Buddhists the domestic affairs were not properly managed without her consent.[3] A woman shared the difficulties of the family and also encouraged her husband. Sometimes she invited troubles due to her bad nature. Therefore, it was understood that only a good houswife could bring prosperity in the house.[4]

The moral character of women had to meet with several challenges. Meeting with a person was not justified for them. The Buddhists take women's beauty as supreme which hypnotizes a person. At last, it diminishes the qualities of a person who fails to recognise its bad results.[5]

Women ranked second position in the family. Due to the sudden death or prolonged absence of husband, women looked after the children and managed the agricultural farms. Sometimes an old husband suspected his young wife. After husband's death a young woman married another person, but some women did not marry. Gradually they came to give shape to the future of their minor children.[6]

In most of the rich families, women had the privilege of receiving honour and respect from their own members. A housewife was warmly welcomed when she took care of others and displayed her qualities in giving final shape to the domestic works.[7] The Jātaka goes to explain how women enjoyed their traditional status under the patronage of their husbands and achieved all kinds of prosperity.[8] It also appears that women of the noble families were treated with honour and man of low origin had no courage to insult them.[9] A girl of the same status was preferred for marriage. Sometimes a housewife abused her mother-in-law and acted against the will of her husband. The Buddhist writers take notice of the seven qualities of women through which stability is obtained in our domestic relationship.[10]

A child is impressed by his mother. Pāṇini tells that the son of a good mother was called *Bhadramātur* while the son of a beautiful mother was known as *Kalyāṇineyas*.[11]

There is an erotic relation between husband and wife. A housewife who is young and beautiful commands her husband by displaying some specific behaviour.[12] By offering food to parents-in-law and displaying loyality to her husband, a woman had become popular among the members of the family. Further, she used to utter sweet words, which granted her all kinds of happiness and peace.[13]

Women from the middle class families understood the feelings of their husbands. They frequently used to offer sitting benches to the *śramaṇas* and paid due courtesy to them. They always kept themselves busy with the domestic works. During the lifetime of husband or after his death, woman was not debarred from the right of property. A skilled housewife engaged the male and female servants for all types of domestic works. She also took keen interest in managing the domestic wealth. It was presumed that a woman devoid of lust and jealousy leads her life well and finally attains heaven.[14]

From the Jātakas, it becomes clear that the merchants of Rājagṛha, Vaiśālī and Vārāṇasi possessed all types of material facilities.

Women of such houses attained proficiency in domestic works. A cultivator's houswife cooked food for the labourers and managed the cattle. Thus she was obedient to her husband. We are informed that a housewife managed the internal affairs while her husband had to look after the external matters.[15]

According to the Buddhist thinkers, prosperity and poverty are linked with the conduct of a woman. She is rewarded with ornaments and fine dresses when she acts well and unites herself with the mentality of her husband.[16]

Among the wellknown families, a girl was married in the family of equal status and fame. A good and kind-hearted housewife had the privilege of serving the senior members of the family with her own hands and never hired servants for such work. But such a pious woman was not left free from mental torture. We are informed that she was compelled to leave her husband after prolonged torture and misbehaviour.[17]

Prosperity in the family had nothing to do she she with the character of an unmarried girl. The Jātaka informs that the daughter of a Seṭṭhi having relations with a domestic servant left her paternal home without considering her future.[18] As a rule, a girl was offered to a suitable boy and was not allowed to marry a boy of low origin.[19]

If a woman conceived through illicit contact, she was not forgiven. The Buddhist community did not tolerate such acts of women. When they came to join the *saṁgha,* they had to pass through minute observations. By adopting such methods, the legal or illegal status of a pregnant woman was determined.[20]

Sometimes, a young girl was offered to an old person without considering his age and strength. An unmatchable marriage never satisfied the couple. A young wife often married another person just after the death of her aged husband.[21]

It becomes evident from the Jātaka that an unmatchable marriage was not favoured by the people. But such marriages were not without reason. A poor family was compelled to offer young girls when it was unable to refund the loan.[22]

The treacherous women invited a lot of troubles. From the Jātaka, it becomes clear that the housewife of a certain *śrāvaka* had entered into sexual contact with a person and disregarded her husband.[23] Sometimes, women treated their husbands with rough tone and behaved with them like a domestic servant. A physically handicapped houswife was exploited for long duration.[24]

Women had lust for sexual pleasure with other persons. Even a pious *brāhmaṇa* had his treacherous wife who used to entertain herself with a man of low origin.[25] Other women also tried to take advantages of their innocent husbands and indulged themselves in sexual pleasure with other men.[26]

The Jātaka makes it clear that the treacherous and disloyal women were not left unchecked for long time. Persons who earned their favour, were also punished. In short, women were not considered as reliable persons and were treated with care. According to the Buddhists, the treacherous women were liable to receive severe punishment when they plunged into sexual contact with other persons. Those women were also not forgiven who cheated their husbands. If they failed to control themselves, more punishment was required for them.[27] In some specific cases, women were exempted from the punishment. Thus according to the Jātaka, women are similar to the river which is meant for the common use. Like the *Dharmaśāstra*, the Buddhists too have not found a woman guilty of intercourse with another person if she loses herself due to deep passion. Therefore, a polluted woman may be accepted again when she is purified with some material objects. But such provisions were restricted to some peculiar cases only.[28]

A majority of women disregarded their husbands and moved for free sex.[29] Urge for sexual pleasure was very common among the wealthy women. The social dignity was challenged by such acts of women. From one of the Jātakas, it becomes clear that the housewife of a certain *brāhmaṇa* moved freely with her lovers. She neglected her husband and offered him rough food.[30] It has been frequently stated that a woman cannot be placed under strict control and she liberates herself.[31] A woman utters sweet words when she intends to cheat her husband. Her sexual urge is never satisfied. Therefore, a person is advised to remain aloof from the association of women; because it produces bad results. A woman comes to our notice when she needs something.[32]

The *kṣatriyas* of the Jātaka period proved to be more sensitive to the purity of their blood. Hence, a *kṣatriya* girl was not allowed to marry a boy of low origin.[33] Somtimes, a young girl of a merchant never tolerated the discourteous treatment.[34] The Jātaka also states that more love and affection towards a young girl changed her motive and she fails in love with a boy of the neighbouring village.[35] It seems that the prosperity of the family had nothing to do with the good or bad character of women. From the Jātaka, it appears that a young girl of a wealthy *brāhmaṇa* had decided to abstain herself from sexual pleasures in order to lead pious life.[36] The Jātaka tells that a woman sometimes surpasses the intellect of her male partner and displays her profound knowledge of the material world.[37]

Women throughout the Jātaka stories have not been considered as means of pleasure only but they also provide a successor to the paternal property. Hence, a housewife without a son was looked down by her father-in-law who searched another girl for his son. Normally a housewife did not tolerate the second wife and sometimes claimed for false pregnancy.[38] Wine-drinking among the wealthy women was also prevalent but it was not tolerated. A drunken woman is reported to have abused her husband and she frequently acted in a very indifferent manner.[39]

A woman devoted to her husband and displaying good character throughout her life was destined to exhibit the glorious tradition of the Indian women. Hence a woman being adorned with all material facilities found herself undressed and unadorned without her husband.[40] Generally a house-holder preferred to select a charming girl for his son.[41] A housewife was admired when she used to utter sweet words and proved to be loyal to her husband.[42] A loving wife had deep love for her husband and used to wash his footprints with water.[43]

Women, in their family set up, earned fame and honour when they displayed their qualities in managing all types of domestic works, although they were not allowed to act against the will of their husbands. The Jātaka criticises those persons who are crippled by their own wives and who do not act freely. A *janapada* also becomes unfit for them when it is governed by women.[44]

On the basis of the Jātaka, it may be stated that an unmarried girl remained under the supervison of either her mother or father. a young girl was suspected of rape and misbehaviour. Therefore, it was necessary to maintain her virginity till her marriage.[45] Marriage with maternal uncle's daughter was not universally accepted, but it got social recognition after some time.[46] Before marriage, most of the young girls were minutely observed. In very special cases, a girl was permitted to select her own husband.[47]

The Jātaka goes to describe how a woman equally shares the good or bad days of her husband. In fact, he meets the challenges of life with the assistance of his loving wife. It is true that the spirit and courage of a housewife are tested in days of adversity.[48]

A widow or divorced woman was permitted for remarriage. Some women neglected such proposals and preferred to look after their children. Conflict between husband and wife does not seem to have discriminated their mutual relation. Some women really felt hesitation in disobeying their first husband.[49] According to the *Jaina Sūtra*, women who intentionally disregarded domestic affairs and acted against the will of the elders were liable to be divorced.[50] According to the Buddhist view, a long gap of communication between husband and wife produces a lot of problems. It further affects the domestic structure and also proves to be damaging to our property. Hence, huband and wife should remain loyal to each other. The pious couples are rewarded with long life, able sons and daughters.[51]

Polygamy had become a symbol of status. A person from the noble class had many women for his pleasure which invited bitterness in the entire domestic structure, although the Jātaka never admires polygamy on account of its antisocial attitude. It also states that a girl should not be offered to a person who is already married.[52] In spite of such injunction, polygamy seems to be deeply rooted in the society. It got popularity among the ruling chiefs. Even the rich merchants were found of keeping many women in their harem. Such practices invited endless hatred and jealousy among women.[53]

Sometimes, a pious woman had to suffer due to the disloyality of her husband who accidently turned his mind towards another lady and kept illicit relations with her.[54] Observing such mentality of husband and wife, the Jātaka tries to explain that a loyal woman in this world is hard to achieve and naturally the same case runs with husband too who takes vow to remain loyal to his wife.[55]

DRESS AND COSMETICS FOR WOMEN

The Jātakas take notice of the different modes of fashion prevailing among the poor and wealthy women. A housewife of a seṭṭhi had to select a number of dresses cosmetics and perfumes. It appears that the social and economic background of the family had its impact on woman's choice for fashion. A poor woman desired for better dresses and cosmetics but she could never meet her demand due to lack of money.

According to the *Therīgāthā*, a wealthy woman was privileged of obtaining luxurious objects for her pleasure.[56] Selection of dresses and cosmetics was frequently done as per colour of skin.[57] On some specific occasions, peculiar types of dresses were urged by women.[58] Husband tried to earn money for such dresses.[59] The *Jaina Sūtra* states that some special dresses for women were chosen in order to mark and celebrate the festivals.[60] A majority of rich women had lust for *Kāśī* cloth. After complete decoration, they were garlands and ornaments.[61]

Women had natural lust for all types of decoration. The *Vinaya* text supplies a list of ornaments which are supposed to have been manufactured for women.[62] The Jātaka tells that bracelets of pure gold were manufactured for women.[63] Pāṇini informs that women wer fond of wearing *Aṅgulīya, Karṇikā, Lalāṭikā* and *Grīveyaka*. It is remarkable to note that such pieces of ornaments have got bold representation in the artistic remains of the Maurya-Śuṅga period.[64]

The economy during the period seems to have been running under the patronage of big merchants. Women of such houses had to select a variety of dresses and ornaments. Ornaments of jewels were reserved for some particular occasions.[65]

Perfumes and fresh flowers formed the major source of decoration. Women believed that the decoration must be done for a loving and delightful personality. Flowers served the cheapest source of cosmetics.[66] From the *Vinaya Piṭaka*, we are informed that cosmetics had its deep impact on the body of women.[67] Some women had dark red polish on nails and adorned themselves with fine dresses and garlands.[68]

The Buddhist Jātaka as well as some passages of the *Therīgāthā* testify the fact that the prostitutes had some typical taste for cosmetics. Their purpose of using cosmetics was to draw attention of the customers.[69] Some women had rich collection of perfumes and they hired a team of maid servants for decorating themselves.[70] A prostitute had to decorate herself with many colourful designs. By adopting peculiar combination of cosmetics, the body of women glittered like pearl.[71]

There are instances to show that most of the rich families had all material objects for cosmetics. Though the life is very short, yet lust for a loving body had attracted the mind of women. For a good bath, women often procured scented powder.[72] Scented oil was needed for hair-dressing.[73] Thus, oil served as major source for hair-style.[74]

Women possessing a rich heritage of cosmetics, often invented new techniques of decoration. The famous *Kāśī* cloth had its combination with sandal paste.[75] The rich women usually sat on confortable beds and got themselves decorated with sandal paste and perfumes.[76]

REFERENCES & NOTES

1. See for details, Prof. Indra ; *The Status of Women in Ancient India*, Banaras, 1955.pp.185-186
   Om Prakash; *Prācīna Bhārata Kā Sāmājika Itihāsa*, Chapter IX, pp.133-148
2. Prof. Indra; *op.cit.*,p.188
3. M.V. (Nālandā), p.80
4. A.N. II (Nālandā), pp.61-62
5. *Ibid*, II., p.331,332 and 384.
6. *Ibid*, III (Nālandā), p.17ff.
7. *Ibid*, p.19
8. *Ibid*, p.76
9. *Jā II* (Hindi Tr.), p.92
10. A.N.III p.222 (Nālandā)
    Jā III (Hindi Tr.), p.71ff.
11. V.S. Agrawal; *Pāṇinikālīna Bhāratavarṣa*, pp. 99-102
12. A.N. III., p.306
13. *Ibid*, p.363
14. *Ibid*, J.C. Jain; *Āgama Sāhitya Men Bhāratīya Samāja*, pp.152-153 ff.
15. K.K. Trivedi; *Prācīna Pāli Sāhitya Men Bhāratīya Samāja*, p.131 ff.

16. *Ibid*, Chapter IV
17. *Therīgāthā,402-403*, Comp. J.C. Jain, *Life in Ancient India as Depicted in Jain Canon*, pp.158-160
18. Jā I (Hindi Tr.), p. 194
19. Hawaldar Tripathi; *Buddha Dharma Aura Bihāra*, p.137
20. *Jā I* (Hindi Tr.), p. 241
21. *Ibid*, pp.339-340
22. *Ibid*, IV, p.9
23. *Ibid*, I, pp.433-434
24. *Ibid*, II, p.,38
25. *Ibid*, II, pp.116-117
26. *Ibid*, p.140
27. *Ibid*, p. 303
28. *Ibid*, p.310
29. *Ibid*, p.320
30. *Ibid*, p.36
31. *Ibid*, p.390
32. *Ibid*, III, p.52 ff.
33. *Ibid*, p.167
34. *Ibid*, p.428
35. *Ibid*, p.36
36. *Ibid*, p.260
37. *Ibid*, IV, p.47 Ga 3,4
38. *Ibid*, p.236
39. *Ibid*, V, p.105 Ga 48
40. *Ibid*, I, p.443 ff.
41. *Ibid*, II, p.305
42. *Ibid*, V, p.15 Ga 18
43. *Ibid*, p.251 Ga 23
44. *Ibid*, I, p.249
45. *Ibid*, II, p.30
46. *Ibid*, p.88
47. *Ibid*, p.323
48. *Ibid*, III, p.236
49. *Ibid*, IV, p.234
50. See for details, J.C.Jain; *op. cit.*, (Hindi), Chapter III
51. Jā IV, (Hindi tr.), p.254 Ga 6,7
52. *Ibid*, p.552
53. *Ibid*, p.526 ff.
54. *Ibid*, V, p.149
55. *Ibid*, p. 184 Ga 34

56. *Vinaya Texts* II, p. 149 ff.I, K.K.Trivedi; *op. cit.*, pp.233-234.
57. Motichandra; *Prācīna Bhāratīya Veśa-Bhūṣā*, p.36 & *Mayyaka Jātaka*
58. *Jā, No.147*
59. *Ibid*, No.547
60. *Ibid*, No.157
61. J.C. Jain, *op.cit.*, (Hindi), p.205
62. *Therīgātha*, 379
63. *The Book of the Discipline*, p.14ft.3
64. *Kumbhakara Jātaka* Ga 2
65. V.S. Agrawal; *op.cit.*, p.137, Comp. Prabhu Dayal Agnihotri ; *Patañjalikālīna Bhārata,p.203*
66. K.K. Trivedi; *op.cit.*, p.260
67. M.V., 6/3/12 (Nālandā)
68. C.V. 5/13/32 (")
69. *Therigāthā*, 459
70. *Ibid*, 72
71. *Ibid*, 145
72. *Ibid*, 253,256, 257, 259
73. Trivedi; *op.cit.*, p.262ff.
74. C.V. 5/1/4 *Samanta Pasādikā* III 1282
75. *Therīgāthā, 960*
76. *Ibid*, 299

Darbhanga

जातकमाला में पारमिता

अञ्जुबाला

बौद्धधर्म के महायान सम्प्रदाय में अष्टाङ्गिक मार्ग का बोधिसत्त्वचर्या के रूप में विकास हुआ। बोधिसत्त्वचर्या ही बुद्धत्व - लाभ की साधना है। महायानी ग्रन्थानुसार बोधिसत्त्व[1] द्वारा पारमिताओं (दानादि) में पूर्णता प्राप्त करना ही बोधिसत्त्वचर्या अथवा बोधिसत्त्व - शिक्षा है। आचार्य बुद्धघोष-कृत जातकट्ठकथा की निदानकथा में वर्णित है कि दीपङ्कर नामक आदि बुद्ध के युग में सुमेध नामक ब्राह्मण ने बुद्धत्व के लिए अभिनीहार (दृढ़ सङ्कल्प) किया। सुमेध द्वारा अश्रान्त परिश्रम करने के बाद ही दस पारमिताएँ प्रकट हुईं।

'पारमिता' (पालि पारमी) पद का अर्थ है सम्पूर्णत्व, परमत्व, सर्वोत्तम स्थिति। ये पारमिताएँ अपने पूर्णत्व की स्थिति में बुद्धपद की प्राप्ति का साधन बनती हैं। वस्तुतः ये हृदय में प्रतिष्ठित बुद्धकारक धर्म, शील, समाधि और प्रज्ञा-इन तीन स्कन्ध मार्ग का ही विकसित रूप है। थेरवादी (पालि) परम्परा में इनकी संख्या दस मानी गई है। वहीं महायान सम्प्रदाय में इन दस का षड्पारमिताओं में ही अन्तर्भाव किया गया है। सर्वप्रथम जातक-कथाएँ ही विविध (547) योनियों में जन्में बोधिसत्त्व के पारमिताओं का अभ्यास करने का वर्णन प्रस्तुत करती हैं। जातक-कथाओं में इन पारमिताओं के माहात्म्य को दर्शाया गया है। वस्तुतः इनकी पूर्णता में ही बुद्धत्व पद की प्राप्ति निहित है। ये वे नैतिक गुण एवं मानवीय आदर्श हैं, जिनका मूलाधार त्याग है। त्याग की विविधता के आधार पर इन पारमिताओं को तीन वर्गों में विभाजित किया जा सकता है।

उपपारमिता

जब पारमिता का पूर्णत्व किसी बाह्य वस्तु के त्याग (दान) पूर्वक किया जाए तो उसे उपपारमिता कहा जाता है जैसे अन्न, धन, वस्त्र आदि का दान।

पारमिता

जब दानादि किसी भी पारमिता की पूर्णता के लिए बोधिसत्त्व द्वारा स्वशरीराङ्ग-त्याग किया जाता है, वह पारमिता कहलाती है जैसे नेत्र, दाँत, रक्त एवं मांस आदि का त्याग।

परमार्थ पारमिता

वह परमभावोपगत गुणविशेष परमार्थ पारमिता कहलाता है, जिसकी पूर्णता बोधिसत्त्व द्वारा जीवितोत्सर्ग (प्राण-त्याग) पूर्वक की जाती है। यही त्याग की पराकाष्ठा है।[2] इस प्रकार उपर्युक्त दसों पारमिताओं के तीन-तीन भेद माने गए हैं। वस्तुतः ये पारमिताएँ बुद्धत्व - प्राप्ति में सर्वाधिक महत्त्वपूर्ण हैं।

जातकमाला (आर्यशूर-कृत)

विशुद्ध संस्कृत तथा अलङ्कृत शैली के काव्यकारों में अग्रगामी कवि आर्यशूर-कृत जातकमाला सुप्रसिद्ध हैं। पालि जातक पर आधृत इस कृति में बुद्ध के पूर्वजन्मों की 34 (चतुस्त्रिंशत्) कथाएँ उपनिषद्ध हैं, जिनमें अनेक योनियों में जन्में बोधिसत्त्व ने परम अनिवार्य दस पारमिताओं का अभ्यास किया। इन समस्त कथाओं का मुख्य प्रयोजन बोधिसत्त्व-कृत उदात्त कर्मों का प्रकाशन करना और विश्व के समक्ष सर्वोच्च आदर्श प्रस्तुत करना है। इन कथाओं के पठन एवं श्रवण से जहाँ मन में बुद्ध के प्रति श्रद्धा व आदर का भाव उत्पन्न होता है वहीं जीवन की कठिनाइयों का सामना करने, शीलाचरण करने और सुखदुःख में तटस्थ रहने की प्रेरणा मिलती है। प्रस्तुत शोध-लेख में बोधिसत्त्व के शोभन कृत्यों का वर्णन करते हुए, दस पारमिताओं को जातकमाला में खोजने का विनम्र प्रयास किया गया है। यहाँ दस पारमिताओं का वर्णन प्रसङ्गप्राप्त है। ये दस पारमिताएँ हैं—

(1) दान-पारमिता

(2) शील-पारमिता

(3) नैष्क्रम्य-पारमिता

(4) प्रज्ञा-पारमिता

(5) वीर्य-पारमिता

(6) क्षान्ति-पारमिता

(7) सत्य-पारमिता

(8) अधिष्ठान-पारमिता

(9) मैत्री-पारमिता तथा

(10) उपेक्षा-पारमिता

इस प्रकार प्रत्येक जातक-कथा किसी भी एक पारमिता को प्रमुख रूप से प्रकट करती है किन्तु कहीं कहीं एक जातक में एक से अधिक पारमिताएँ भी द्रष्टव्य हैं।

1. दान पारमिता

पारमिताओं में प्रथम एवं शीर्षस्थ दान-पारमिता महायान की प्रवर्तिका है । दान का सामान्य अर्थ 'त्याग' है, त्याग युक्त चेतना ही दान है । अभिधर्मकोश के अनुसार 'दीयते येन तद्दानम् पूजानुग्रहकामनया' ।[3] वही दान सर्वोत्तम है जिसमें चित्त-सौमनस्य, ज्ञान और कुशल (अलोभ, अद्वेष, अमोह) हेतु—तीनों का समावेश होता है । अर्थात् दान, दानफल की इच्छा (स्पृहा) से रहित होना चाहिए । निदान-कथा में इसकी उपमा ऐसे जलाप्लावित, उलटे हुए घट से दी गई है जो अपने को पूर्ण रिक्त करता हुआ पुनः जल पाने की आशा न रखकर जल-त्याग करता है ।[4] अतएव फलासक्ति रहित धन, पुत्र, शरीराङ्ग आदि का सर्वस्व परित्याग ही दानपारमिता का पूर्णत्व है । शान्तिदेव-कृत शिक्षा-समुच्चय के अनुसार-'दानं हि बोधिसत्त्वस्य बोधिरिति ।'[5] जातकमाला में बोधिसत्त्व द्वारा किए गए ऐसे उदात्त दान-कृत्यों की अनेक कथाएँ (दृष्टान्त) उदाहरणार्थ प्रस्तुत हैं । सर्वप्रथम बोधिसत्त्व द्वारा अन्न, धन, वस्त्रादि बाह्य वस्तुओं के त्यागपूर्वक दानरूप उपपारमिताएँ द्रष्टव्य हैं यथा—

(क) कुल्माषपिण्डी-जातक (3/21-23), श्रेष्ठि-जातक (4), अविषह्यश्रेष्ठि-जातक (5/15,23), अगस्त्य-जातक (7), दुम्मेघ-जातक (10) आदि ।

(i) कुल्माषपिण्डी-जातक[6] में प्रसन्न चित्त से सत्पात्र को अल्प कुलथी की दाल (साग) का दान करने के परिणामस्वरूप बोधिसत्त्व ने अग्रिम जन्म में वैभवशाली कोशल देश का स्वामित्व (राजा-पद) पाया ।

(ii) श्रेष्ठि-जातक[7] के अनुसार श्रेष्ठि-कुलोत्पन्न बोधिसत्त्व को दान देने से रोकते हुए पापी मार (विघ्न) ने प्रचण्ड ज्वालाओं से युक्त महारौरव नामक नरक तैयार किया किन्तु उन्होंने भयभीत हुए बिना उस नरक को पार करके भी, निस्पृह महादान (अन्न) दिया । उन्होंने कहा कि मेरा यह दान आत्मसुख के लिए नहीं, अपितु लोककल्याण (भावना) के लिए है । **दानं हि मे लोकहितार्थमिष्टं नेदं स्वसौख्योदयसाधनाय ।**[8]

(iii) अगस्त्य-जातक[9] में अगस्त्य नामक तपस्वी-रूप में बोधिसत्त्व ने तपोवन में निवास किया । वहाँ भी आए हुए अतिथि को निरन्तर पाँच दिनों तक अपने भोजन (उबाले हुए पत्ते) का दान किया । इसमें उदात्त दान-भावना का प्रतिपादन हुआ है ।[10] इस प्रकार उपर्युद्धृत उद्धरणों में अन्न भोजनादि के त्याग द्वारा दान उपपारमिता स्पष्ट हैं ।

(ख) तदनन्तर यहाँ वे कथाएँ सङ्कलित हैं जिनमें बोधिसत्त्व ने शरीराङ्ग —नेत्र, बाहु, मांसादि का प्रसन्नतापूर्वक त्याग किया । यथा—

शिबि-जातक (2), मैत्रीबल-जातक (8) तथा विश्वन्तर-जातक (9)

(i) दान पारमिता का सर्वश्रेष्ठ उदाहरण सुप्रसिद्ध शिबि-जातक[11] में स्पष्ट है । राजा शिवि की दानवीरता बौद्ध ग्रन्थों में ही नहीं अपितु पुराणों में भी प्रसिद्ध है । यहाँ वर्णित जातक-कथानुसार बोधिसत्त्व (शिवि-कुमार) की दानप्रियता से विस्मित हुए शक्र ने नेत्रहीन ब्राह्मण का रूप धारण किया और याचक रूप में बोधिसत्त्व से एक

नेत्र की याचना की । नेत्रत्याग की उदात्त भावना से प्रसन्न होकर बोधिसत्त्व ने कहा-'आप मेरी एक आँख चाहते हैं, मैं आपको अपनी दोनों आँखें देता हूँ ।' आकाङ्क्षमाणाय मदेकमक्षि ददामि चक्षुर्द्वयमप्यहं ते ।[12] यहाँ याचक को अपने दोनों नेत्र सहर्ष दान करते हुए बोधिसत्त्व ने दानपारमिता पूर्ण की ।

(ग) यहाँ बोधिसत्व द्वारा अपने प्राणों के त्याग द्वारा दान-परमार्थ पारमिता में पूर्णत्व प्राप्त करने की कथाओं को उपस्थित किया गया है यथा—

व्याघ्री-जातक (1), शश-जातक (6), महाकपि-जातक (27) तथा हस्ति-जातक (30) ।

(i) व्याघ्री-जातक[13] नामक सुप्रसिद्ध कथा बोधिसत्त्व के जीवित-त्याग का उत्कृष्ट उदाहरण प्रस्तुत करती है । इसमें बोधसत्त्व (आचार्य) ने एक समय वनगिरि में अपने नवप्रसूत शिशुओं को आहारनिमित्त देखती हुई क्षुधापीड़ित बाघिन को देखा । तब करुणावान् बोधिसत्त्व ने स्वयं को उस बाघिन के भोजन के लिए पहाड़ से गिरा दिया । इस प्रकार उन्होंने आत्मोत्सर्ग पूर्वक दान-परमार्थ पारमिता में पूर्णत्व प्राप्त किया ।

(ii) शश-जातक[14] कथा दान-परमार्थ पारमिता को प्रकट करती है । इसमें शशकयोनि में जन्म लेकर बोधिसत्त्व ने अपने शरीर से अतिथि का स्वागत करते हुए उन्हें भोजनार्थ आमन्त्रित करते हुए कहा—

यदस्ति यस्येप्सिनसाधनं धनं स तन्नियुङ्क्तेऽर्थिसमागमोत्सवे ।
न चास्ति देहादधिकं च मे धनं प्रतीच्छ सर्वस्वमिदं यतो मम ।।[15]

जिसके पास जो उपयोगी साधन होता है, वह उसी से अतिथि का सत्कार करता है । मेरे पास इस शरीर से अधिक कुछ नहीं है । अतएव आप मेरे इस (शरीरोत्सर्ग-रूप) सर्वस्व को स्वीकार करें ।

(iii) महाकपि-जातक[16] में वानरयोनि में उत्पन्न हुए बोधिसत्त्व ने अपने प्राणों को देकर भी अपने आश्रित वानर-समूह की सैनिकों से रक्षा की ।

(iv) हस्ति-जातक[17] में हाथी के रूप में जन्में बोधिसत्त्व ने मरुभूमि में भटकते हुए क्षुधार्त 700 मनुष्यों के प्राण अपना शरीर देकर बचाए । अपने शरीर को पर्वत से गिराकर वे उन मनुष्यों के लिए भोजन-रूप बने । एवम् उपर्य्युद्धृत कथाएँ दान-परमार्थ पारमिता के चरमोत्कर्ष को सुन्दर व अद्भुत रूप से प्रस्तुत करती हैं ।

2. शील पारमिता

शील अथवा सदाचार बौद्ध साधना का मूलाधार है । इसी पर ब्रह्मचर्य जीवन की सफलता तथा बोधिसत्त्वचर्या अवलम्बित है । व्यापक अर्थ में शील से अभिप्राय कुशल कार्यों के सम्पादन से है । संसार में शील ही श्रेष्ठ एवम् उत्तम आचरण का आधार है । शं।ल का कायेन, वाचा तथा मनसा पालन (संयमसम्पन्न होकर) करना अनिवार्य है । निदानकथा में शील-परिपालन के विषय में कहा गया है 'जिस प्रकार टिटहरी अपने अण्डों की, चमरी गाय अपनी पूँछ की, माता अपने एकमात्र पुत्र की और काना अपने एक नेत्र की रक्षा जीवन की चिन्ता

न करते हुए भी (प्रयत्नपूर्वक) करता है, उसी प्रकार शील की एकमात्र रक्षा करना अनिवार्य है।'[18] बौद्धधर्म में गृहस्थों के लिए 'पञ्चशील' और भिक्षुओं के लिए 'दसशील' का पालन परम कर्त्तव्य माना गया है। धर्माचरण के मूलमन्त्र ये दस कुशल कर्म निम्नलिखित हैं—

(i) प्राणातिपात-विरति (अहिंसा)

(ii) अदत्तादान-विरति (अचोरी)

(iii) मृषावाद-विरति (सत्यभाषण)

(iv) काममिथ्याचार-विरति (अव्यभिचार)

(v) सुरामैरेय-विरति (मद्यपान न करना)

(vi) नृत्यगीतवादनत्रय-विरति

(vii) गन्धमाल्यविलेपन-विरति

(viii) उच्चशयनमहाशयन-विरति

(ix) अकालभोजन-विरति (संयमित आहार)

(x) जातरूपरजतप्रतिग्रहण-विरति (सुवर्ण ग्रहण न करना)

कुशल कर्मों का सम्पादन चित्तपरिशोधन-हेतु परमावश्यक है। जातक-कथाओं में शील सदाचरण के महत्त्व को सर्वत्र दर्शाया गया है। जातकमाला में शीलपारमिता के अभ्यास में संलग्न बोधिसत्त्व के उत्कृष्ट कृत्यों का अनेक कथाओं में वर्णन प्राप्त है यथा—

अगस्त्य-जातक (7), विश्वन्तर-जातक (9), यज्ञ-जातक (10), कुम्भ-जातक (11), ब्राह्मण-जातक (12), उन्मादयन्ती-जातक (13/34), चुड्डबोधि-जातक (21), रुरु-जातक (26/38-44) और क्षान्ति-जातक (28)।

(i) विश्वन्तर-जातक[19] शील पारमिता का उत्कृष्ट दृष्टान्त है। इस के अनुसार महादानी विश्वन्तर राजपुत्र (बोधिसत्त्व) ने दानानुरागवश मङ्गल हाथी, राज्यसिंहासन, सम्पत्ति, राजमहल आदि वस्तुओं का त्याग करके[20] तपोवन का आश्रय लिया। तपोवन में उपस्थित ब्राह्मण (याचक) की परिचर्या के लिए दोनों बच्चे भी दान कर दिए। ब्राह्मण के द्वारा पीटे जाने पर वे पिता को पुकारते हुए कहते हैं—

अयं मां ब्राह्मणस्तात लतया हन्ति निर्दयः।
न चायं ब्राह्मणो व्यक्तं धार्मिका ब्राह्मणाः किल॥
यक्षोऽयं ब्राह्मणच्छद्मा नूनं हरति खादितुम्।
नीयमानौ पिशाचेन तात किं नावुपेक्षसे॥[21]

ब्राह्मण के कपट वेष में यह यक्ष निश्चय ही खाने के लिए हमारा अपहरण कर रहा है। यह पिशाच हमें लेकर जा रहा है, पिता जी ! आप हमारी उपेक्षा क्यों कर रहे हैं ?

ऐसी करुणामय पुकार को सुनकर भी बोधिसत्त्व ने सज्जन-धर्म का अनुसरण करते हुए क्रोध नहीं किया। उनकी सहनशीलता एवं क्षमाशीलता उनकी शीलपारमिता की परिचायिका है।

(ii) ब्राह्मण-जातक[22] में गुरु ने अपने शिष्यों के आचरण एवं शील की परीक्षा करने के लिए उनसे कहा कि 'मेरे दारिद्र्य-दुःख को दूर करने के लिए छिपाकर धन लाओ।' सभी शिष्यों ने गुरु की आज्ञा (अनुचित कर्म) को अपना कर्त्तव्य समझकर माना किन्तु शुद्धप्रकृति (शिष्य) बोधिसत्त्व ने चोरी को अधर्म माना। इस प्रकार प्रस्तुत कथा धर्मानुचारी, शीलवान् बोधिसत्त्व के उदात्त कृत्य एवं शीलपारमिता के महत्व को प्रकाशित करती है। वस्तुतः यहाँ शील पारमिता का चरमोत्कर्ष स्पष्ट है।

3. नैष्क्रम्य पारमिता

समस्त बौद्धवाङ्मय में 'नैष्क्रम्य' पद निष्क्रमण, अभिनिष्क्रमण अथवा वैराग्यभाव से गृहत्याग करने के अर्थ में प्रयुक्त हुआ है। नैष्क्रम्य (पालि नेक्खम्म) का सामान्य अर्थ ही संसार-त्याग है।[23] इस प्रकार नैष्क्रम्य पारमिता से अभिप्राय है जन्म मरण रूपी चक्र से मुक्ति पाने के लिए अनासक्त होकर गृहत्याग करना और इसका चरमोत्कर्ष धनवैभव युक्त राज्य को भी तृणवत् छोड़ने में है। निदानकथा में वर्णित है कि 'जिस प्रकार बहुत समय तक बन्धनागार में रहने वाले मनुष्य को उसके प्रति स्नेह नहीं रहता और वह उससे निकलने का प्रयत्न बार बार करता है उसी प्रकार सभी भवों (जन्मों) को बन्धनागार के समान जानकर मनुष्य को उनसे मुक्त होने के लिए नैष्क्रम्याभिमुख होना चाहिए।'[24]

ऐसी अनेक जातक-कथाएँ उपलब्ध हैं जिनमें मनुष्ययोनि में उत्पन्न बोधिसत्त्व गृह तथा राज्य-त्याग करके आध्यात्मिक जीवन में प्रवृत्त होते हैं यथा—

अगस्त्य-जातक (7), विश्वन्तर-जातक (9/27), अपुत्र-जातक (18/20), बिस-जातक (19), श्रेष्ठि-जातक (20/11), चुड्डबोधि-जातक (21), अयोगृह-जातक (32/45-46)। इनमें से यहाँ कुछ जातककथाएँ प्रस्तुत हैं।

(i) अगस्त्य-जातक[25] के अनुसार विपुल धन सम्पत्ति के स्वामी अगस्त्य ब्राह्मण (बोधिसत्त्व) ने गृहस्थ जीवन के दोषों और तपोमय जीवन के गुणों को जाना। तब उन्होंने चञ्चल धन को तृणवत् त्याग कर तापसोचित प्रवज्या ग्रहण की।[26] एवं संसार की असारता को जानने वाले बोधिसत्त्व ने नैष्क्रम्य पारमिता का अभ्यास किया।

(ii) श्रेष्ठि-जातक[27] नैष्क्रम्य पारमिता का सर्वोत्तम उदाहरण है। इसमें बोधिसत्त्व ने किसी राजा के यहाँ कोषाध्यक्ष होकर जन्म लिया। एक समय यह किंवदन्ती प्रसिद्ध हो गई कि बोधिसत्त्व घर छोड़कर प्रव्रजित हो गए हैं। ऐसी किंवदन्ती (जनप्रवाद मात्र) के श्रवण से ही बोधिसत्त्व ने विजन वन में निवास करने का दृढ़

सङ्कल्प किया। अतएव यहाँ जनप्रवाद मात्र को कार्य रूप में परिणत करना, सांसारिक सुखों को त्याग कर वन का आश्रय लेना ही नैष्क्रम्य पारमिता के परिचायक हैं।

4. प्रज्ञा पारमिता

प्रज्ञा का अर्थ है 'यथार्थ ज्ञान' अथवा 'भूततथता'। प्रज्ञा पारमिता का सभी पारमिताओं में सर्वश्रेष्ठ स्थान है। इसके अभ्यास द्वारा ही यथार्थ ज्ञान होता है कि समस्त पदार्थ अनित्य, अनात्म और दुःखमय हैं। संसार से निर्वेद (विरक्ति) होने पर बोधिसत्त्व निर्वाण-मार्ग पर प्रवृत्त हो जाते हैं।

निदानकथा में प्रज्ञापारमिता के लिए प्रेरित करते हुए कहा गया है कि 'जिस प्रकार भिक्षु हीनादि भाव को त्यागकर सभी घरों में समान रूप से जाकर भिक्षा प्राप्त करते हैं, उसी प्रकार उच्च निम्न की भावना से रहित होकर बोधिसत्त्व को सभी विद्वज्जनों से तत्त्व की गवेषणा करते हुए प्रज्ञापारमिता में पूर्णत्व प्राप्त करना चाहिए।[28] जातकमाला की अनेक कथाओं में यह पारमिता द्रष्टव्य है यथा—

अगस्त्य-जातक (7), मैत्रीबल-जातक (8/55), विश्वन्तर-जातक (9), सुपारग-जातक (14), अपुत्र-जातक (18/20), बिस-जातक (19), चुड्डबोधि-जातक (21), महाबोधि-जातक (23), क्षान्ति-जातक (28/21), ब्रह्म-जातक (29), अयोगृह-जातक (32/7-9, 14, 41) आदि।

(i) अगस्त्य-जातक[29] के अनुसार ब्राह्मणकुलोत्पन्न बोधिसत्त्व ने समस्त वेद-वेदाङ्गों का अध्ययन किया। उन्होंने गृहस्थ जीवन को प्रमाद का घर, शान्ति-विरोधी, विपत्ति-मूल और अतृप्तिजनक माना और मृत्यु की अनिवार्यता को जानकर उन्होंने कहा—

पुनःपुनर्जातिरतीव दुःखं जराविपद्व्याधिविरूपताश्च।
मर्तव्यमित्याकुलता च बुद्धेर्लोकानतस्त्रातुमिति स्थितोऽस्मि॥[30]

बार बार जन्म कष्टकारक है, रूप को कुरूप करने वाली वृद्धावस्था और रोग दुःखकारक है। 'मरना ही है' ऐसा सोचकर ही बुद्धि व्याकुल हो जाती है। अतएव प्राणियों की रक्षा के लिए मैं स्थित हूँ। यहाँ सांसारिक निःसारता को जानने वाले बोधिसत्त्व ने प्रज्ञापारमिता का अभ्यास किया।

(ii) महाबोधि-जातक[31] में परिव्राजक बोधिसत्त्व ने मिथ्यावादी विचारों का अकाट्य तर्कों से खण्डन किया और प्रज्ञा के आधार पर धर्मपरायण होकर लोककल्याण करने का उपदेश दिया।

(iii) अयोगृह-जातक[32] कथानुसार विनयसम्पन्न राजवंश में जन्मे बोधिसत्त्व ने कौमुदी-महोत्सव के शुभपर्व पर नगर की शोभा का आनन्द लेने के अवसर पर वैराग्य का अनुभव किया और सोचा कि जब मृत्यु अजेय शत्रु है तो मनुष्य के लिए आनन्द का अवसर ही कहाँ है? यथा—

कृपणा बत लोकस्य चलत्वविरसा स्थितिः ।
यदियं कौमुदीलक्ष्मीः स्मर्तव्यैव भविष्यति ।।[33]

अस्थिरता के कारण संसार की स्थिति दुःखमय और दयनीय है । शीघ्र ही कौमुदी-महोत्सव की यह शोभा भी स्मरण-शेष रह जाएगी ।

इमामवेत्याप्रतिवार्यरौद्रतां कृतान्तशत्रोर्भवने न मे मतिः ।[34]

मृत्यु रूपी शत्रु की रौद्रता का निवारण नहीं किया जा सकता, यह जानकर मेरा घर में रहने का विचार नहीं है । इस प्रकार यथार्थ ज्ञान हो जाने पर बोधिसत्त्व ने तपोवन के आश्रयपूर्वक प्रज्ञापारमिता का अभ्यास किया ।

5. वीर्य पारमिता

वीर्य पद का अर्थ है श्रम, परिश्रम, प्रयत्न तथा पराक्रम । वीर्य पारमिता से अभिप्राय है-प्राणियों की रक्षा पूर्ण उत्साह से प्रमाद रहित होकर करना और आध्यात्मिक साधना के लिए प्रयत्नरत एवम् उत्साहशील रहना । निदानकथा में इसका दृष्टान्त देते हुए बताया गया है कि 'जिस प्रकार सिंह सभी अवस्थाओं में दृढ़ उत्साह पूर्वक रहता है उसी प्रकार सभी योनियों तथा अवस्थाओं में दृढ़ उद्योगी, अनासक्त तथा वीर्यवान् होकर बुद्धत्व प्राप्ति करनी चाहिए ।'[35]

जातकमाला में अनेक कथाएँ वीर्यपारमिता की प्रतिपादक हैं, क्योंकि उत्साह के बिना किसी भी पारमिता की पूर्णता नहीं हो सकती । यथा—

व्याघ्री-जातक (1), शिबि-जातक (2), श्रेष्ठि-जातक (4), शश-जातक (6), मैत्रीबल-जातक (8), सुपारग-जातक (14), हंस-जातक (22), महाकपि-जातक (27) और सुतसोम-जातक (31) आदि ।

(i) सुपारग-जातक[36] में नाविक-रूप में उत्पन्न हुए बोधिसत्त्व के प्रयत्नशील होने का परिचय मिलता है । इसमें उन्होंने भयङ्कर, प्रचण्ड वेगवान् बडवानल में घिरे जलयान को अपने पुण्यबल से सकुशल लौटाया । एवं विपत्तिग्रस्त मनुष्यों की रक्षा करके बोधिसत्त्व ने वीर्य पारमिता का अनुशीलन किया ।

6. क्षान्ति पारमिता

'क्षान्ति' पद सहनशीलता एवं क्षमाशीलता के अर्थ में प्रयुक्त हुआ है । क्रोध न करते हुए शत्रु को भी क्षमा कर देना क्षान्ति पारमिता है । निदानकथानुसार 'जिस प्रकार पृथ्वी पवित्र अथवा अपवित्र वस्तु को फेंकने वालों के प्रति समरस रहती है, दोनों प्रकार की वस्तुओं को सहनकर स्वीकार कर लेती है, इसी प्रकार निन्दा-प्रशंसा, मान-अपमान आदि को अनासक्त भाव से सहना ही क्षान्ति पारमिता है ।'[37]

जातकमाला की निम्नोक्त कथाओं में इसके दृष्टान्त उपलब्ध हैं यथा—

विश्वन्तर-जातक (9), चुड्डबोधि-जातक (21), महाकपि-जातक (24), शरभ-जातक (25), रुरु-जातक (26), क्षान्ति-जातक (28/23, 29, 55), अयोग्रह-जातक (32/11-14, 16), महिष-जातक (33) और शतपत्र-जातक (34)।

(i) चुड्डबोधि-जातक[38] कथा में तपस्वी चुड्डबोधि (बोधिसत्त्व) की पत्नी (प्रव्रजिता) के शोभन रूप से आकर्षित होकर नृप द्वारा उसका अपहरण कर लिया जाता है। इस पर भी बोधिसत्त्व क्रोध किए बिना राजा को क्षमा कर देते हैं और शान्ति तथा उपदेशपूर्वक उन्हें क्रोध के दुष्परिणामों[39] से अवगत कराते हैं। वस्तुतः यह कथा बोधिसत्त्व की क्षमाशीलता एवं क्षान्ति पारमिता की परिचायक है।

(ii) क्षान्ति-जातक[40] क्षमाशीलता के चरमोत्कर्ष का सर्वश्रेष्ठ उदाहरण है। इसमें क्षान्तिवादी (बोधिसत्त्व) तपस्वी के प्रति राजा ने दुर्व्यवहार किया। ईर्ष्यालु राजा ने अपनी स्त्रियों से उन्हें आवृत देखकर प्रवचन देने वाले बोधिसत्त्व पर शस्त्र से प्रहार किए और क्रूरतापूर्वक दोनों हाथ, नाक, कान तथा पैर काट दिए, इतने पर भी बोधिसत्त्व की क्षमा अक्षुण्ण बनी रही। बोधिसत्त्व नृशंस राजा को आशीर्वाद देते हुए बोले—

चिरं जीवत्वसौ राजा मा चैनं पापमागमत्॥[41]

'वह राजा चिरकाल तक जिए और उन्हें (कोई) पाप न लगे।' इस प्रकार प्रस्तुत दृष्टान्त क्षान्ति पारमिता में पूर्णत्व का परिचायक है।

7. सत्य पारमिता

सत्य-पारमिता से अभिप्राय है 'सत्यभाषण' अर्थात् सत्य की रक्षा में अपने प्राणों की भी चिन्ता न करना। सत्यपारमिता का अर्थ हुआ प्राणप्रण से भी सत्यरक्षण में बद्धचित्त रहना। दसशील (शिक्षापदों) में तृतीय (मृषावाद-विरति) असत्य भाषण से विरति है। भयङ्कर भय, प्रलोभन अथवा इच्छा वश असत्य कथन नहीं करना चाहिए। निदानकथानुसार 'जिस प्रकार शुक्र (औषधि) तारा कभी भी अपने मार्ग को छोड़कर अन्य किसी मार्ग से नहीं जाता, उसी प्रकार सत्य के अतिरिक्त कोई मार्ग नहीं है।'[42] जातकमाला में सत्यपारमिता के अनेक दृष्टान्त वर्णित हैं यथा—

शिबि-जातक (2/36-37), सुपारग-जातक (14), मत्स्य-जातक (15), वर्तकापोतक-जातक (16), श्रेष्ठि-जातक (20), सुतसोम-जातक (31/22, 43-45, 57-58) आदि।

(i) सुतसोम-जातक[43] में सत्य पारमिता में पूर्णता सिद्ध होती है। इसमें राजकुमार सौदास को राजा सुतसोम (बोधिसत्त्व) ने सत्यनिष्ठा और सदुपदेश द्वारा प्राणिहिंसा तथा नर-मांस-भक्षण से निवृत्त किया। सत्य के कारण ही सौदास ने उन्हें सौ राजकुमारों (बन्दी) सहित मुक्त कर दिया। अन्ततोगत्वा बोधिसत्त्व ने सौदास

को सत्यवचनों के गुणों का महत्त्व बताया। वस्तुतः सत्यवचन सज्जनों का अभीष्ट है, पुण्य और कीर्ति का आलय है। एवम् अपने जीवन, सुख और ऐश्वर्य की उपेक्षा करके सत्य की रक्षा करने वाले बोधिसत्त्व की सत्यपारमिता दर्शनीय है।

जातकमाला में शिबि-जातक (2/36-37), सुपारग-जातक (14), मत्स्य-जातक (15) और वर्तका-पोतक-जातक (16) आदि कथाओं में 'सत्य-क्रिया' का प्रतिपादन हुआ है। बोधिसत्त्व सत्यादि जिन पारमिताओं में पूर्णत्व प्राप्त कर चुके, उनके बल पर वे अपने अथवा लोगों के कल्याणार्थ सत्यक्रिया करते हैं यथा—

(ii) सुपारग-जातक[44] में बोधिसत्त्व (नाविक) ने बडवानल से अपने जलयान की रक्षा के लिए 'सत्य-क्रिया' करते हुए कहा—

स्मरामि यत आत्मानं यतः प्राप्तोऽस्मि विज्ञताम्।
नाभिजानामि सञ्चिन्त्य प्राणिनं हिंसितुं क्वचित्॥
अनेन सत्यवाक्येन मम पुण्यबलेन च।
बडवामुखमप्राप्य स्वस्ति नौर्विनिवर्तताम्॥[45]

'होश सम्भालने से लेकर, ध्यान करने पर भी मुझे ज्ञात नहीं होता कि मैंने कभी किसी प्राणी की हिंसा की हो' इस सत्यवचन और मेरे पुण्यबल से जहाज बडवानल में प्रविष्ट हुए बिना ही सकुशल लौट जाए। इस सत्यबल (क्रिया) से उन्होंने अनेक विपत्तिग्रस्त मनुष्यों के प्राण बचाए, अतः यहाँ सत्य पारमिता स्पष्ट है।

8. अधिष्ठान पारमिता

'अधिष्ठान' का अर्थ दृढ़ निश्चय है। कुशल-कर्म एवं जन (पर) कल्याण में दृढ़निश्चय रहना अधिष्ठान पारमिता है। निदानकथा में इसके विषय में वर्णित है कि 'जिस प्रकार पर्वत सभी दिशाओं से प्रताड़ित वायु द्वारा भी प्रकम्पित नहीं होता, उसी प्रकार लक्ष्य-विनिश्चय के प्रति अडिग तथा अचल रहकर ही अभीप्सित पदार्थ की प्राप्ति की जा सकती है।'[46] इस प्रकार विमुक्ति, बुद्ध-पद और सर्वज्ञता-प्राप्ति के लिए दृढ़ सङ्कल्प रहना अधिष्ठान पारमिता में पूर्णत्व प्राप्त करना है। जातकमाला में इसको प्रकाशित करने वाली कथाएँ निम्नलिखित हैं यथा—

व्याघ्री-जातक (1/29), शिवि-जातक (2), श्रेष्ठि-जातक (4), अविषह्यश्रेष्ठि-जातक (5), विश्वन्तर-जातक (9), श्रेष्ठि-जातक (20), हंस-जातक (22), महाकपि-जातक (27/9) तथा सुतसोम-जातक (31)।

(i) शिबि-जातक[47] में अधिष्ठान पारमिता स्पष्ट है। इसके अनुसार (बोधिसत्त्व) राजा शिवि, याचक ब्राह्मण (शक्र) को नेत्रदान करने के लिए दृढ़ सङ्कल्प हैं। राजा के अमात्यों, प्रधानमन्त्री आदि द्वारा उन्हें नेत्रदान से रोकते हुए अनेक प्रकार से समझाया जाता है किन्तु वे अपनी दान-प्रतिज्ञा पर स्थिर तथा दृढ़सङ्कल्प रहते हुए बोले—

दास्यामीति प्रतिज्ञाय योऽन्यथा कुरुते मनः ।
कार्पण्यानिश्चितमतेः कः स्यात्पापतरस्ततः ।।[48]

दूँगा, ऐसी प्रतिज्ञा करके जो अपने विचार को बदलता है, जो कृपणतावश अपने निश्चय को छिन्न करता है, उससे बढ़कर पापी कौन है ?

इस प्रकार सर्वज्ञताप्राप्ति के उपायभूत विभिन्न शीलादि पारमिताओं के पूर्णत्व में बोधिसत्त्व स्थिर-निश्चय रहे । अतः यहाँ अधिष्ठान पारमिता सिद्ध होती है ।

9. मैत्री पारमिता

बौद्धधर्म में प्राणिमात्र के प्रति मैत्री अथवा सौहार्द भाव पर विशेष बल दिया गया है । ब्रह्मविहारों में मैत्री का प्रथम स्थान है । प्राणियों के प्रति करुणा, उदारता, अहिंसा तथा कल्याण की भावना ही वस्तुतः मैत्री पारमिता है । निदानकथा में इसकी उपमा जल से दी गई है 'जिस प्रकार जल पापी व पुण्यात्मा दोनों के प्रति समान भाव रखते हुए शीतलता प्रदान करता है, उसी प्रकार शत्रु अथवा मित्र सभी प्राणियों के प्रति समान मैत्री-भाव से युक्त होना चाहिए' ।[49] जातकमाला की कथाएँ इस पारमिता में संलग्न बोधिसत्त्व के उत्कृष्ट चरित्र को प्रकट करती हैं यथा—

व्याघ्री-जातक (1), शिबि-जातक (2), मैत्रीबल-जातक (8), यज्ञ-जातक (10), शक्र-जातक (11), सुपारग-जातक (14), मत्स्य-जातक (15), हंस-जातक (22/25, 35, 44), महाकपि-जातक (24) तथा (27) और क्षान्ति-जातक (28/24) ।

(i) हंस-जातक[50] मैत्री पारमिता के सर्वश्रेष्ठ दृष्टान्त के रूप में प्रस्तुत है । इसमें हंसों के राजा धृतराष्ट्र के रूप में जन्में बोधिसत्त्व की मुक्ति के लिए हंस-सेनापति सुमुख अपने आप को मूल्य-रूप (बोधिसत्त्व के बदले) में अर्पित करते हैं । सौहार्द की चरमोत्कृष्टता का परिचायक उनका वचन यहाँ द्रष्टव्य है जिसमें हंसराज को जाल में फाँसने वाले व्याध के प्रति सुमुख कहते हैं—

एकेन यदि तुष्टोसि तत्त्यजैनं गृहाण माम् ।।[51]

'यदि एक (हंसश्रेष्ठ) से ही सन्तुष्ट हो तो इन्हें छोड़ दो, मुझे पकड़ लो ।' अतएव ऐसे कृतज्ञतायुक्त, धैर्यपूर्ण एवं मधुर मित्रवचनों से कठोरहृदय व्याध भी द्रवीभूत हो गया । उसने दोनों हंसों को मुक्त कर दिया । वस्तुतः यह कथा मैत्री व पारमिता का शोभन दृष्टान्त है ।

10. उपेक्षा पारमिता

पारमिता के सन्दर्भ में 'उपेक्षा' का अभिप्राय समभाव, समरस, मध्यस्थ, तटस्थ भाव से है अर्थात् लाभ-हानि, यश-अपयश, सम्मान-अपमान, सुख-दुःखादि सभी अवस्थाओं में एक समान रहना उपेक्षा पारमिता

है । असुख अदु:ख का नाम ही उपेक्षा है । निदानकथानुसार 'जिस प्रकार पृथ्वी शुचि तथा अशुचि के फेंके जाने पर मध्यस्थ बनी रहती है, उसी प्रकार सुख दु:ख के प्रति तटस्थ बने रहना ही उपेक्षा है' ।[52]

जातकमाला की अनेक कथाएँ इसकी सुन्दर निदर्शन हैं यथा—

बिस-जातक (19), चुड्डबोधि-जातक (21), महाकपि-जातक (24 तथा 27), शरभ-जातक (25), रुरु-जातक (26), क्षान्ति-जातक (28/31 से पूर्व व पश्चात् के गद्यांश) और अयोगृह-जातक (32) ।

(i) चुड्डबोधि-जातक[53]-कथानुसार किसी राजा द्वारा अपहृत बोधिसत्त्व की प्रव्रजिता पत्नी ने भय से करुण विलाप किया । सैनिकों ने घसीट कर उनका अपमान किया किन्तु तब भी (ऐसे अपमान किए जाने पर) बोधिसत्त्व क्रोध को शान्त करके क्षोभरहित होकर पूर्ववत् स्थिर रहे । इस प्रकार प्रतिकूल आचरण करने वाले राजा के प्रति बोधिसत्त्व की मध्यस्थता उनकी उत्कृष्ट उपेक्षा पारमिता की परिचायक है ।

ये समस्त जातक कथाएँ भगवान् बुद्ध के पूर्व जन्मों की घटनाओं के रूप में श्रोताओं के मन व मस्तिष्क को प्रभावित करती हैं । इनमें आध्यात्मिक आनन्द, मानव हृदय की भावनाओं के साथ-साथ परोपकार एवं त्याग (बलिदान) के आदर्श भी निहित हैं । नैतिक शिक्षा देने वाली ये कथाएँ अमूल्य हैं ।

वस्तुत: पारमिता के माहात्म्य की प्रकाशक जातक-कथाएँ पारमिता पद को पूर्णत: सार्थक करती हैं । ये दस पारमिताएँ ही दस बुद्धकारक धर्म भी हैं जिनका बोधिसत्त्व ने चार असंख्येय एक लाख वर्ष पर्यन्त विभिन्न योनियों में परिपालन किया । इन दस पारमिताओं के अभ्यास एवम् इनमें पूर्णता द्वारा बोधिसत्त्व बुद्धपद अथवा सर्वज्ञता के अधिकारी बने ।

सन्दर्भ-सङ्केत

1. बोधि (ज्ञान) के लिए प्रयत्नशील प्राणी, जो भविष्य में 'बुद्ध' होगा, 'बोधिसत्त्व' कहलाता है ।
2. 'अङ्गपरिच्चागो पारमियो नाम, बहिरभण्डपरिच्चागो उपपारमियो नाम, जीवितपरिच्चागो परमत्थपारमियो नामाति' । निदानकथा, महेश तिवारी संस्करण, पृ. 62
3. अभिधर्मकोश (वसुबन्धु-कृत), चतुर्थ कोशस्थान, 113 पूर्वार्द्ध, पृ.740-741
4. निदानकथा, दूरे निदान, महेश तिवारी संस्करण, पृ.48
5. शिक्षासमुच्चय (शान्तिदेव-कृत), रत्नमेघ, पृ.34
6. जातकमाला (आर्यशूर-कृत), जातक कथा-3, पृ.24-31
7. जा.मा., जा.क.-4, पृ.30-37
8. जा.मा.- 4/16 का उत्तरार्द्ध
9. जा.मा., जा.क.- 7, पृ.56-69

10. जा.मा.-7/8
11. जा.मा.,जा.क.-2, पृ.10-25
12. जा.मा.- 2/13 का उत्तरार्द्ध
13. जा.मा.,जा.क.-1, पृ.1-11,
14. जा.मा.,जा.क.- 6, पृ.46-57
15. जा.मा.- 6/30
16. जा.मा.,जा.क.-27,पृ.292-301
17. जा.मा.,जा.क.- 30, पृ.332-345
18. निदानकथा,दूरे निदान,पृ.50
19. जा.मा.,जा.क.-9, पृ.86-113
20. जा.मा.- 9/6
21. जा.मा.- 9/65-66
22. जा.मा.,जा.क.- 12, पृ.130-137
23. पालि-हिन्दी-कोश, आनन्द कौसल्यायन,पृ.179
24. निदानकथा,दूरे निदान,पृ.50-53
25. जा.मा.,जा.क.-7, पृ.56-69
26. जा.मा.- 7/2 के बाद गद्यांश,पृ.56
27. जा.मा.,जा.क.- 20, पृ.196-207
28. निदानकथा,दूरे निदान,पृ.52
29. जा.मा.,जा.क.- 7, पृ.56-69
30. जा.मा.- 7/12
31. जा.मा.,जा.क.- 23,पृ.238-259
32. जा.मा.,जा.क.- 32, पृ. 312-385
33. जा.मा.- 32/7
34. जा.मा.- 32/41 का पूर्वार्द्ध
35. निदानकथा,दूरे निदान,पृ.54.
36. जा.मा.,जा.क.- 14, पृ.150-161
37. निदानकथा,दूरे निदान,पृ.54-57
38. जा.मा.,जा.क.- 21, पृ.206-217
39. जा.मा.- 21/22-34
40. जा.मा.,जा.क.- 28, पृ.302-319.

41. जा.मा.- 28/62 का उत्तरार्द्ध
42. निदानकथा, दूरे निदान, पृ.56-58
43. जा.मा., जा.क.- 31, पृ.345-373
44. जा.मा., जा.क.- 14, पृ.150-161
45. जा.मा.- 14/30-31
46. निदानकथा, दूरे निदान, पृ.58
47. जा.मा., जा.क.- 2, पृ.9-25
48. जा.मा.- 2/22
49. निदानकथा, दूरे निदान, पृ.60
50. जा.मा., जा.क.- 22, पृ.216-239
51. जा.मा.- 22/47 का उत्तरार्द्ध
52. निदानकथा, दूरे निदान, पृ.60-63
53. जा.मा., जा.क.- 21, पृ.206-217

दिल्ली

जातकमाला में अलङ्कार

अञ्जुबाला

कवि आर्यशूर-कृत जातकमाला प्रथम ऐसा संस्कृत बौद्ध-ग्रन्थ है जिसमें बुद्ध-उपदेशों को पाणिनीय संस्कृत भाषा में चम्पू शैली में कवि ने संसार के समक्ष प्रस्तुत करने का स्तुत्य प्रयास किया । यह कृति गद्य-पद्य-मयी चम्पू शैली में 27 विभिन्न छन्दों में उपनिबद्ध है । जातक जो जन्—निष्ठार्थक क्त प्रत्यय तथा स्वार्थ में क प्रत्यय से बना है, का अर्थ 'बीते हुए जन्म की कथा' है । इस ग्रन्थ में विभिन्न योनियों में जन्मे गौतम बुद्ध के पूर्वजन्मों की 34 कथाएं हैं । इन सभी कथाओं में प्रधान पात्र बोधिसत्त्व हैं । कवि ने अपने काल के विषय में कुछ नहीं लिखा किन्तु बाह्यतथ्यों के आधार पर इनका काल 350 ई.—400 ई. के लगभग माना गया है । यद्यपि इस ग्रन्थ का उद्देश्य नैतिक तथा आध्यात्मिक पूर्णता है तथापि इसमें खोजने पर जो अलङ्कार पाए गए वे स्वाभाविक हैं। इन शब्दार्थोभयालङ्कारों को इस शोधपत्र में प्रस्तुत करने का प्रयास किया गया है ।

अलङ्कारों का काव्य में महत्त्वपूर्ण स्थान है । गद्य हो अथवा पद्य, उभयत्र अलङ्कारों का प्रयोग होना स्वाभाविक होता है । अलङ्कार कथन की ललित भङ्गिमा है । ये अलङ्कार तीन वर्गों में विभाजित हैं—शब्दालङ्कार, अर्थालङ्कार तथा उभयालङ्कार । जातकमाला ग्रन्थ में आर्यशूर ने अनेक अलङ्कारों का सुन्दर उपन्यास किया है ।

अनुप्रास

काव्यप्रकाश—

वर्णसाम्यमनुप्रासः ।

साहित्यदर्पण—

अनुप्रासः शब्दसाम्यं वैषम्येऽपि स्वरस्य यत् ।[1]

जहाँ स्वरों में असमानता होने पर भी यदि केवल व्यञ्जनों की समता हो तो वहाँ अनुप्रास अलङ्कार होता है । उदाहरणार्थ—

धनस्य निःसारलघोः स सारो
यद्दीयते लोकहितोन्मुखेन ।
निधानतां याति हि दीयमान-
मदीयमानं निधनैकनिष्ठम् ।।[2]

तुच्छ और असार धन का इतना ही सार है कि यह लोकहित के लिए दान दिया जाता है, क्योंकि जो कुछ दिया जाता है वह (अक्षय) निधि हो जाता है और न दिया जाने वाला धन नष्ट हो जाता है।

प्रस्तुत पद्य में स्वरों में असमानता रहते हुए भी अनेक व्यञ्जन समान दिखाई देते हैं जैसे—स, र, य, त, न ध, म। अतएव यहाँ अनुप्रासालङ्कार स्पष्ट है। अनुप्रास के अनेक भेद किये गये हैं जिनके उदाहरण जातकमाला में द्रष्टव्य हैं जैसे—लाटानुप्रास—२/१८, छेकानुप्रास—2/50, श्रुत्यनुप्रास—7/17, अन्त्यानुप्रास—14/3,22/23 आदि।

उपमा

काव्यप्रकाश—

साधर्म्यमुपमा भेदे पूर्णा लुप्ता च।

साहित्यदर्पण—

साम्यं वाच्यमवैधर्म्यं वाक्यैक्य उपमा द्वयोः॥[3]

जहाँ उपमेय और उपमान का परस्पर भेद होने पर भी दोनों की गुण, क्रियादि रूप एक धर्म के कारण समानता हो (सम्बन्ध हो), वहाँ उपमालङ्कार रहता है।

इस अलङ्कार का प्रयोग जातकमाला में बहुत मिलता है। यथा—

बोधिसत्त्वस्तु तां दृष्ट्वा धीरोऽपि करुणावशात्।
चकम्पे परदुःखेन महीकम्पादिवाद्रिराट्॥[4]

उस (व्याघ्री) को देखकर बोधसत्त्व धीर होने पर भी करुणावश दूसरे के दुःख से ऐसे कम्पित हुए जैसे कि महाकम्पन (भूकम्प) से गिरिराज काँप उठता है।

यहाँ उपमेय-बोधिसत्त्व को उपमान-गिरिराज के समान बताया गया है। दोनों में क्रिया रूप समान धर्म है-कम्पन और उपमावाची शब्द है-इव। इस प्रकार चारों तत्त्वों से युक्त यहाँ पूर्णोपमालङ्कार है। अन्यत्र यह अलङ्कार दर्शनीय है—2/6, 6/2, 33, 11/1,7-8, 12/21.

मालोपमा

काव्यप्रकाश—

एकस्यैव बहूपमाने.पादाने मालोपमा।

साहित्यदर्पण—

मालोपमा यदेकस्योपमानं बहु दृश्यते।[5]

यह अलङ्कार वहाँ होता है जहाँ एक उपमेय के अनेक उपमान विद्यमान रहते हैं। यथा—

तदभ्रवद्व्योमनि मारुतेरितं
पतत्रिसेनेव वितानवत्क्वचित्।
विसृत्य माला ग्रथितेव कुत्रचि-
त्समं समन्तान्नृपतेर्व्यकीर्यत ॥[6]

मैत्रीबल-जातक से उद्धृत इस पद्य में उन पुष्पों का वर्णन है जो वृक्षों द्वारा बरसाए गए।

वायु द्वारा प्रेरित वे फूल आकाश में कहीं बादल के समान, कहीं पक्षियों के समूह के समान, कहीं चँदोवे (वितान) के समान और कहीं गुथी हुई विशाल माला के समान एक साथ ही राजा के चारों ओर फैल गए।

यहाँ उपमेय एक है-पुष्प, जिनकी उपमा विभिन्न उपमानों-बादल, पक्षिसमूह, वितान तथा ग्रथित माला द्वारा की गई है। अतएव यहाँ मालोपमालङ्कार घटित होता है।

इसके अतिरिक्त अन्यत्र 8/11 और 13/3 के बाद के गद्यांशों में मालोपमा स्पष्ट है।

यमक

काव्यप्रकाश—

अर्थे सत्यर्थभिन्नानां वर्णानां सा पुनः श्रुतिः ॥

साहित्यदर्पण—

सत्यर्थे पृथगर्थायाः स्वरव्यञ्जनसंहतेः।
क्रमेण तेनैवावृत्तिर्यमकं विनिगद्यते ॥[7]

जहाँ अर्थ रहने पर भिन्न अर्थ वाले स्वर एवं व्यञ्जन समुदाय की पहले ही क्रम से आवृत्ति हो, वहाँ यमक अलङ्कार होता है। यथा—

अथ प्रववृते तत्र भीरूणां धृतिदारुणः।
अन्योन्यायुधनिष्पेषजर्जरावरणो रणः ॥[8]

तब वहाँ कायरों का धैर्य (संयम) विदीर्ण करने वाला संग्राम आरम्भ हुआ, जिसमें एक-दूसरे के शस्त्रों की चोट से (योद्धाओं के) कवच चूर (नष्ट) हो रहे थे।

उपर्युक्त पद्य में 'रणः' पद की आवृत्ति हुई है। इसमें प्रयुक्त प्रथम रण निरर्थक है और दूसरा सार्थक है। अतएव यहाँ यमकालङ्कार घटित होता है।

इसी प्रकार यह 3/5, 7/17, 14/19 में भी स्पष्ट है।

रूपक

काव्यप्रकाश—

तद्रूपकमभेदोयमुपमानोपमेययोः।

साहित्यदर्पण—

रूपकं रूपितारोपाद्विषये निरपह्नवे ।[9]

बिना छिपाए विषय (उपमेय) पर विषयी (उपमान) का अभेदारोप रूपक अलङ्कार कहलाता है । यथा—

त्वमत्र सन्मानससारथी रथी
स्व एव देहो गुणसूरथो रथः ।
अरूक्षताक्षो दमदानचक्रवान्
समन्वितः पुण्यमनीषयेषया ।।[10]

ब्रह्मजातकोद्धृत प्रस्तुत पद्य में बोधिसत्त्व ने राजा को धर्मोपदेश करते हुए कहा—

गुणों को उत्पन्न करने वाला आपका शरीर ही रथ है, जिसके आप रथी हैं । आपका उत्तम मन सारथि और मैत्री इसकी धुरी है । दान और संयम इसके चक्के हैं । पुण्य की इच्छा ही इसकी ईषा है ।

यहाँ राजा के शरीर (विषय) पर रथ (विषयी) का आरोप किया गया है । इसी प्रकार मन पर सारथि, मैत्री पर धुरी, दान एवं संयम पर चक्कों तथा पुण्याभिलाषा पर ईषा का आरोप बिना छिपाए किया गया है । अतएव यहाँ रूपकालङ्कार घटित होता है ।

अन्यत्र—2/16, 16/4, 19/30, 29/56 में भी रूपक दर्शनीय है ।

उत्प्रेक्षा

काव्यप्रकाश—

सम्भावनमथोत्प्रेक्षा प्रकृतस्य समेन यत् ।

साहित्यदर्पण—

भवेत्सम्भावनोत्प्रेक्षा प्रकृतस्य परात्मना ।।[11]

जहाँ अप्रकृत के रूप में प्रकृत की सम्भावना की जाए वहाँ उत्प्रेक्षा अलङ्कार होता है । यथा—

असावापूर्णशोभेन मण्डलेन हसन्निव ।
निवेदयति साधूनां चन्द्रमाः पोषधोत्सवम् ।।[12]

यह (अपने) पूर्णमण्डल की शोभा से मानो हँसता हुआ चन्द्रमा साधुओं को पोषध व्रत की सूचना दे रहा है ।

यहाँ चन्द्रमा का हँसना और सूचना देना-इन दोनों क्रियाओं की सम्भावना की गई है क्योंकि ये क्रियाएँ मनुष्य में होती हैं चन्द्रमा में नहीं । इस प्रकार प्रकृत की अप्रकृत के रूप में सम्भावना होने से उत्प्रेक्षालङ्कार स्पष्ट है ।

अन्यत्र द्रष्टव्य—1/7, 13/12, 14/32, 16/6

अर्थान्तरन्यास

काव्यप्रकाश—

सामान्यं वा विशेषो वा तदन्येन समर्थ्यते ।

यत्तु सोऽर्थान्तरन्यासः साधर्म्येणेतरेण वा ॥

साहित्यदर्पण—

सामान्यं वा विशेषेण विशेषस्तेन वा यदि ।

कार्यं च कारणेनेदं कार्येण च समर्थ्यते ॥[13]

यह वह अलङ्कार है जिसे साधर्म्य या वैधर्म्य से सामान्य का विशेष से, विशेष का सामान्य से, कार्य का कारण से या कारण का कार्य से समर्थन कहा गया है ।

यथा—

आदेयतरतां यान्ति कुलरूपगुणाद्गुणाः ।

आश्रयातिशयेनेव चन्द्रस्य किरणाङ्कुराः ॥[14]

सद्गुण किसी (उच्च) कुल या (सुन्दराकृति) रूप को प्राप्त कर और भी अधिक उपादेय हो जाता है । आश्रय की अतिशयता के कारण चन्द्रकिरणों की दीप्ति बढ़ती ही है ।

यहाँ सद्गुण रूपी सामान्य का चन्द्रकिरण आदि विशेष से समर्थन-रूप अर्थान्तरन्यास अलङ्कार दृष्टिगोचर होता है ।

अन्यत्र द्रष्टव्य—11/8, 22/88, 25/23.

परिसंख्या

काव्यप्रकाश—

किञ्चित्पृष्टमपृष्टं वा कथितं यत्प्रकल्पते ।

तादृगन्यव्यपोहाय परिसंख्या तु सा स्मृता ॥

साहित्यदर्पण—

प्रश्नादप्रश्नतो वापि कथिताद्वस्तुनो भवेत् ।

तादृगन्यव्यपोहश्चेच्छाब्द आर्थोऽथवा तदा ॥ परिसंख्या ॥[15]

कहीं प्रश्नपूर्वक अथवा बिना प्रश्न के ही वस्तु को कहे और उसी के सामान अन्य का व्यवच्छेद हो, वहाँ परिसंख्या अलङ्कार होता है । यथा—

धर्मश्च रक्षति नरं न धनं बलं वा ।

धर्मः सुखाय महते न विभूतिसिद्धिः ।[16]

धर्म ही मनुष्य की रक्षा करता है न कि धन या बल। धर्म से ही महासुख है, न कि सम्पत्ति की प्राप्ति से।

यहाँ बिना प्रश्न के 'धर्म' की विद्यमानता कहकर, धन और बल का व्यवच्छेद किया गया है जो शाब्द है। अतएव यहाँ परिसंख्या अलङ्कार स्पष्ट है।

अन्यत्र द्रष्टव्य—12/4, 19/10, 28/18, 46.

पर्याय

काव्यप्रकाश—

एकं क्रमेणानेकस्मिन् पर्यायः। अन्यस्ततोऽन्यथा॥

साहित्यदर्पण—

क्वचिदेकमनेकस्मिन् अनेकं चैकगं क्रमात्।
भवति क्रियते वा चेत्तदा पर्याय इष्यते॥[17]

जहाँ एक वस्तु क्रम से अनेक में अथवा अनेक वस्तुएं क्रम से एक में होती हैं, वहाँ पर्यायालङ्कार होता है। यथा—

निर्दुर्जनान्यनुपभुक्तसरित्तरूणि
नानाविहंगविरुतानि मृगाकुलानि।
वैडूर्यकुट्टिममनोहरशाद्वलानि
क्रीडावनाधिकसुखानि तपोवनानि॥[18]

दुर्जन रहित, निर्मल नदियों व पवित्र वृक्षों से युक्त, नाना पक्षियों से निनादित, मृगसमूह-युक्त, वैदूर्य-खचित फर्श के समान मनोहर दूर्वाच्छादित (तृणयुक्त) भूमि से युक्त (राजप्रासादों के कृत्रिम) क्रीडा-उद्यानों से अधिक तपोवन सुखकर हैं।

यहाँ एक तपोवन में अनेक वस्तुओं का क्रमशः सम्पादन होने से पर्यायालङ्कार है।

अन्यत्र द्रष्टव्य—12/4, 17/24, 28/36.

उल्लेख

काव्यप्रकाश—अनुपलब्ध।

साहित्यदर्पण—

क्वचिद् भेदाद् ग्रहीतृणां विषयाणां तथा क्वचित्।
एकस्यानेकधोल्लेखो यः स उल्लेख उच्यते॥[19]

जहाँ ग्रहीतृ-भेद या विषय-भेद से एक वस्तु का अनेकधा ग्रहण हो वहाँ उल्लेख अलङ्कार होता है।

यथा—

स ब्रह्मवद्ब्रह्मविदां बभूव
राजेव राज्ञां बहुमानपात्रम्।
साक्षात्सहस्राक्ष इव प्रजानां
ज्ञानार्थिनामर्थचरः पितेव ॥[20]

वह ब्रह्म-वेत्ताओं के लिए ब्रह्म के समान, राजाओं के लिए आदर के पात्र राजा के समान, प्रजाओं के लिए साक्षात् इन्द्र के समान और विद्यार्थियों के लिए अनुकूल व उपकारी पिता के समान थे।

प्रस्तुत पद्य में एक प्राणी (बोधिसत्त्व) के लिए ज्ञातृभेद से अनेक प्रकार का ग्रहण यथा—ब्रह्म, राजा, इन्द्र और पिता किया गया है। यहाँ उल्लेख अलङ्कार उपयुक्त है।

अन्यत्र द्रष्टव्य—31/32-34.

विषम

काव्यप्रकाश—

क्वचिद्यदतिवैधर्म्यान्न श्लेषो घटनामियात्।
कर्तुः क्रियाफलावाप्तिर्नैवानर्थश्च यद्भवेत्॥
गुणक्रियाभ्यां कार्यस्य कारणस्य गुणक्रिये।
क्रमेण च विरुद्धे यत्स एष विषमो मतः॥

साहित्यदर्पण—

गुणौ क्रिये वा चेत् स्यातां विरुद्धे हेतुकार्ययोः।
यद्वारब्धस्य वैफल्यमनर्थस्य च सम्भवः॥
विरूपयोः संघटना या च तद्विषमं मतम्॥[21]

इसके 4 प्रकार हैं—

1. अत्यन्त वैधर्म्य के कारण सम्बन्ध न बनना।

2. कर्त्ता को अपनी क्रिया का अभीष्ट फल प्राप्त न हो, व अनर्थ हो।

3. कार्य कारण के अनुरूप हो, फिर भी उन दोनों की क्रियाएं विरुद्ध हों।

4. कार्य कारण के अनुरूप हो तो भी उन दोनों के गुण विरुद्ध हों।

यथा—तृतीय प्रकार—

दृष्टावदानो व्यसनोदयेषु
वाष्पोद्गमान्मूर्त इवोपलब्धः ।
संरूढमूलोऽपि सुहृत्स्वभावः
शाठ्यं प्रयात्यत्र विनानुवृत्त्या ।।[22]

जिस मित्रता का पराक्रम विपत्ति में मैंने देखा था वह इन (बन्धुओं) के आँसुओं से मानों मूर्तरूपेण उपस्थित है किन्तु वह बद्धमूल मित्रता भी (आज) अनुकूल न होने से शठता हो रही है ।

यहाँ गृहत्याग-रूप कारण के अनुरूप वाष्पोद्गम-कार्य है किन्तु फिर भी दोनों की क्रियाएं विरुद्ध हैं । मित्रता सदैव सुखकर, अनुकूल होती है जो यहाँ शठता में परिणत हो रही है । ऐसा विरोध होने से यहाँ विषमालङ्कार घटित होता है ।

अन्यत्र—24/21.

स्वभावोक्ति

काव्यप्रकाश—

स्वभावोक्तिस्तु डिम्भादेः स्वक्रियारूपवर्णनम् ।

साहित्यदर्पण—

स्वभावोक्तिः दुरूहार्थस्वक्रियारूपवर्णनम् ।[23]

कविजन-संवेद्य, दुरूह (सूक्ष्म, कल्पनाशील) पदार्थों के स्वरूप या क्रियाओं का वर्णन करना स्वभावोक्ति अलङ्कार होता है । यथा—

मुक्ता विमुक्ता इव तैर्विमुक्ता
धारा निपेतुः प्रशशाम रेणुः ।
गन्धश्चचारानिभृतो धरण्यां
विकीर्यमाणो जलदानिलेन ।।[24]

(अपने सम्पुटों से) गिरते हुए मोतियों (की पंक्ति) के समान, मेघों से जल-धाराएं गिरीं । धूल शान्त हो गई । पृथिवी से तेज गन्ध निकली, जिसे बादलों के साथ बहने वाली वायु ने (चारों ओर) बिखेर दिया ।

यहाँ वर्षा का स्वाभाविक वर्णन होने से स्वभावोक्ति अलङ्कार है ।

अन्यत्र द्रष्टव्य—8/16, 11/5, 14/1, 17/20.

विशेषोक्ति

काव्यप्रकाश—

विशेषोक्तिरखण्डेषु कारणेषु फलावचः ।

साहित्यदर्पण—

सति हेतौ फलाभावे विशेषोक्तिस्तथा द्विधा ।[25]

जहाँ कारण विद्यमान होने पर भी कार्य का अभाव वर्णित हो, वहाँ विशेषोक्ति अलङ्कार होता है ।

यथा—

युवापि वृद्धोपशमाभिराम-
स्तेजस्व्यपि क्षान्तिसुखस्वभावः ।
विद्वानपि ज्ञानमदानभिज्ञः
श्रिया समृद्धोऽप्यवलेपशून्यः ।।[26]

युवा होने पर भी वृद्धोचित शान्ति से युक्त था, तेजस्वी होने पर भी क्षमाशील, विद्वान् होकर भी ज्ञान-मद से अनभिज्ञ और लक्ष्मीपात्र होकर भी अभिमान-शून्य था ।

यहाँ अनुक्त-निमित्ता विशेषोक्ति अलङ्कार है क्योंकि यौवन, तेज, विद्या, श्री आदि कारणों के होने पर भी क्रमशः उद्दण्डता, क्षमाराहित्य, गर्व तथा अभिमान-रूप कार्यों के अभाव का वर्णन है ।

अन्यत्र द्रष्टव्य—17/1, 21/22, 29.

विभावना

काव्यप्रकाश—

क्रियायाः प्रतिषेधेऽपि फलव्यक्तिर्विभावना ।

साहित्यदर्पण—

विभावना विना हेतुं कार्योत्पत्तिर्यदुच्यते ।[27]

जहाँ कारण के अभाव में भी कार्योत्पत्ति वर्णित हो वहाँ विभावना अलङ्कार होता है । यथा—

यस्यान्नमेतत्तु स एव राजा विनैव राजत्वपरिश्रमेण ।।[28]

जिसे ये फल प्राप्त है वही राजा है, राज्य-सञ्चालन में होने वाले परिश्रम के बिना ही राजा है ।

यहाँ परिश्रमरूपी कारण के अभाव में भी राजारूपी फल के वर्णन होने से विभावना अलङ्कार स्पष्ट है ।

अन्यत्र द्रष्टव्य—11/2, 21/22.

व्यतिरेक

काव्यप्रकाश—

उपमानाद्यदन्यस्य व्यतिरेकः स एव सः ।

साहित्यदर्पण—

आधिक्यमुपमेयस्योपमानान्न्यूनताऽथवा । व्यतिरेकः ।[29]

उपमान की अपेक्षा अन्य उपमेय के आधिक्य या न्यूनत्व के वर्णन में व्यतिरेक अलङ्कार होता है । यथा—

सुदृष्टकर्मा निपुणोऽपि शल्यहृन्न तत्प्रयत्नादपि शल्यमुद्धरेत् ।
यदुज्जहारानभियोगसिद्ध्या स मेधया जन्मशतानुबद्ध्या ।।[30]

सुपरीक्षित निपुण शल्यहारक प्रयत्नपूर्वक भी उस शल्य को नहीं निकाल सकता है, जिसे (शतपत्रपक्षि) उन्होंने जन्मपरम्परा से अनायास प्राप्त बुद्धि से निकाल दिया ।

यहाँ (उपमान) शल्यहारक की अपेक्षा (उपमेय) बोधिसत्त्व के गुणों का उत्कर्ष किया गया है । अतएव व्यतिरेक अलङ्कार है ।

यथासंख्य

काव्यप्रकाश—

यथासंख्यं क्रमेणैव क्रमिकाणां समन्वयः ।

साहित्यदर्पण—

यथासंख्यमनूद्देश उद्दिष्टानां क्रमेण यत् ।।[31]

जहाँ पूर्वोद्दिष्ट पदार्थों का क्रमशः पुनः कथन हो वहाँ यथासंख्य अलङ्कार होता है यथा—

गार्हस्थ्यं महदस्वास्थ्यं सधनस्याधनस्य वा ।
एकस्य रक्षणायासादितरस्यार्जनश्रमात् ।।[32]

धनी और निर्धन दोनों के लिए ही गृहस्थ जीवन बड़ा कष्टदायक है । एक को (धन) रक्षा में कष्ट होता है और दूसरे को उपार्जन में परिश्रम करना पड़ता है ।

यहाँ पूर्वार्द्ध में धनी और निर्धन एक बार कह दिया गया है । उत्तरार्द्ध में पुनः दोनों का यथासंख्य उद्देश है अर्थात् धनी व्यक्ति को धन-रक्षा में और निर्धन को धनोपार्जन में कष्ट होता है ऐसा अर्थ प्रयुक्त करने से यहाँ यथासंख्य अलङ्कार है ।

अन्यत्र द्रष्टव्य—3/2.

आर्यशूर-प्रणीत जातकमाला में उपन्यस्त उपरिविवेचित अलङ्कारों ने इस ग्रन्थ को अप्रतिम सौन्दर्य प्रदान किया है ।

सन्दर्भ-सङ्केत

1. काव्यप्रकाश—9/79, साहित्यदर्पण—10/3
2. जातकमाला—2/50
3. का.प्र.—10/87, सा.द.—10/14
4. जातकमाला—1/16
5. का.प्र.—10/90 के बाद, सा.द.—10/26
6. जा.मा.—8/62
7. का.प्र—9/83, सा.द.—10/8
8. जा.मा.—11/4
9. का.प्र.—10/93, सा.द.—10/28
10. जा.मा.—29/55
11. का.प्र.—10/92, सा.द.—10/40
12. जा.मा.—6/6
13. का.प्र.—10/109, सा.द.—10/61
14. जा.मा.—18/4
15. का.प्र.—10/119, सा.द.—10/81
16. जा.मा.—32/47
17. का.प्र.—10/31, सा.द.—10/79
18. जा.मा.—9/33
19. सा.द.—10/37
20. जा.मा.—1/5
21. का.प्र.—10/126-127, सा.द.—10/69-70
22. जा.मा.—20/28
23. का.प्र.—10/111, सा.द.—10/92
24. जा.मा.—15/11
25. का.प्र.—10/108, सा.द.—10/67
26. जा.मा.—9/3
27. का.प्र.—10/107, सा.द.—10/65
28. जा.मा.—27/6

29. का.प्र.—10/19, सा.द.—10/52
30. जा.मा.—34/6
31. का.प्र.—10/22, सा.द.—10/79
32. जा.मा.—18/11

दिल्ली

जातकमाला में नायकगत सात्त्विक गुण

अञ्जुबाला

संस्कृत शास्त्रकारों ने नायक में कतिपय सात्त्विक गुणों की उद्भावना की है जो नायक के मन की विशेष अवस्थाएँ हैं। सर्वप्रथम आदि आचार्य भरतमुनि सत्त्व को समाहित मन में उत्पन्न मानते हुए मन की समाधि अवस्था में ही सत्त्व-निष्पत्ति बताते हैं। आचार्य भरत-कृत **नाट्यशास्त्र** के अनुसार-'सत्त्वं नाम मनःप्रभवम्। सत्त्व समाहितमनस्त्वादुच्यते। मनसः समाधौ सत्त्वनिष्पत्तिर्भवति।'[1] इनके अनुसार अव्यक्त रूप सत्त्व रसों (तथा भावों) को उचित रीति से रोमाञ्च, अश्रु आदि गुणों के द्वारा भावाश्रित होकर अभिव्यक्त भी करता है—

अव्यक्तरूपं सत्त्वं हि विज्ञेयं भावसंश्रयम्।

यथास्थानरसोपेतं रोमाञ्चास्रादिभिर्गुणैः ॥[2]

आचार्य धनिक ने अपने ग्रन्थ **दशरूपक** में सत्त्व की परिभाषा देते हुए कहा है कि दूसरे के दुःख और हर्षादि की भावना में अन्तःकरण का अत्यन्त अनुकूल हो जाना 'सत्त्व' है—'परगतदुःखहर्षादिभावनायामत्यन्तानुकूलान्तःकरणत्वं सत्त्वम्'।[3] अन्य सभी आचायों ने इसी प्रकार अन्तःकरण की भावना विशेष को ही सत्त्वसंज्ञा से अभिहित किया है अर्थात् सत्त्व (सात्त्विक गुण) का सम्बन्ध मानसिक अवस्थाविशेष से स्वीकार किया है किन्तु आचार्य हेमचन्द्र ने शरीर के विकारों से उत्पन्न भाव को सत्त्व बताया है—'सत्त्वं देहविकारस्तस्माज्जाताः'।[4] यहाँ मानसिक अवस्थाविशेष के गुणों को ही सात्त्विक गुण मानना अधिक उचित प्रतीत होता है।

आचार्य भरत से लेकर सभी आचार्य सात्त्विक गुणों की संख्या आठ स्वीकार करते हैं—शोभा, विलास, माधुर्य, स्थैर्य (धैर्य), गाम्भीर्य, ललित, औदार्य तथा तेज—

शोभा विलासो माधुर्यं स्थैर्यं गाम्भीर्यमेव च।

ललितौदार्यतेजांसि सत्त्वभेदास्तु पौरुषाः ॥[5]

आचार्य भरत ने अभिनय के प्रसङ्ग (नाट्यशास्त्रीय दृष्टिकोण) में इनकी उद्भावना की तथापि इनका सर्वत्र (काव्यादि में भी) विशेष महत्त्व है। कविआर्यशूर-कृत जातकमाला संस्कृतनिष्ठ ऐसा बौद्ध ग्रन्थ है जिसमें भगवान् बुद्ध के पूर्वजन्मों की अलग अलग 34 कथाएँ गुम्फित हैं। इन सभी कथाओं में प्रधाननायक[6] (नेता) बोधिसत्त्व हैं। बोधिसत्त्व के महाकरुणा, त्यागभावना और निरभिलाषिता-ये गुण उनकी श्रेष्ठ मनोवृत्ति के परिचायक हैं। पारमिताओं के पूर्णत्व में संलग्न वे जनकल्याण के लिए बद्धचित्त सदैव स्वसुखों को तिलाञ्जलि

देते हुए जीवन यापन करते हैं। इनमें सर्वत्र उनके महान् और दुष्कर कार्यों तथा असह्य मनोबल का ज्ञान प्रवाहित होता है। बोधिसत्त्व स्वयं गुणों के रत्नाकर हैं।उनमें इन सात्त्विक गुणों का अस्तित्व स्वाभाविक है क्योंकि ये गुण तो अन्तःकरण की विशेष अवस्था के द्योतक हैं। आर्यशूर ने बोधिसत्त्व को सर्वत्र गुणवान् (गुणों के आश्रय) के रूप में प्रस्तुत किया है। यथा—

शीलश्रुतत्यागदयादमानां तेजः क्षमाधीधृतिसंनतीनाम्।
अनुन्नतिह्रीमतिकान्तिकीर्तिदाक्षिण्यमेधाबलशुक्लतानाम् ॥
तेषां च तेषां स गुणोदयानामलङ्कृतानामिव यौवनेन।
विशुद्धतौदार्यमनोहराणां चन्द्रः कलानामिव संश्रयोऽभूत् ॥[7]

कवि आर्यशूर की कृति में नायकगत इन सात्त्विक गुणों को ढूँढने का विनम्र प्रयास प्रस्तुत लेख में किया गया है। इन समस्त आठों सात्त्विक गुणों का एक नायक में समावेश हो, ऐसा अनिवार्य नहीं है। बौद्ध धर्म-प्रचार की दृष्टि से रची गई इस कृति में बोधिसत्त्व धर्मरक्षक व धर्मपालक के रूप में चित्रित हैं। यहाँ शोभा आदि का क्रमशः सलक्षण विवेचन प्रसङ्गप्राप्त है।

1. शोभा

नाट्यशास्त्र—

दाक्ष्यं शौर्यमथोत्साहो नीचार्थेषु जुगुप्सनम्।
उत्तमैश्च गुणैः स्पर्धा यतः शोभेति सा स्मृता ॥

दशरूपक—

नीचे घृणाधिके स्पर्धा शोभायां शौर्यदक्षते।

काव्यानुशासन—

दाक्ष्यशौर्योत्साहनीचजुगुप्सोत्तमस्पर्धागमिका शोभा।

भावप्रकाशन—

दक्षता शौर्यमुत्साहो नीचे कुत्साधिके मुहुः।
स्पर्धाधिक्रियते यत्र सा शोभेति प्रकीर्तिता ॥

साहित्यदर्पण—

शूरता दक्षता सत्यं महोत्साहोऽनुरागिता।
नीचे घृणाधिके स्पर्धा यतः शोभेति तां विदुः ॥[8]

शोभा नामक यह सात्त्विक गुण वहाँ होता है जहाँ नायक में शौर्य, दक्षता, उत्साह, सत्य, नीच के प्रति घृणा, उच्च कार्यों में स्पर्धा और अनुरागिता पाई जाती है। उदाहरणार्थ—

(1) शौर्य-शोभा

अन्त्रैः स्वैरपि संयताग्रचरणो मूर्च्छाविरामक्षणे
स्वाधीनव्रणिताङ्गशस्त्रनिचितो रोमोद्गमं वर्मयन्।
भग्नानुद्वलयन्निजान्परभटान्सन्तर्जयन्निष्ठुरं
धन्यो धाम जयाश्रियः पृथुरणस्तम्भे पताकायते ॥[9]

(यद्यपि) उस वीर के पैरों के अग्रभाग अँतडियों से बँध गये हैं (तो भी) मूर्च्छा समाप्त होते ही वे उठ खडे होते हैं। उनका शरीर घाव व संलग्न शस्त्रों से युक्त है। वीरता-सञ्चार होने से खड़े हुए रोंगटों का मानों कवच धारण किए हुए हैं। हारे हुए सैनिकों को पुनः उत्साहित करते हुए, शत्रु-सैनिकों को निष्ठुरता पूर्वक फटकार रहे हैं। वह विजयलक्ष्मी का निवास स्थान उत्कृष्ट वीर धन्य है, जो उस महान् युद्धस्थल के स्तम्भ पर पताकावत् फहरा रहा है।

रणस्थल पर घायल हुआ नायक गिरकर मूर्च्छित हो गया और मूर्च्छा के समाप्त होते ही पुनः रणस्थल में आ गया। आचार्य धनिक ने इस पद्य में धराधीश मुञ्ज के शौर्य का वर्णन किया है। अतएव यहाँ 'शौर्य-शोभा' सात्त्विक गुण स्पष्ट है।

(2) अनुरागवशिता शोभा

अहमेव मतो महीपतेरिति सर्वः प्रकृतिष्वचिन्तयत्।
उदधेरिव निम्नगाशतेष्वभवन्नास्य विमानना क्वचित् ॥[10]

महाराज (अज) का मैं ही अन्तरङ्ग हूँ, यह बात सभी मन्त्री आदि समझते थे। जैसे समुद्र सब नदियों के जल को अपने में समा लेता है, इसी प्रकार महाराज भी सबकी बात आदरपूर्वक सुनते थे, किसी की अवहेलना नहीं करते थे।

महाराज अज की समस्त मन्त्रियों के प्रति स्वाभाविक आत्मीयता अनुरागवश है। अतः उपर्युक्त पद्य अज राजा की 'अनुरागजन्य शोभा' का सुन्दर निदर्शन है।

यहाँ **जातकमाला** में नायक (बोधिसत्त्व) के दाक्ष्य (चतुरता), शौर्य, उत्साह, सत्य, नीच के प्रति घृणा (दया), उच्च के प्रति स्पर्धा और अनुरागवशिता शोभा—सात्त्विक गुण का क्रमशः विवेचन प्रस्तुत है।

(1) दाक्ष्य-शोभा

नाथः पृथिव्याः स जितेन्द्रियारिर्भुक्तावगीतेषु फलेष्वसक्तः।
प्रजाहितेष्वाहितसर्वभावो धर्मैककार्यो मुनिवद् बभूव ॥
विवेद लोकस्य हि स स्वभावं प्रधानचर्यानुकृतिप्रधानम्।
श्रेयः समाधित्सुरतः प्रजासु विशेषतो धर्मविधौ ससञ्जे ॥

ददौ धनं शीलविधिं समाददे क्षमां निषेवे जगदर्थमैहत।

प्रजाहिताध्याशयसौम्यदर्शनः स मूर्तिमान्धर्म इव व्यरोचत ।।[11]

वह जितेन्द्रिय पृथिवीपति उच्छिष्ट एवं निन्दित भोगों में अनासक्त एवं प्रजाहित-कार्यों में दत्तचित्त था धर्माचरण ही उनका एकमात्र कार्य था । उनकी वृत्ति मुनि-सदृश हो गयी थी । यह जानकर कि प्रधान पुरुष (राजा) के आचरण का अनुसरण ही लोगों (प्रजा) का स्वभाव हो गया है, वह प्रजाओं के श्रेय की इच्छा से स्वयं विशेष रूप में धर्माचरण में संलग्न हुए । उन्होंने धन-दान किया, शीलाश्रय लिया, क्षमा का सेवन और जग-कल्याण की कामना की । प्रजा-हित-चिन्तन से सौम्यदर्शन वे राजा मूर्तिमान धर्म के समान सुशोभित हुए ।

उपर्य्युद्धृत तीन पद्यों में चक्रवर्ती सम्राट् के रूप में जन्में बोधिसत्त्व के उत्तम एवं शोभन गुणों का वर्णन उनके धर्माचरण तथा प्रजाकल्याण में दाक्ष्य का परिचायक है । वह प्रजा के आशय को जानने में कुशल हैं । प्रजा-हित में व्यग्रमानस राजा के दान, शील, सत्य, क्षमादि से समृद्ध कार्य उनकी निपुणता और चारित्रिक उत्कर्ष के प्रतिपादक हैं । अतएव यहाँ नायकगत 'दाक्ष्य-शोभा' नामक सात्त्विक गुण स्पष्ट है ।

जातकमाला में यह सात्त्विक गुण अनेक स्थलों पर उपलब्ध होता है यथा—2/1-2, 3/1, 8/1, 10/32, 13/1-3.

(2) शौर्य-शोभा

अथ प्रतप्तासुरशस्त्रसायकैर्भयात्प्रदुद्राव सुरेन्द्रवाहिनी।

रथेन विष्टभ्य बलं तु विद्विषां, सुरेन्द्र एकः समरे व्यतिष्ठत ।।[12]

देवेन्द्र-रूप में उत्पन्न बोधिसत्त्व हज़ारों उत्तम घोड़ों से जुते हुए, देदीप्यमान शस्त्रों से सुशोभित, सुवर्ण निर्मित रथ पर आरूढ हुए और चतुरङ्गिणी सेना को लेकर असुरों का सामना किया ।) तब (युद्ध भूमि में) राक्षसों की प्रचण्ड तलवारों तथा तीरों से डरकर देवेन्द्र की सेना को रोककर समर में स्थिर रहे ।

प्रस्तुत पद्य में देवेन्द्र-रूप बोधिसत्त्व का दुर्जयत्व सूचित है । सेना के भाग जाने पर अकेले ही युद्धक्षेत्र में स्थिर रहना उनके 'शौर्य-शोभा' नामक सात्त्विक गुण का प्रतिपादक है ।

अन्यत्र द्रष्टव्य- 1/26-29,31-33, 8/11.

(3) उत्साह-शोभा

अयं पाशेन महता संयतश्चरणे त्वया।

गुणैरस्य तु बद्धोऽहमतो दृढतरैर्हृदि ।।

नो चेदिच्छसि मे दुःखं तत्कुरुष्व ममार्थनाम्।

एकेन यदि तुष्टोसि तत्त्यजैनं गृहाण माम् ।।[13]

तुमने महाबन्धन से इन (बोधिसत्त्व) के चरण को बाँधा है, किन्तु इससे दृढतर इनके गुणों से मेरा हृदय बँधा हुआ है। यदि मेरा दुःख (अनिष्ट) नहीं चाहते हो तो मेरी प्रार्थना पूर्ण करो। यदि तुम एक से सन्तुष्ट हो तो इन्हें छोड़ दो, मुझे पकड़ लो।

सच्चा मित्र विपत्ति में कभी साथ नहीं छोड़ता। अपने मित्र (हंसराज) को विपत्ति में देखकर सुमुख नामक हंस-सेनापति ने अपने प्राणों की चिन्ता नहीं की और समीप आए व्याध से अनुरोध किया कि 'मेरे बदले मेरे मित्र धृतराष्ट्र (बोधिसत्त्व) को छोड़ दो' ऐसे जीवननिरपेक्ष, स्वामिभक्त मित्र की बोधिसत्त्व के लिए मधुर वाणी से क्रूर व्याध का हृदय भी मृदु हो गया। यह उनके पराक्रम, उत्साह एवं वीरत्व आदि गुणों को अभिव्यक्त करता है। वस्तुतः इनमें बोधिसत्त्व की सङ्गति, पवित्र व्यक्तित्व और गुणों का ही माहात्म्य है। एवम् उपर्य्युद्धृत पद्य सुमुख हंस-सेनापति (बोधिसत्त्व-मित्र) के 'उत्साह-शोभा' रूप सात्त्विक गुण के निदर्शक हैं।

अन्यत्र द्रष्टव्य - 9/25, 27, 77.

(4) उच्च कार्यों में स्पर्धा-रूप शोभा

दानोद्भवः कीर्तिमयः सुगन्धस्तस्यार्थिना वागनिलप्रकीर्णः।
मदं जहारान्यनराधिपानां गन्धद्विपस्येव परद्विपानाम्॥[14]

दानोत्पन्न उन (शिवि नामक बोधिसत्त्व) की कीर्तिमय सुगन्ध ने, जिसे याचकों ने अपनी वाणी रूपी हवा से (दिशाओं में) फैलाया, दूसरे राजाओं के मद का अपहरण किया, जिस प्रकार गन्ध-कुञ्जर की सुगन्ध (हवा में फैलकर) दूसरे हाथियों का अभिमान चूर्ण करती है।

प्रस्तुत पद्य शिवि राजा के दानमय कार्यों का वर्णन करता है। उनकी दान-कीर्ति ने अन्य राजाओं का अभिमान चूर-चूर कर दिया। बोधिसत्त्व के जीवन का उद्देश्य याचकों को इच्छित वस्तु देकर आनन्दित करना है, इसी प्रकृति से उच्चकार्यों में उनके 'स्पर्धा-रूप शोभा' गुण की अभिव्यक्ति यहाँ हो रही है।

अन्यत्र द्रष्टव्य - 1/3, 9/77 का उत्तरार्द्ध, 31/31.

(5) नीच कार्यों के प्रति घृणा (दया) - रूप शोभा

अमृष्यमाणः स जगद्गतानां दुःखोदयानां प्रसृतावलेपम्।
दानेषुवर्षी करुणोरुचापस्तैर्युद्धसंरम्भमिवाजगाम॥[15]

वे (बोधिसत्त्व) संसार में दुःखों (के कारणों) का अनुचित प्रसार नहीं सह सकते थे अतएव करुणा का विशाल धनुष लेकर दानरूपी तीरों की वर्षा करते हुए उन्होनें मानों उनसे घोर युद्ध किया।

बोधिसत्त्व (युवराज विश्वन्तर के रूप में जन्मे) की त्रिलोकव्याप्त कीर्ति और उनके दानानुराग से प्रभावित याचकगण प्रतिदिन खिंचे आते थे और पूर्णमनोरथ होकर आनन्दित होते थे। ज्ञानगरिमासम्पन्न महासत्त्व के लिए प्रकृतिवश दुःखों का प्रसार असह्य था। अतएव करुणावश उन्होंने याचको की पीडा दान-कर्म से दूर की। यहाँ

बोधिसत्त्व दु:खों से मानों युद्ध करते हुए दर्शाये गये हैं । उनका यह पौरुष उनके 'नीच कार्यों के प्रति घृणा अथवा दया रूप शोभा' सात्त्विक गुण का परिचायक है ।

अन्यत्र द्रष्टव्य- 13/19-20.

(6) अनुरागवशिता शोभा

अनेकदु:खायतने शरीरे सदा कृतघ्नेऽपि नराधिपस्य ।

गतेऽर्थिसम्माननसाधनत्वं हर्षानुकूलं ग्रहणं बभूव ॥[16]

यद्यपि यह शरीर सदा कृतघ्न रहने वाला और अनेक दु:खों का घर है तथापि याचकों के आदर सत्कार का साधन सिद्ध हुआ, ऐसा सोचकर (बोधिसत्त्व) राजा को बहुत आनन्द हुआ ।

यहाँ बोधिसत्त्व—मैत्रीबल नामक राजा के दानानुराग की अतिशयता सूचित हो रही है । अपने शरीर-मांस और रक्त का दान यक्षों को देने के आनन्द से उनके नेत्र व मुखमण्डल खिल उठे और हृदय दान देने की प्रसन्नता से आपूर्ण हो गया । धर्मानुरागी, दानवीर तथा महाकारुणिक बोधिसत्त्व का अनुराग स्वाभाविक है । इस प्रकार यहाँ 'अनुरागवशिता शोभा' नामक सात्त्विक गुण स्पष्ट है । इसके अतिरिक्त दान-औदार्य रूप सात्त्विक गुण भी व्यञ्जित है ।

अन्यत्र द्रष्टव्य-2/3, 31/95.

2. विलास

नाट्यशास्त्र—

धीरसञ्चारिणी दृष्टिर्गतिर्गोवृषभाञ्चिता ।

स्मितपूर्वमथालापो विलास इति कीर्तितः ॥

दशरूपक—

गतिः सधैर्या दृष्टिश्च विलासे सस्मितं वचः ॥

काव्यानुशासन—

धीरे गतिदृष्टी सस्मितं वचो विलासः ॥

भावप्रकाशन—

वृषयानं स्मितालापो विलास इति कथ्यते ॥

साहित्यदर्पण—

धीरा दृष्टिर्गतिश्चित्रा विलासे सस्मितं वचः ।[17]

जहाँ नायक की दृष्टि में धैर्य, गति में गो तथा वृषभ के समान विचित्रता, वाणी में माधुर्य (मधुरवाणी), स्मितपूर्वक भाषण, शुभाकृति और सम्पद् विपद् में समता होती है, वहाँ 'विलास' नामक सात्त्विक गुण कहा जाता है यथा—

सुधासोदारवाचस्ते स्मितपूर्वाभिभाषण: ।
को नामार्थी न तुष्टः स्यादलं तावद्धनागमैः ।।[18]

मुस्कुराते हुए अमृत-सदृश आपके मीठे कथन से ही ऐसा कौन याचक है जो सन्तुष्ट नहीं हो जाता, फिर आगे धनप्राप्ति की बात ही क्यों कही जाए ?

(1) उत्तप्तचामीकरसंनिकाशं श्रीमद्वपुर्व्यक्तपदाक्षरा वाक् ।
धर्माभिजातो विनयो नयश्च काव्यप्यमू केवलहंसवेषौ ।।[19]

तपे हुए (प्रदीप्त) सोने के समान शोभन शरीर, स्पष्ट अक्षरों वाली वाणी, धैर्य-जन्य विनम्रता और नीति से युक्त वे (दोनों बोधिसत्त्व हंस-राज तथा उनका हंस-सेनापति) केवल हंस के वेष (मात्र) में थे, (किन्तु वस्तुत:) वे कोई (महात्मा पुरुष) थे ।

यहाँ बोधिसत्त्व की रूपराशि और शुभाकृति का मनोरम चित्रण उनके 'विलास' सात्त्विक गुण का द्योतक है । अन्यत्र द्रष्टव्य- 2/9 के बाद गद्यांश, 3/19, 5/16, 6/1, 24, 7/7-8, 8/40, 22/65 के बाद, 25/9, 28/14 के बाद, 30/34-36, 31/4, 33/आरम्भिक गद्यांश ।

3. माधुर्य

नाट्यशास्त्र—

अभ्यासात्करणानां तु श्लिष्टत्वं यत्र जायते ।
महत्स्वपि विकारेषु तन्माधुर्यमिति स्मृतम् ।।

दशरूपक—

श्लक्ष्णो विकारो माधुर्यं संक्षोभे सुमहत्यपि ।

काव्यानुशासन—

क्षोभेऽप्यनुल्बणत्वं माधुर्यम् ।।

भावप्रकाशन—

माधुर्यं चेष्टितालापस्पर्शानां स्पृहणीयता ।

साहित्यदर्पण—

संक्षोभेष्वप्यनुद्वेगो माधुर्यं परिकीर्तितम् ।[20]

मानसिक क्षोभ के कारणों के उपस्थित रहने पर भी नायक के मन में स्वस्थता और शान्ति बनी रहें तो वहाँ 'माधुर्य' सात्त्विक गुण कहा जाता है यथा—

अपराधिन्यपि जने साधुः साध्वेव वर्तते ।

छेत्तारमपि गन्धेन वासयत्येव चन्दनः ।।[21]

सज्जन पुरुष अपराध करने वाले पुरुष से भी सज्जनता का ही व्यवहार करेगें क्योंकि चन्दन का वृक्ष (उसे) काटने वाले को भी अपनी सुगन्ध से सुवासित ही करता है ।

कवि आर्यशूर ने मानसिक क्षोभ को साक्षात् मृत्यु माना है, आयु के क्षय को नहीं । इसलिए विद्वान् प्राण-सङ्कट में भी मन में क्षोभ नहीं करते ।[22]

(1) अथापराह्णसमये धर्मश्रवणार्थमृषयस्ते यथोचितं बोधिसत्त्वस्य पर्णशालां समभिगता ददृश्वांसश्चैनं कृशतरशरीरं परिक्षामकपोलनयनं परिम्लानवदनशोभमसम्पूर्णस्वरगाम्भीर्यं परिक्षीणमप्यपरिक्षीणधैर्यप्रशम-गुणमभिनवेन्दुप्रियदर्शनम् । बोधिसत्त्वोऽपि च महासत्त्वस्तथैव निःसंक्षोभप्रशान्तचित्तो बभूव ।[23]

(बिस-जातक-कथानुसार ब्राह्मणरूप बोधिसत्त्व की स्थिरता व शान्ति की परीक्षाहेतु इन्द्र ने उनके भोजन को निरन्तर पाँच दिनों तक छिपा दिया ।) जब अपराह्णकाल में धर्मोपदेश-श्रवण-हेतु ऋषि (जन) पूर्ववत् बोधिसत्त्व की पर्णशाला में गये तो (वहाँ) देखा कि उन (बोधिसत्त्व) का शरीर दुबला हो गया है, गाल व नेत्र धँस गए, मुख-शोभा मुरझा गई और वाणी की गम्भीरता खण्डित हो गई है । क्षीण (शरीर) होने पर भी शान्ति और धैर्य क्षीण नहीं हुआ है । वे महासत्त्व बोधिसत्त्व उसी प्रकार क्षोभरहित और शान्तचित रहे ।

उपर्युद्धृत गद्यांश में मानसिक क्षोभ (क्रोध) के कारण के होने पर भी बोधिसत्त्व के मन की पूर्ववत् स्वस्थता, धैर्य और प्रशमता उनके 'माधुर्य' सात्त्विक गुण की व्यञ्जक है ।

अन्यत्र द्रष्टव्य- 9/3, 21/17 के बाद गद्यांश, 25/8, 33/5.

4. गाम्भीर्य

नाट्यशास्त्र—

यस्य प्रभावादाकारा रोषहर्षभयादिषु ।

भावेषु नोपलभ्यन्ते गाम्भीर्यमिति शंसितम् ।।

दशरूपक—

गाम्भीर्यं यत्प्रभावेन विकारो नोपलक्ष्यते ।

काव्यानुशासन—

हर्षादिविकारानुपलम्भकृद्गाम्भीर्यम् ।।

भावप्रकाशन—

अविज्ञातेङ्गिताकारो भावो गाम्भीर्यमुच्यते ।

साहित्यदर्पण—

भीशोकक्रोधहर्षाद्यैर्गाम्भीर्यं निर्विकारता ।।[24]

हर्ष, भय, शोक, क्रोधादि भावावेशों के आने पर भी जब मुखाकृति पर किसी प्रकार का मानसिक विकार परिलक्षित नहीं होता तो वह 'गाम्भीर्य' नामक सात्त्विक गुण कहा जाता है । यथा—

आकर्ण्योपहतां सीतां रावणेन रघूद्वहः ।

न रुरोद न चुक्रोश लक्ष्मणं प्रैक्षतादशत् ।।[25]

श्रीराम ने सीता को रावण के द्वारा हर (अपहरण) लेने का समाचार सुनकर न तो रुदन किया न क्रोध ही किया, केवल थोड़ा झुककर लक्ष्मण की ओर देखने लगे ।

(1) महाकपि-जातक में बोधिसत्त्व (कपिराज) अपने बन्धुजनों की प्राणरक्षा-हेतु वृक्ष-शाखा को पकड़ कर पुल-रूप बन गए । समस्त वानर-गण उनके शरीर का आश्रय लेकर वृक्ष से उतरकर सुरक्षित स्थान पर पहुँच गए । क्षत विक्षत शरीर वाले बोधिसत्त्व उसी प्रकार सेतु बने हुए वहाँ आनन्दित हुए । विस्मित हुए राजा ने जब इसका कारण उनसे पूछा तब वे बोले—

कामं शरीरं क्षितिप क्षतं मे मनः परस्वास्थ्यमुपागतं तु ।

अकारि येषां चिरमाधिपत्यं तेषां मयार्तिर्विनिवर्तितेति ।।

जित्वाहवे विद्विषतः सदर्पान् गात्रेष्वलङ्कारवदुद्वहन्ति ।

वीरा यथा विक्रमचिह्नशोभां प्रीत्या तथेमां रुजमुद्वहामि ।।[26]

हे राजन् ! अवश्य ही मेरा शरीर क्षतविक्षत हुआ किन्तु मेरा चित्त अत्यन्त स्वस्थ (प्रसन्न) हुआ । मैं चिरकाल तक जिनका अधिपति रहा, (मैंने) उन के दुःखों को दूर किया । मैं इस घाव को आनन्दपूर्वक उसी प्रकार धारण करता हूँ जिस प्रकार युद्ध में अभिमानी शत्रुओं को जीतकर वीरपुरुष पराक्रम-चिह्न (घाव) को अलङ्कार के समान धारण करते हैं ।

उपर्युक्त पद्यों में घायल शरीर और अत्यन्त पीडा को सहने वाले बोधिसत्त्व महाकपि की मुखाकृति मानसिक विकार से रहित है । वे आत्मसन्तोष, शान्ति और निर्मलयश से सुशोभित हुए । अतएव वे 'गाम्भीर्य' सात्त्विकगुणालङ्कृत हैं ।

अन्यत्र द्रष्टव्य- 8/47 के पश्चात् गद्यांश, 28/55-57, 32/6 के बाद गद्यांश, 7,14.

5. स्थैर्य (धैर्य)

नाट्यशास्त्र—

धर्मार्थकामसंयुक्ताच्छुभाशुभसमुत्थितात् ।

व्यवसायादचलनं स्थैर्यमित्यभिधीयते ।।

दशरूपक—

व्यवसायादचलनं स्थैर्यं विघ्नकुलादपि ।

काव्यानुशासन—

विघ्नेऽप्यचलनं स्थैर्यम् ।।

भावप्रकाशन—

शुभेऽशुभेऽर्थे तद्धैर्यं व्यवसायादचलनम् ।।

सहित्यदर्पण—

व्यवसायादचलनं धैर्यं विघ्ने महत्यपि ।।[27]

जब नायक अनेक महान् विघ्नों के आने पर भी अपने कर्त्तव्य-पथ से विचलित नहीं होता, धैर्य रखता है, तब 'स्थैर्य' अथवा 'धैर्य' नामक सात्त्विक गुण कहलाता है यथा—

सम्पत्स्वापत्सु तुल्यात्मा रामो धैर्य्यकुलाचलः ।
विकारैः कैश्च नाक्षिप्तो वेदार्थ इव हेतुभिः ।।[28]

श्रीराम धैर्य के कुलपर्वत हैं, जो सम्पत्ति और आपत्ति में समान रूप से स्थिर रहते हैं । इन पर विकारों का कुछ भी प्रभाव नहीं पड़ता जैसे वेदों का अर्थ दुष्ट हेतुओं से आक्षिप्त नहीं होता ।

(1) कामं पतामि नरकं स्फुरदुग्रवह्नि
ज्वालावलीढशिथिलावनतेन मूर्ध्ना ।
न त्वर्थिनां प्रणयदर्शितसौहृदानां
सम्मानकालमवमानानया हरिष्ये ।।[29]

मैं (बोधिसत्त्व) इस भीषण देदीप्यमान अग्निमय नरक में (स्वेच्छा से) जाऊँगा, चाहे ज्वालाओं के स्पर्श से मेरा मस्तक (जलकर) लटक जाए किन्तु जिन याचकों ने प्रार्थना द्वारा मित्रता प्रकट की है, उनके प्रति आदर सत्कार का समय उनके तिरस्कार में नहीं बिताउँगा ।

बोधिसत्त्व श्रेष्ठि की दानशीलता ऐसी अजस्रधार है जो अनेक विघ्नों के उपस्थित होने पर भी बाधित नहीं होती । द्वार पर उपस्थित याचक को भिक्षार्थ अन्न देने के लिए व्यग्रचित बोधिसत्त्व वहाँ मार (विघ्न) द्वारा बनाए महानरक (महारौरव) की उपेक्षा करके प्रसन्नमन से उन्हें भोजन देते हैं । यहाँ दानकार्य से रोकने वाले विघ्न (माररूप शैतान) के प्रति बोधिसत्त्व की स्पष्टोक्ति उनके 'स्थैर्य' सात्त्विक गुण की परिचायिका है ।

(2) आनम्यमानानि धनूंषि दृष्ट्वा विनिष्पतद्दीप्तशिलीमुखानि ।
भीमस्वनज्यान्यविचिन्त्य वेगादस्मात्तरोः शैलमिमं गतोऽस्मि ।।[30]

झुकाये जाते हुए धनुषों को, जिनसे देदीप्यमान तीर निकल रहे थे, देखकर तथा प्रत्यञ्चा के भयङ्कर टङ्कार की चिन्ता न करते हुए मैं (बोधिसत्त्व) वेगपूर्वक इस वृक्ष से पहाड़ पर चला गया ।

यहाँ बोधिसत्त्व प्रजा-संरक्षण-रूप कार्य में बद्धचित्त हैं। राजा के कर्त्तव्यरूप प्रजापालन और त्यागभावना को उन्होनें चरितार्थ किया। स्वयं कष्ट सहकर भी आश्रितों के सन्ताप को शान्त किया। भयङ्कर तीरों से विचलित हुए बिना वानरगण की रक्षा द्वारा जिस धैर्य और साहस का उन्होनें परिचय दिया, वह उनके 'स्थैर्य' अथवा 'धैर्य' सात्त्विक गुण को अभिव्यक्त करता है।

अन्यत्र द्रष्टव्य- 1/17, 11/13, 25/1, 26/4-6, 31/42 के बाद गद्यांश।

6. ललित

नाट्यशास्त्र—

अबुद्धिपूर्वकं यत्तु सुकुमारस्वभावजम्।
शृङ्गाराकारचेष्टत्वं ललितं तत् प्रकीर्तितम्॥

दशरूपक—

शृङ्गाराकारचेष्टत्वं सहजं ललितं मृदु।

काव्यानुशासन—

मृदुः शृङ्गारचेष्टा ललितम्॥

भावप्रकाशन—

चेष्टितं यस्य शृङ्गारमयं तल्ललितं भवेत्॥

साहित्यदर्पण—

वाग्वेशयोर्मधुरता तद्वच्छृङ्गारचेष्टितं ललितम्।[31]

जहाँ वाणी तथा वेष में मधुरता हो और शृङ्गार के अनुरूप चेष्टाएँ की जाएं, उस प्रकार के नायक के गुण को 'ललित' नामक सात्त्विक गुण कहा जाता है यथा—

स तिष्ठति सदा धीमाञ्छास्त्रचिन्तासुधारसैः।
स्वबिम्बैरिव भित्तिस्थैः पण्डितैः परिवारितः॥[32]

वह बुद्धिमान् पुरुष शास्त्र के चिन्तन-रूपी अमृत का आस्वादन करते हुए भित्तियों पर स्थित दर्पणों में प्रतिबिम्बित अपने जैसे ही पण्डितों से घिरा रहता है।

अन्वर्थरम्याक्षरसौकुमार्यमहो कृतं नाम यथेदमस्याः।
उन्मादयन्तीति शुचिस्मितायास्तथा हि सोन्मादमिवाकरोन्माम्॥
धृत्या महत्यापि निगुह्यमानः स भूपतेस्तस्य मनोविकारः।
मुखेन चिन्तास्तिमितेक्षणेन कार्श्येन च व्यक्तिमुपजगाम॥[33]

इस शुभ्र मुस्कान वाली का यह जो उन्मादयन्ती (उन्मत्त करने वाली) नाम है, वह यथार्थ में मधुर और कोमल है। इसने मुझे भी मानों उन्मत्त कर दिया है। बहुत धैर्य (प्रयत्न) पूर्वक छिपाने पर भी राजा का मानसिक विकार (कामचिह्न) चिन्ताओं के कारण निश्चल नयनों वाले मुखमण्डल से और शारीरिक दुर्बलता से प्रकट हो गया।

उन्मादयन्ती-जातकोद्धृत उपर्युक्त पद्यों के अनुसार जितेन्द्रिय बोधिसत्त्व (राजा) को भी सांसारिक भाव विकल करते हैं। यहाँ वर्णित उनकी अवस्था 'ललित' नामक सात्त्विक गुण की अभिव्यञ्जक है।

अन्यत्र द्रष्टव्य- 8/14, 28/5-6.

7. औदार्य

नाट्यशास्त्र—

दानमभ्युपपत्तिश्च तथा च प्रियभाषणम्।
स्वजने वा परे वाऽपि तदौदार्यमिति स्मृतम्॥

दशरूपक—

प्रियोक्त्याऽऽजीविताद् दानमौदार्यं सदुपग्रहः।

काव्यानुशासन—

स्वपरेषु दानाभ्युपपत्तिसंभाषणान्यौदार्यम्॥

भावप्रकाशन—

प्रियालापस्मितोदारं दानमौदार्यमुच्यते।

साहित्यदर्पण—

दानं सप्रियभाषणमौदार्यं शत्रुमित्रयोः समता॥[34]

स्वजन और परजन दोनों के प्रति दान-भावना तथा प्रियभाषण एवं सबके प्रति उदार व्यवहार व समता के भाव को 'औदार्य' नामक सात्त्विक गुण कहा जाता है। आचार्य रामचन्द्र और गुणचन्द्र के अनुसार शत्रु अथवा मित्र का प्राणप्रण से भी उपकार करना औदार्य है—**औदार्यं शत्रुमित्राणां प्राणितेनाप्युपग्रहः**। यथा—

परात्मीयविभागोऽयं मोहः क्लिश्नात्यपण्डितम्।
प्रीतिः सर्वत्र धीरस्य ज्योत्स्नेवास्ते सुधानिधेः॥[35]

यह मेरा है और यह पराया है, ऐसी भावना (विभाजन) मूर्ख को कष्ट देती है। धीर मनुष्य चन्द्रमा की प्रभा के समान अपनी प्रीति सभी पर (समान) रखता है।

जातक-कथाओं में सर्वत्र बोधिसत्त्व की उदात्त दान-भावना का वर्णन है। बोधिसत्त्व के अनुसार धन को घर में छिपाकर रखने से अधिक याचकों को दान देने से आनन्द मिलता है।[36]

(1) दान-औदार्य

(1) कदा नु गात्रैरपि नाम कुर्यां हितं परेषामिति यश्च मेऽभूत् ।
मनोरथस्तत्सफलीक्रियां च संबोधिमग्र्यामपि चाविदूरे ॥
न स्पर्धया नैव यशोभिलाषान्न स्वर्गलाभान्न च राज्यहेतोः ।
नात्यन्तिकेऽप्यात्मसुखे यथायं ममादरोऽन्यत्र परार्थसिद्धेः ॥[37]

यह जो मेरा मनोरथ था कि कब अपने शरीर (उत्सर्ग) द्वारा भी अन्यों का हित करूँगा, उसे अब पूर्ण करुँगा और निकट भविष्य में ही सम्यक् संबोधि (बुद्धत्व) प्राप्त करूँगा । (यह सब) स्पर्धा, यशोभिलाषा, स्वर्गप्राप्ति या राज्य के लिए नहीं हैं । परोपकार के अतिरिक्त अन्य किसी भी चीज में, आत्यन्तिक आत्मसुख की प्राप्ति में भी मेरी यह अभिरुचि नहीं है ।

बोधिसत्त्व (ब्राह्मण) आर्तत्राता और महाकारुणिक हैं । उनकी करुणा शक्ति ही उनके लौह पुरुषत्व की उत्प्रेरक है, वे क्षुधापीडित व्याघ्री, जो अपने नवप्रसूत शिशुओं को आहारवत् देखती हुई उन्हें खाने को उद्यत है, को अपना शरीर भोजनार्थ दान करते हैं । उनकी ऐसी विशालहृदयता उनके 'दान-औदार्य' नामक सात्त्विक गुण की परिचायिका है ।

(2) न सन्ति मुद्गा न तिला न तण्डुला वने विवृद्धस्य शशस्य केचन ।
शरीरमेतत्त्वनलाभिसंस्कृतं ममोपयुज्याद्य तपोवने वस ॥
यदस्ति यस्येप्सितसाधनं धनं स तन्नियुङ्क्तेऽर्थिसमागमोत्सवे ।
न चास्ति देहादधिकं च मे धनं प्रतीच्छ सर्वस्वमिदं यतो मम ॥[38]

मैं शशक (बोधिसत्त्व) जङ्गल में पला, बड़ा हुआ, मेरे पास न (तो) मूँग है, न तिल और न तण्डुल किन्तु यह शरीर है । अग्नि में पकाकर आप इसका उपयोग करें और वन में ठहरें । जिसके पास जो भी उपयोगी साधन होता है वह उसी से अतिथि का सत्कार करता है । अतः आप मेरे इस सर्वस्व (शरीर) को स्वीकार करें ।

अतिथिसत्कार के लिए शरीर-दान से बढ़कर भला और क्या दान होगा ? आचार्य रामचन्द्र और गुणचन्द्र के अनुसार जो मित्र अथवा शत्रु का अपने प्राणों से भी उपकार करना रूप औदार्य है, वह यहाँ सम्यक् रूपेण उपन्यस्त है । आत्मोत्सर्ग का यह सुन्दर दृष्टान्त बोधिसत्त्व के 'दान-औदार्य' रूप सात्त्विक गुण का व्यञ्जक है ।

अन्यत्र द्रष्टव्य- 1/33, 2/3-5, 4/18 के बाद गद्यांश, 5/23,27, 7/1-2, 8/22,43, 9/6,25, 10/22-23, 20/आरम्भिक गद्यांश, 27/11, 30/14,17.

(2) अभ्युपपत्ति-औदार्य

(1) यत्त्वस्ति पुण्यं मम किंचिदेवं कान्तारमग्नं जनमुज्जिहीर्षोः ।
संसारकान्तारगतस्य तेन लोकस्य निस्तारयिता भवेयम् ॥[39]

मैं (हाथी-बोधिसत्त्व) मरुभूमि में फँसे हुए लोगों का उद्धार करना चाहता हूँ। इसमें यदि कुछ पुण्य प्राप्त हो तो उससे मैं संसाररूपी मरुभूमि में फँसे हुए लोगों का उद्धारक हो जाऊँ।

हस्ति-जातक की कथा के अनुसार नागवन में भटकते हुए भूखप्यास से व्याकुल तथा शोकाभिभूत 700 मनुष्यों को करुणावान् महासत्त्व (हस्ति) ने अभयसूचक प्रियवचन कहे। वे उदार, मधुर तथा सान्त्वनापूर्ण इन वचनों से विपत्तिग्रस्त मनुष्यों के शोक के प्रत्याख्यान में बद्धचित्त हैं। उनकी उदार व्यवहार युक्त ऐसी मधुरभाषिता उनके 'अभ्युपपत्ति-औदार्य' नामक सात्त्विक गुण की सूचक है।

अन्यत्र द्रष्टव्य- 2/28, 4/3, 5/2,12, 8/31, 11/11, 13/2, 17/1-2, 22/42,47, 24/11-12, 25/8, 26/35, 28/56-57, 31/42, 33/10-15.

(3) सम्भाषण-औदार्य

(1) दुष्करं पुरुषादोऽसावुदारं चाकरोन्मयि।
मद्वचःप्रत्ययाद्यो मां व्यसृजद्वशमागतम्॥
लब्धं तत्कारणाच्चेदं मया तात सुभाषितम्।
उपकारी विशेषेण सोऽनुकम्प्यो मया यतः॥[40]

यद्यपि मैं (सुतसोम) उस (सौदास नरभक्षी) के वश में आ गया था, तो भी मेरे वचनों पर विश्वास करके उसने मुझे छोड़ दिया। उसने मेरे प्रति यह दुष्कर उदारता प्रकट की। हे तात! उसी के कारण मैनें यह (अमूल्य) सुभाषित पाए। वह मेरा उपकारी है, अतः विशेष अनुकम्पा का पात्र है।

सुतसोम-जातक-कथानुसार बोधिसत्त्व सुतसोम राजपुत्र अपने वचनों की रक्षा के लिए प्राणों की चिन्ता किए बिना नरभक्षी सौदास (राक्षस) के पास लौट आए। ऐसा अद्‌भुत दृश्य देखकर क्रूर सौदास ने स्वयम् उनके धैर्य एवं सत्यरक्षण की प्रशंसा की। अतएव यहाँ बोधिसत्त्व सुतसोम के सम्भाषण में 'औदार्य' नामक सात्त्विक गुण स्पष्ट है।

(2) अतः कृपामत्र कुरुष्व मा रुषं यदीप्सितं चैवमनेन किंचन।
कुरुष्व तेनैनमवन्ध्यसाहसं स्थितं त्वदाज्ञाप्रवणं हि मे शिरः॥[41]

अतएव इस (कृतघ्न मनुष्य) पर दया करें, क्रोध नहीं। इसने जो कुछ पाने की आशा की थी, वह इसे देकर इसका साहस सफल करें। आप (राजा) की आज्ञा के लिए मेरा (बोधिसत्त्व का) मस्तक झुका है।

परम करुणाशील बोधिसत्त्व रुरुमृग अपने अपकारी (शत्रु) कृतघ्न व्यक्ति के प्रति भी क्षमावान् हैं। उन्होनें राजा से उसे उचित धन देने का अनुरोध किया। दयावान् परोपकारी पशुयोनि में जन्में बोधिसत्त्व के ये उदार वचन उनके 'सम्भाषण-औदार्य' रूप सात्त्विक गुण के द्योतक हैं।

अन्यत्र द्रष्टव्य- 22/92.

8 तेज

नाट्यशास्त्र—

अधिक्षेपावमानादेः प्रयुक्तस्य परेण यत्।
प्राणात्ययेऽप्यसहनं तत्तेजः समुदाहृतम्॥

दशरूपक—

अधिक्षेपाद्यसहनं तेजः प्राणात्ययेष्वपि।

काव्यानुशासन—

पराधिक्षेपाद्यसहनं तेजः।

भावप्रकाशन—

अवमानासहत्वं यत्ततेजस्समुदाहृतम्।

साहित्यदर्पण—

अधिक्षेपापमानादेः प्रयुक्तस्य परेण यत्।
प्राणात्ययेऽप्यसहनं तत्तेजः समुदाहृतम्॥[42]

प्राणों का सङ्कट आ जाने पर भी जब नायक शत्रु आदि द्वारा किए गए अपमान आदि को सहन नहीं करता, तब वह 'तेज' नामक सात्त्विक गुण कहा जाता है यथा—

आज्ञास्तु ते त्रिदशनाथ दशाननस्य
सन्धौ विदेहदुहितुश्च समागमेऽस्मिन्।
प्रत्याशयान्तिकगतस्य विभीषणस्य
लङ्कां प्रदाय न विना धृतिमेति रामः॥[43]

हे देवाधिराज इन्द्र ! आपकी चाहे यह आज्ञा ही क्यों न हो और मुझे जिससे रावण के साथ सन्धि और सीता की प्राप्ति ही चाहे क्यों न हो जाती हो किन्तु राज्यप्राप्ति की आशा से मेरी शरण लेने वाले विभीषण को बिना लङ्का का राज्य प्रदान किए राम को शान्ति नहीं मिलेगी।

जातक-कथाओं में बोधिसत्त्व का यह गुण केवल भावात्मक वर्णन में उपलब्ध होता है जहाँ उन्हें अकुशलों (बुरे कर्मो) के प्रति कठोर प्रवृत्ति का प्रस्तुत किया गया है यथा—

(1) स्यादत्र मे यः प्रतिकूलवर्ती
दर्पोद्भवादप्रतिसंख्यया वा।
व्यक्तं न मुच्येत स जीवतो मे
धाराघनस्येव घनस्य रेणुः॥[44]

अभिमान या अज्ञान से जो यहाँ मेरे प्रतिकूल आचरण करेगा उस (क्रोध) को मैं जीवित रहकर नहीं छोड़ूँगा, जिस प्रकार जलधारा बरसाने वाले मेघ धूल को नहीं छोड़ते हैं ।

चुड्डबोधि-जातक से सङ्कलित प्रस्तुत पद्य में बोधिसत्त्व चुड्डबोधि परिव्राजक के क्रोध के प्रति ऐसे उत्तेजक वचन वर्णित है । यहाँ क्रोध भावात्मक शत्रु-रूप है जो बोधिसत्त्व के (प्रति) प्रतिकूल आचरण करने को तैयार है । इसे बोधिसत्त्व ने प्रयत्नपूर्वक वश में किया । अतएव (क्षमा, शान्ति के आर्दश द्वारा) यहाँ 'तेज' नामक सात्त्विक गुण को प्रतिपादित किया गया है ।

यहाँ आचार्यों द्वारा स्वीकृत अष्ट सात्त्विक गुणों का प्रधान पात्र बोधिसत्त्व के प्रसङ्ग में विवेचन किया गया । इस प्रकार उपर्य्युद्धृत समस्त कथाएं उनके अष्ट सात्त्विक गुणों का सुन्दर निदर्शन प्रस्तुत करती हैं । इन सात्त्विक गुणों का महत्त्व स्वयं कवि आर्यशूर के ही शब्दों में—

अलङ्क्रियन्ते कुसुमैर्महीरुहा-
स्तडिद्गुणैस्तोयविलम्बिनो घनाः ।
सरांसि मत्तभ्रमरैः सरोरुहै-
र्गुणैर्विशेषाधिगतैस्तु देहिनः ।।[45]

वृक्ष फूलों से अलङ्कृत होते हैं, जलभार से लटकते हुए मेघ बिजली से सुशोभित होते हैं, सरोवर मत्त भ्रमरों से युक्त कमलों से मण्डित होते हैं और प्राणी विशेष रूप से प्राप्त गुणों से शोभायमान होते हैं ।

सन्दर्भ-सङ्केत

1. नाट्यशास्त्र (भरतमुनि-कृत), सप्तम अध्याय, पृ.429
2. ना.शा.- 24/3
3. दशरूपक (धनिक-कृत), 4/5 पर अवलोक टीका
4. काव्यानुशासन (हेमचन्द्र-कृत), 7/2 पर वृत्ति
5. ना.शा.- 24/31
6. नायक √ नी+ण्वुल् प्रत्यय, नीयते इति 'नायकः' । मार्गदर्शक ।
   त्यागी कृती कुलीनः सुश्रीको रूपयौवनोत्साही ।
   दक्षोऽनुरक्तलोकस्तेजोवैदग्ध्यशीलवान्नेता ॥ सा.द.- 3/30
7. जा.मा.- 31/1-2 -
8. ना.शा.24/32, द.रू.2/11, काव्यानु.7/3, भा.प्र.1/65, सा.द.3/51
9. द.रु.- 2/10 पर अवलोक (स्वयं वृत्तिकार धनिक-कृत पद्य), पृ.94-95
10. सा.द. (श्री शालग्राम शास्त्री-कृत व्याख्या सहित संस्करणोद्धृत), पृ. 70

11. जा.मा.- 10/1-3
12. जा.मा.- 11/10
13. जा.मा.- 22/42,47
14. जा.मा.- 2/6
15. जा.मा.- 9/5
16. जा.मा.- 8/43
17. ना.शा.24/33, द.रू.2/11, काव्यानु.7/4, भा.प्र.1/66, सा.द.3/52
18. नाटकलक्षणरत्नकोश (सागरनन्दी -कृत) ,पृ.140
19. जा.मा.- 22/4
20. ना.शा.24/34, द.रू.2/12, काव्यानु.7/6, भा.प्र.1/67, सा.द.3/52
21. नाटकलक्षणरत्नकोश-पृ.140
22. मनः संक्षोभ एवेष्टो मृत्युर्नायुः क्षयः सताम् ।
जीवितार्थेऽपि नायान्ति मनःक्षोभमतो बुधाः ॥ जा.मा.- 19/10
23. जा.मा.- 19/10 के बाद गद्यांश
24. ना.शा.24/36, द.रू.2/12, काव्यानु.7/8, भा.प्र.1/69, सा.द.3/53
25. नाटकलक्षणरत्नकोश,पृ.141
26. जा.मा.- 27/25-26
27. ना.शा.24/35, द.रू.2/13, काव्यानु.7/7, भा.प्र.1/68, सा.द.3/53
28. नाटकलक्षणरत्नकोश,पृ.141
29. जा.मा.- 4/18
30 जा.मा.- 27/20
31. ना.शा.24/37, द.रू.2/14, काव्यानु.7/5, भा.प्र.1/69, सा.द.3/55
32. नाटकलक्षणरत्नकोश,पृ.142
33. जा.मा.- 13/12,16
34. ना.शा.24/38, द.रू.2/14, काव्यानु.7/9, भा.प्र.1/70, सा.द.3/55
35. नाटकलक्षणरत्नकोश,पृ.142
36. न हि तां कुरुते प्रीतिं विभूतिर्भवनाश्रिता ।
संक्रम्यमाणार्थिजने सैव दानप्रियस्य याम् ॥ जा.मा.- 9/6
37. जा.मा.- 1/29-30
38. जा.मा.- 6/29-30
39. जा.मा.- 30/22

40. जा.मा.- 31/42-43

41. जा.मा.- 26/34

42. ना.शा.24/39, द.रू.2/13, काव्यानु.7/10, भा.प्र.1/71, सा.द.3/54

43. नाटकलक्षणरत्नकोश (राघवाभ्युदयोद्धृत),पृ.142-143

44. जा.मा.-21/11

45. जा.मा.-28/19

दिल्ली

APPENDIX I

Papers Related to Buddhism & Buddhist Studies Presented at International Conferences

Papers related to Buddhism & Buddhist Studies Presented at International Conferences held abroad

Sushma Kulshreshtha
Anju Bala

IV WORLD SANSKRIT CONFERENCE

WEIMAR,G.D.R.
May 23-30,1979

1. ***Mejor, Marek (Warsaw)***
   Some New Remarks on the *'Pratītya-samutpāda.*
2. ***Pezzali, Amalia(Bologna,Italy)***
   The Works of Nāgārjuna, The Great Buddhist Philosopher of the *Mādhyamika* School.
3. ***Pobozniak, Tadeusz (Cracow)***
   Milindapañha.
4. ***Sundermann, Werner (Berlin)***
   The Parthian Language and the Diffusion of Buddhist Terms of Indian Origin

VI WORLD SANSKRIT CONFERENCE

PENNSYLVANIA UNIVERSITY, PHILADELPHIA, U.S.A.
October,1984

5. ***Banerjee, Biswanath***
   Sanskrit Language and Buddhist Writers.
6. ***Bronkhorst, Johannes***
   Souls and Wholes.

7. *Caillat, Colette*

Idiosyncracies of language and style in Aśoka's Rock-Edicts at Girnar.

8. *Caudhary, K.*

Buddha Icon and Aśoka

9. *Gomez, Luis O.*

Exegetical Categories in Kamalaśīla's *Ṭikā* to the *Avikalpapraveśa*.

10. *Hayes, Richard P.*

Re-examination of Dharmakīrti's *Svabhāva-hetu*.

11. *Jaini, Padmanabh*

The Apocryphal *Jātakas* : Southeast Asian Buddhism.

12. *Lang, Karen C.*

Gender-Related Imagery in the *Theragāthā* and *Therīgāthā*.

13. *Lienhard, Siegfried*

A Nepalese Painted Scroll illustrating the *Siṃhalāvadāna* (with slides).

14. *McDermott, James P.*

The *Kathāvatthu Niyāma* Debates.

15. *Mishra, Kameshwar Nath*

The Unpublished *Tattvasiddhi* of Śāntarakṣita : a Resume.

16. *Nihom, M.*

Hallucinatory Background of the Buddhist Tantras.

17. *Niyogi, Puspa*

Accounts of Foreign Travellers on the organization of Monasteries in Ancient Bengal and Bihar.

18. *Roth, Gustav*

The seven Daughters of King *Kṛkī*.

19. *Sharma, Shree Niwas*

The Religio-Philosophical Vision of Aśoka and Global Welfare.

20. *Steinkellner, Emst*

Remarks on *niścitagrahaṇa*.

21. ***Tewari, Prema***
Gauḍapada and Buddhism.

22. ***Vyas, R.T.***
Yājñavalkya and Buddha.

23. ***Wayman, Alex***
Imperatives in Buddhist Tantra Mantras.

VIII CONFERENCE OF THE INTERNATIONAL ASSOCIATION OF BUDDHIST STUDIES, UNIVERSITY OF CALIFORNIA, BERKELEY, U.S.A.

August 8-10,1987

24. ***Ames, W. (Washington)***
Philosophy and Soteriology in Nāgārjuna's *Mūlamādhyamikakārikās*.

25. ***Bhaskar, B.J. (Nagpur)***
Kṣaṇikavāda as Understood by Jaina Philosophers.

26. ***Bonneux, A. (Ghent)***
Subāhuparipṛcchā.

27. ***Bronkhorst,D. (Leiden)***
The Date of *Pañcavastuka*.

28. ***Broucke,P.Van den (Ghent)***
Daishokongo.

29. ***Buck, Harry M. (Wilson College)***
Eyes of Compasion and Eyes of Judgment.

30. ***Buswell, R. (California, Los Angeles)***
K'an-hua Ch'an as the Evolution of a Practical Subitism in Chinese Buddhism.

31. ***Carter, J.R. (Colgate)***
Faith in the Wake of the *Dhammapada*.

32. ***Carter, M.L. (Wisconsin)***
The Mystery of the Udayana Buddha.

33. *Chandra, Ramesh (Patna)*

The Concept of Compassion and the Picture of Global Unity.

34. *Ching, J. (Toronto)*

Ch'i-Sung and the Buddhist Confucian Dialogue.

35. *Cousins, L.S. (Manchester)*

Emptiness.

36. *Dargyay, E. (Calgary)*

Buddhaguhya and the Bodhisattva Monarchy of Tibet.

37. *Davidson, R. M. (California, Berkeley)*

Paramārtha's Hermenutic on the *Hsienyang sheng chiao lun.*

38. *Dessein, B. (Ghent)*

Nāgārjuna's *Shih-erhmen Lun.*

39. *Eckel, D. (Harvard)*

Tarkajvala III : The Structure of a *Mādhyamika* Philosophical System.

40. *Ganguly, S. (Delhi)*

Aspects of the *Wei-Shih* Philosophy of Huan-tsang.

41. *Gokhale, G. (Wake Forest)*

The Image World of the *Milindapañha.*

42. *Gomez, L. (Michigan)*

Structure and Meaning of a *Pāli Sutta.*

43. *Gupta, R. (Visva-Bharati)*

Agent-Causation and Event-Causation : The Buddhist Naiyayika Controversy.

44. *Huang, C.C. (Mount Holyoke College)*

The Confucian Revival and Sung Anti-Buddhism.

45. *Hui Wan, Ven.Shig (Taiwan)*

The Educational Theory of the *Samādhi* of Neither Walking Nor Sitting.

46. ***Ichimura, S. (Berkeley)***

A New Approach to the Philosophical Linkage between *Mādhyamika* and *Yogācāra* Systems in terms of *Māyā-dṛṣṭānta.*

47. ***Ishihara, John S. (Calgary)***

A Buddhist Social Ethics.

48. ***Kaplan, S. (Manhattan College)***

The Inadequacy of the Traditional *Yogācāra* Simile : A Holographic Analysis of Vasubandhu's Three *Svabhāvas.*

49. ***Kawazoe, Yoshiyuki (Tohoku)***

The Computer and Sanskrit Textual Studies : The *Lotus Sūtra* Project of Tohoku University.

50. ***Keenan, J. (Middlebury College)***

Asaṅga's *Yogācāra* Understanding of *Mādhyamika* Thought.

51. ***Khare, B. (California, San Bernadino)***

Epistemology of Nāgārjuna.

52. ***Kimura, H. (Ghents)***

Some Deities of the *Māyājāla-tantra.*

53. ***Kloppenborg, R. (Utrecht)***

The Composition of the *Bodhicaryāvatāra.*

54. ***Kubo, T. (Tokyo)***

The Concept of Bodhisattva Practice as Depicted in the *Lotus Sūtra* and Its Place in Buddhist Philosophy.

55. ***Ku, C. (Singapore)***

The Development of the Concept of the Cakravartin in China.

56. ***Kulshreshtha, Abha (Delhi, India)***

Some Legal Problems and Their Remedies in Buddhist Literature.

57. ***Kulshreshtha, Sushma (Delhi, India)***

Music and Dance in Buddhist Literature.

58. ***Lahiri, L. (Delhi, India)***

The Complex of Buddhist Grottoes at Da-Zu in China.

59. *Lang, K. (Virginia)*

Buddhist Influence in the Use of the Term *Prapañcopāsanā* in the *Māṇḍūkya Upaniṣad* and *Gauḍapādīya Kārikās*.

60. *Leese, M. (Berkeley)*

The Pillar as a Central Concept in Indian Buddhism.

61. *Lindtner, C. (Denmark)*

Bhavya's Theory of Four Truths.

62. *Liu, M.W. (Hong Kong)*

The *Lotus Sūtra* and the *Garland Sūtra* According to the T'ient'ai and Hua-Yen Schools of Chinese Buddhism.

63. *Macdonald, A.W. (Paris)*

Buddha-isation and Lama-isation : Or what Happened at La-phyi?

64. *Mammitzsch, U. (Western Washington)*

On the Definition and classification of Mandala in the Sino-Japanese Tradition.

65. *Payne, R. (Berkeley)*

Homa in the *Mahāvairocana Sūtra* : The Development of a Tantric Buddhist Ritual.

66. *Redmond, G.P. (Cleveland)*

Dukkha and Desire : Parallel Concepts in Buddhist Philosophy and Marcel Proust's *A Al Recherche du Temp Perdu*.

67. *Sarao, K.T.S. (Cambridge)*

Urban Centres Reflected in Early Buddhist Literature.

68. *Sharma, R.M. (Punjab)*

Śūnya and *Brahman*.

69. *Shih, Heng-Ching (San Francisco)*

The Nature of the *Tathāgata garbha* : An Expression of Monism or Emptiness.

70. *Shih Jen-hua, Ven. (Taiwan)*

The Creative Spirit in Buddhist Art.

71. ***Shukla, B.W. (Lucknow)***

Some Buddhist Remains and Antiquities of Kumaun and Garhwal Hills of Uttar Pradesh—Their relationship with Tibet and Nepal.

72. ***Steben, B. (Toronto)***

The Records of Pointing at the Moon (Chin Yueh lu) as a Repository of Ch'an Insights into the Nature of the Mind.

73. ***Steinman, Brigitte (Paris)***

On Tamang Buddhism.

74. ***Stevens, J. (Toronto)***

The Role of *Bodhidharma* in Zen Art.

75. ***Takasaki, J. (Tokyo/Waseda)***

On *Upādāna* : *Alayavijñāna* and its two kinds of *Upādāna.*

76. ***Tanaka, K. (Berkeley)***

On Ching-Ying Hui Yuan's Contribution to Chinese Pure Land Buddhism.

77. ***Tsukamoto, Keisho.***

The Computer and Sanskrit Textual Studies : The *Lotus Sūtra* Project of Tohoku University.

78. ***Upreti, K. (Delhi, India)***

The Historical Bearing of the Buddhist-Sanskrit Literature of the Transitional Phase.

79. ***Virottam, B. (Ranchi, India)***

Buddhism and the Chotanagpur Tribes.

80. ***Wang, Ven.S. (Taiwan)***

The Concept of Filial Piety in the *Sūtra* of Bodhisattva Ksitigarbha's Fundamental Vow.

81. ***Willemen, C. (Ghent)***

Tsa-pao tsung ching.

82. ***Yamazaki, Moriichi***

The Computer and Sanskrit Textual Studies : The *Lotus Sūtra* Project of Tohoku University.

83. ***Yeh, Ah-Yueh (National Taiwan University)***
The Theories of the *Abhūtaparikalpa* and *Prajñāpāramitā* in the *Madhyantavibhaṅga-bhāṣya.*

84. ***Yugama, A. (Tokyo)***
Textual Studies.

VII WORLD SANSKRIT CONFERENCE

THE KERN INSTITUTE, UNIVERSITY OF LEIDEN, LEIDEN, THE NETHERLANDS. August, 1987

85. ***Aramaki, Noritoshi***
Some Precursors of the Subconscious desire (*gṛddhā*) in the *Attadaṇḍasutta.*

86. ***Gail, Adalbert J.***
The Vehicles of the Indian Gods, Hindu and Buddhist.

87. ***Ichimura, Shohei***
Did the *Mādhyamika* and the *Vedāntin* find a common ground for fair games of refutation or dialogue?

88. ***Imanishi, Junkichi***
On the Concept of *Satkāyadṛṣṭi* (*Sakkāyadiṭṭhi*).

89. ***Jha, Makhan***
History of Hindu Sacred *Tīrthas* (Places of Pilgrimage) of India and Nepal with special reference to Kashi & Janakpur.

90. ***Kloppenborg, Ria***
The Composition of the *Bodhicaryāvatāra* : An analysis of the text in the light of Buddhist Spiritual Practice.

91. ***Kulshreshtha, Sushma*** (Delhi, India)
Music and Dance in Buddhist Literature.

92. ***Lang, Karen***
On the expression *advitīyaṃ Śivadvāram* in *Catuḥśataka* XII : 13.

93. ***Matsumura, Hisashi***
Lexical notes on the *Vinaya.*

94. ***Mejor, M.***
The Problem of the two Vasubandhus reconsidered.

95. ***Mishra, Kameshwar Nath.***
Advaya(=Non-dualism) in Buddhist Sanskrit.

96. ***Mishra, Y.K. (Magadh, Bodhgaya)***
Ancient University of Vikramaśilā : An archaeological study.

97. ***Oetke, Claus***
On Some non-formal aspects of the proofs in the *Mūlamādhyamikakārikās*.

98. ***Padoux, Andre***
The body in Tantric Ritual : The Case of the *Mudrās*.

99. ***Pereira, Jose***
The four noble truths in Vasubandhu.

100. ***Pou, Saveros***
Sanskrit, Pāli and Khmer-Pāli in Combodia.

101. ***Prasad, K.D.***
Cultural History of Gaya.

102. ***Prets, Ernst***
Remarks on the Structure of *Sādhanam* in the *Abhidharma-samuccaya*.

103. ***Ruegg, D. Seyfort***
The Literary-historical Problem of Bhāvaviveka/*Bhavya*.

104. ***Sarao, K.T.S. (Cambridge, U.K.)***
Who and What Produced Earliest Buddhism.

105. ***Sengupta, Sudha***
Some Fragments of Buddhist Sanskrit Manuscripts from Gilgit.

106. ***Shukla, K.(Gorakhpur, India)***
Dharmakīrti, Kumārila and Śaṅkara : A study in their logical and metaphysical Approaches.

107. ***Singh, Ram Binod***
Gayā *Tīrtha* as depicted in Traditional Literature.

108. *Stein Kellner, Ernst*

Is Dharmakīrti a Mādhyamika?

109. *Tsuda, Sh. (Japan)*

Original Meaning of Śīnyatā and its Magāyānic transformation.

110. *Verboom, A. (Institut Kern, Leiden)*

The importance of the GilGit-Manuscript of the *Pañcaviṃśatisāhasrikāprajñāpāramitāsūtra.*

111. *Vetter, T.E.*

Some Remarks on older parts of the *Suttanipāta.*

112. *Wayman, Alexander*

The three Pratyekabuddha Paths per Asaṅga.

113. *Yuyama, A. (Tokyo, Japan)*

Some Remarks on Traditional Sanskrit Studies in Premeiji Japan.

XXXIII ICANAS

XXXIII INTERNATIONAL CONGRESS OF ASIAN & NORTH AFRICAN STUDIES

UNIVERSITY OF TORONTO

TORONTO, CANADA

August 19-25, 1990

114. *Boisvert, Mathieu*

A New Perspective on the *Paṭiccasamuppāda.*

115. *Chang, Yun-Shik*

Confucianization of a Kingdom : The Case of Choson Dynasty Korea.

116. *Chung, Edward Y.J.*

Yi Yulgok, a Neo-Confucian Political Reformer in 16th Century Korea.

117. *Corless, Roger J.*

Coterminous Epistemology and Coinherent Ontology : Nāgārjuna and Athunasius.

118. *Fukui, Fumimasa*

Avatar Chinois et Japonais d'un role bouddhiste Indien de Commentateur, *dujiang.*

119. *Graham, Patricia J.*

Professional Buddhist Painting of the Late Tokugawa Period.

120. *Hirakawa, Akira*

Changing Petals of the Lotus.

121. *Iida, Shutaro*

Dōgen's Lotus : An Aspect of the Shobogenzo.

122. *Indorf, Pinna*

A Cultural Interpretation of a Buddhist Tradition, *Bai Sema.*

123. *Jan, Yun-hua*

The Place of T'ien -t'ai Doctrines in Yen-shou's (904-975 A.D.) Thought.

124. *Junghare, Indira*

Buddhism and Hinduism : Cultural Interaction in Combodia and Laos.

125. *Karetzeky, Patricia Eichenbaum*

The Iconography of the First Sermon

126. *Katsura, Shoryu*

Diṅgnāga and Dharmakīrti on the determination of Logical Connection.

127. *Keenan, John*

Mahāyāna Theology.

128. *Keenan, John P.*

The Prospects for a *Mahāyāna* Theology.

129. *Kim, Young-ho*

Some Forms of Comparative Religion in Korean Tration : The Buddhist Response to the Confucian Challenge.

130. *Kloppenberg, Ria*

Buddhist Views on Suicide.

131. ***Kubo, Tsugunari***

What is the Buddha as Depicted in the *Lotus Sūtra* Like, *e.g.*, *"....buddho'grasattvaḥ"*?

132. ***Kulshreshtha, Sushma***

Glimpses of Music in the *Buddhacarita* of Aśvaghoṣa.

133. ***Kumar, Bimlendra.***

Buddhist Philosophy of Relation as Energy.

134. ***Kyodo, Jiko.***

A Study of the Buddhist Manuscripts of Dun-huang : Classification and Method.

135. ***Lancaster, Lewis***

The Social Dimension to Buddhist and Christian Doctrines.

136. ***Leese, Marilyn Edwards***

Imported Visions and Indigenous Interpretations : Central Jāvā's Buddhist Monuments.

137. ***Leidy, Denise Patry***

Beyond Likeness : Biography in Buddhist Portraiture.

138. ***Lida, Shotaru (Vancouver)***

The *Lotus Sūtra*.

139. ***Mammitzsch, Ulrich***

Mandala - the Changing Nature and function of an *Imago Mundi*.

140. ***Maruyama, Takao***

The Doctrine of the one Vehicle between India and China : The *Lotus Sūtra* Commentaries.

141. ***Mather, Richard***

The Interaction of Buddhism with Local Traditions During China's Middle Ages.

142. ***Matthews, Robin***

Faith and *Mahāyāna* Theology.

143. ***McLaughlin, Michael C.***

A Buddhist Epistemological Challenge to the Universality of Lonergan's Cognitional Model.

144. ***Menezer, Pascol Marian***

Contribution of Pali Classical Literature (11th -14th Century A.D.) to Buddhist Religion and Culture.

145. ***Mishra, Yugal Kishor***

Aṅga, a Mahājanapada of Eastern India.

146. ***Mittal, Kewal Krishan***

Status of the Individual in the Buddhist Raligio-Philosophic thought.

147. ***Mochizuki, Ryoko***

Horiami Koetsu (1558-16637) Lotus : His Faith and Art.

148. ***Mullick, Chandika Charan***

Sculptures of Nālanda : A Review.

149. ***Nakada, Naomichi***

Samatha and Nabhi as Referred in Chinese Buddhist Work-Tendai's *The Makashikan.*

150. ***Ning, Qiang***

From India to China : Comparison Among the Compositions of Some *Jātakas*.

151. ***Ogasawara, Ryugen***

The Vicissitudes of the Sotozen Buddhist Tradition.

152. ***Pan, Cedric Hung-chao***

Nietzsche's Overman and Buddhist Bodhisattva.

153. ***Robbins, Robert Lee***

A Re-examination of Diṅgnāga's Concept of *Svasamvedana.*

154. ***Sarao, Karam***

The Chronology of Kings From the Buddha to the Mauryas.

155. ***Shah, Jitendra B.***

Nāgārjuna is Mahāyānist, with Special Reference to Major Jain Works.

156. ***Sharma, Tulsi Ram***

The Relation between *Pratītyasamutpāda* and *Śūnyatā*.

157. *Shim, Jae-ryong*

Contemporary Korean Buddhism at the Crossroads of Cultural Contacts : From Protection to Liberation.

158. *Shyam, Lalit*

A Study of Salient Features of Buddhist Art and Culture.

159. *Smith, R.Morton.*

What was one's own Language? *Vinaya* 139.

160. *Srivastava, V.C.*

Interaction Between Buddhism and Hellenism in Afghanistan.

161. *Steben, Barry*

The Critique of Buddhism in the thought of Nakae Toju.

162. *Takasaki, Jikido*

Buddha, the Compassionate *(Karuṇātman)*

163. *Tang, Jian*

Medieval Chinese and Sanskrit : Historical Linguistic Contacts through Translations of *Mahāyāna* Buddhist Scriptures.

164. *Tiwary, Mahesh*

Peace Factors within (Buddha's View).

165. *Wang, Yao*

Tibetan Opera *Dri-Med Kun-Idan*--A Symbol of Buddhist Culture in Tibet.

166. *Wolter, Albert F.*

Kamakura Responses to Sung Buddhism : Eisai and Dogen on the three Teachings.

167. *Yamaori, Tetsuo*

Two Petals of the Lotus : A Case Look at Poetics and Politics in Japan.

168. *Yeh, Ah-yueh*

A Study on the Theories of the Bodhisattva's "*Daśavidha-dharma-dhātavas*" from the Viewpoint of the *Madhyanta-vibhāga-bhāṣya*.

169. *Yuyama, Akira*

A Critical Survey of Recent Researches on the *Lotus Sūtra.*

VIII WORLD SANSKRIT CONFERENCE

UNIVERSITY OF VIENNA,

VIENNA, AUSTRIA

August-September, 1990

170. *Banerjee, Mal (Santiniketan)*

Impact of the Sanskrit Avadānas on motifs of the Tibetan Dance-Dramas.

171. *Banerjee, Man (Calcutta)*

On some interesting Manuscripts preserved in the Asiatic Socıety, Calcutta.

172. *Basant, P.K. (New Delhi)*

Through the gateways of Sanchi : A view of the Early Buddhism.

173. *Eimer, Helmut (Bonn, Federal Republic of Germany)*

The Classification of the Buddhist *Tantras* according to the *Vajrajñānasamuccya.*

174. *Fastiggi, R.L. (St. Edward's University, Austi', Texas, U.S.A.)*

Some aspects of Buddhology in the *Lotus Sūtra.*

175. *Ganguly, K.Chakraborty (Calcutta)*

The Buddhist Theory of the Relation of Causality (*Tadutpatti*) and Essential Identity (*Tādātmya*) as determinant of *Vyāpti-Nyāya* critique.

176. *Gombrich, R. (Oxford University, Oxford, U.K.)*

Dating the Buddha.

177. *Hartmann, J.U. (Göttingen, West Germany)*

Remarks on the *Dīrghāgama* Transmitted in Eastern Turkistan.

178. *Isoda, H. (Sendai, Japan)*

A study of the commentaries on the *Abhisamayālaṃkāra.*

179. ***Kawasaki, Shinjo (Tsukuba, Japan)***
Principle of Life according to Bhavya.

180. ***Lienhard, S. (Stockholm, Sweden)***
Avalokiteśvara in the wick of the Night-lamp.

181. ***Manne, J. (La Conversions/Luty)***
On a Departure Formula in the Pali Canon and its translation.

182. ***Mejor, M. (Warsaw, Poland)***
On Vasubandhu's *Pratītyasamutpādavyākhyā*.

183. ***Mishra, K.K. (New Delhi,India)***
The Concept of Rebirth as reflected in the *Jātakamālā* of Āryaśūra.

184. ***Mishra, K.N. (Sarnath, Varanasi)***
Titles Quoted by Śāntarakṣita in his *Tattvasiddhi* : An appraisal.

185. ***Nakatani, H. (Kobe, Japan)***
Dharmapada Verses transmitted.

186. ***Norman, K.R. (Cambridge, U.K.)***
The Pāli Cannon and the development of writing in India.

187. ***Oetke, C. (Hamburg, West Germany)***
Doctrine and Argument in *Vijñānavāda*-Buddhism.

188. ***Sarao, K.T.S. (New Delhi, India)***
Ācāriyaparamparā and Date of the Buddha.

189. ***Sato, M. (Morioka, Japan)***
The Mutual influences between Buddhism and Śaivism in Kashmir.

IX WORLD SANSKRIT CONFERENCE, LA TROBE UNIVERSITY MELBOURNE, VICTORIA, AUSTRALIA

January 9-15,1994

190. ***Agrawal, M.M.***
Dharmakīrti and Bhāmaha.

191. ***A..lon, Mark***

Some Oral Features of the Portions of Pāli Canonical *Sutta* Texts.

192. ***Barua, S.***

A Study of Consciousness : Buddhist Perspective.

193. ***Chapple, C.K.***

Haribhadra's Response to Buddhism, Vedānta and Tantra in his *Yogadṛṣṭisamuccaya.*

194. ***Devaki, H.P.***

The Influence of Early Buddhist-Yoga on the *Yogasūtra* of Patañjali

195. ***Fenner, Peter (Deakin)***

Orthodox and Unorthodox Responses and the Relationship between Method and Wisdom in Buddhism.

196. ***Franco, Eli***

Faith and Reason in the Buddhist Epistemological Tradition.

197. ***Harrison, P.***

Keeping the Magic under Wraps : Reflections on the Fourth *Pārājika* of the Buddhist *Vinaya.*

198. ***Isaacson, H.***

Yogaratnamālā, Muktāvalī and *Ratnāvalī :* Notes on three Sanskrit Commentaries on the *Hevajratantra.*

199. ***Junghare, Indira Y.***

Sanskritic Buddhism of Southeast Asia with Special Reference to Combodia and Laos.

200 ***Kumar, Bimalendra***

Relation as Energy in Buddhism.

201. ***Menezes, P.***

A Comparative Study of Pali Buddhist Texts and Sanskrit Buddhist Texts.

202. ***Mishra, Kameshwar Nath***

Modern Sanskrit Buddhist Poetry : An Appraisal.

203. *Mishra, Kameshwar Nath*

The Buddhist Hybrid Sanskrit vs. the *Mlecchabhāṣā*.

204. *Prasad, S.*

Practice of Buddhism in Daily and Secular life.

205. *Rana, Chander Prabha*

Buddhist View of *Kalpana* and *Abhilapa*

206. *Saito, Akira*

On the Difference between the Two Versions of Śāntideva's *Bodhi(sattva)caryāvatāra*.

207. *Sarin, S.*

Atinītita, a Formula for *Unmīlita* in Khmer Buddhist Ritual.

208. *Schalk, Peter*

The Beginning of Buddhism in Tamilakam.

209. *Sharma, Mahesh Chandra*

The Influence of the *Raghuvaṃśa* of Kālidāsa on *Padyacūdāmaṇi* (Sanskrit Buddhist Epic *Siddhārthacaritam*) of Buddhaghoṣa.

210. *Singh, L.P.*

Concept of Maitreya : An analysis and reflection.

211. *Skilling, P.*

Sanskrit Buddhist Inscriptions in South-East Asia.

212. *Suneson, C.*

On the term *Vāmalokāyatika* found in two Central Asian Mss. of the *Saddharmapuṇḍarīkasūtra* and its Chinese interpretation.

213. *Templeman, David*

Some Contributions to the Study of a *gaṇacakra* drawn from a Sixteenth Century Tibetan Source.

Delhi

APPENDIX II

CONTRIBUTORS

1. Anju Bala (Ms.)

Research Scholar
Department of Buddhist Studies
University of Delhi, Delhi-110007

2. Bajracharya, Naresh Man

Jhwafahal, Cha 2-553, Wa. No. 27
Kathmando-3, Nepal &

Research Scholar
Department of Buddhist Studies
University of Delhi, Delhi-110007

3. Bauddha, Sanghamitra (Ms.)

Research Scholar
Department of Buddhist Studies
University of Delhi, Delhi-110007

4. Chandra, Lokesh (Prof.)

Ex. Member of Parliament (Rajya Sabha)
Director, International Academy of Indian Culture, J-22, Hauz Khas Enclave
New Delhi-110016

5. Chandra, Meena (Mrs.)

Research Scholar, Department of Sanskrit
University of Delhi, Delhi-110007

6. **Gaur, Veena (Dr.)**

Research Associate
Department of Buddhist Studies
University of Delhi, Delhi-110007

7. **Hira Lal**

Proprietor, Amar Printing Press
8/25, Double Storey
Vijay Nagar, Delhi-110009

8. **Inder Raj (Lucky)**

8/25, Double Storey, Vijay Nagar
Delhi-110009

9. **Kantawala, S.G. (Dr.)**

Ex. Director, Oriental Research Institute &
Ex. Professor & Head, Sanskrit Department,
M.S. University of Baroda, Baroda (Gujrat)

10. **Kulshreshtha, Abha (Ms.)**

M.B.I.M. (London)
Advocate, Delhi High Court
102-104, Lawyers' Chambers
Western Wing, Tis Hazari Court
Delhi-110054

11. **Kulshreshtha, Sushma (Dr.), D.Litt.**

F.R.A.S. (London)
Visiting University Professor
Department of Sanskrit
Ranchi University, Ranchi-834008 (Bihar)

12. **Mishra, Kamlakant (Dr.), D.Litt.**

Director, Rashtriya Sanskrit Sansthan
A-4, Vishal Enclave, New Delhi-110027

13. Mittal, Kewal Krishan (Dr.)

Professor & Ex. Head
Department of Buddhist Studies
University of Delhi, Delhi-110007

14. Pavagadhi, Subhra Barua (Dr.)

Lecturer
Department of Buddhist Studies
University of Delhi, Delhi-110007

15. Sarao, K.T.S. (Dr.)

Ph.D. (Cantab), F.R.A.S. (London)
Professor & Head
Department of Buddhist Studies
University of Delhi, Delhi-110007

16. Shahi, S.M.P.N. Singh (Dr.)

Reader in English
Ranchi University, Ranchi-834008 (Bihar)

17. Sharma, T.R. (Dr.)

Head of the Sanskrit Department
Khalsa College
University of Delhi, Delhi-110007

18. Shukla, Chandrakant (Dr.), D. Litt.

Professor & Head, Department of Sanskrit
Ranchi College, Ranchi University
Ranchi-834008 (Bihar)

19. Singh, Priyasen (Dr.)

Department of Buddhist Studies
University of Delhi, Delhi-110007

20. Singh, Sanghasen (Dr.)

Professor & Ex. Head
Department of Buddhist Studies
University of Delhi, Delhi-110007

21. Sobti, Harcharan Singh (Dr.)

Reader & Head of the Panjabi Department
Dayal Singh College (Evening)
University of Delhi

22. Soonthorndhammathada, Phra (Dr.)

Vice-Chancellor
Nong-Khai Buddhist University
Bangkok, Thiland

23. Srivastava, Urmila (Dr.)

Head of the Sanskrit Department
Arya Kanya Degree College
Allahabad University, Allahabad (U.P.)

24. Trivedi, Krishnakant (Dr.)

Bihar Education Service
Mithila Research Institute
Darbhanga (Bihar)

25. Unni, N.P. (Dr.)

Professor & Head
Department of Sanskrit, Kerala University
Kariavattom, Trivendrum (Kerala)

PUBLICATION COMMITTEE

1. **Kulshreshtha, Abha (Ms.)**
   President

   M.B.I.M. (London)
   Manika-Dhawal
   KC/12 B, Ashok Vihar
   Delhi-110052

2. **Chandra, Meena (Mrs.)**

   Research Scholar
   Department of Sanskrit
   University of Delhi
   Delhi-11007

3. **Anju Bala (Ms.)**
   Secretary

   Member, Executive Committee
   Kalidasa Academy of Sanskrit
   Music & Fine Arts, Delhi-110052